LGBT Identity and Online New Media

A landmark anthology, *LGBT Identity and Online New Media* is the first to critically introduce and examine constructions of LGBT identity within new media. Almost entirely composed of original essays, this anthology analyzes new media against the historical, generic, and iconic influences of older media such as television, film, and print to discern the unique possibilities that new media offer for the construction of LGBT identity. While some of the new media discussed are MySpace, Facebook, Youtube.com, gay men's health websites, gay message boards, and transsexual craigslist ads, among others, a few of the many possibilities include opportunities for virtual coming out, connecting to and constructing communities, establishing identity ideals, and composition of self-narratives via blogs. In detailing the possibilities of these constructions, the collection also presents a theoretically sophisticated dissection of the effects, issues, influences, benefits, and disadvantages of the constructions themselves.

The result is a pioneering interdisciplinary study that will prove essential reading for anyone interested in the topics of gender, sexuality, and identity as they intersect with media studies, cultural studies, sociology, and notably politics.

Christopher Pullen is Senior Lecturer in Media Studies at Bournemouth University in the UK. He has published widely on issues of identity and the media. He is the author of *Documenting Gay Men: Identity and Performance in Reality Television and Documentary Film* and *Gay Identity, New Storytelling and the Media*.

Margaret Cooper is a Sociologist at Southern Illinois University whose work on gender identity has been internationally published in journals, textbooks, and various collections. An activist for LGBT rights, women's rights, and civil rights for twenty-five years, she is also the former recipient of the Humanitarian of the Year Award in Nashville, Tennessee.

LGBT Identity and Online New Media

Edited by
Christopher Pullen and
Margaret Cooper

Routledge
Taylor & Francis Group
NEW YORK AND LONDON

First published 2010
by Routledge
270 Madison Avenue, New York, NY 10016

Simultaneously published in the UK
by Routledge
2 Park Square, Milton Park, Abingdon, Oxon OX14 4RN

Routledge is an imprint of the Taylor & Francis Group, an informa business

© 2010 Taylor & Francis

Typeset in Perpetua and GillSans by Swales & Willis Ltd, Exeter, Devon
Printed and bound in the United States of America
on acid-free paper by Walsworth Publishing Company, Marceline, MO

All rights reserved. No part of this book may be reprinted or reproduced or utilized in any form or by any electronic, mechanical, or other means, now known or hereafter invented, including photocopying and recording, or in any information storage or retrieval system, without permission in writing from the publishers.

Trademark Notice: Product or corporate names may be trademarks or registered trademarks, and are used only for identification and explanation without intent to infringe.

Library of Congress Cataloging in Publication Data
LGBT identity & online new media / Christopher Pullen & Margaret Cooper, editors.
  p. cm.
  Includes bibliographical references and index.
  1.Sexual minorities—Identity. 2. Social media. I. Pullen, Christopher, 1959– II. Cooper, Margaret, 1964– III. Title: LGBT identity and online new media.
  HQ73.L43 2010
  306.76—dc22
  2009038288

ISBN10: 0–415–99866–2 (hbk)
ISBN10: 0–415–99867–0 (pbk)
ISBN10: 0–203–85543–4 (ebk)

ISBN13: 978–0–415–99866–6 (hbk)
ISBN13: 978–0–415–99867–3 (pbk)
ISBN13: 978–0–203–85543–0 (ebk)

For LGBT youth at school, and especially those who are the subject of homophobic abuse. Also in remembrance of Lawrence King.

Contents

List of Figures and Tables x
Preface xi
Acknowledgements xiii

Introduction 1

PART I
Active Youth

1 The Murder of Lawrence King and LGBT Online
   Stimulations of Narrative Copresence 17
   CHRISTOPHER PULLEN

2 "A YouTube of One's Own?": "Coming Out" Videos as
   Rhetorical Action 37
   JONATHAN ALEXANDER AND ELIZABETH LOSH

3 YouTube Courtship: The Private Ins and Public Outs
   of Chris and Nickas 51
   DAMON LINDLER LAZZARA

4 Virtually Supportive: Self-Disclosure of Minority
   Sexualities through Online Social Networking Sites 62
   BRUCE E. DRUSHEL

PART II
Commodity Networks

5 Lesbians Who Are Married to Men: Identity,
   Collective Stories, and the Internet Online Community 75
   MARGARET COOPER

6	A Very Personal World: Advertisement and Identity of Trans-persons on Craigslist DANIEL FARR	87
7	The Facebook Revolution: LGBT Identity and Activism MARGARET COOPER AND KRISTINA DZARA	100
8	PlanetOut and the Dichotomies of Queer Media Conglomeration BEN ASLINGER	113
9	Commercial Closet Association: LGBT Identities in Mainstream Advertising IAN DAVIES	125

PART III
Fan Cultures

10	Queering Brad Pitt: The Struggle between Gay Fans and the Hollywood Machine to Control Star Discourse and Image on the Web RONALD GREGG	139
11	Internet Fandom, Queer Discourse, and Identities ROSALIND HANMER	147
12	Transconversations: New Media, Community, and Identity MONICA EDWARDS	159
13	Out and About: Slash Fic, Re-imagined Texts, and Queer Commentaries RICHARD BERGER	173
14	Identity Unmoored: Yaoi in the West MARK MCHARRY	185

PART IV
Body Discourses

15 Look at Me! Images, Validation, and Cultural Currency
    on Gaydar   201
    SHARIF MOWLABOCUS

16 Gay Men's Use of Online Pictures in Fat-Affirming Groups   215
    JASON WHITESEL

17 "Compartmentalize Your Life": Advising Army Men on
    RealJock.com   230
    NOAH TSIKA

18 "Stephanie Is Wired: Who Shall Turn Him On?"   245
    TRUDY BARBER

19 Health Information, STDs, and the Internet: Implications
    for Gay Men   258
    JOSEPH CLIFT

PART V
Community Spaces

20 The Demise of the Gay Enclave, Communication
    Infrastructure Theory, and the Transformation of Gay
    Public Space   271
    NIKKI USHER AND ELEANOR MORRISON

21 From Websites to Wal-Mart: Youth, Identity Work, and
    the Queering of Boundary Publics in *Small Town, USA*   288
    MARY L. GRAY

    Notes on Contributors   299
    Index   304

Figures and Tables

Figures

1.1	Lawrence King	18
1.2	Adrian L. Acosta	26
1.3	"Remember Lawrence King"	27
14.1	*Endless Waltz*	187
14.2	*Mite, mite!*	192
16.1	"Absolut Beefy"	219
16.2	"Underwear: Calvin Klein—Belly: Burger King"	222

Table

6.1	Percentage Distributions Among the Different Types of Personal Ads	92

Preface

Christopher Pullen

This book offers a critical introduction into Lesbian, Gay, Bisexual, and Transgender (LGBT) identity within online new media. In a contemporary age, where identity is often played out within online and virtual environments as much as face to face encounters, this book explores the evolving citizenship potential of LGBT identity, which is increasingly apparent within the World Wide Web. LGBTs are for the first time not only experiencing more optimistic life chances in the contemporary (developed) world (such as the *limited* legislative advances in same sex marriage,[1] and anti-hate crime laws protecting diverse sexuality),[2] but also they are engaging in new opportunities for identity affirmation and investigation, online. From the potential of social networking and political mobilization, to that of identity experimentation and activity, this book explores the significance of "self reflexivity" for LGBT identity, inherent in contemporary constructions of personal self and community within modern society.

This book argues that LGBT identity is evolving as a community form, at the same time that it is increasingly distanced from the need for a physical social space, in the mediation and evocation of its messages, politics, and textures. The tension of the virtual and immediate, in contrast with the physical and disconnected, is a central axis of engagement in attempting to understand the accelerating development of these new "advances."

Presenting the work of a wide range of authors, who offer a variety of insights through their own research and discipline specialism, this book develops a discussion which mediates key theories, such as queer theory, social construction, audience reading, and identity politics, pertinent for LGBT identity. Exploring tensions and dynamics between these theories, a focal point of investigation is the examination of the productive and cultural potential of new media producers. This reveals the diverse yet coalescent nature of LGBT identity, exhibited through varying levels of engagement. Such cohesion is explored through the framework of this book, which foregrounds the impact of youth and social agency, the dynamic of social networking and issues of commodity, the iconic and interactive potential of fan-based culture, the discursive, performative and "well being" significance of the body, and the dynamic of community "physical" social space.

LGBT Identity and Online New Media offers new insight into examinations of imagined democracy played out through the internet and the World Wide Web. In offering the prospect of new voices to the historically silenced, othered, and disconnected, new opportunities online are presented to LGBTs in the formation of ideal worlds and the construction of sites of resistance, revealing an evolution in terms of understanding.

Notes

1 The world's first legally recognized same sex marriages were performed on January 14, 2001 in Toronto. They were deemed to be legal, as of that date, by order of the Court of Appeal for Ontario on June 10, 2003, setting off court victories across Canada [leading to national legislation offering gay marriage in July 2005]. The Netherlands became the first country to legalize same sex marriage, on April 1, 2001 (Equal Marriage 2008). A number of other countries have also adopted gay marriage. At the time of writing, Belgium, Norway, South Africa, Spain, and Sweden all offer same sex marriage, as do a growing number of U.S states (such as Massachusetts, Connecticut, Iowa, Vermont, and New Hampshire).
2 For example, the development of The Law Enforcement Hate Crimes Act in the United States (Govtrack 2009).

References

Equal Marriage. 2008. http://www.samesexmarriage.ca/equality/world.html#netherlands. [Accessed November 22, 2008]

Govtrack. 2009. http://www.govtrack.us/congress/bill.xpd?bill=h111-1913 [Accessed August 4, 2009]

Acknowledgements

Christopher Pullen

I would like to express admiration for emerging LGBT youth, who offer enduring inspiration for my research. Through expressing more carefree and confident lives, in many instances I would argue that they are leading the way in changing our world. Despite facing historically embedded challenges and oppression, they are embarking on new pathways of innovation, bravery, and commitment, which we can all learn from.

I would particularly like to thank my co-editor Margaret Cooper, as her work on rural lesbians and opportunities of online new media (presented at the Popular Culture Conference in Boston 2007) stimulated our meeting, leading to our partnership as editors and the formation of this book. Also I would like to express deep gratitude to Matthew Byrnie at Routledge for his admirable support in commissioning this book, and to Matt's assistant Stan Spring for his exceptional dedication.

Significantly, Margaret and I would like to thank our contributors for their hard work in forming this book. We are inspired by their dedication, insight, and passion. Our involvement with them has not only been pleasurable and rewarding, but also we would consider them as close allies and friends.

Also, we would like to note the contribution of José Luís Terrón Blanco, Sarah Boslaugh, Nishan Bernard Dharmaindra, Jana Funke, Terri He, Gareth Longstaff, Richard Pearce, Kristin Scherrer, Ramon García Sedó, and Naida Zukic, who were involved in the project in the early stages of its development, but for various reasons were unable to contribute. In addition we would like to thank Adrian L. Acosta, André Beja, Michael W. E. Edwards and *The Advocate*, *Limina*, Mid-America American Studies Association, Palgrave, Thomas Peele, and Kitsune Steele for the provision of valuable media and permissions in the formation of this book.

Furthermore, I would like to thank various friends and colleagues (including many at Bournemouth University) who have inspired and supported my research: Richard Berger, Hugh Chignell, Fiona Cownie, Adam Cox, Karl Curling, Christopher Frankland, Dimple Godiwala, Robin Griffiths, Graeme Harper,

Su Holmes, Alex Hunt, Andrew Ireland, Deborah Jermyn, Stephen Jukes, James R. Keller, Shaun Kimber, Leno Pisano, the editors of *Media, Culture and Society*, Barry Richards, Christabel Scaife (of Palgrave), Leslie Strayner, Sean Street, and Steve Wilson (of McFarland).

Finally, I would like to mention the enduring support of my family Ian, Cleo, and Max. Ian (Davies) is not only my dedicated partner (of over 23 years) and a contributor to this book, but he is also an insightful and caring humanist, educator, and editor; and the ultimate inspiration behind my work.

Margaret Cooper

I would especially like to thank my wonderful partner in life, Tina Pierson, for teaching me how to love profoundly, and our daughter, Julia Grace, for showing me the beauty in life. I love you both and thank God daily for you. You bring joy to my life.

I would also like to express my gratitude to my father, Bill Cooper, for his unconditional love. Many thanks to our daughter, Jessica. We love you. Thanks to my parents-in-law, Bud and Brenda Pierson for their assistance and support, to my mentors, Rob Benford, Jennifer Dunn, and Kathy Ward at Southern Illinois University, Joan Krenzin, Steve Groce, and Judy Woodring at Western Kentucky University, to my biological and chosen families, especially Laura Wellington for her undying encouragement and belief, Mary Wilder for being the sister I never had, Wolf Greenwell for his generosity, and Linda Copeland for a lifetime of friendship, wisdom, and laughter.

Thanks also to Kathy McMichen, David Jordan, Deanna Henley, and Vada Powell. Tina and I will never forget the great kindness you have shown us.

A special thank you to Christopher Pullen for his great vision.

Finally, thank you, Mom and Christine. We know you are still with us.

Introduction

Christopher Pullen

Introduction

Anthony Giddens (1995 [originally 1992]) tells us that:

> Intimacy should not be understood as an interactional description, but a cluster of prerogatives and responsibilities that define agendas of practical activity.
>
> (p. 190)

The engagement of lesbian, gay, bisexual and transgender citizens using the internet displays evidence of social agency, which in Giddens's terms reveals a "Transformation of Intimacy" in the expression of the personal self within the public sphere. This offers new opportunities for action and coalescence, allowing for the showcasing of diverse sexuality. The internet and the World Wide Web *seemingly* reveal a patchwork of new social worlds, offering scope beyond the virtual and the disconnected. Whether this is concerned with identity, representation, production, consumption, or self regulation,[1] LGBTs are defining new pathways distant from historical confines.

LGBTs are actively engaging in a contemporary medium, which although not necessarily technologically determined, has offered provision to a minority, involving user interactivity and self production oriented modes. LGBTs have stimulated online opportunities to test their identities within virtual environments, and to make connections previously unimagined. This may be evident (though not necessarily ideal or universally approved) in the provision, for example, of:

- opportunities for virtual coming out,
- engagement in dating, or sexual encounter,
- the easy access to pornography,
- composing self narratives through blogging,
- connecting to and constructing communities,
- establishing identity ideals,
- the potential to mobilize political ideologies,

- the potential to contribute to historical foundations,
- the opportunity to evaluate preferred service providers manufactures and employers.[2]

Personal access and multi user domains (MUDs) have stimulated a new electronic age for LGBT identity, where the historical isolation and rejection of sexual diversity seems relatively distant. Marking a shift away from the "hold of the local," to quote Anthony Giddens (1995), the "dissembedding mechanism" of online new media in the conditions of late modernity, stimulates new pathways for sexual identity which seem connected. We are living in a world where the discursive potential of an "imagined gay community" (Pullen 2007), *seems* vividly real through online interactivity and identity affirmation.

This book offers a contemporary examination of the potential of LGBT identity within online new media, evident in the presentation of diverse interdisciplinary essays, produced by scholars of mostly western oriented provenance. Although the global potential of new media is clearly contiguous with non western identity, this collection of work aims to provide a foundation within Anglo-centric worlds, which acknowledges the primacy and contention of dominant western voices in global media. Whilst I consider that non western identity and contexts of youth are prime constituents in the emerging political mobilizations for gay and lesbian identity (Pullen 2009), the discussion within this book places in context the superior commodity, and privilege, of online western media producers.[3]

The book is organized under the headings of "Active Youth," "Commodity Networks," "Fan Cultures," "Body Discourses," and "Community Spaces" (further discussed below). At the same time it foregrounds the conflicting perspectives which might be apparent in an examination of the virtual and the substantial, alongside the theoretical and the subjective. Hence a new voice is expressed here in the examination of online new media, extending prior discourses for LGBT identity, which have been largely founded on queer theory, social construction and identity politics. However, *LGBT Identity and Online New Media* is not an attempt to offer a new "queer oriented" examination of the internet and the World Wide Web foregrounding technology and sexuality, as evident in the term "cyberqueer" first discussed by Nina Wakeford (1997) (see also O'Riordan and Phillips 2007). Instead this book is a multivalent platform for the identity concerns for LGBTs, stimulating a focus on the meaning of community.

Whilst inevitably there are preceding texts which appear directly influential, such as Kate O'Riordan's and David J. Phillips's *Queer Online: Media, Technology and Sexuality* (2007) (briefly alluded to above), Jonathan Alexander's "Queer Webs" issue of the *International Journal of Gay and Lesbian Studies* (2002) and Chris Berry's, Fran Martin's and Audrey Yue's *Mobile Cultures: New Media in Queer Asia* (2003), we would also consider that any foundation in new media should consider the issue of "convergence." Hence Henry Jenkins's work *Convergence Culture: Where Old and New Media Collide* (2006) is relevant in revealing the multivalent nature of media, which enables not only the blending of diverse and historically influential generic forms, but also the way in which new media is an evolution of preceding media such as radio, television, film and print. This is related to the convergence of form, and its interconnection to identity.

For example within the arena of TV form, which is highly influential in the convergence of online new media, the work of Raymond Williams (1974), John Ellis (2000), Roger Silverstone (1994), Lynn Spigel (1992) and John Thornton Caldwell (1995) might also be considered in evaluating, issues of flow, segmentation, domesticity, family, and contemporary aesthetics. LGBT narratives within online new media rely on histories of form and delivery which are foundational and contextual. This may be evident in the construction of the video blog, which on YouTube has engendered a new world of "TV" channels formed by vernacular and casual producers (see Chapters 1, 2 and 3). In addition, such forms of personal and confessional address inevitably should relate to issues self disclosure, intimacy, and therapeutic potential, which may not only be seen in theories of contemporary society such as the "Transformation of Intimacy" (Giddens 1995) (discussed above), but also are evident within discussions of televisual and documentary form (see Pullen 2007; Renov 2004; Shattuc 1997; White 1992). Consequently any understanding of online new media must consider its textual and generic precursors, in terms of form, address and framing. Whilst the ground-breaking work of primary new media theorists such as Shelly Turkle (1995), David Gauntlett (2004), and Howard Rheingold (1993), who coined the provocative term "The Virtual Community," are inevitably contextual to this book, they are not necessarily wholly foundational. The convergence of form and its relationship to identity potential is central, melding generic and textual precursors.

Therefore the ground-breaking LGBT historical and identity work of Richard Dyer (1984, 1990) Vito Russo (1981), Steven Capsuto (2000) Joshua Gamson (1998), Larry Gross (2001) Roger Streitmatter (1995) and Edward Alwood (1996) within film, television, radio and print media should be considered as informative to recent new media "queer" theorists (discussed above). In addition, any understanding of LGBT identity within the media must contextualize the substantial investigations of queer theory and social construction. Hence paradigmatic writers within queer theory such as Judith Butler (1999 [originally 1990]), Eve Kosovsky Sedgwick (1990), Steven Seidman (1996), and Mark Warner (1993), should be considered alongside those within social construction such as Michel Foucault (1998 [originally 1976]), Anthony Giddens (1992, 1995) (discussed above), Mary McIntosh (1996), Ken Plummer (1997 [originally 1995]), and Jeffrey Weeks (1990, 2000), in this estimation.[4]

The tension between queer theory and its advocacy of identity deconstruction, in contrast with social construction, and its propensity for coalescence, should be a prime ingredient in any examination of "LGBT identity." The term is deployed to represent not only the potential of lesbian, gay, bisexual, and transgender citizens, as an identity construct of sexual diversity, but also to foreground the subcultural challenge and the philosophy of "queer" life. Hence the tension between deconstruction and cohesion is inevitably a process rather than a fixed point of energy or investigation. This process of identity, inherent within any evaluation of LGBT lives (in theoretical and practical terms), must consider the diversity of the components which make up this fragmented coalescence, and the constituents of power.

Therefore the primacy of gay and lesbian discourses should be acknowledged, as foundational and also as problematic within the composition of LGBT. Although identity politics (Rimmerman 2002), and issues of sexual citizenship (Bell and Binnie 2000) are central, these are founded on a gay and lesbian civil rights movement, which potentially subordinates bisexual and transgender voices. As Brett Beemyn and Erich Steinman (2002) tell us "[s]ince the late twentieth century, bisexuality has seemed to be both everywhere and nowhere in popular culture" (p. 3), evident in the contentious conflation of the oppositional identities of heterosexuality and homosexuality (see also Tucker 1995). Bisexual and transgender identities are often not an easy fit within political ideologies. As Surya Munro's and Lorna Warren's (2004) discussion on "transgendering citizenship" reveals, diverse models of sexual and feminist citizenship are not necessarily harmonious with transgender identity, and there is a need to address the assimilationist and oppositional potentials. LGBT identity is a contentious construction, which whilst it is used to affirm sexual diversity, is largely composed of diverse and often contrapuntal constituents.[5]

Despite this, an overarching philosophy of LGBT identity should be related to its potential as an affirmative celebration of sexual diversity. This book explores such potential on varying levels of theoretical and philosophical engagement. LGBT potential may be related to contemporary narrative and the opportunity of "new storytelling" (Pullen 2009) and to "intimate citizenship" (Plummer 1997, 2003), extending from Anthony Giddens's evaluation of "the transformation of intimacy" (1995) within modern society (discussed above). This offers coalescence for LGBT identity, in the intimate expression of (albeit polyvalent) self identity within public space. John D'Emilio's (1983) evaluation of gay and lesbian community is helpful here. He argues that historically:

> [A] subculture of gay men and lesbians was evolving in American cities that would help create a collective sense of consciousness among its participants and [this would] strengthen their sense of identification within a group.
>
> (p. 13)

I suggest that this is a precursor to the enhanced identity expression of LGBTs within online arenas. Furthermore this can be related to the erosion of the divide between public and private spheres (Habermas 1962), intensified through intimate disclosure and public exhibition within new media. I argue that not only new media offers for LGBT identity an oppositional, or proletarian, public sphere (Livingstone and Lunt 1994; Negt and Kluge 1993 [originally 1972]) where dissenting voices may be heard, but also that LGBT community takes form through agency as "counterpublics" (Warner 2002). As Michael Warner affirms:

> [P]eople address publics, they engage in struggles—at varying levels of salience to consciousness, from calculated tacit to mute cognitive noise— over the conditions that bring them together as a public. The making of publics is a metapragmatic work newly taken up by every text in every reading.
> (p. 12)

Through online new media, LGBTs offer personal expressions of self, in the construction of a public identity. This as Warner suggests, relates to diverse textual forms, in the constitution of an identity. At the same time there is an awareness of speaking to a public, offering some sense of democracy. However in terms of a "direct versus a representative" democracy (see Graham 1999), the representatives of political power might be new media producers engaging in citizenry through the internet, challenging the direct and oppressive power of heteronormativity. This involves LGBTs presenting themselves to a public, as politically oriented identity (albeit unelected by consensus).

As within all media, this involves addressing a general public, as much as a subaltern public. This sense of a larger public, of different constitutive factors, consequently not only relates to LGBTs themselves, but also to their relationship, and address, to wider society. In terms of "modern power," this can be enabling, and performative. As Nancy Fraser (1989) tells us, relating Michel Foucault's (1998) ideas:

> [Modern power] is more penetrating than earlier forms of power. It gets hold of its objects at the deepest level—in their gestures, habits, bodies and desires. .... Taken in combination, these characteristics define the operation of modern power as what Foucault calls "self amplifying."
> (p. 24)

Such potential for "modern power" to flow though varying contexts of social life foregrounds the opportunity of "self amplification" though online new media. The constitution of LGBT may suggest a disorganized force, but through the connection of intimate storytelling and community identification, transgressive ideas progress. LGBTs may appear as a patchwork quilt of different colors, patterns and textures: despite this the domestic form of the social fabric inherent in LGBT offers union and context. It reveals the coalescent potential of social movements evident in "stories of change" (Davis 2002), played out through the narrative expression of self within community.

Self Identity Politics and the Structure of the Book

Self expression is the inherent theme within this book, relating the potential of new media to offer discursive space for identity and identification stimulations. This is evident in terms of author investigation and textual relationships, foregrounding an identity politics approach. Although Diana Fuss (1995) tells us that "any identity politics need to come to terms with the complicated and meaningful ways that identity is continually compromised, imperiled, one might even say *embarrassed* by identification" (p. 10), the process of self identification is important here, in the provision of deeper and reflexive insight. This might be related to the potentially subjective context of the authors, who identity with their subject texts, but offer self reflexive visions of analysis. As David Swartz (1997) reports discussing Pierre Bourdieu's (1990) discussions on reflexive sociology:

> First, one needs to control for the values, dispositions, attitudes, and perceptions [i.e. Bourdieu's notion of "habitus" (1984 [originally 1979])] that the researcher brings from his or her social background to the object of inquiry. This means cultivating a critical awareness of the social location of the researcher (e.g., class origins, race or gender) in a particular historical context and how this background may shape and influence the inquiry.
>
> (p. 272)

Consequently, in union with the subjects and representational contexts of this book, the authors presented here largely identify as LGBT (or "queer") themselves, or as heterosexuals who offer feminist and transgressive examinations of sexual identity. Hence the control and critical context for the "values, dispositions, attitudes, and perceptions" of the researchers evident within this book are that we announce a political affinity with "queer politics," yet deploy our various interdisciplinary methodologies with the intent of objectivity. Although Edward Said (1995 [originally 1978]) would appropriately announce "it is true that no production of knowledge in the human sciences can ever ignore or disclaim its author's involvement as a human subject in [their] own circumstances" (p. 11), I would argue that the author's relationship to the texts discussed here offers insights of reflexive identification which are enabling and useful.

Evoking Anthony Giddens's (1992) concept of the "reflexive project of the self," as scholars concerned for LGBT identity, Margaret Cooper and I (as the editors of this book) present a cohesive and intimate narrative of contemporary society, which is informed by union and relationship with the subject text. In this sense, to address Bourdieu's and Said's concerns, we are telling stories of ourselves and/or of our political concerns (as LGBT (or "queer") predominantly, in partnership with counter cultural heterosexuals), within the rigor of academia.

The architecture of self storytelling is hence an endemic theme within the authors' intents, and resonant within the textual content of this book, relating the identity concerns of LGBTs online. This is primarily evident in the structure of the book, which foreshadows issues of social agency, networking potential, audience decoding, corporeal deconstruction and physical environment, inherent in the divisions of "Active Youth," "Commodity Networks," "Fan Cultures," "Body Discourses" and "Community Spaces." Within these sections, diverse essays are brought together, revealing not only subject and representational confluence, but also theoretical axis and political ideology.

"Active Youth" is the first section, and focuses on the contemporary themes of social agency within youth, and representational concerns. We argue that youth are not only the prime users and innovators of the internet, but also that LGBT youth are engaging intensely in new opportunities of social action. All the essays within this section foreground this multivalent potential. The first chapter (written by myself) reflects on issues of homophobia in school, which in the extreme may lead to murder. This offers an examination of the murder of Lawrence King, foregrounding a discussion on LGBT responses to the incident. The chapter considers how new media as a discursive tool is potentially transgressive and offers political awareness examining material which is mostly posited on YouTube. The following two chapters by Jonathan Alexander and Elizabeth Losh, and Damon Lindler Lazzara, respectively, similarly focus on the potential of the vernacular video and the video blog. In the former, issues of coming out are discussed, in terms of youth experimenting with this (and at times parodying this). In the latter, an online dating romance is played out between same sex potential partners, revealing "normative" issues of courtship enabled through new technology. Bruce Drushel's examination of youth engagement within social networking sites, exploring issues of identification and the use of language, reveals a complex arena of subjectivity and agency.

"Commodity Networks" is the second section, and concerns both the potential of social networking, and commodity issues evident in "commercial" connectivity. The potential to connect to diverse individuals in the formation of community offers both the affirmation of identity, and opportunities to test out concepts or imaginations of the self. Also, issues of service and production are inevitably central. Margaret Cooper's chapter focuses on the networking possibilities of rural "married" lesbians, and explores new positive notions of self here. At the same time it foregrounds the potential to overcome geographical limitations, and oppressions. The following two chapters by Daniel Farr, and Margaret Cooper and Kristina Dzara, focus further on this potential, examining leading social networking sites Craigslist and Facebook, respectively. Whilst the former chapter foregrounds the changing strategies and opportunities for "trans-persons," the latter explores issues of LGBT identity management, and the potential of activism. Ben Aslinger's discussion on the media conglomerate PlanetOut further develops the discussion concerning the opportunity of material bases, and issues of commercial history. This extends the debate concerning commodity, evident in networking, and marketing. Ian Davies presents the final chapter in this section, offering further insight into the connection between identity and the advertising industry. Exploring the web site The Commercial Closet Association, he foregrounds the contentious relationship between community use and identity potential often played out and parodied in commercials.

"Fan Cultures" is the third section, and is concerned with the relationship between LGBT audiences and iconic references of popular culture, such as evaluations of celebrities, and readings of textual forms. Often LGBTs are represented as possessing an intense relation with the identity of the "star" (Dyer 2001), and likely to deploy the determination of "queer reading" (Sinfield 1994) in reconstructing celebrity personae. Ron Gregg's chapter offers a foundational discussion, exploring Hollywood star identity within an historical setting, and the problem of "queer" identity. The following two chapters by Rosalind Hanmer and Monica Edwards, respectively, explore the stimulating potential of television drama, and active audience engagement with this through new media. With the former exploring *Xena the Warrior Princess* and issues of community, and the latter foregrounding *The L Word* and issues of transgender identity, they respectively offer an historical mythological setting and a contemporary vision. Richard Berger's chapter directly explores the notion of "slash fiction," a genre where popular narratives are reconstructed by vernacular writers in fan appreciation (often in subversion), and LGBT potential within this. Finally, Mark McHarry's chapter offers a detailed investigation of "Yaoi" homoerotic works created by fans of Japanese *manga* (graphic novels) and *anime* (animation). His analysis negotiates the provocative issues of male effeminacy and childhood, within the representational reconstructions.

"Body Discourses" is the fourth section, and concerns the iconic representation and use of the physical form with regard to issues of currency, agency, and concern. Inevitably for LGBTs, the physical body and notions of its discursive and social potential provides not only a locus of identity which might require management, but also a vulnerable resource which may not necessarily be contained or protected. Sharif Mowlabocus's chapter explores the dating site Gaydar, considering issues of intimate physical display, designed to court attention, within the textual disseminations. Issues of authenticity and imagined currency are central here, establishing an arena and vocabulary within this form. The following two chapters by Jason Whitesel and Noah Tsika, respectively, foreground discussions on the male body image, and value judgments that may be made. The former considers issues surrounding the transgressive and countercultural currency of the "overweight" male body within iconic representations. The latter foregrounds the athletic physical form in relationship to some gay men's interest in the armed forces, and explores notions of "authentic" male identity, as directly connected to masculinity. Trudy Barber's chapter presents an independent research concerning virtual identity, and the potential to play out roles of sexuality. Through examining issues of performativity within the online and offline body, a central focus is placed upon discourses of transgender identity, as game play. Our closing chapter is by Joseph Clift, and foregrounds a contemporary discussion concerning the body in terms of health and the sexual engagement of MSM (men who have sex with men, irrespective of social identity) through social networking. Offering an educational and "well being" perspective, the statistics and analysis provide insight and advocate caution concerning the spread of STDs (sexually transmitted diseases).

"Community Spaces" is the fifth, and final, section of the book, and concerns relationships between physical social space, and the emerging context of online new media. The presence of community and the iconic and utilitarian use of physical social space, is a locus of both identity and production. Nikki Usher's and Eleanor Morrison's chapter explores the historical and theoretical constitution of the gay neighborhood focusing on the Castro in San Francisco as a case study, and considers issues of transformation stimulated by varying forces, including online new media. Mary L. Gray's chapter similarly foregrounds the use of public space, in the examination of social networking relative to youth and opportunities for affirmation.

The diverse analysis of the chapters understandably represents a spectrum of voices within polyvalent form. My task as an editor, with Margaret Cooper, has been to collect and organize a wealth of opinion, investigation and ultimately dissemination. Inevitably as LGBTs concerned for social identity, our organization has framed these discussions foregrounding a political concern for the oppression of LGBT identity, illuminating the potential of online new media to represent new possibilities for agency, ultimately leading to change.

Conclusion

Online new media is a convergent form, which can be related to preceding historical and generic influences of other media, such as radio, television, film, and print. It can also be placed in context with antecedent issues of representation, which for LGBTs have been reductive within various media. In addition, recent contexts of address and stimulation are relevant, such as the opportunity for self disclosure, and its therapeutic potential, within television and documentary form. In these historical places, whilst recent opportunities have occurred (particularly within documentary (Pullen 2007)), LGBTs have generally been subject to oppressive strategies, architectural within dominant mainstream media, offering dissonance more than harmony.

Whilst online new media appears to offer increasing democratic scope for LGBTs, it is the journey that we have taken which informs the way ahead, as much as the imagined destination. This equates to a need to understand issues such as the subjectivity of "queer" identity, the potential of social construction, and the contemporary setting of self reflexivity. Although LGBT identity seems fragmented and disconnected (exhibiting the primacy of gay and lesbian discourse, and displaying an adjunct relationship to bisexuality and transgender identity, discussed above), it is the knowledge of self, and of the histories and forms of the past, which we can learn from.

Such agency should involve "emancipatory politics," which Anthony Giddens (1992) suggests:

> ... involves two main elements: the effort to shed shackles from the past, thereby permitting a transformative attitude towards the future; and the aim of overcoming the illegitimate domination of some individuals or groups by others.
>
> (p. 210)

Emancipatory politics is executed this way by LGBTs concerned for their identity, offering a sense of moving forward in transformation, and working towards overcoming oppression. Online new media provides an arena for this in the display and potential of intimacy, which in the conditions of late modernity stimulates LGBT identity in new and productive ways. LGBT identity within online new media offers new scope, particularly when it is reflective, contextual, and continuously self aware.

However, as a closing note to this introduction, and in some senses as an afterword, although I argue that online identity is largely enabling, I would like to express certain concern, which might be called the *ambivalence* of online new media for LGBTs.

The technology of the internet and the World Wide Web offers both a site of opportunity and contention for LGBT identity. The advent of new communication technology has enabled the construction of new vivid electronic arenas of networking, community and identity. At the same time evoking Nikki Usher's and Eleanor Morrison's findings (in Chapter 20), engagement within new virtual forms reveals a certain migration from a need for LGBT presence in real physical social space. This is evident in virtual and online social (and sexual) encounters subverting the need to venture into real community spaces, where physical community might meet by social chance (e.g. in community venues such as youth clubs, cafes, bars, night clubs, book stores, and varying locations of political gathering and social leisure). In this way, the internet holds up an ideal for new connections and identity stimulations, which might create new social settings, yet at the same time it may limit the need for real social space in establishing new forms of communication.

Consequently, whilst this book reveals the stimulation of new connections for LGBT identity, at the same time we might consider the potential loss to some extent of real physical community. I suggest that the way ahead may be a strategy of visibility inspired by an old world order, yet embracing new online possibilities. Visibility is the essential ingredient in the establishment, development and endurance, of any community. Although the "disembedding mechanism" (Giddens 1995) of online new media frees us from the "hold of the local," in essence what is needed is to change "real" local environments, as much as to venture into "virtual" global cyberspace. Our increasingly bold presence on the internet and the World Wide Web needs not only to offer identity connections, but also to contribute to the reconstruction of everyday physical living space, which ideally should be democratic and all encompassing.

Notes

1. I am offering resonance to Paul du Gay et al.'s (1997) "circuit of culture," modifying regulation to "self" regulation.
2. The extent of potential for LGBTs is diverse. The Advocate's *Gay and Lesbian Online: more than 4,000 web sites from bears to lesbian chic and circuit parties to domestic partnership* (Dawson 2003), provides an extensive sample arena.
3. Chapter 14 (by Mark McHarry) is the main exception, as this focuses on media production of Japanese provenance. However, in terms of the non western analogy employed here, Japan may be considered as an industrialized 'western oriented' country.
4. This is not to say that queer theory and social construction are disconnected, nor that the authors mentioned here fit comfortably within this distinction (e.g. Foucault is often considered as a queer theorist).
5. We should also consider issues of asexuality and intersexuality within this (see Grabham 2007, and Scherrer 2008).

References

Alexander, J. 2002. Introduction to the special issue: Queer webs: Representation of LGBT people and communities on the world wide web. *International Journal of Sexuality and Gender Studies* 7(2/3): 77–84.
Alwood, E. 1996. *Straight news: Gays, lesbians, and the news media.* New York: Columbia University Press.
Beemyn, B., and Steinman, E. 2002. *Bisexual men in culture and society.* New York: Haworth Press.
Bell, D., and Binnie, J. 2000. *The sexual citizen: Queer politics and beyond.* Cambridge: Polity.
Berry, C., Martin, F., and Yue, A., eds. 2003. *Mobile cultures: New media in queer Asia.* Durham. NC: Duke University Press.
Bourdieu, P. 1984 [1979]. *Distinction: A social critique of the judgement of taste.* Trans. R. Nice. London: Routledge.
Bourdieu, P. 1990. *In other words: Essays toward a reflexive sociology.* Stanford, CA: Stanford University Press.
Butler, J. 1999 [1990]. *Gender trouble,* rep. London: Routledge.
Caldwell, J. T. 1995. *Televisuality: Style crisis and authority in American television.* New York: Rutgers University Press.

Capsuto, S. 2000. *Alternate channels: The uncensored story of gay and lesbian images on radio and television*. New York: Ballantine Books.
Davis, J. E., ed. 2002. *Stories of change: Narrative and social movements*. Albany: State University of New York Press.
Dawson, J. 2003. *Gay and lesbian online: More than 4,000 from bears to lesbian chic and circuit parties to domestic partnership*, 5th ed. Los Angeles: Advocate Books.
D'Emilio, J. 1983. *Sexual politics, sexual communities: The making of a homosexual minority in the United States 1940–1970*. Chicago: University of Chicago Press.
du Gay, P., Hall, S., Janes, L., Mackay, H., and Negus, K., eds. 1997. *Doing cultural studies: The story of the Sony Walkman*. London: Sage.
Dyer, R., ed. 1984. *Gays and film*, rev. ed. New York: Zoetrope.
Dyer, R. 1990. *Now you see it: Studies on lesbian and gay film*. London: Routledge.
Dyer, R. 2001. *Stars*, rep. London: British Film Institute.
Ellis, J. 2000. *Seeing things: Television in an age of uncertainty*. London: I. B. Tauris.
Fraser, N. 1989. *Unruly practices: Power, discourse and gender in contemporary social theory*. Minnesota: University of Minnesota Press.
Foucault, M. 1998 [1976]. *The history of sexuality, Vol. 1*. Trans. Robert Hurley, rep. London: Penguin.
Fuss, D. 1995. *Identification papers*. New York: Routledge.
Gamson, J. 1998. *Freaks talk back: Tabloid talk shows and sexual nonconformity*. Chicago: Chicago University Press.
Gauntlett, D., and Horsley, R., eds. 2004. *Web Studies*. London: Arnold.
Giddens, A. 1992. *Modernity and self identity: Self and society in the late modern age*, rep. Cambridge: Polity Press.
Giddens, A. 1995 [1992]. *The transformation of intimacy: Sexuality, love and eroticism in modern societies*, rep. Cambridge: Polity Press.
Grabham, E. 2007. Citizen bodies, intersex citizenship. *Sexualities* 10 (February): 29–48.
Graham, G. 1999. *The internet:// a philosophical enquiry*. London: Routledge.
Gross, L. 2001. *Up from visibility: Lesbians, gay men, and the media in America*. New York: Columbia University Press.
Habermas, J. 1962. *The structural transformation of the public sphere: An inquiry into a category of bourgeois society*, trans. T. Burger and F. Lawrence. Cambridge: Polity Press.
Jenkins, H. 2006. *Convergence culture: Where old and new media collide*. New York: New York University Press.
Livingstone, S., and Lunt, P. 1994. *Talk on television: Audience participation and public debate*. London: Routledge.
McIntosh, M. 1996. The homosexual role. In *Queer theory/sociology*, edited by S. Seidman. Oxford: Blackwell Press, 33–63.
Munro, S., and Warren, L. 2004. Transgendering citizenship. *Sexualities* 7(3): 345–362.
Negt, O., and Kluge A. 1993 [1972]. *Public sphere and experience: Towards an analysis of the bourgeois and proletarian public sphere*, rep. Minneapolis: University of Minnesota Press.
O' Riordan, K., and Phillips, D. J., eds. 2007. *Queer online: Media, technology and sexuality*. New York: Peter Lang.
Plummer, K. 1997. *Telling sexual stories: Power, change and social worlds*, rep. London: Routledge.

Plummer, K. 2003. *Intimate citizenship: Private decisions and public dialogues*. Seattle: University of Washington Press.

Pullen, C. 2007. *Documenting gay men: Identity and performance in reality television and documentary film*. Jefferson, NC: McFarland.

Pullen, C. 2009. *Gay identity, new storytelling and the media*. Basingstoke: Palgrave Macmillan.

Renov, M. 2004. *The subject of documentary*. Minneapolis: University of Minnesota Press.

Rheingold, H. 1993. *The virtual community: Homesteading on the electronic frontier*, rev. ed. Reading, MA: Addison-Wesley.

Rimmerman, C. A. 2002. *From identity to politics: The lesbian and gay movements in the United States*. Philadelphia: Temple University Press.

Russo, V. 1981. *The celluloid closet*. New York: Harper & Row.

Said, E. W. 1995 [1978]. *Orientalism: Western conceptions of the Orient*. London: Penguin.

Scherrer, K. 2008. Coming to an asexual identity: Negotiating identity, negotiating desire. *Sexualities* 11(5): 621–641.

Sedgwick, E. K. 1990. *The epistemology of the closet*. Berkley: University of California Press.

Seidman, S., ed. 1996. *Queer theory/sociology*. Oxford: Blackwell.

Shattuc, J. 1997. *The talking cure: TV talk shows and women*. New York: Routledge.

Silverstone, R. 1994. *Television and everyday life*. London: Routledge.

Sinfield, A. 1994. *Cultural politics—Queer reading*. Philadelphia: University of Philadelphia Press.

Spigel, L. 1992. *Make room for TV: Television and the family ideal in postwar America*. Chicago: University of Chicago Press.

Streitmatter, R. 1995. *Unspeakable: The rise of the gay and lesbian press*. Winchester: Faber and Faber.

Swartz, D. 1997. *Culture and power: The sociology of Pierre Bourdieu*. Chicago: Chicago University Press.

Tucker, N., ed. 1995. *Bisexual politics: Theories, queries and visions*. New York: Haworth Press.

Turkle, S. 1995. *Life on the screen: Identity in the age of the internet*. New York: Simon and Schuster.

Wakeford, N. 1997. Cyberqueer. In *The lesbian and gay studies reader*, edited by S. R. Munt and A. Medhurst. London: Cassell, 20–38.

Warner, M., ed. 1993. *Fear of a queer planet*. Minneapolis: University of Minnesota Press.

Warner, M. 2002. *Publics and counterpublics*. New York: Zone Books.

Weeks, J. 1990. *Coming out: Homosexual politics in Britain from the nineteenth century to present*, rev. ed. London: Quartet Books.

Weeks, J. 2000. *Making sexual history*. Cambridge: Polity Press.

White, M. 1992. *Tele-advising*. Chapel Hill: University of North Carolina Press.

Williams, R. 1974. *Television: Technology and cultural form*. London: Collins.

Part I

Active Youth

Chapter 1

The Murder of Lawrence King and LGBT Online Stimulations of Narrative Copresence

Christopher Pullen

Introduction

On February 12, 2008 (in Oxnard, California) a young male teenager Lawrence King (aged 15), who presented an effeminate and sexually ambiguous identity, was murdered in cold blood at school by a fellow classmate, Brandon McInerney (aged 14).[1] A few days later in response to the tragedy at E. O. Green Junior High, Ellen DeGeneres, in an emotionally charged state, on her popular network daytime talk show (*The Ellen DeGeneres Show*, Warner Bros, 2003–, US) told her audience:

> Days before [the murder], Larry asked his killer to be his valentine. [pause, studio audience responds with emotional shock "ohhh"]. I don't want to be political, this is not political, I am not a political person, but this is personal to me. A boy has been killed and a number of lives have been ruined. And somewhere along the line the killer (Brandon) got the message that it's so threatening and so awful and horrific that Larry would want to be his valentine that killing Larry seemed to be the right thing to do. And when the message out there is so horrible, that to be gay, you can get killed for it, we need to change the message.
> [pause, audience applause].

Ellen DeGeneres' heartfelt and "political" response (despite attestations otherwise), speaking of a need to "change the message," not only reached large-scale audiences through the television broadcast network, but it also formed a principal point of access and identification on YouTube (2009a), as a video sequence receiving over a million hits.[2] The media coverage of Lawrence King's story, although following in the precedence of the murder of gay youth Matthew Shepard (in Wyoming in 1998) and the world wide attention awarded at that time which stimulated anti hate crime legislation,[3] received very limited coverage. Only *The Advocate* (the popular gay and lesbian newspaper) foregrounded his story as a central social concern, devoting their front page cover to this (see Figure 1.1), at the same time questioning the imagined over-confidence of LGBT society which might inappropriately support a youth to express sexual diversity at such an early age, and become vulnerable (see Broverman 2008).

Figure 1.1 Image of Lawrence King appearing on the front cover of the *Advocate*, April 8, 2008, addressing concerns of culpability in LGBT society encouraging him to experiment with his sexual identity. Image courtesy of *The Advocate* and LPI Media Inc.

However despite *The Advocate's* reflective concern, mainstream media offered very little debate. Nevertheless, vernacular online media commentary, and particularly video web content posted on YouTube, explored Lawrence's significance as a gay identified youth, and as the victim of a hate crime. Largely these involved intimate responses and took the form of tribute montages, at times in direct response to Lawrence's murder, and also commenting on Ellen DeGeneres' notable "political" stance on the event.

A substantial point of reference in the new media content was redressing the lack of mainstream media coverage for the event. This offered moments of self reflexive personal reflection enabled though contemporary media technology, suggesting copresence, "as a sense of being with others" (Zhao 2003) in terms of narrative understanding, revealing empathy and shared experience. Many LGBT new media producers (discussed below), reiterated personal stories of similarly growing up as outsiders at school, establishing Lawrence King as an icon of bravery, in his self confidence of sexual identity. Although new media memorial content produced by his family (Remember Larry 2009), emphasized the loss of a valued family member, and foregrounded an archive of family snapshots revealing Lawrence growing up (which were copied by audiences and used in later news media tributes to him (see below)), direct allusions to a gay identity, or the support of the positive nature of diverse identity, were avoided. Despite this, Lawrence's reported presentation of a shame free, gender ambiguous identity, and his status as the victim of a hate crime, encouraged new media producers and commentators to construct Lawrence as an inspirational icon of gay youth identity.

This chapter consequently explores the context of Lawrence King's murder in relation to his status as a victim of a hate crime and his potential construction as a gay teen. At the same time it examines the agency of new media producers concerned for the loss of Lawrence, revealing personal intimations of sharing and narrative copresence. However, as alluded to above, it is important to note that there is a disjuncture between a sympathetic LGBT construction of Lawrence, and his family's preferred reading of him as disconnected from gay identity.[4] Therefore the discussion which follows acknowledges the subjective nature of Lawrence King's construction as a gay teen as outside his family, potentially appearing in direct contrast to the representation of Matthew Shepard who was murdered in not that dissimilar circumstances (see Loffreda 2000; Patterson 2005; Pullen 2007), but who was presented by his family as a beloved gay son. Although Lawrence is reported by peers and teachers to have identified as gay, and potentially may have been transgender in his desire to wear female clothing,[5] including a brown pair of stiletto heeled shoes which he bought with a gift card given to him by a gay youth organization (see Setoodeh 2009), as a youth who was troubled he may be read as an unstable identity. Despite this, the narrative of his brave, troubled, and tragic life offered a site of emotive connection. Irrespective of an assured gay (or transgender) identity, his "life story" (Plummer 2001) of transgression, bravery, and ultimate punishment stimulated audiences to reflect.

However, before investigating selected evidence of the new media content in memorial of Lawrence King, produced by Ellen DeGeneres, the Gay Lesbian Straight Education Network (GLSEN), Logo Online, Waymon Hudson,[6] Adrian L. Acosta and YouTube producers "live4life1984," and "Truting" (all discussed below), it is important to consider the context of gay youth at school. This not only offers an insight into the circumstances which may have led to Lawrence's death, but also it potentially offers resonance and motive in reviewing the stimulations of new media producers. In these circumstances, LGBT youth feel ostracized and distanced from normative potentials.

Gay Teen Identity: Denial, Rejection, and Symbolic Violence

Ritch Savin-Williams tells us in his groundbreaking book *And Then I Became Gay: Young Men's Stories* (1998) that:

> Despite the inherent value of romantic relationships, many [gay male] adolescents despair of being given the opportunity to establish anything other than clandestine sexual intimacies with another male.
>
> (p. 160)

Through the presentation of personal narratives, Savin-Williams reveals not only the desire of gay male youths to find romantic partners but also that opportunities for open engagement rarely occur. As outsiders to dominant expressions of romance which reveal the binary dynamic as centered on male and female, same sex potential is denied. When LGBT youths challenge the normative rules of romance, this leaves them vulnerable to the threat posed by heterosexual peers, with "the penalty for crossing the line of 'normalcy' [resulting] in emotional and physical pain" (Savin-Williams 1998, p. 161). Clearly Lawrence King's experience involved this, which is particularly evident in his desire to find a male valentine date, and his tragic rejection by Brandon McInerney, in the formation of an ultimate punishment for crossing the boundaries of normalcy.

Significantly LGBT youth need support networks, however as Gerald Unks (1995) observes:

> [A major] factor contributing to the marginalization of homosexual adolescents is their lack of viable support groups. While virtually all students of any other identifiable group have advocates and support in the high school, homosexual students typically have none.
>
> (p. 7)

This leads not only to a failure for the gay teen to find a positive sense of homosexual identity, but also it reveals the disparity in experience and expectation offered to non-heterosexuals. Although in Lawrence's case there were some supporters of his attempts to explore his identity: teachers who would reassure him of the everyday nature of diverse identity and orientation (such as assistant principal at E. O Junior High, Joy Epstein (Setoodeh 2009)), and institutions both educational and social (such as an LGBT youth group who were concerned for his welfare), ultimately he was not offered adequate care.

This may be related to the larger issue of the need for social and cultural security for LGBT youth. Generally in schools, there are not adequate social mechanisms designed to protect emerging LGBT citizens.[7] Debates within "normative" family and society practically ignore the existence of a non-heterosexual youth, or child.[8] This is particularly relevant with the issue of growing up at home where, as Caitlin Ryan and Diane Futterman (1998) report:

> As [gay and lesbian youth] develop cognitively many ... begin to understand the nature of their difference and society's negative reaction to it. In identifying and learning to manage stigma, lesbian and gay adolescents face additional, highly complex challenges and tasks. Unlike their heterosexual peers, lesbian and gay adolescents are the only social minority who must learn to manage a stigmatized identity without active support and modeling from parents and family.
>
> (p. 9)

Gay and lesbian youth are subject to stigma, and find ways to deal with this often in isolation, without the support of family. Lawrence King's attempts to deal with his stigma apparently took the form of constructing a "larger than life" identity, performed in a way which might have appeared as entertaining, yet provocative. As Ramin Setoodeh (2009) reports:

> Girls [at school] would take photos of [Lawrence] on their camera phones and discuss him with their friends. ..[Furthermore] [d]uring lunch [at school], he'd sidle up to the popular boys' table and say in a high pitched voice, "Mind if I sit here?" In the locker room, where he was often ridiculed, he got even by telling boys, "You look hot," while they were changing, according to the mother of a student.

I would argue that such a performed persona, though easily assumed to be calculated to attract attention and to cause entertainment or disruption, reveals much about issues in the management of a stigmatized identity (see Goffman 1986 [originally 1963]; Plummer 1975). LGBT youth as the subject of oppression and rejection, often need to find ways to "make it through the day." Lawrence King's apparent over confidence, flamboyance, and imagined effrontery need not have been considered as a problem by teachers and peers, but it may be accepted as an understandable response to social and cultural rejection. For Lawrence this was apparent not only in school, but also in his status as a child cared for by the welfare system, outside of normative ideas of family support.

Generally, LGBT youth are situated on the periphery of normative concerns, and not able to draw benefit from heterosexual networks of support and identification. Furthermore, foregrounding Pierre Bourdieu's and Jean Claude Passeron's (2000 [originally 1977]) ideas, they are subject to the "pedagogic action" which is achieved by "pedagogic work" within educational systems, leaving them vulnerable to "symbolic violence."

Educational discourses which construct the diversity of sexuality as outside the norm (or subject to special attention), reveal the "symbolic violence" of the cultural capital, founded on idealized concepts of legitimacy and authority. Pierre Bourdieu considers that "pedagogic work" contributes to this, in the rejection of difference, as outside hierarchy. As Richard Jenkins (2007 [originally 1992]) tells us further exploring Pierre Bourdieu's work in this area:

> Pedagogic work, and its results, are a substitute for physical constraint and coercion; it is produced out of or by pedagogic authority and subsequently reinforces it. Bourdieu argues that the experience—as a pupil—of pedagogic work is the objective condition which generates the misrecognition of culture as arbitrary and bestows upon it the taken-for-granted quality of naturalness.
>
> (p. 107)

Lawrence's status as a pupil, who would be subject to the authority and the institution of education which supports normative expectations of gender, displays evidence of "pedagogic work" in the construction of him as in opposition to "naturalness." Bourdieu would consider this as the "misrecognition" of educational culture as non political and benign, for it is founded upon agreed sets of ideas which distance certain components (such as diversity of sexuality), but potentially implies that these are understood. Lawrence King, like many LGBT youths, was situated in an untenable position, not only subject to symbolic violence, but also marginalized by institutional limitations.

Such marginalization may be considered through relating the larger notion of power. Whilst I have argued elsewhere (Pullen 2007, 2009) that power offers a fluid social constructionist potential in Foucaultian terms (Foucault 1998 [originally 1976]), that we all may possess discursive power which may be capillary (Fraser 1989), resistant, and productive, equally it has the potential to be oppressive and reductive. As David Swartz tells us further exploring Pierre Bourdieu's ideas:

> Bourdieu thinks of symbolic power as "*worldmaking* power," for it involves the capacity to impose the "legitimate vision of the social world and of its divisions." Because symbolic power legitimizes existing economic and political

relations, it contributes to the intergenerational reproduction of inegalitarian social arrangements.

(Swartz 1997, p. 89)

Citizens of gender and sexual diversity are subject to unequal social, cultural, and legislative arrangements, which place them "outside" and encourage divisions. Although schools generally suggest an environment of equality for children and youth, only legitimate ideas of identity are prioritized, and secondary notions are subjugated. However as Bourdieu (2008 [originally 1983]) attests:

> Symbolic power does not reside in "symbolic systems" in the form of an "illocutionary force" but that it is defined in and through a given relation between those who exercise power and those who submit to it, i.e. in the very structure of the field in which belief is produced and reproduced.
>
> (p. 170)

In this sense "belief" and submission to normative frames provides the essential relationship in the exertion of symbolic violence. Those who discount the potential or the value of the individual citizens of gender and sexual diversity are complicit in the continuance of oppression. Although schools are constructed as imagined democratic environments, they are subject to dominant notions of identity, and consequently they expel and reject outsiders through dominant notions of authority. As Bourdieu and Passeron (2000) state:

> [H]ow could such a system of education continue to exist, did it not, through the traditional form of communication which it sets up, continue to serve the classes or groups from whom it derives its authority[?]
>
> (p. 114)

I argue that in response to such dominant authority inherent in educational systems, the new media producers discussed below challenge evident symbolic violence, in order to encourage change and progress.

Such agency might be related to an expression of copresence with the narrative of Lawrence King. Extending concepts such as the potential of audience identification in the witness of traumatic events, largely played out through the reception of images and contemporary media, this offers narrative stimulation. Relating to media images such as those published on the internet foregrounding the childhood of Lawrence King (Remember Larry 2009), through bearing narrative witness and stimulating copresence, as Frances Guerin and Roger Hallas (2007) tell us: "these material images do not merely depict the historical world, they participate in its transformation" (p. 4). Furthermore, this process of copresence "as a sense of being there" (Zhao 2003), reveals evidence of Anthony

Giddens's notion of the "reflexive project of the self" (Giddens 1992), where the individual reflects on personal identity concerns, connecting the self to the event.

In addition, Ken Plummer's (1997 [originally 1995], 2003) concept of "intimate citizenship" and my own hypothesis of "new storytelling" (Pullen 2009) are relevant here, where individuals foreground personal life stories in new media production, contributing to discourses. As Giddens (1992) tells us, "In conditions of modernity, in sum, the media does not mirror realities but in some part forms them" (p. 27), through reflexive agency. The texts discussed here exhibit contemporary ideas of audience identification, copresence, and witness. Through foregrounding the personal self within the political and public frame, the "pedagogic action" (Bourdieu and Passeron 2000) is challenged and reformed by individual storytellers in a process of self representation, within diverse narrative forms.

Reflecting and Constructing Lawrence King: Citizenship, Copresence, and Silence

Whilst Ellen Degeneres' video extract from her talk show achieved the most substantial viewership on the internet (discussed in the introduction), and notably many of the responses to Lawrence King's murder were stimulated by her political stance, a number of subsidiary videos similarly placed the personal narrative of the media producer in context. Potentially following, or at least resonant with DeGeneres' essential narrative: "Larry was not a second class citizen. I am not a second class citizen. It's OK to be gay," the discussion below foregrounds the intimate personal voice as copresent with Larry's story, in political witness and participation.

Such participation was primarily evident in the dedication of the Gay, Lesbian and Straight Education Network's (GLSEN) National Day of Silence (GLSEN 2009a) held on April 25, 2008, to the memory of Lawrence King. This is an annual day of silence in remembrance of victims of hate crimes, mostly supported by students from schools and colleges across the United States of America (Day of Silence 2009). The Day of Silence web site, which foregrounds LGBT youth, reports not only that its recent National School Climate Survey (GLSEN 2009b) "found that four out of five LGBT students report verbal, sexual or physical harassment at school and 29% report missing at least a day of school in the past month out of fear for their personal safety," but attests that "The Day of Silence is one way students and their allies are making anti-LGBT bullying, harassment, and name-calling unacceptable in America's schools." In support of the Day of Silence GLSEN produced their own video advertisement (YouTube 2009b). Also, Logo Online produced a public service advertisement in memory of Lawrence King focusing on bullying in school (YouTube 2009c), and Adrian L. Acosta (under the name of "drawlove") recorded the Day of Silence in New York in a commemorative video posted on YouTube (2009d). The discussion continues by further examining these frameworks, and later relates the video work of Waymon Hudson, and YouTube producers "live4life1984" and "Truting."

GLSEN's and Logo Online's public service advertisements (YouTube 2009b, 2009c) both foreground the significance of role models, in offering a mixture of iconic identities in support of LGBTs at school. The former centralizes pop star Lance Bass (previously of the boy band NSYNC) as sole narrator, with a supporting diverse cast of students who may be identified as LGBT and straight. The latter foregrounds actress Portia de Rossi (Ellen DeGeneres' marriage partner)[9] sharing the dialogue with a number of celebrities, including actor T. R. Knight and pop star Janet Jackson. Both videos focus on the issue of silence and the context of violence; the GLSEN PSA promoting the call to silence for the Day of Silence itself, and the Logo Online PSA exploring Lawrence's case, telling us "no one is safe till we are all safe." These videos foreground a sense of union focusing on diverse citizenship, linking popular cultural iconic celebrity to the everyday school child, and acknowledging the rights of all individuals to explore and express identity in a safe environment. This is highlighted in the Logo Online video where Portia de Rossi tells us "Imagine if wearing make up or a dress could get you killed. For 15 year old Lawrence King that's just what happened," and actor T. R. Knight adds "If you think that gay teens like Lawrence King are safe in our schools, then you are wrong." Whilst the narrative of the Logo Online video continues with a call to action, asking students to speak out against potential bullying in school, generally the idea of coalescence in respect for diversity is central.

Adrian L. Acosta[10] extends this to another level, by recording the events of the National Day of Silence in New York, on 25 April, 2008. Relating the community vigil in Christopher Street Park, New York on that day between 6pm and 8pm, we are presented with a succession of still photographic images in sympathetic montage with no source sound, but simply accompanied by a gently meditative acoustic guitar ballad titled *Exploring the Blue,* with a lead female vocal.[11] The iconic images support various themes which might be connected to the gay and lesbian community. The location of Christopher Park is foregrounded as the camera momentarily focuses on the sign (New York City Department Parks 2009) which is preceded by a succession of iconic New York street signs. This includes Christopher Street, where the notorious Stonewall riots took place in 1969, founding the LGBT civil rights movement in the United States, if not the world (see Clendinen and Nagourney 1999). Monochrome images predominate: but there are two exceptions, offered in vivid color; a rainbow tie and a red commemorative T shirt. The rainbow tie appears as a staged image for the title frame, and is placed across a man's face, his mouth taped shut in a symbolic allusion to silence (see Figure 1.2). Perhaps more significantly, the red commemorative T shirt carrying the script "Remember Lawrence King: Day of Silence" (viewed from the back) is a source image from the demonstration, and is central (see Figure 1.3). This focused use of color counterpoints the sparsity of the monochrome palette. Whilst this framework connotes somber darkness and sincerity in respect of Lawrence's death, it also brings to mind the discourse of the film *Schindler's List* (Steven Spielberg, 1993, US) for its emotive power in foregrounding persecution. In *Schindler's List,* a scarlet coat worn by a little girl is the single incidence of color. When in a later scene, it is cast upon a heap of clothing taken from children who are about to be exterminated in the concentration camps in Nazi Germany, it has a powerful, unspoken significance. The red T shirt at the New York demonstration is similarly framed, as isolated, anonymous, and iconic of separation and distance.

Besides the reference to mood in the color palette, still images are presented of various members of the public respecting the silence, formed as if they are unaware of being photographed, and deep in thought. Many are framed within the traditional decorative iron fencing of Christopher Park, including demonstration participants inside the park and those looking out, suggesting a distinction of community and boundaries that may be apparent. Furthermore, the representation of demonstrators reveals diversity in community constitution. This is evident not only in the representation of those who could potentially be identified as part of a subculture or of an artistic persuasion (who might be considered as supporters of the gay community), but also in the observation that a very wide range of social types of different ages are present, including the foregrounding of the police as supporting the event. This apparent range of diverse

Figure 1.2 Adrian L. Acosta, depicted in an opening image of his YouTube tribute to The Day of Silence in New York, April 25, 2008, in memory of the murder of Lawrence King. Image courtesy of Adrian L. Acosta.

Figure 1.3 An image from Adrian L. Acosta's YouTube tribute to The Day of Silence in New York, April 25, 2008, in memory of the murder of Lawrence King, featuring the "Remember Lawrence King" commemorative T shirt (appears as red with monochrome background). Image courtesy of Adrian L. Acosta.

citizenship offers a sense of togetherness and political cohesion, in tribute to Lawrence and in opposition to homophobia.

Such a public display of cohesion, however is framed within the personal as the video closes, where we see a staged image (of Adrian L. Acosta) emulating the GLSEN PSA video (briefly discussed above), where youths had simulated the idea of silence by holding a single index finger to the mouth. This is then followed with a potential reference to the Logo Online PSA, in its closing textual message of "Dedicated to all those who have fallen the victim of hate crimes. Let us stop the violence today." Adrian L. Acosta's recording and tribute to the National Day of Silence in New York appears to emulate and extend preceding media textual forms. Acosta's work offers a narrative sense of copresence, where "being there" involves not only empathy and understanding, but also a call to action. It is apparent in the recording of the event, in the tone of the production, and in the carefully thought out allusions. Such a sense of personal presence is further evident in the work of Waymon Hudson, and his tribute to Lawrence King.

Waymon Hudson is a "political consultant [who] deals with communications through modern media and youth outreach, [focusing on] social networking sites and Youtube" (Hudson 2008).[12] Hudson describes Lawrence King and the surrounding events in his "video blog," telling us:

He was gay. He liked to wear make-up and jewelry and heels to school, and was bullied [and] teased a lot because of it. What has really been shocking to me is the lack of outrage and anger, and the lack of media coverage of it, within the mainstream media. The gay blogs and LGBT media has really been buzzing about it, but it doesn't seem to be picking up much traction in mainstream media, which is really bothersome to me, because I can't remember when there was a violent school shooting like this, that didn't get 24/7 news coverage. But it seems because this happened to a young gay man, and that makes a lot of people uncomfortable, they don't want to talk about it. They want to brush it under the rug. … When you look at the picture of Lawrence and you read his story, I know I personally see myself in it. He was just like me. In school I was teased because I was too girly. I was called gay, I was beat up a lot, and luckily I made it out OK, but Lawrence didn't.

(YouTube 2009e; The Homo Politico 2008)

Through using his own personal language, setting his image in a confessional manner direct to video camera, Waymon offers a heartfelt interpretation of Lawrence King's murder. Notably, he not only offers insight into the context of media coverage, or its absence, but also he places himself within the frame both literally and metaphorically. We are presented with a political agency, which engages with the potential of "intimate citizenship" (Plummer 1997, 2003) offering democratic scope in personal storytelling. Also Waymon's discourse recognizes the oppression of the "pedagogic action" and "symbolic violence" (Bourdieu 2008; Bourdieu and Passeron 2000) inherent in school environments for gay and lesbian youth. Waymon reacts to Lawrence's story not only expressing his discontent with mainstream media, but also peeling back the layers of potential within LGBT youth, which are so devalued in dominant narratives.

However, not all responses to Lawrence King's murder were necessarily sympathetic: some new media respondents failed to see the deeper human and political context. If we consider the forum contribution of "TxnMom" in response to an MTV article reporting on Lawrence King and the Day of Silence (Harris 2009), we are told:

Middle school is a crazy time for kids. Most are insecure about their own sexual identity, many are undeveloped and terrified of being mocked. ….Why are middle-schoolers [sic] allowed to "flaunt" their sexuality in school? Hetero- or homo-, kids should not be allowed to dress provocatively.

(TxnMom, cited in response to Harris 2009)

Although making some valid points, and criticizing the role of both parents and teachers (in the larger text), this forum contributor presents a biased evaluation. To call for the prohibition of the "flaunting" of sexuality implies a restriction on diverse sexuality, rather than to suppress imagined "normative" sexual interests (such as heterosexuality). The terms "flaunt" and "dress provocatively" imply an unexpressed judgment, as if sexuality were unnatural, undesirable, even dangerous and shameful, inviting punishment. Whilst heterosexual overt sexual display may be potentially considered as a threat, it is only "provocative" if it is unsolicited, and extraordinary. In these terms I argue that diverse sexuality would always be seen as provocative, whilst sexually provocative heterosexual behavior is often accepted as ritualistic, normal behavior in the advance towards adulthood. This characterizes those of diverse sexuality as oppressed, to be unfavorably considered as provocative, in general terms.

Furthermore it is difficult to assess whether Lawrence's behavior was in fact in any way provocative (even though his father attests that it was),[13] because such provocative behavior must be taken in the context of defending a stigmatized identity (see discussion earlier). Consequently, any evaluation of "ideal reforms" needs to be considered as potentially untenable, as they are framed though an educational environment exhibiting "pedagogic action" (Bourdieu and Passeron 2000) which prioritizes heterosexual lives, and does not fully support outsiders. This setting within dominant institutional culture engenders all diversity to be considered as "provocative."

I argue that a call to action in response to the allegation of provocation, as exhibited by the video material produced by GLSEN, Logo Online, Adrian L. Acosta and Waymon Hudson (discussed above), can be largely related to the issue of personal and domestic montage, placing the self within the political frame. Domestic montage is developed further in the commodity use and reframing of childhood images of Lawrence King which were published on the web, and notably apparent on the official Lawrence King family website (Remember Larry 2009). These are evident in a number of personal video productions on YouTube, where Lawrence's childhood images were used in montage. I would like to consider two examples of this as my final case study, produced by YouTube producers "live4life1984" and "Truting."

The video productions of "live4life1984" (YouTube 2009f) and "Truting" (YouTube 2009g) employ the use of domestic childhood images of Lawrence King, contrasting this with sympathetic and/or contextual audio tracks. "live4life1984" uses the pop song *Stay the Same* by Joey McIntyre (previously of the boy band New Kids on the Block), an emotive ballad with refrains such as "Don't you ever wish you were someone else, you were meant to be the way you are exactly". "Truting" uses the pop song *Do You Really Want to Hurt Me?* by Culture Club (headed by openly gay male pop star icon, Boy George), which offers an upbeat tempo, yet focuses on the misunderstanding of sexual diversity with the line "this boy loves without a reason," and repeating the title line and "Do you really want to make my cry?" frequently. Whilst "live4life1984" features the pop song *Stay the Same* as the exclusive audio component, "Truting" blends *Do You*

Really Want to Hurt Me? with an audio track which sounds like a police radio/telephone recording of members of staff at E. O. Green Junior High School (where Lawrence King was murdered) reporting the discovery of the event. In this sense the former relies on the exclusive diegetic of the song to complement the visuals produced, whilst the latter blends an "unnerving" meeting of an up-tempo pop song and the reporting of a murder.

However, despite different approaches to the audio track, both cases prioritize the iconic domestic family images of Lawrence King, counterpointing his life as an everyday child growing up. Images of Lawrence having a haircut, playing baseball, going on holiday, receiving presents for Christmas, and holding a fossil in his hand, are used in successive montage to complement the audio tracks. Whilst this suggests an emotive connotation, foregrounding loss, at the same time there is an historical and archival property in these representations. "Truting" offers a graphic realism within this. In the closing of the video there is a single image of children outside the school where Lawrence was murdered laying floral tributes, and the accompanying audio track dominantly shifts to prioritize the police/school recording. This foregrounds the dialogue:

POLICE RADIO: We have police there now. We do have somebody on the phone that is with the victim, who is trying to help them. . . . .
SCHOOL: We need an ambulance. . . . .
POLICE RADIO: They should be there staging anytime now. OK? . . . .
SCHOOL: We have the gun. The school psychologist has the gun. . . . .
POLICE RADIO: What kind of a school is that?

This sequence adds a sober closure, resolving the dissonance between the upbeat popular song and the police radio track. It focuses not only on the sense of impossibility and tragic circumstance, but also on the responsibility of the authorities. The juxtaposition of the school psychologist with the murder weapon, and the presentation of the police as unaware as to the constitution of the school, offers a political commentary on institutional failure.

In contrast "live4life1984" focuses more on personal agency and social responsibility. The video blends images of memorials, vigils, and tributes to the memory of Lawrence King, besides including contextual images of Ellen DeGeneres, Portia de Rossi, the Logo Network, the Day of Silence, and GLSEN (as discussed above). In addition, in a more intimate focus "live4life1984" offers religious and new age iconography of spirituality (such as images of praying hands, a silhouetted crucifix, doves ascending, and a rainbow). Furthermore, the producer not only places himself within the frame in the introduction to the video, but also he features himself within the montage, as a still image with the caption: "someone who cares."

This contribution also connects with the wider potential of self therapy, within media production. It is highly apparent in an open letter written to Lawrence

King, by the producer behind "live4life1984," Christian Shojamanesh (2009). Christian tells Lawrence:

> I admire you so much because you have something I've never had when I was your age in school … confidence and courage. I "came out" when I was 14. I made the mistake of telling people who I thought were some friends and some family members who don't know the definition of the word secret. As a result, I was tortured on a daily basis. One incident that sticks out in my mind is walking through the park behind school going home and 2 boys had knocked me down and dragged me through the mud. After that one of them had pushed my head into the water adding so much pressure screaming "You f**king faggot!" and then pushed me backwards back on to the ground. I gasped for air and screamed at them they took off running. Larry, I feel the pain you went through from the kids at school.
>
> (Shojamanesh 2009)

Christian's identification with Lawrence's narrative is emotionally charged. It reveals intimate expressions of empathy and understanding, which are contextual to Waymon Hudson's tribute Lawrence King (discussed above), yet offers even more personal intensity.

Personal disclosures such as this might seem inappropriate (considering Lawrence's family's lack of support for his gay identity), but I argue that such disclosures reveal the potential for depth in self storytelling. New media producers and writers, such as Christian, may be related to the larger process of "autobiographical thinking." Anthony Giddens (1992) not only describes this as a central element of self therapy (which is apparent in Christian's video and letter), but also asserts that "autobiographical thinking" should be considered as a process which may engender change. As Giddens (1992) tells us:

> … for developing a coherent sense of one's life history is a prime means of escaping the thrall of the past and opening oneself out to the future. The author of the autobiography is enjoined to go back as far as possible into early childhood and set up lines of potential development to encompass the future.
>
> (p. 72)

Christian and the variety of other openly LGBT media producers discussed here, to a lesser or greater degree, through autobiographical expression, foregrounded their narrative copresence with the horror of Lawrence King's murder. This involved reflecting on personal stories in contrast or union with those of Lawrence King. I argue that such reflection stimulates a pathway towards future progress, in the personal and copresent rejection of homophobia.

Conclusion

Whilst we are unable to ascertain a fixed and essential sexual identity for Lawrence, inevitably the discourse of his life, and the consistency of reports, leads us to qualify his status as an icon for gay youth and sexual diversity. Lawrence should be considered as a brave and valued member of society, who through the tragic circumstances of his demise, inadvertently generated discourses to wide audiences, evoking the challenge, yet ultimate endurance and resolve of LGBT youth.

Many new media producers have displayed empathy for Lawrence's personal story, at the same time relating their own connection to this, in the process of copresence. It is important to note however, that the new media responses discussed here are of varying constitution. The work of Ellen DeGeneres, GLSEN, Logo Online, Adrian L. Acosta, and Waymon Hudson all recognized the context of dominant institution, and the need for professionalism, aesthetic quality, and eloquence, within challenges to the establishment. It's possible to argue that these producers are aware of the "pedagogic action" (Bourdieu and Passeron 2000) embedded within educational systems, which demand robust content of a certain caliber, and tone, in counteraction. These *composed responses* offer "appropriate" allusions and engagements, in their constructions. In contrast, the productions of "live4life1984" and "Truting" may be considered as emotive and instinctive in essence. It is possible to consider these contributions as *spontaneous responses* of copresence, which peel back the layers of a deeper "unprepared" human conscience and essence. Whilst these might be considered by some as unstable and unprofessional productions, I argue that they foreground the intuitive and therapeutic nature of new media engagements. This is resonant of Anthony Giddens' (1995 [originally 1992]) concept of the "transformation of intimacy," indicative of a contemporary society displaced from hierarchy, and engaged in self reflexivity. Ultimately institutional forces are challenged through the intimate display of various individuals, foregrounded within "composed" and "spontaneous" forms of online new media narrative copresence. I argue that these actions have the potential to challenge the dominance of "pedagogic action" (Bourdieu and Passeron 2000) which can subjugate LGBT youth, offering little comfort, acceptance or welcome.

Lawrence King, like Matthew Shepard, represents an icon within tragic histories of brutality, denial, and institutional failure, foregrounding the lack of care for LGBT youth within dominant cultural and social worlds. The courage of Lawrence King in the expression of his sexuality, and the dignity of Matthew Shepard's parents in their support of their beloved son, in many ways inspires a wider sense of social belonging that surpasses the limitations of simple acceptance. This is primarily evident in considering the motives and agency of family members, and the responsibilities that we should all hold.

After Lawrence's death, his family agreed that his bodily organs could be donated for transplantation.[14] In a tragic irony of his affection for Brandon, who became his killer, his heart was donated to a ten year old girl on February 14,

Valentine's Day (Setoodeh 2009). This allusion to love lost, the agency of the family and the commodity of the self, foregrounds the tragedy of Lawrence's story. Often family take for granted the subjugation of LGBT youth, automatically denying their personal life chances, in favor of preserving traditional identity forms. Families, and wider society, might better support LGBT youth not as an emerging "lifestyle" which needs to be understood but rather as an expression of deep commitment to knowledge of self, and an acknowledgement of common humanity. We are living in a new era of LGBT identity, which is largely led by new confident voices within youth. Lawrence's contribution is that he offered an icon of bravery, hope and confidence in self. Although his story is tragic, his legacy may be a testament for a better definition of self worth connectivity, and shared humanity in exploring self and other relations.

Notes

1 At the time of writing the trial of Brandon McInerney has not yet been held. However on July 23, 2009 Towleroad (2009) reports that "McInerney [was] charged as an adult with first-degree murder. [T]he judge said the charge was appropriate, along with an allegation that it was a hate crime." However, it is likely that McInerney will appeal to be tried in the juvenile courts. Should he be successful, this would reduce the context of the alleged hate crime, and the scale of possible punishments awarded.
2 At August 4, 2009 Ellen DeGeneres' YouTube video post (YouTube 2009a) had received 1,190,412 hits. Also within the calculation between July 26 and August 4, 2009 9,049 hits took place, equating to an average of over 1,000 new hits per day almost a year and a half after the event (February 12, 2008), connoting its continuing contemporary resonance.
3 The Law Enforcement Hate Crimes Act, also known as the Matthew Shepard Act, is currently in progress within the United States (see Matthew Shepard 2009; Govtrack 2009).
4 In fact Ramin Setoodeh (2009) reports that although Lawrence King's (estranged) father, Greg King, does not feel sympathy for his son's killer, he "does believe [that] his son sexually harassed [his eventual killer]," contentiously acknowledging an acceptable motive. Furthermore, he is considered as "resentful that the gay community has appropriated his son's murder as part of a larger cause" (Setoodeh 2009), expressing discontent as "it makes a poster child out of [his] son" (Greg King, cited in Setoodeh 2009).
5 On the day that Lawrence was murdered, he reportedly came to school wearing traditional male teen clothing (tennis shoes, baggy pants, a loose sweater over a collared shirt (Setoodeh 2009)), suggesting that prior to this he had been threatened about his gender ambiguous appearance.
6 See Pullen (2009), where I further discuss Waymon Hudson's contribution to "new storytelling," and also relate his response to the murder of Lawrence King.
7 This is also related to the wider issue of homophobia in school, and cultural and social influences, such as the media and its preferred heterosexual discourse (see Frankland 2009; Stonewall 2009)

8 The revolutionary documentary maker Deborah Chasnoff makes positive attempts to address this (see Pullen 2007, 2009), where she foregrounds an educational need for knowledge of the gay community within school, and to address issues of bullying and stereotyping, thereby acknowledging the inevitable existence of gay children.
9 Ellen Degeneres and Portia de Rossi were married in California in August 2008 (People 2009) before the passage of Proposition 8 (in November 2008) which halted the progress of gay marriage in California, but allowed those same sex couples who had already married to retain the status as legal spouses. At the time of writing, there are continuing legal challenges to the passing of Proposition 8, including a federal strategy against the Defense of Marriage Act of 1996 (see Boston Globe 2009).
10 Adrian L. Acosta not only produces work on YouTube under the name "drawlove" and uses the pseudonym of Amnesia Sparkles as a drag artist, but also he is an artist, photographer, performer, and writer (see AdrianAcosta 2009; AmnesisSparkles 2009; GenderFun 2009)
11 "Exploring the Blue" is composed by Irish songwriter Luka Bloom, but is performed by YouTube producer "369bee" (YouTube 2009h).
12 Waymon Hudson founded the web site "Fight OUT Loud" (2008a) with his partner Anthony Niedweiki, a law professor and lawyer. "Fight OUT Loud" is a "national non-profit organization dedicated to empowering the [LGBT] community to fight discrimination and hate" (Fight OUT Loud 2008). "The Homo Politico" (2008) is Waymon Hudson's weblog site, linked to "Fight OUT Loud," which foregrounds his personal reports on homophobia. This includes a diverse range of subjects, of international and local concern.
13 See note 4 above.
14 Lawrence died after two days in hospital, when his family gave permission to turn off his life support machine, after brain death was confirmed.

References

AdrianAcosta. 2009. www.AdrianAcosta.com [Accessed August 4, 2009]
AmnesiaSparkles. 2009. www.AmnesiaSparkles.com [Accessed August 4, 2009]
Boston Globe. 2009. Mass. is 1st to fight US marriage. http://www.boston.com/news/local/massachusetts/articles/2009/07/09/mass_to_challenge_us_marriage_law/ [Accessed July 28, 2009]
Bourdieu, P. 2008 [1983]. *Language and symbolic power,* rep. Cambridge: Polity Press.
Bourdieu, P., and Passeron, J. C. 2000 [1977]. *Reproduction in education, culture and society,* rep. London: Sage.
Broverman, N. 2008. Mixed messages. *The Advocate,* Issue 1005, April 8: 28–33.
Clendinen, D., and Nagourney, A. 1999. *Out for good.* Simon and Schuster: New York.
Day of Silence. 2009. http://www.dayofsilence.org/index.cfm [Accessed August 20, 2009]
Fight OUT Loud. 2008. http://www.fightoutloud.org/ [Accessed July 24, 2008]
Foucault, M. 1998 [1976]. *The history of sexuality, Vol. 1,* trans. Robert Hurley, rep. London: Penguin.
Frankland, C. 2009. Representing the gay identity within children's media. Unpublished graduate dissertation, Bournemouth University, UK.

Fraser, N. 1989. *Unruly practices: Power, discourse and gender in contemporary social theory.* Minneapolis: University of Minnesota Press.

GenderFun. 2009. www.GenderFun.com [Accessed August, 2009]

Giddens, A. 1992. *Modernity and self identity: Self and society in the late modern age*, rep. Cambridge: Polity Press.

Giddens, A. 1995 [1992]. *The transformation of intimacy: Sexuality, love and eroticism in modern societies*, rep. Cambridge: Polity Press.

GLSEN. 2009a http://www.dayofsilence.org/content/news.html [Accessed July 28, 2009]

GLSEN. 2009b National school climate survey. http://www.glsen.org/cgi-bin/iowa/all/library/record/1927.html [Accessed July 28, 2009]

Goffman, E. 1986 [1963]. *Stigma: Notes on the management of spoiled identity*, rep. London: Penguin.

Govtrack. 2009. http://www.govtrack.us/congress/bill.xpd?bill=h111-1913 [Accessed August 4, 2009]

Guerin, F., and Hallas, R. 2007. *The image and the witness: Trauma, memory and visual culture.* London: Wallflower Press.

Harris, C. 2009. Lawrence King—Student who was murdered for being gay—To be honored with national day of silence. http://www.mtv.com/news/articles/1582039/20080221/id_0.jhtml# [Accessed 26 July 2009]

Homo Politico. 2008. http://homopolitico.tumblr.com/. [Accessed July 24, 2008]

Hudson, W. 2008. Personal communication. June 10.

Jenkins, R. 2007 [1992]. *Pierre Bourdieu*, rep. London: Routledge.

Loffreda, B. 2000. *Losing Matt Shepard: Life in the aftermath of anti-gay murder.* New York: Columbia University Press.

Matthew Shepard. 2009. http://www.matthewshepard.org/site/PageServer?pagename=Erase_Hate_Crimes_Legislation [Accessed August 4, 2009]

National Day of Silence. 2009. http://www.dayofsilence.org/index.cfm [Accessed 28 July 2009]

New York City Department Parks. 2009. http://www.nycgovparks.org/parks/M012/ [Accessed July 29, 2009]

Patterson, R. 2005. *The whole world was watching: Living in the light of Matthew Shepard.* New York: Advocate Books.

People. 2009. First look: Ellen and Portia's wedding album by Julie Jordan. http://www.people.com/people/article/0,,20220057,00.html [Accessed August 4, 2009]

Plummer, K. 1975. *Sexual stigma: An interactionist account.* London: Routledge and Kegan Paul.

Plummer, K. 1997 [1995]. *Telling sexual stories: Power, change and social worlds*, rep. London: Routledge.

Plummer, K. 2001. *Documents of life: An invitation to a critical humanism.* London: Sage.

Plummer, K. 2003. *Intimate citizenship: Private decisions and public dialogues.* Seattle: University of Washington Press.

Pullen, C. 2007. *Documenting gay men: Identity and performance in reality television and documentary film.* Jefferson, NC: McFarland.

Pullen, C. 2009. *Gay identity, new storytelling and the media.* Basingstoke: Palgrave Macmillan.

Remember Larry. 2009. http://www.rememberlarry.com/ [Accessed July 31, 2009]

Ryan, C., and Futterman, D. 1998. *Lesbian and gay youth: Care and counseling.* New York: Columbia University Press.

Savin-Williams, R. C. 1998. *And then I became gay: Young men's stories.* London: Routledge.

Setoodeh, R. 2009. Young, gay and murdered. *Newsweek,* July 28, 2008. http://www.newsweek.com/id/147790/page/1 [Accessed August 4, 2009]

Shojamanesh, C. 2009. My letter to Lawrence King (1993–2008) http://www.geocities.com/spiritualboy7/larry.html [Accessed July 30, 2009]

Stonewall. 2009. Tuned out: The BBC's portrayal of lesbian and gay people. http://www.stonewall.org.uk/documents/tuned_out_pdf_1.pdf [Accessed August 20, 2009]

Swartz, D. 1997. *Culture and power: The sociology of Pierre Bourdieu.* Chicago: Chicago University Press.

Towleroad. 2009. http://www.towleroad.com/2009/07/brandon-mcinerney-will-be-tried-as-adult-in-lawrence-king-murder.html [Accessed August 4, 2009]

Unks, G., ed. 1995. *The gay teen: Educational practice and theory for lesbian, gay, and bisexual adolescents.* New York: Routledge.

YouTube. 2009a. Ellen DeGeneres discusses the recent tragic death. http://www.youtube.com/watch?v=QcMEL3_YsVI [Accessed July 28, 2009]

YouTube. 2009b. Lance Bass PSA for day of silence. http://www.youtube.com/watch?v=ah5eUz6iT9s [Accessed July 28, 2009]

YouTube. 2009c. LOGO's Lawrence King PSA. http://www.youtube.com/watch?v=qUsEgG5musk [Accessed July 28, 2009]

YouTube. 2009d. Lawrence King Vigil NYC 4-25-08 day of silence. http://www.youtube.com/watch?v=flWy7iFduiU [Accessed July 28, 2009]

YouTube. 2009e. http://www.youtube.com/watch?v=1wy4EAigSBw. [Accessed July 24, 2009]

YouTube. 2009f. To: Lawrence "Larry" King (revised). http://www.youtube.com/watch?v=DgSe9Io4uf0 [Accessed July 30, 2009]

YouTube. 2009g. Lawrence King tribute—very sad. http://www.youtube.com/watch?v=o42_UpP_uB0 [Accessed July 30, 2009]

YouTube. 2009h. Exploring the Blue covered by Cathy and Frank. http://www.youtube.com/watch?v=o0yR4zEeKzs [Accessed August 4, 2009]

Zhao, Shanyang. 2003. Toward a taxonomy of copresence. *Presence: Teleoperators and Virtual Environments* 12(5) (October). http://www.mitpressjournals.org/toc/pres/12/5 [Accessed July 28, 2009] societal critique by an extremely heterogeneous population of alternative content-creators and disseminators (Juhasz 2008). As such, we ask, with new media scholars and queer theorists, what kinds of normative discourses discipline the production of coming out videos, as well as what kinds of productive resistances form in response to pressures to produce (and reproduce) particular coming out narratives through the affordances of "vlogging." While our survey here can only be partial, we contend that our observations represent some significant trends in the rhetorical construction and performance of coming out in popular video formats. We conclude with a consideration of the emergence of databases organizing and archiving coming out videos and what such databases may suggest about these videos' rhetorical efficacy in aggregate

Situating Coming Out Videos in Identities and Communities Online

For many lesbian, gay, bisexual, and transgender people, particularly those in rural or isolated areas, the Internet has been an important, even vital venue for connecting with others and for establishing a sense of identity and community. Particularly in a queer diaspora where notions of community and contexts of identity are central, these must often be constructed through information steadily gleaned, sometimes at great personal and political cost, from places outside one's home of origin (Frank et al. 2000; Meem et al. 2009). Certainly, much queer activity online is about "hooking up," but it is also about establishing, and asserting, identity and community. As such, much scholarship about queer activity online has focused on issues of representation. How and to what effect do LGBT/queer people represent themselves online? What kinds of representational practices are used by queers (and by non-queers) to figure queerness? What kinds of work—socially, culturally, personally, and politically—do such representations do? What are their possibilities and limitations?

Coming out videos often make these questions of representation quite explicit, particularly because the specific media form promises access to an unmediated truth by a confessing subject who seems to be offering a moment of intimate disclosure of an authentic identity hidden by a social mask, while also emphasizing how gender and sexuality are performed for the camera much as they are staged in offline environments. Often the speaker describes his or her journey of assembling "clues" to personal sexuality that goes back to early experiences. In many coming out videos the performative quality of the speech act also reminds the viewer that an actual change of state takes place through the speaker's rhetoric. As apples33ds (2008) explains in his text description of his video, the digital replication of this revelation not only marks a life-changing rhetorical occasion but may actually constitute it: "This is my coming out story . . . which may even be a coming out video . . . people actually finding out through this video." His video includes a seemingly self-contained recognizable and even predictable "story," but the circumstances of its dissemination online may also create other narratives of recognition and discovery that take place outside the frame of his composition via the computer screens of others. For example, in beginning his video, apples33ds situates his rhetoric within an entire community of similar content-creators before addressing audience members in his personal circle who may be surprised by his declaration:

> Hello, this is John. I'm doing this video because last week these videos really helped me in my circumstances. I'm gay, and I came out on the weekend. I had come out once before and that was to a friend on St. Patrick's Day this year. For anybody that's watching that knows me that I haven't told I guess this will be a shock to you. I don't know. Just let me know if you see this, so we can talk about it.

Kate O'Riordan and David J. Phillips write in their introduction to *Queer Online: Media, Technology, and Sexuality* that much scholarship analyzing queer representation online "highlight[s] the ongoing importance of place, space, embodiment, and everyday life in the construction and production of queer techno-practices" (2007, p. 4). We can see the relevance of "place, space, embodiment, and everyday life" in this and any number of other coming out videos; apples33ds acknowledges the dissemination of other coming out videos in cyberspace as crucial in helping him frame his own narrative as well as offering him a sense of potential community from which to speak more authoritatively as a queer subject. Interestingly, his is also an invitation to connect not just digitally but materially, face to face, in the ongoing construction and reconstruction of his identity and community.

While such declarations seem intimately personal—note the halting nature of apples33ds speech in his video—these are not stories without structure. Ken Plummer posits in *Telling Sexual Stories* that a gay or lesbian subjectivity often finds initial public expression in a coming out narrative that asserts "truth" about oneself; such stories usually "use some kind of causal language, sense a linear progression, [and] talk with . . . language [as though their tellers] are 'discovering a truth'" (1994, p. 83). Plummer suggests that "Stories are often, if not usually, conservative and preservative—tapping into [a] dominant worldview" (p. 178). That worldview often finds expression as a narrative with certain key, frequently reproduced elements: "young gay person discovers his/her difference, or the 'truth' about him/herself at an early age, struggles with telling close friends and family, finds various levels of acceptance and rejection, accommodates accordingly, and learns to love his/her life" (Alexander 2002, p. 87). The repetition of such stories creates a commonality of experience and community.

But since these are also *video* coming out narratives, they follow some of the emerging rhetorical conventions of homemade, self-sponsored video production. For example, like a large category of instructional videos on YouTube, many of these coming out videos use conventions from DIY or how-to genres. For example, GDProphetXVII (2007) promises to enumerate useful tips, by counting off "how I did it, how I dealt with it, and what it has done to me." Gay-God (2007) has created an entire FAQ, which has garnered over one million views, that covers frequently asked questions about coming out. He appears as an authoritative figure on the subject, speaking before a rainbow flag to the camera, where he expresses his expectation that "this video will help you with any of your coming out problems."

Rhetorically, the *kairos* or "appropriate timing" of coming out is a significant consideration for many LGBT YouTube users. In GayGod's video, for instance, the Q&A structure begins with a question about timing and rhetorical occasion: "When is the best time to come out?"

> Okay so the best time to come out is when you are a little older and independent and on your own, because when you are dependent on your parents they can take away privileges. Like let's say you have a car or a cell phone, and it's under their name, they can take it away from you. I know from experience that when I came out of the closet, my mom could took away my computer, which meant my life basically, because I was on the computer all the time talking to my friends, you know going on MySpace, all that fun stuff. But she took it away from me. Because she could. Because she thought it would teach me a lesson.

GayGod warns that one of the consequences of coming out could be the sacrifice of access to sustaining online social networks, particularly when authority figures have already been swayed by the rhetoric of moral panics about use of the Internet by young people. As Sarah Banet-Weiser (2004) has argued, the online activities of minors necessarily challenge ideologies that romanticize and desexualize childhood. While the sexually explicit and nominally gated content posted on video-sharing sites like GayTube (offering mostly pornographic content) assumes closed access to specific knowledge communities, content on YouTube is not labeled as "adult," so young and old, as well as gay and straight, may view and respond to the video content that is presented. Thus, young queers are often active vloggers who try to manage a number of online identities while incorporating an explicit consciousness of camerawork, editing software, and the reception practices circulating around other YouTube videos. For instance, they know that "sensitive" material can elicit hostile comments, so gay YouTubers posting their own coming out videos learn how to respond to those who leave comments—both positive and negative—on their channels. As such, they learn to manage identities in the growing social networks that characterize the lives of many young people, gay and straight, in the net-saturated spaces of the Global

North. For gay youth, however, these social networks are often more than just online "hang out" spots or ways to keep track of friends and family; they offer access to online communities, narratives for negotiating coming out and its consequences, and emotional and psychological support, particularly if such might not be immediately present. They serve importantly as a testing ground for first steps in coming out "IRL" or "in real life."

The Marketplace of Identities: Queer Critiques on YouTube

Certainly, the dissemination of recognizable identities has been important for queers to connect online and form community and even engage in political activism. Just as important has been the possibilities opened up for people to explore different sexual subjectivities online before trying them out "in real life." For example, Tom Boellstorff has argued that *Second Life*, like other virtual communities, can serve as a testing ground, in which gays and lesbians could "grow comfortable with a gay or lesbian identity before coming out in the real world" (2008, p. 165). Although this has obviously enabled an extension of the erotic palette and imaginations of those with access and time to engage in virtual sexual play, we wonder what other kinds of queer work could be done (and perhaps is already being done) by those involved in multimedia concerned with the representations of queerness. In other words, within concepts of queer identity there is not only a move toward community and a desire for experimental play, but also a gesture of critique—a critique of the normalizing categorizations of people into gay and straight. Such is a critique, in short, of the heteronormative, of the proliferation of sexual subjectivities coupled with regimes of power that reproduce certain kinds of families, certain kind of acceptable intimacies, certain kinds of authorized lives.

In *Coming Out Stories*, the Logo online network has created a series of webisodes consisting of commercially produced videos that normalize, naturalize, reify, and commoditize the coming out experience by showcasing the narratives of telegenic celebrities and public figures. For example, reality show star Jackie Warner of *Workout* on the Bravo network describes how her high school relationship with a cheerleader "rocked my world." Actor Wilson Cruz recounts rehearsing his disclosure in front of a mirror while brushing his teeth as an experience of what he twice calls "ownership." *Coming Out Stories* also includes reality-TV style episodes that invite the viewer to "[s]ee how Karen's mom takes the news when Karen tells her she's a lesbian," or watch as "Chris comes out publicly to the community of West Sacramento, as the Mayor." Audiences are drawn in to what television scholar Annette Hill (2005) has characterized as a hybrid form that mixes fact and fiction, documentary and drama in which sections are organized into conventional story arcs around revelations to loved ones and employers.

Scenes are shot to cut between characters in ways that mimic the exchanges of captive contest participants; for instance, in a scene in which a public speaking professor comes out to his cancer-stricken sister, the audience is invited to "[s]ee more of Tom's story as he comes out to his sister and hear what she has to say."

Commercial interests are hardly the sole proprietors and producers of such sleek and polished videos. From the nonprofit sector, in service of political advocacy for marriage equality, the Human Rights Campaign has invited people to share videos about their experiences of coming out. To encourage similar modes of production, HRC posts model coming out stories with celebrities, pastors, philanthropists, and sports figures. In one video, show business gossip blogger Perez Hilton appears in his closet urging others to take action. Not surprisingly, none of the model videos show children—either the children of LGBT people or of minors identifying as LGBT. One HRC video that received over a half-million views was produced by stand-up comic and writer Mary C. Matthews. Alongside her longtime partner Jen Weidenbaum, Matthews had previously achieved fame for making a video that asked Democratic candidates in the CNN/YouTube debate, "If you were president of United States, would you allow us to be married, [long pause] to each other?" Matthews' HRC video about coming out is carefully scripted to emphasize the framing of her coming out narrative (Matthews 2007), which starts with recounting her anxieties about telling her mother after her first same-sex kiss brings two simultaneous revelations—"this is awesome" and "my mother can never know"—and ends with her imagining "the next nineteen-year-old woman kissing another woman" and thinking "I can't wait to tell my mother." The video uses music, editing, humor, and linguistic play, in which Matthews describes her actual coming out as more of a "cornering," to create a rhetorical set piece that is timeless and universal in its address.

Plummer suggests that such an emphasis on revealing a long-hidden, essential truth of unchanging and fixed identity, as opposed to an emphasis on sexual agency and play, may be a reaction to perceptions of flux, instability, and constant change associated with a postmodern, multicultural era:

> At both millennium and century's end, when a strong sense of massive and rapid social change is in the air, stories take on a crucial symbolic role—uniting groups against common enemies, establishing new concerns, mapping the social order to come. Stories mark out identities; identities mark out differences; differences define 'the other'; and 'the other' helps structure the moral life of culture, group and individual.
>
> (1994, p. 178)

Such expertly produced videos comfort viewers by reminding them of familiar broadcast genres, such as public service announcements or episodes of reality TV shows, and they emphasize the linearity or the cyclic nature of a coming out story that seems to contain no extraneous details or unintended addressees. With their high production values, glossy look, and expert editing, they seem to speak to obvious truths about coming out, perennial narrative norms in the coming out story, and even the necessity of coming out as the most powerful (and empowering) personal and political strategy to promote tolerance of lesbians and gays. Furthermore, although formalized advocacy campaigns may also encourage the production of personal stories and first-person narratives about coming out, they tend to highlight those that feature celebrities or professional spokespeople and limit both who can speak and to whom the message can be addressed. In the process, rhetorical moves in the coming out narrative and aesthetic standards of attraction are reproduced and reified.

While both offer access to information about queerness, and the possibility of sexual play, and they have constituted important dimensions of many people's experience of the Internet, some scholars have raised critical red flags that signal limitations, even dangers, in thinking about what happens when queers go online. Echoing the work of cyberscholars writing about race and online identity, such as Lisa Nakamura, O'Riordan argues that,

> although the ideal cybersubject as fluid and the ideal queer subject as fluid converge in fictions [about cyberspace] and critiques such as [Sherry] Turkle's, there is more evidence to suggest that online queer communities are stratified into fixed identity hierarchies, and anxiety about bodily identity is a strong determinant in online queer formations.
>
> (2007, p. 26)

Citing the work of Joshua Gamson, O'Riordan connects the substantial commercial dimensions of the Internet, particularly the Web, to the formation and reification of marketable categories of identity: "The successful formation of online queer communities has also fragmented into prescriptive identity menus, which serve commercial marketing purposes as much as they are expressive" (2007, p. 27).

Although commercially produced videos may superficially seem similar to their amateur counterparts, they are fundamentally different from vernacular productions that are often created as "response" videos to online content. Unsponsored coming out videos on YouTube are frequently characterized by their rhetorical engagement with the flux of compositional and reception practices in online communities oriented around the creation and remediation of vernacular video. Home-made videos make explicit the difficulties of managing multiple, sometimes even competing networked publics and of editing the self, and they frequently go "off message" in ways constitutive of their discursive practices. For example, many YouTube users actually upload multiple iterations of their coming out stories, so that no definitive version may be said to ultimately exist. This is evident in the case of pablootheverge (2009), where he describes coming out to family members when drunk at a wedding:

> I know I've done this before. Em. Probably the most of you is like tired of watching all these coming out videos. But . . . now that I've watched my coming out video again, it's like there is something missing there. What I mean is I didn't talk about my coming out thing, my coming out story. Because it was like me talking about me coming out to my parents, and they already knew about me.

Fellow YouTuber Eric Thor (2007) similarly begins with exaggerated self-deprecation and anticipated audience resistance to message redundancy: "This is going to be like the most edited video of all time. It's going to be pretty long and boring. And it's just pretty much a revision of one of my older videos, 'It's Okay to be Gay.'"

Indeed, unlike linear narratives of commercially produced videos, many amateur YouTube videos emphasize themes of contingency and accident in describing their first-person narrator's choices of first sexual partners, straight confidantes, and even the circumstances of retelling.[2] For example, ManoXpiano (2009) introduces his story about how "apparently everyone knew I was gay before I did" with an explanation of his video's spontaneous composition in response to viewing the videos of others:

> Hi. Uh. It's Mano. Uh. I've just been looking at videos. You know, the coming out stories and that. And uh I thought just thought I'd jump on the bagwagon, bandwagon, and uh tell my coming out story, if I have one. I haven't really thought about this. I thought I'd just make a video.

Along the same lines, Amz15 (2008) posted two coming out videos, the second of which she labeled as "sober edition lol." She subsequently uploaded a video with the title "Sexual Identity Crisis," which demonstrates how the conventional narrative of the coming out story comes under pressure. As she herself admits, the quality of the footage is also marred by environmental conditions: "WARNING: a lil cursing.. and music can b a lil loud.. sorry! if you cant hear much.. parents was about..=S." In the video Amz describes an attitude of unresolved questioning and desperation for advice from fellow YouTubers rather than a coherent coming-of-age story about sexual awakening and maturity:

> Biologically I am female. Clearly . . . Female but yeah. I do have my girly moments once in a blue moon. But I really don't feel female. At all. I mean, I thought I could swap between both genders of male and female, but you know cause I might be gender queer. Which is I'm still learning the concept

of meaning . . . gender queer. Because I've been hearing a lot about it lately especially on YouTube. It's on my mind I kind of am thinking if I am possibly gender queer.

Having done initial research on YouTube, Amz15 now wishes to harness the site's collective dynamic by "crowd sourcing" for an answer to her dilemma. She also conveys her desire for input via the accompanying text: "I need advice.. on my sexual identity crisis eep!"

In addition to acknowledging its benefits for community building through such knowledge sharing and pooling of experience, some scholars also see in cyberspace the potential to create fluid and challenging representations of queerness—representations that, like cyberspace itself, figured sexuality as complex, changing, dynamic.[3] Cyberspace as a domain of identity play complements, if not parallels, similar dimensions of queer theory that gesture toward the fluidity and performative play of sexualities and identities. O'Riordan summarizes such a position by suggesting that "The cybersubject, assumed as a fluid performative freed from embodied constraints . . . intersects with the ideal queer subject as trans, bisexual" (2007, p. 26). As Joshua Berman and Amy Bruckman (2001) asserted in their work on the Turing Test, one could adopt a variety of online identities to "play" at different subject positions, experimenting and experiencing (even if virtually) what the "other" is like. This might also engage in virtual role play that challenges one's own sense of sexuality as fixed, immutable, and essential. Such work suggests rich possibilities for exploring the contrast between, on one hand, critiquing the emergence of marketable and fixed identity categories, and, on the other, lauding the Internet as a space of unrestrained sexual play. In between the constructions of identity and the deconstructions of freeplay lies the potential for understanding the representation of queerness on the Internet as a complex endeavor with many different ramifications for identity, community, and political action.

Strength in Numbers? Possible Futures for the Coming Out Video

While the number of personal, self-sponsored and corporately sponsored coming out videos suggests a valuation of the personal narrative in establishing identity, forming community, and even potentially shaping the political, we should keep in mind that individual videos are rarely viewed and infrequently commented upon. Thus such videos may have more affective and political power in aggregate, as YouTube makes available a venue for "database watching" that allows users to experience a rapid sampling of files of digital video that are sequenced by metadata and the site's ranking and grouping algorithms, rather than arranged by the coherent plotlines and sustained attention that govern a conventional cinematic experience. Recognizing the potential power of the aggregate, the Human Rights Campaign has attempted to spur the production of a more orderly database of clips than what emerges by happenstance on YouTube to provide an online reference source for LGBT community members and their supporters and present both the diversity and the common morphology of the coming out experience. In the visual logic of their National Coming Out Day (hrcmedia 2007) video, these separate video diaries function much like the discrete panels of the AIDS quilt that serves to memorialize departed community members.

In ways very different from the HRC, vernacular video makers have also used many-to-many means to create more improvised coming out databases, ones that might lack the attention to political rhetoric of empowerment through normative behavior that are so central to the HRC models. For example, GDProphetXVII posted a video called "Coming Out Archive" that received seventy-six separate response videos as part of a related digital collection of coming out stories that are grouped together by YouTube's keyword logic:

> So since a lot of people asked me how to come out and all that I figured it might be good if maybe we started like a video archive of coming out stories, of stories where we came out to our families, to our friends, everything, but also stories of people coming out to us and how we have been allies to others, because that's a really important aspect of it all too, and so if you could video respond to this your coming out story, your ally story, anything you want regarding coming out, and then maybe hopefully one day all these videos might help someone come out for themselves and if it does then we've all done good.

In introducing the collective scholarly project of formulating "database aesthetics," Victoria Vesna has claimed that "[d]atabases and archives serve as ready-made commentaries on our contemporary social and political lives" (2007, p. xi). In the same collection, however, Lev Manovich has argued "a database can support narrative, but there is nothing in the logic of the medium itself that would foster its generation" (Vesna 2007, p. 47). Databases of coming out videos similarly provide commentary on queer lived experience, although they may lack a coherent narrative that emphasizes sequence and singularity.

Furthermore, as Geert Lovink (2008) has pointed out in *Zero Comments*, in the era of database-watching not every online artifact of communication generates a response from the public. Unlike GDProphetXVII's successful efforts to shape a coming out archive, Paigehope (2008) has a very different experience. Her video, which opens with her lip synching to the song "I'm Coming Out," does not receive a single response video, even when she specifically solicits the posting of coming out videos from others:

> "Okay. So. Okay. Um. Best song ever. I'm coming out by Diana Ross. Okay so I thought I would start a YouTube video response chain thing. Um. I want

your stories of coming out either if your bisexual or lesbian or gay or whatever Coming out stories. Please let's share and be happy! whew!"

While the aggregation of coming out videos suggests rhetorical power, potency, and strength in numbers, the actual mechanism of calling up videos on YouTube through the interface of its search and browsing features depends on the logic of keywords, metadata, statistics, and sponsorship arrangements. Thus the aggregation of polymorphous and seemingly unregulated coming out videos on YouTube may still be subject to architectures of corporate control that can contain and filter out certain forms of queer expression. Moreover, the communities of interest that gravitate toward coming out videos may also include abusive homophobes eager to suppress queer rhetoric now that they are able to locate them more easily and interfere with meaningful communication under the cover of online anonymity. For instance, the comments to GayGod's videos are at times hostile and derogatory. Given the presence of both online homophobes and the potential for corporate control of content, vlogging remains both a rhetorically rich and vexed venue for coming out narratives. On one hand, as we have seen, those with access to time and technological competence can produce home-grown videos that speak to specific circumstances of LGBT life in the West; such videos reveal diverse sexualities, diverse genders, and diverse intimacies. On the other hand, they elicit heteronormative responses that can be damaging, and that might cause hosts to censor the kinds of information disseminated on their servers, and content-creators to remove such videos from their channels.

Nonetheless, we expect that coming out videos will continue to be a robust genre that invites production, elaboration, response, and remediation. Unlike ephemeral memes that quickly fade with the movement of fads or fan culture online, coming out videos are in their very nature rhetorical: they presume the presence of an addressee, they are oriented around a transformative speech act, they respond to discourses around community building, and they recognize enduring ambiguities in the construction of sexual orientation, sexuality, and gender. Eventually the YouTube platform may encourage more content creators to produce hoaxes, parodies, mash-ups, and digitally composited homages, but we would argue that those forms of production could also invite queer participation that contests normative ideas about authenticity and stability and could allow subversive rhetoric to be seen, disseminated, and iterated.

Notes

1 For example, see reihiasguy's playlist (2009) for numerous examples associated with a single curatorial YouTube user.
2 Following Plummer, Alexander suggests in an earlier article that the "newer [coming out narratives], compared to the 'coming out' stories of late mid-century for instance, are less linear, less revelatory of a 'truth' about one's sexuality, and even less clearly

identified or concerned with articulating specific identity 'modes,' such as gay or lesbian as opposed to straight. Further, these stories often problematize traditional assimilationist (and heteronormative) figurings of sexuality and sexual orientation as part of one's private, as opposed to public, life" (2002, p. 92). Such an insight might apply as well to the YouTube "coming out" videos we analyze in this chapter.

3 Here, we are using the term "cyberspace" as it is used in Mark Nunes' *The Cyberspaces of Everyday Life* to indicate discourse practices associated with common computer-mediated communication rather than futuristic 3-D environments.

References

Alexander, J. 2002. Introduction to the Special Issue: Queer Webs representations of LGBT people and communities on the World Wide Web. *International Journal of Sexuality and Gender Studies* 7(2/3): 77–84.

apples33ds. 2008. *Re:* Coming out archive. http://www.youtube.com/watch?v=ZAkiL0TtFFI [Accessed July 19, 2009]

Amz15. 2008. Sexual identity crisis! http://www.youtube.com/watch?v=RrCiqG3XOG0 [Accessed April 21, 2009]

Banet-Weiser, S. 2004. Surfin' the net: Children, parental obsolescence, and citizenship. In *Technological visions: The hopes and fears that shape new technologies*, edited by M. Sturken, D. Thomas, and S. J. Ball-Rokeach, illustrated edition. Philadelphia, PA: Temple University Press.

Berman, J. and Bruckman A. 2001. The Turing Game: Exploring identity in an online environment. *Convergence* 7(3): 83–102.

Boellstorff, T. 2008. *Coming of age in second life: An anthropologist explores the virtually human*. Princeton, NJ: Princeton University Press.

boyd, d. 2006. apophenia: End of the year top five. *Zephoria.*: http://www.zephoria.org/thoughts/archives/2006/12/28/end_of_the_year.html [Accessed June 30, 2009]

Coming Out Stories. 2009. Video clips, photos, episode guide, cast & more. Logo Online. http://www.logoonline.com/shows/dyn/coming_out_stories/series.jhtml [Accessed April 18, 2009]

Frank, M., Patton, C., and Sánchez-Eppler, B., eds. 2000. *Queer diasporas.* Durham: Duke University Press

GayGod. 2007. Coming out. http://www.youtube.com/watch?v=WkkRbVZ-5RE [Accessed April 18, 2009]

GDProphetXVII. 2007. Coming out archive. http://www.youtube.com/watch?v=2t-R_cZxR8g [Accessed April 18, 2009]

Hill, A. 2005. *Reality TV: Factual entertainment and television audiences*. London: Routledge.

hrcmedia. 2007. National Coming Out Day 2007. http://www.youtube.com/watch?v=fSTtGSUJHMs [Accessed April 18, 2009]

Jenkins, H. 2008. Learning from YouTube: An interview with Alex Juhasz (Part Two) Center for Future Civic Media. http://civic.mit.edu/blog/henry/learning-from-youtube-an-interview-with-alex-juhasz-part-two [Accessed April 18, 2009]

Juhasz, A. 2008. *TOUR #3: POPULARITY! Who doesn't want to be prom queen?* http://www.youtube.com/watch?v=U-XuCRO1Ecw [Accessed April 21, 2009]

Lovink, G. 2008. *Zero comments: Blogging and critical internet culture.* New York: Routledge.

manoXpiano. 2009. Coming out story. http://www.youtube.com/watch?v=OJh4Sd8Hklo [Accessed July 1, 2009]

Matthews, M. 2007. Re: National Coming Out Day 2007. http://www.youtube.com/watch?v=BBrO9Ge7FEE [Accessed April 18, 2009]

Meem, D. T., Gibson, M. A., and Alexander, J. F. 2009. *Finding out: An introduction to LGBT Studies.* Thousand Oaks, CA: Sage.

Nunes, M. 2006. *Cyberspaces of everyday life.* Minneapolis: University of Minnesota Press.

O'Riordan, K., and Phillips, D. J. 2007. *Queer online: Media technology and sexuality.* New York: Peter Lang.

Pabloontheverge. 2009. Coming out (Vol. 2) This is basically what you shouldn't do! lol. http://www.youtube.com/watch?v=HRfcGuJEYXs [Accessed June 30, 2009]

Paigehope. 2008. Coming out. http://www.youtube.com/watch?v=mnTkiHUOOo4 [Accessed June 30, 2009]

Plummer, K. 1994. *Telling sexual stories*, 1st ed. New York: Routledge.

RavenMae. 2007. National Coming Out Day (late). http://www.youtube.com/watch?v=Y7vpD9jpTxc [Accessed April 18, 2009]

reihiasguy. 2009. Playlist. http://www.youtube.com/view_play_list?p=CB0ACC36C9864B5E [Accessed August 15, 2009]

Thor, Eric. 2007. Eric Thor on coming out gay. http://www.youtube.com/watch?v=lzw1I4bp73M [Accessed April 18, 2009]

Vesna, V. 2007. *Database aesthetics: Art in the age of information overflow*, 1st ed. Minneapolis: University of Minnesota Press.

x44jackal44x. 2009. Coming out of the closet (: (APRIL FOOLS). http://www.youtube.com/watch?v=bm3NbrbfUiY [Accessed April 18, 2009]

Chapter 3

YouTube Courtship
The Private Ins and Public Outs of Chris and Nickas

Damon Lindler Lazzara

Since the 1980s, gay men have used online identities to seek friendship, sex, and partnership, first through private electronic bulletin board systems, later through for-profit, corporate services such as CompuServe, GEnie, and America Online, and then through the mainstream Internet. In 2005, the public video-sharing website youtube.com expanded the means by which they could construct and disseminate their identities, as well as how they could pair with suitable mates: through full-color, sound-enhanced videos known as "video-logs," or "vlogs"—a derivation of the terms "web-logs" or "blogs." Video-logging on YouTube may have begun as the electronic performance of private lives in the public sphere, but video-loggers soon harnessed the medium to form relationships outside cyberspace. The courtship of YouTube users nickasarbata and littleBIGGERchris, both gay male video-loggers (see littleBIGGERchris 2009a and nickasarbata 2009a) who claim in their videos to be in their twenties, embodies this phenomenon, which synthesises performed identity and community participation. Since their "real-life" meeting July 30, 2007 (littleBIGGERchris 2009h), the two began cohabitating in New York City October 8, 2007 (nickasarbata 2009f). When presented against a theoretical backdrop concerning performativity, simulation, tradition, and democracy, and in light of an early Internet survey of LGBT youth, their story may foreshadow the course and character of other such relationships that rely on complex and public mediating mechanisms to legitimize LGBT identities and interactions, especially as increasing numbers of the LGBT population come of age, come out, and come together online.

Antecedents

In 2004, Holleran wrote that the "gayness" of young LGBT people in the twenty-first century had become "virtually unrecognizable—evaporated, almost into assimilation and cyberspace" (p. 12). His intention was to highlight the decrease in public demonstrations of gay activism in opposition to heterosexist discrimination. Rather than a "gender-free, communitarian world" the gay liberation movement achieved an "unprecedented growth of gay capitalism and a new masculinity" which did not necessarily include overt activism (Adam 1987, p. 97). Ironically, signs which had once challenged heteronormativity became integrated into it, partly manifesting in what would become known as "metrosexuality" or a keener and more accepted attentiveness among heterosexual men to the fashion and beauty savvy once stereotypically reserved for homosexual men. Needless to say, the profit-making opportunities offered by a beautified heterosexual masculinity were not lost on the market. But certain goals of the gay liberation movement—among them equality, mutual acceptance, and the freedom of self-expression—did not entirely dissolve into a capitalistic "new masculinity." Nor did the perceptible "gayness" of young LGBT people simply disappear. Instead, cyberspace became an outlet, without physical boundaries, for these goals and identities. Doubtless the segue between Stonewall and YouTube courtship did not occur in a single generation; and it did not occur without notice from twentieth- and twenty-first-century critical and theoretical literature, much of which appeared before the current Internet existed.

As early as 1968, McLuhan was observing the "rearview mirror" phenomenon in the media, a metaphor he coined to explain how the present could not be revealed until it had become the past, and why established traditions, rather than pressing realities, tend to dominate the present (p. 18). The "rearview mirror" may account for the gravitation of two twenty-first-century gay men toward "old-fashioned" notions of courtship, romantic love, and partnership, despite their radical method for achieving them. Geertz's articulation of culture as the common understandings of a group that both emerges from and shapes social interactions also finds apt applicability in an online context, in which interactivity is magnified (1973, p. 92). Baudrillard's 1976 *Symbolic Exchange and Death*, while considering the symbolic representation of the sexual carnival in "The Body, or the Mass Grave of Signs" interwove a critique of capitalism, commercialism, sex, and sexuality, all of which dramatically collide on the Internet, where sex and romance are "sold" in an atmosphere of a carnivalesque bazaar (2004, pp. 101–121). To that end, in his "Precession of Simulacra," Baudrillard wrote that "[s]imulation is the dominant schema of the current . . . phase [which operates] on the structural law of value" (2004, p. 50). Foucault's *History of Sexuality: An Introduction* (1990) expanded on sexuality as commerce, and assessed the LGBT struggle to develop a healthy, non-self-destructive sexual identity within cultures that privilege heterosexuality (pp. 36–38), an escape from which may be found through an outlet of lesser resistance, which in this case is the Internet.

Butler's *Gender Trouble* (1990) explicated gender performativity as "constituted by the very 'expressions' that are said to be its results" (p. 25), generalizing that a subject's communicative actions are "not expressive but performative" (p. 141), and, one might venture, well-suited to a medium of performance. Turkle's *Life on the Screen* (1997) proposed that the "disjuncture between [postmodern] theory . . . and lived experience" is one of the "main reasons why we tend to settle back into older, centralized ways of looking at things" (p. 15). Still, she wrote, "We have moved from a modernist culture of calculation toward a postmodernist culture of simulation" (p. 26) in which "virtual space relationships . . . become intense very quickly because the participants feel isolated in a . . . world with its own rules" (p. 206). Those aware of their position in this lawless frontier begin to reach back to tradition for the preservation and perpetuation of "earlier notions of an authentic and coherent identity" that are inextricably bound to "tribalistic rituals" of seeking community input, advice, mediation, and approval (Wilcox 1991, p. 348).

Most recently, Rak's "The Digital Queer" (2005) explored the genre, rhetoric, and ideologies of the LGBT text web-log, much of which translates to video-logging. Rak connected "beliefs about the value and rights of the individual [which] remain at the core of most blogging" with the tendency for "self disclosure . . . even when this could be dangerous" (p. 172). Despite its distancing from physical reality, online web-logging "works to produce gay identity . . . as an experience of the absolute in everyday life" (p. 178). The LGBT web-logger's output, in the context of an online democracy of equally valuable and equally honest sovereign agents, affirms both the validity of the individual and the legitimacy of the community. Similar backgrounds and life histories bind this community of web-loggers, enabling them to imbue the authenticity of physical reality and shared actual experience into the detached realities of the web-log. The totalizing and universalizing energies underpinning the democratic spirit of web-logs, however, discount the latent and inevitable conflicts that erupt between web-loggers, regardless of their similarities. Thus far, though, similarities have overpowered differences, perhaps due to the sheer and growing numbers of LGBT online.

The documentation of these numbers, as well as the anticipation for YouTube courtship, is in the inaugural 1997 *!Outproud!-Oasis Magazine Internet Survey of Queer and Questioning Youth* (Kryzan and Walsh 1998). This recorded what Internet-savvy LGBT youth, now in their twenties and thirties, were saying about themselves during their adolescent years. Tellingly, 60 percent of the surveyed were visitors to the sponsoring *Oasis Magazine* site, an early clearinghouse for web-logging with an operating model similar to that of YouTube, though text-based and LGBT-specific. The *Survey*'s subsection "The Internet" revealed 45 percent of the surveyed reported their Internet use spanned from one to three years, with 47 percent logging on for "one or two" hours each day (pp. 17–18). Fifty-one percent reported coming out online before coming out in "real life," and 68 percent reported that the Internet "helped them to accept their sexual orientation" (p. 18). Despite the *Survey*'s sample limitations (p. 4), it demonstrates a decade-old Internet presence of LGBT youth in an evolving pursuit of personal and social fulfillment online.

Though writing from perspectives different from that of the current study, Kimbali and Lyotard bring cohesion to the literature germane to the online activities of littleBIGGERchris and nickasarbata. Kimbali observed "an increasing number are forced to accomplish their transitions [between life stages] alone and with private symbols" (in Van Gennep 1960, p. xviii). The privatization of symbols resonates with Lyotard's definition of the postmodern condition as the fall of "great metanarratives" (1979, p. xxiv). If courtship leading to strong, partnered romantic relationships is among the "great metanarratives," then it is not surprising that the LGBT generation now coming into adulthood employs private symbols within the now-flexible framework of a waning-yet-familiar metanarrative of romantic love. It also seems that this demographic is not content to accept traditional metanarratives merely interspersed with private symbols, and is in fact reinventing the courtship-romance-love metanarrative to suit the online community in which they are participating and concurrently (re)creating. Their activities corroborate and elaborate on Giddens's argument that modernity's "transformation of intimacy" has yielded "pure relationship . . . entered into for its own sake [and] continued only in so far as it is thought by both parties to deliver enough satisfactions for each individual to stay within it" (1992, p. 58).

The Courtship

On June 30, 2007, littleBIGGERchris, a self-described "wee Irish-Mexican insomniac pushing 30," wrote a comment on nickasarbata's YouTube channel: "Nick—I found your profile somehow and sat and watched about 30 of your videos today [. . .] The only acceptable thing left for us to do is become boyfriends . . ." Over the next three days, littleBIGGERchris interacted with nickasarbata, a Swedish-American who spent several years in Spain before returning to Iowa in 2007. LittleBIGGERchris also exchanged messages about nickasarbata with other YouTube users via messages written on their public YouTube channels. He then posted his first public video dedicated to nickasarbata, "For Nickas Arbata," on July 3, in which he confessed his love and insisted that the object of his affection had no need for "any other boys." LittleBIGGERchris then mimicked threatening competing suitors with a pair of scissors and the words "back off" (littleBIGGERchris 2009b). In less than two minutes, he had established a pattern of elaborate, professional-quality video production with overdubbed popular music, television and film quotes, and the quick editing that offer a pastiche of contemporary visual media. Through his participation in these styles of visual representation, littleBIGGERchris conveyed a consciousness of his cultural milieu, placing himself and his viewers in a very precise generational context and reinforcing its most identifiable traits (Geertz 1973).

Most of the textual comments about littleBIGGERchris's first attempt at piquing nickasarbata's curiosity are positive and supportive, but one is poignant in terms of the reclamation and reformation of the romantic metanarrative, that of user "pvampire," who wrote that "watching this was like a real life fairy tale" (littleBIGGERchris 2009b). Nickasarbata replied to littleBIGGERchris's overture in two videos on July 5 and 6, in which he confirmed that littleBIGGERchris was "his type" and addressed the "hurtful" comments of other users, such as "Tanblondalex" who wrote, "I just was surprised and disappointed with your taste [. . .] [F]orgive me for having higher expectations of you" (nickasarbata 2009b, 2009c). Most of the comments left for nickasarbata's videos were also positive and supportive, such as one by user "sarraksartaj." "[L]et's face it, insanely romantic stuff like this doesn't happen to everyone!!" (nickasarbata 2009c). Emboldened by the chatter about him, littleBIGGERchris wrote on nickasarbata's profile page that "the battle for nick's heart is ON!" He then clarified his position on July 6 with a video directed toward anyone who challenged his quest for nickasarbata. "I'm going after you and your boy . . . the internet is big enough for ALL of us to share our love for NICKAS," he displayed in text foregrounding a lip-synced musical performance (littleBIGGERchris 2009d). The July 6 video would become one of four in a series entitled "Boyfriending Nick" in which littleBIGGERchris argued his case for nickasarbata to leave Iowa and to move to New York City to cohabitate with him (littleBIGGERchris 2009c, 2009d, 2009e, 2009f).

User "SeeBassTian" commented on one of these videos, asking rhetorically, "[I]s this the future of courtship? potential suitors trade videos and solicit personal references? it's definitely entertaining, but a little impersonal," to which littleBIGGERchris answered, "the videos definitely might seem impersonal, but nick caught the energy behind them . . . [W]hat the youtubers don't get to witness are the 7hr phone conversations, the many . . . messages during work, and the constant wondering about each other" (littleBIGGERchris 2009e). What the "youtubers" do witness in the second of the "Boyfriending Nick" series is a procession of friends and well-known YouTube video-loggers (a "precession of simulacra" in their own right) who vouch for the quality of littleBIGGERchris's character, material possessions, and sexual prowess. His friend, "Jax" alluding to her most important criterion for nickasarbata's decision to "boyfriend" littleBIGGERchris, said that the two would make "the hottest couple" in Greenwich Village. In this instance "Jax," though only one individual, becomes an extension and representative of the community of mediated LGBT Internet identities who have converged around this particular narrative. Her presence as an exponent of possessed attractiveness in coupling reinforces the supremacy of the semiotic sexual marketplace that sells a commodified sexual product and entices others to join in the act of the exchange (Baudrillard 2004). Her words are the mantra of a new tradition whose believers require a seamless switchover from relationships on the screen to relationships in physical reality: simulate, manipulate, use to one's satisfaction in ways impossible in a closeted culture.

On July 14 nickasarbata posted a video in response to littleBIGGERchris's "Boyfriending Nick" series after littleBIGGERchris couriered him a package, eliciting heightened controversy among the proto-couple's viewers. Nickasarbata said that despite some skepticism surrounding littleBIGGERchris's advances, his videos were "well received with [him]" (nickasarbata 2009d). He then itemized the contents of the package: a greeting card, spiced cinnamon candies known as "Red Hots," a CD, a map of Manhattan, and a condom—accompanied by a sarcastic "no comment" (nickasarbata 2009d). After discussing the package, he confidently announced his intention to visit littleBIGGERchris in New York City (nickasarbata 2009d). In a textual aside at the end of the video, nickasarbata made an insightful observation, especially given the blinding powers of infatuation, of his own situation: "In these modern times . . . there are no rules, there is no protocol to follow [. . .] Chris is using new technologies to aid him in his quest to boyfriend me. I think his combination of creativity and dedication is . . . extremely romantic" (nickasarbata 2009d). Yet these "modern times" do exhibit rules of romantic engagement. They are rules both parties understand, at least instinctually, as they have thus far succeeded in communicating their interests to each other and to their viewers.

In new and unfamiliar territory, individuals seeking relationships, and ultimately love, may revert to the traditions that are their cultural inheritance (Wilcox 1991). Although no demographic studies yet exist regarding the LGBT involvement in YouTube, anecdotally the site is predominantly Western and English-speaking. Consciously or not, YouTube users in this demographic carry with them post-revolutionary, post-democratic beliefs articulated by Rak and others about the value of the individual and peer group. Instead of venturing into a new medium alone, LGBT youth seek connections, not only toward objects of affection, but also toward networks of prospective advisors, of diverse authority and age. From these new authorities, the uninitiated may receive warnings which expose the dangers of affording undue trust to the unknown. Several viewers reacted strongly to littleBIGGERchris's forthrightness and nickasarbata's relaxed acceptance thereof. User "lemondrop10" wrote that he "loved watching [nickasarbata's] videos" but "just cannot any longer" after surviving an Internet wooing which had soured (nickasarbata 2009d). User "laws9g" and nickasarbata engaged in a heated exchange in which the former demanded of the latter, "If you do not care what people think why are you on here showing your life?" This was a pointed jab at nickasarbata's dismissive attitude toward viewers who did not share his sense of optimism. He countered: "I just make video blogs [. . .] I'm going to do what I think is right and what I want. Negativity can stay away." Laws9g replied: "Good for you. You should not care about what we think. You will be the one who will have to live with your decision" (nickasarbata 2009d). Nickasarbata ended the conversation, but this was only the beginning of friction between the couple and their YouTube community that would come to a head after their first face-to-face encounter.

LittleBIGGERchris began a countdown for nickasarbata's arrival in New York City with the video "Boyfriending Nick: The Countdown" (littleBIGGERchris

2009g). LittleBIGGERchris does not speak, but he does indicate the date of nickasarbata's arrival on a dry-erase board in shots interspersed with captions indicating his enthusiasm. The commentators to this video contribute only praise and approval, and user "Samostorm" nearly appeals to destiny, writing, "He is doomed! . . . in a good way" (littleBIGGERchris 2009g). Extrapolating the romantic metanarrative to its logical end, user "vtremaine" wrote, "You two need to hurry so I can be in a wedding!!!!" LittleBIGGERchris responded enthusiastically with details about the wedding rings the two had chosen (littleBIGGERchris 2009g). By this time, the mounting sentiment for the union of the two men had become infectious, so much so that some had begun to openly share their internalization of and identification with the impending event as if they were personally involved. User "aubied" wrote, "I want a littleBIGGERchris all to myself!" and user "jcmantaray" wrote, "Is it weird that i kinda want to be there whenever you two meet? [I] just want to cheer you two on!" (littleBIGGERchris 2009g). User "JVinManch" sounded a note of jealousy, writing, "I would love my [boyfriend] to be that happy to see me" (littleBIGGERchris 2009g).

LittleBIGGERchris made a final anticipatory video July 30, the morning he was to meet nickasarbata at La Guardia International Airport, in which he said, "Next time you see me, I will have the adorable, beautiful, blond, blond, Swedish boy from Iowa, Nick, sitting right next to me, hopefully for the rest of my life" (littleBIGGERchris 2009h). Responding to the story arc which had unfolded thus far, and to the YouTube users both in favor of and opposed to the impending first acquaintance, user "nimoss" wrote, "ok so to the haters who complain that this whole thing is crazy: will you just chill out and enjoy the moment these two beautiful human beings are having? who needs the jaded cynicism. up with love, people!" (littleBIGGERchris 2009h). These words bring to mind that the simulated, commodified signs produced by littleBIGGERchris and nickasarbata and also standing in for them are intended for viewers' consumption as "enjoyment" (Baudrillard 2004). Also in these words is an aspiration toward the concreteness of love as a countermeasure to the "cynicism" of disbelievers—a concreteness nimoss vehemently prescribes not only for littleBIGGERchris and nickasarbata, but also for their viewership (Rak 2005).

On July 30, 2007, nickasarbata arrived in New York City, and was met by littleBIGGERchris at La Guardia Airport. By July 31, littleBIGGERchris had produced a video of the much-anticipated event. In it, nickasarbata is featured against the background of littleBIGGERchris's living room, bantering with a friend on the telephone. LittleBIGGERchris then addressed his viewers: "Nick is here . . . I really don't even have time to be making this video [. . .] But everybody wants to know what's going on [. . .] He's incredible; we're having the best time!" Then, playfully shunning his virtual community, he said, "We have no more time for you. We have to spend it together" (littleBIGGERchris 2009i). Nonetheless, littleBIGGERchris provides four minutes of footage chronicling his day with nickasarbata, including time spent in Central Park and an inebriated after-dinner conversation between them when nickasarbata declared his first day with littleBIGGERchris, "from start to finish, perfect" (littleBIGGERchris 2009i). He added, "Now it's bed time, and there will be no cameras involved in that" (littleBIGGERchris 2009i). The collective endeavor was complete, and user "TheWatcher108" appropriately commented: "Thank you so much for video. I love it and [am] glad we could be part of it. it is US here on youtube that brought you together after all isnit it" [sic] (littleBIGGERchris 2009i).

Tension, Possession, and the Future

During their courtship, littleBIGGERchris and nickasarbata openly quarreled with various commentators, and vice-versa. The comment above by user "TheWatcher108" offered the most contentious contribution: What did littleBIGGERchris and nickasarbata owe their viewers, and what did their viewers owe them? The immediate intimacy engendered by online contact, especially when augmented by the illusion of proximity through the simulated moving human image and speaking human voice, accelerates the development of a sense of acquaintance and friendship (Turkle 1997). This intimacy also accelerates the development of trust, albeit not at the same rate and under the same conditions for everyone. Consequently, YouTube commentators may assume that their opinions are valued and respected by others. In fact, as in the offline world, they are likely to offend with their unsolicited commentary. Such is the inspiration for two videos by littleBIGGERchris and nickasarbata, directed precisely at users they deemed too involved in their "private" lives.

LittleBIGGERchris was the first to address online encroachment into his affairs. While reporting a trip to Iowa to visit nickasarbata, he digressed: "People have been very curious, wanting to know more. I can't blame anybody because, obviously, I put these videos out there in the beginning" (littleBIGGERchris 2009j). He responded to the pressing question of sexual contact between him and nickasarbata: "I'm not going to tell you, [but] would you get on a plane to fly to another city you've never been to just to shake hands with somebody?" (littleBIGGERchris 2009j). He continued: "While I really do enjoy that so many people have things to say, I don't really care that much. But if you're supporting us, that's awesome. Please keep doing that" (littleBIGGERchris 2009j). While discouraging his viewers from asking personal questions, littleBIGGERchris coyly answers those questions. His mixed messages betray tension between the traditional impulse for privacy and the online compulsion to over-disclose. Apparently, according to the ambivalence of his words against the mixing of the private and public, and the strength of his deeds in favour of it, littleBIGGERchris indeed cares what other people think or say about his life on the screen. At the least, he cares that others watch.

Nickasarbata's tirade against intrusive curiosity is not so ambivalent. In a video entitled "Unhappy withYOUtube"—capitals intended—he said:

> "People onYouTube watch my videos; they think they know me because they watch my videos and what I have chosen to put on the Internet.They feel like they have a personal relationship with me. I really don't have interest in 500 strangers watching [my videos] and thinking they know me."
>
> (nickasarbata 2009e)

Nevertheless, after only a brief respite of protest, nickasarbata continued to share his videos and comments with theYouTube community. Both littleBIGGERchris and nickasarbata wrestled with the issue of possession. They may have struck an uneasy balance between public and private life, but the question of who possesses their lives (even if only the fraction they shared with others onYouTube) remains unanswered. Without the vast, public audience for their courtship, it is not clear if either man would have engaged so enthusiastically in the process. With YouTube, however, they and others have been able to enjoy interactions through which the impact of their online identities was transmitted to those of similar backgrounds and interests, and then transmitted back in a feedback loop. In other words, the online lives of YouTube users may very well, at least to a degree, belong to each other.

To believe in the communal ownership of theYouTube LGBT courtship metanarrative, it may be necessary to concede that not all involved in the enterprise necessarily agree on what it is that they want or need the metanarrative to accomplish. Fiske's reading of audience reactions to Madonna posited that the productions of popular culture can provide resources of "pluralized" meanings that encompass the "homogeneity and coherence" of the existing, commodified cultural order, as well as the "struggle over the meanings of cultural experience" (Fiske 1989, p. 89). A text, while constructed and disseminated with one set of intentions, and bearing the mark of a long history of semiotic sexual exchange, may, for audiences, be received completely differently due to their particular needs. The intricate dance between hegemony and counter-hegemony in popular culture nourishes theYouTube community, which in turn nurtured the courtship of littleBIGGERchris and nickasarbata. And the internalized shaping of the received message according to recipients' needs may justify the disconnect between the stated objectives of littleBIGGERchris's or nickasarbata's videos and the reactions of the audience. On a broader scale, the disconnect may be symptomatic of the tensions resulting from the integration of tradition and radicalism in an entirely new frontier rife with experimental possibilities, typically democratic in nature, but subject to inharmonious struggle.

Though a far cry from the radical idealism of the gay liberation movement of the 1960s and 1970s, the community orientation of online LGBT life includes unmistakable aspects of this movement, among them an unabashed gay pride. On YouTube, the LGBT community may seek and find equality, acceptance, and the freedom of self-expression, as well as a reconstruction of traditional romantic metanarratives that they themselves create. This reconstruction is not without the friction that occurs at the site of waning traditions and on the cusp of new cultural movements: as comfortable as littleBIGGERchris, nickasarbata, or other YouTube courtship participants may be with the performance of their romantic interest, they will inevitably encounter elements of tradition that conflict with the new rules of their electronic frontier. Partly to blame is the system of sexual commoditization into which they have entered toward the end of the twentieth century and into the first decade of the twenty-first century. Recent theoretical and critical interest in the effect of electronic media on human interaction also complicates the online LGBT landscape, exposing the complex performative aspects of online identity, the encroachment of simulation into everyday interactions, the recapitulation of tradition in a radicalized world, and the re-articulation of democracy. Evidently, finding love and maintaining it within an accepting community, even on the Internet, is no easy task. Nonetheless, if recent trends are reliable indicators, then first contact through the medium of ultimate privacy and ultimate transparency is the future of many kinds of relationships for the LGBT and others on the Internet. Those interested in finding connections online, as well as those interested in exploring connections online, would be well advised to expand their awareness of the provenance of the human operating system—as much as of the technological operating system—behind the YouTube courtship of littleBIGGERchris and nickasarbata.

References

Adam, B. 1987. *The rise of a gay and lesbian movement*. Boston: Twayne Publishers.
Baudrillard, J. 2004. *Symbolic exchange and death*. London: Sage Publications.
Butler, J. 1990. *Gender trouble: Feminism and the subversion of identity*. New York: Routledge.
Fiske, J. 1989. *Reading popular culture*. New York: Routledge.
Foucault, M. 1990. *The history of sexuality: An introduction*. New York: Vintage Press.
Geertz, C. 1973. *The interpretation of cultures*. New York: Basics Books.
Giddens, A. 1992. *The transformation of intimacy*. Stanford: Stanford University Press,
Holleran, A. 2004. The day after. *Gay and Lesbian Review* 11(1): 12–17.
Kryzan, C., and Walsh, J. 1998. *The !OutProud! /Oasis internet survey of queer and questioning youth: August to October 1997* [Online]. http://www.outproud.org/survey/index.html. [Accessed August 21, 2009]
littleBIGGERchris. 2009a. http://www.youtube.com/littleBIGGERchris [Accessed August 21, 2009]
littleBIGGERchris. 2009b. For Nickas Arbata. 3 July 2007. http://www.youtube.com/watch?v=xJmaLB7lB6g [Accessed August 21, 2009]

littleBIGGERchris. 2009c. Boyfriending Nick: attempt #1. 5 July 2007. http://www.youtube.com/watch?v=GgXiPzsKsi4 [Accessed August 21, 2009]

littleBIGGERchris. 2009d. Boyfriending Nick: For the Naysayers. 6 July 2007. http://www.youtube.com/watch?v=rPxQDmM8h5E [Accessed August 21, 2009]

littleBIGGERchris. 2009e. Boyfriending Nick: attempt #2. 13 July 2007. http://www.youtube.com/watch?v=FO6ntyx7nOc [Accessed August 21, 2009]

littleBIGGERchris. 2009f. Boyfriending Nick: attempt #3. 15 July 2007. http://www.youtube.com/watch?v=z7F049iL_CA [Accessed August 21, 2009]

littleBIGGERchris. 2009g. Boyfriending Nick: The Countdown. 25 July 2007. http://www.youtube.com/watch?v=Ev61X_p43dQ [Accessed August 21, 2009]

littleBIGGERchris. 2009h. Getting Nick. 30 July 2007. http://www.youtube.com/watch?v=xUSrbhbAq5g [Accessed August 21, 2009]

littleBIGGERchris. 2009i. Chris & Nick: adventure #1. 31 July 2007. http://www.youtube.com/watch?v=tij5YH7BURE [Accessed August 21, 2009]

littleBIGGERchris. 2009j. Iowabound. 18 August 2007. http://www.youtube.com/watch?v=LiX3jaDdAc0 [Accessed August 21, 2009]

Lyotard, J. 1984. *The postmodern condition: A report on knowledge*. Minneapolis: University of Minnesota Press.

McLuhan, M., and Fiore, Q. 1968. *War and peace in the global village*. Columbus, OH: McGraw Hill.

nickasarbata. 2009a http://www.youtube.com/nickasarbata [Accessed August 21, 2009]

nickasarbata. 2009b. Laundry. 5 July 2007. http://www.youtube.com/watch?v=wt-ebNsIV8I [Accessed August 21, 2009]

nickasarbata. 2009c. It's shorter and it's cut, but it's back! 6 July 2007. http://www.youtube.com/watch?v=59I2smSmMdg [Accessed August 21, 2009]

nickasarbata. 2009d. Boyfriending Nick: A Surprise from Chris. 14 July 2007. http://www.youtube.com/watch?v=upq01Ev7vr4 [Accessed August 21, 2009]

nickasarbata. 2009e. Unhappy with YOUtube. 29 September 2007. http://www.youtube.com/watch?v=N4kotCHkJ3I [Accessed August 21, 2009]

nickasarbata. 2009f. Hola Nueva York! 8 October 2007. http://www.youtube.com/watch?v=FyTZwiB0tVE [Accessed August 21, 2009]

Rak, J. 2005. The digital queer: Weblogs and internet identity. *Biography* 28(1): 166–182.

Turkle, S. 1997. *Life on the screen: Identity in the age of the internet*. New York: Simon & Schuster.

Van Gennep, A. 1960. *The rites of passage*. Chicago: University of Chicago Press.

Wilcox, L. 1991. Baudrillard, DeLillo's White Noise, and the end of the heroic narrative. *Contemporary Literature* 32(3): 346–365.

Chapter 4

Virtually Supportive
Self-Disclosure of Minority Sexualities through Online Social Networking Sites

Bruce E. Drushel

Nearly four decades after nights of riots outside the Stonewall Inn in Greenwich Village and their symbolism as the most visible first battle in a war against antiqueer oppression captured the imaginations of lesbians, gays, bisexuals, and transgender people in much of the world, and a half-decade after the U.S. Supreme Court overturned the basis for the criminalization of homosexual behavior (*Lawrence v. Texas* see U.S. Supreme Court 2003), the disclosure of same-sex attraction by sexual minorities remains a topic of interest both in the social scientific literature and in the popular media. Increased social acceptance of "queerness" evinced by its more frequent, diverse, and positive representation in the media, as well as by its political potency, means those who realize their same-sex attraction earlier in life less often have cause to try to repress or secrete their identity (Vary 2006), though a social support network of other "queers" still is considered important to the coming-out process (Gonsiorek and Rudolph 1991). Increasingly, self-disclosure of minority sexual identity is made in adolescence and young adulthood. Coincidentally, online social networking websites such as MySpace and Facebook, in the few short years since their introduction in 2003, have grown immensely popular among teens and young adults especially. They present the possibility of providing a virtual social support function in an environment which appears non-geographically restricted.

This chapter examines the use of social networking sites as sources of social support for self-disclosure of minority sexual identities, and also explores the influence of these sites upon the discourse of those identities, particularly through their co-mingling of positive and pejorative uses of the term "gay."

Coming Out

Sexual identity has been defined as "the enduring sense of oneself as a sexual being which fits a culturally created category and accounts for one's sexual fantasies, attraction, and behaviors" (Savin-Williams 1995, p. 166). Self-identification as a sexual minority and subsequent disclosure to another person typically is not a single event, but rather a protracted process that Gonsiorek and Rudolph (1991) believe "is characterized by unpredictability, starts, stops, backtracking, and denial" (pp. 164–165). Frequently, that process begins with emotional destabilization, such as feelings of alienation and confusion, and an ultimate realization of its connection to the person's sexuality (Savin-Williams 1995).

The precise process frequently is conceived of as one of a multiple stages, or steps. Among the most well-regarded descriptions is Cass's Homosexuality Identity Model (Cass 1979), which examines the cognitive phases a lesbian, gay, or bisexual person goes through in developing an understanding of his or her sexual orientation. Ideally, the person coming out is able to work through the internalized homophobia that characterizes the early stages of the process, which Cass called Identity Confusion and Identity Tolerance, through a lesbian or gay social support network. Such a network, according to Gonsiorek and Rudolph (1991), provides positive feedback, empowerment, and a sense of community.

Though seminal studies such as those by Boxer et al. (1989) and Savin-Williams (1990) have put the age of first disclosure somewhere between the early high school and early college years, Egan (2000) notes that recent work suggests that gay teens are coming out at younger and younger ages, at least in part because of the support and interactivity offered by the Internet. A recent survey by the queer newsmagazine *The Advocate* of 3,225 of its readers confirms the age range indeed may be younger: 40 percent reported having come out by age 18, 37 percent came out between 19 and 25, and just 23 precent came out after age 25. Fully 17 percent claimed to have come out before they entered high school (Lam 2006).

The very nature of what "coming out" means may be evolving. There have been suggestions in the popular media that "gay" as an identity in the twenty-first century may not have the relevance it enjoyed during much of the twentieth century. The conclusion David Levithan draws from his recent collection of pieces written by queer youth is that they increasingly define themselves as individuals, and less according to a gay/straight dichotomy. Encouraged by popular culture texts accepting of gay imagery and stories and performances that co-mingle the heteronormative and the queer, teens and young adults who realize they are not traditionally straight increasingly reject "gay" as an identity in favor of sexuality that is open, or undefined (Vary 2006). By contrast, the survey of readers of *The Advocate*, 84 percent of whom were 25 or older, showed 89 percent identified as either "gay" or "lesbian." Thirty percent considered their sexual or gender identity to be "primary" or "essential;" 53 percent considered it "significant" (Lam 2006).

Social Capital

While the notion that individuals derive benefits from their personal associations with other individuals and groups is historical, it was first conceptualized as "social capital" in 1916 by a West Virginia education administrator to encourage community involvement in rural schools (Putnam 2000). The term appeared sporadically in print in the 1960s and 1970s, before Bourdieu (1986) defined it as a form of capital related to economic and cultural capital. Though its definition has varied as the concept has gained currency in a number of disciplines, in a widely accepted version, it is "the sum of the resources, actual or virtual, that accrue to an individual or a group by virtue of possessing a durable network of more or less institutionalized relationships of mutual acquaintance and recognition" (Bourdieu and Wacquant 1992, p. 14).

Putnam (2000) has distinguished between two types of social capital. Bridging social capital is a series of loose connections among individuals that provide useful information or new perspectives, but little in the way of emotional support. Conversely, bonding social capital exists among individuals in emotionally close relationships, including family and close friends. Ellison et al. (2007) suggest the existence of a third type of social capital, maintained social capital, which they define as the ability to stay connected with members of a previously-inhabited community.

Social Networking Websites

The use of the internet as a social support network has a rich, if not lengthy, tradition, beginning with chat rooms on the Internet Relay Channels (IRC) and virtual bulletin boards. The first of the modern interactive social networking websites was Friendster, which was founded by Jonathan Abrams in March of 2002. Approximately a year later, Harvard student Aaron Greenspan started houseSYSTEM, a site used by several thousand of his fellow students for various college-related online tasks. In September of 2003, he announced the addition of a feature called "the Face Book," which allowed students to quickly locate each other. Later in the year, other Harvard students would begin similar projects, ConnectU and Facebook (Markoff 2007). The latter was founded by Mark Zuckerberg, and it has become one of the best-known of the social networking sites, with over 58 million active users (Rosenbloom 2007). The students who began ConnectU have sued Zuckerberg in the federal court, claiming he stole the idea from them (Markoff 2007).

The success of Friendster and Facebook spurred the launch of other social networking sites, some of which target specialized markets and functions. LinkedIn, for instance, focuses on professional networking. MySpace pages historically targeted those who share political interests and leisure and entertainment pursuits, though its user base has broadened significantly since its inception. Friendster, whose original purpose was romantic interconnections, became a popular site for political organizing during the 2004 presidential election campaign. And Facebook, which initially limited its membership to college and university students, now has divisions devoted to high-school students and commercial ventures (Ellison et al. 2007).

There also is evidence of social networking sites' specialization by ethnicity of user. One recent study concluded that Latino students were significantly less likely to use Facebook, and much more likely to use MySpace, while white, Asian, and Asian-American students were much more likely to use Facebook and significantly less likely to use MySpace (Rosenbloom 2007). Increasingly, African-Americans, Latinos and Latinas, and Asian-Americans who are sexual minorities may be gravitating to yet another specialized social networking site, DowneLink.com (Vary 2006), which claims to have 400,000 users, 72 percent of whom are from ethnicities other than Caucasian. The site was founded in 2004 and was acquired by Viacom in 2007.

While the communities of users of social networking sites once were a small percentage of those online and dominated by teens and college-age adults, they are growing and increasingly are made up of young adults. A private online consumer survey from early 2007 revealed users of the sites had increased by nearly one-third to 43 percent of those 13 and older. A large part of the increase was attributed to adults 18 to 34, while teen users actually declined. The survey's sponsor predicted continued growth in the number of sites and in their use by young and middle-aged adults (Mcilroy 2007).

Online Communities and Social Capital

Early research into the social implications of online communities focused on the presumption that individuals would use technology to forge new connections independent of geographical considerations (Wellman et al. 1996) rather than to reinforce existing ones. Parks and Floyd (1996) believed that relationships begun online eventually could develop offline. Anecdotal evidence of this exists in the practice of members of the IRC Gay Ohio chat room meeting monthly at a bar in Columbus in the mid-1990s. More broadly, 46 percent of *Advocate* readers meet the people they date via websites and 32 percent use online personal ads (Lam 2006).

Because of the contemporary emergence of social networking sites and their recent burgeoning popularity, scholarly studies of them have only recently begun to be published. Ellison et al. (2007) note that initial unpublished work seems to be focusing on issues of identity and privacy. Facebook, which is the sixth most-visited website in the United States, has particularly attracted interest from social scientists. A *New York Times* article from late 2007 noted that scholars from institutions such as Indiana, Northwestern, Penn State, Tufts, and the University of Texas were conducting research into topics ranging from identity, self-esteem, and popularity to relationships, collective action, and political engagement. But though Facebook effectively facilitates scholarly work by erecting no barriers to studies, results of those studies may not be able to be generalized beyond its user base, because those with Facebook profiles do not represent the ethnicity, educational background, and income of the population as a whole.

Social networking sites may be of particular value to gay, lesbian, and bisexual teens and young adults. In his study of online behaviors of queer youth, around the time MySpace and Facebook were being developed, Alexander (2004) found users were writing online in complex and provocative ways, far beyond simply coming out. The online world was becoming a space for exploring and re-configuring issues of sexuality and identity. He also found a notable lack of traditional visual markers of queer culture, such as rainbow flags and pink triangles, at youth-composed websites. The study found evidence of the rejection of traditional labels for sexuality in the tendency of users to organize content around sex or political issues rather than around discrete identities.

Sexual Identities on MySpace

Though Facebook and MySpace both are popular social networking websites, and while both host groups distinguished by interest area and allow construction of social networks through designating other users as "friends," they handle access to information about users very differently. At Facebook, detailed profiles about users tend not to be available outside of social networks, while MySpace allows searches by keyword of profiles from outside of networks. So while Facebook facilitates scholarly study of networks, MySpace is better suited for study of the use of language in profiles and by groups. In addition, figures from January of 2008 indicate MySpace is more widely used than Facebook, with more than 68 million unique visitors in a single month compared with half as many for Facebook (Bulik 2008).

Given the popularity of MySpace among adolescents and especially young adults, and given its potential attractiveness as a virtual support network to individuals in that cohort who may be in the coming out process or otherwise defining their sexual identities, the author investigated the use of terms denoting sexual identity such as "gay," "lesbian," "bisexual," "homosexual," and "queer" in the site's profiles. These would likely be the search terms entered by users, in an effort to locate online friends or other potentially supportive users. Searching them could provide not only evidence of the perceptions that people may have of these terms (and of individuals to whom they refer), but also it may provide evidence either of continued endorsement of conventionally accepted terms for minority sexual identities, or the rejection of them. This leads to the study's first research question:

> R_1: How does the frequency of use of the sexual identity terms "homosexual," "gay," "lesbian," "bisexual," and "queer" in MySpace profile pages compare to use of "open" and "questioning" or the rejection of labels for sexual identity?

Anecdotally, the author has encountered frequent use by college-age adults of "homosexual," conventionally regarded by LGBT persons as a medical oriented and politically charged term, in place of "gay." One Stanford University linguist has argued that such younger individuals increasingly think of their sexuality more diffusely so that "gay" has related and specific meanings that may not be universally agreed upon (Vary 2006). These seem to include more pejorative uses that equate "gay" with "strange" or "uncool." Thus, results of such an investigation also could suggest a connection between how an identity term preferred by many in the LGBT community is used and its apparent increasing rejection by younger sexual minorities. This leads to the study's second research question:

> R_2: Is the term "gay" more often used as a description of sexual identity or as a pejorative term not related to the sexual identity of the owner of the MySpace profile?

The best indicators of the accumulation of social capital by MySpace users are the list of "friends," or other users "added" to a profile by the user. "Friends" may be family members and close friends of the user from offline; they also may be more casual acquaintances and users who want only to be associated with another user, perceived to be popular or attractive, or both. "Friends" who also appear in the list of messages left at a user's profile page are more likely to fall into the former group; those who are absent from the message list, the latter. Putnam's (2000) distinction between bridging social capital and bonding social capital seems to be represented in "friends" who are casual online acquaintances as opposed to those who are close friends and family, respectively. Finally, "friends" who appear frequently in the message list over a longer period of time may be not just close friends and family, but also illustrations of Ellison's (2007) concept of maintained capital. Hence, the third research question:

> R_3: What will be the relationships among the amount of bridging social capital, bonding social capital, and maintained social capital as judged from the numbers of "friends," their geographic proximity, and messages from "friends" received on MySpace profile pages?

Method

The author conducted a series of searches of user groups and user profiles at the MySpace website in March of 2008. Each was intended to simulate the type of search a teen or young adult in the throes of self-identifying as a sexual minority might make in an effort to locate a virtual support network. The first search was of the listing of "Gay, Lesbian, Bi Groups" hosted by MySpace. Its focus was the context in which descriptors such as "gay," "lesbian," "bisexual," and "queer" were used. A second search in the "All" group listing used "gay," "lesbian," "bisexual," and "queer" as keywords and had a similar focus. Four additional searches of user profiles examined the network of "friends" for users self-identifying as "gay," "bi," "straight," and "not sure," which was the MySpace profile option most closely resembling "open" and "questioning." In each case, five profiles were selected at random, the geographic location and list of "comments" from "friends" for each noted, and for each profile, ten "friends" were selected at random and their location noted. The author's assumption was that users with friends demonstrated evidence of bridging social capital, users with friends in the same geographic location knew or had the opportunity to know those friends offline and thus demonstrated evidence of bonding social capital, and finally users with friends who left written comments at the user's profile page demonstrated evidence of maintained social capital.

Results

The search of "Gay, Lesbian, Bi Groups" returned a listing of 43,290 distinct groups, the largest of which was "Support Same Sex Marriage" with 159,390 members. Most had descriptive names, such as "Boys into Briefs" and "Just Bi Girls." Others had names with positive connotations about their members, including "Hot Guys With Hot Bodies" and "Mid-Atlantic Bisexual and Lesbian Beauties." A few had names with political connotations, such as "Support Gay Rights" and "Erase the Hate." None among the largest of the 26 groups, each of which had memberships greater than 10,000, had names with negative connotations. The second search in the "All" category using "gay" as a keyword yielded a listing of much smaller groups, many with just one member, with more pejorative uses of the keyword. These included "Wow This is Gay I Wish I Could Delete it," "Yuma's Fuckin Gay (For People Who Hate Yuma)," and "Your Scene is Gay (Your Scene is Bullshit)."

The broader search of all MySpace pages using "gay" yielded approximately 1,010,000 hits. Generally speaking, the connotations either were positive or neutral. Among the pages returned by the search were a video titled "Gay Robot," a video titled "Gay Dialect for the Serious Actor," and one devoted to gay and lesbian news. A similar search of pages using "lesbian" returned approximately 466,000 hits, most of them positive. Representative among the early ones on the list were the gay and lesbian news page, an entry promoting a "private" site (for which an invitation from a member was required) where users could meet bisexual women and lesbians, and a listing of employment opportunities for which lesbians were sought. The broad search using "bisexual" returned 75,400 hits. Again, most of those early on the list—and hence more likely to be perused by users—were positive or neutral, including the video "Bisexual Cyborg," and informational sites such as "Bisexual Resource Center," and "MySpace Bisexual Network."

A search using the term "homosexual," on the other hand, yielded approximately 92,000 hits and tended to return pages more negative in tone. These included the positive (but somewhat stereotypical) "House of Homosexual Culture," an anti-gay video called "Homosexual Can't Be Christian," and an animated short called "Sasper the Homosexual Ghost."

Users self-identifying as gay had an average of 129 friends each. Sixty percent of friends were located in a town nearby the user, indicating users were accumulating both bridging and bonding social capital. Forty of those friends on average, or nearly 31 percent, had left at least one comment at the profile page, suggesting maintained capital.

Users self-identifying as bisexual had an average of 254 friends each, nearly twice as many as gay users. Fifty percent of those friends were located in a town nearby, offering evidence of bridging and bonding capital. An average of 26 friends, or 10 percent, wrote comments on each user's profile page. Bisexual users thus demonstrated less maintained capital.

Users electing to define their sexuality as uncertain had an average of 158 friends each, fully half of whom lived nearby the user. Thirty-one, or 20 percent, of those friends left comments at the user's profile page, placing uncertain users between gay users and bisexual users in maintained capital.

Straight users had an average of 168 friends each, roughly the same number as those self-identifying as uncertain. On average, 60 percent lived nearby the user, similar to user friends from the other three groups. An average of 32, or 19 percent, of friends wrote comments and thus offered evidence of maintained capital among straight users.

Discussion

The author's search of groups and user profiles at the MySpace social networking site is illuminating in terms of the usefulness of the site both for those who have self-identified as gay, lesbian, or bisexual and for those exploring their sexual identities. The choice of users to identify as either gay, lesbian or bisexual seems still to be quite common, since searches of profiles in which the user used one of those labels in each case returned the maximum number of profiles allowed, 3,000. The remaining choices, "not sure" and "straight," also returned 3,000. The lack of a way to assess the exact number in each of the five categories presented a formidable roadblock in attempts to answer the first of the research questions,

> R_1: How does the frequency of use of the sexual identity terms "homosexual," "gay," "lesbian," "bisexual," and "queer" in MySpace profile pages compare to use of "open" and "questioning" or the rejection of labels for sexual identity?

The fact that at least 12,000 MySpace users elect one of four specific labels tells us only that at least some users are not reluctant to be associated with a definitive descriptor of sexuality, though the fact that 3,000 selected "not sure" also indicates many are. It might be surmised, however, that had there been a groundswell of complaints from users about rigid sexuality categories, MySpace likely would have revised the standard profile options, given the available mechanisms for feedback.

The MySpace groups clustered in the "gay, lesbian, and bi" section and containing the search terms "gay," "lesbian," "bisexual," and "queer" likely to be the first encountered by one doing a search are both varied and positive; the groups containing the same search terms but part of the broader MySpace listing were much less likely to be positive, though their tone and extremely small memberships marked them as more marginalized or less serious in viewpoint. Moreover, the pages returned by the search terms suggest that the labels viewed within the queer communities as more conventionally acceptable—gay, lesbian, bisexual, and queer—still are more widely and more positively used than "homosexual." Thus, the tentative answer to the question

> R2: Is the term "gay" more often used as a description of sexual identity or as a pejorative term not related to the sexual identity of the owner of the MySpace profile?

seems to be that, while "gay" frequently is being used as a synonym for "strange" or "stupid" or "uncool" by mainstream MySpace users, it seems to retain its positive connotation among queer users.

Th study's final research question was:

> R3: What will be the relationships among the amount of bridging social capital, bonding social capital, and maintained social capital as judged from the numbers of "friends," messages from "friends," and length of time over which messages are received on MySpace profile pages?

This addressed the formation and maintenance of social capital by users as measured by the number of friends listed on their profile pages, the number of friends in close geographic proximity to each user, and evidence of ongoing online contact between users and their friends.

Because once a MySpace user is accepted as a "friend" by a fellow user both may exchange messages and other content, a user with many "friends" has the potential at least for the amassing of bridging, bonding, and maintained social capital. Whether that social capital is realized depends upon the motivation of the "friend" in seeking to be added to a user's list and the degree of discrimination exhibited by the user in adding friends. A user's "friend" could be anyone from a complete unknown who is geographically distanced but who is attracted to the user's picture or profile, to an unknown from the same area who is seeking new friendships or romantic relationships that are geographically close, to an offline acquaintance eager to maintain or expand the relationship online. Users similarly may add as friends only those they know offline as a shield against online predators or other unwanted attention. Or, they may welcome as friends "unknowns" from their geographical area in hopes of expanding the ranks of their offline friendships. Or, they may indiscriminately add all those who so request, perhaps in hopes that large numbers of friends will suggest they are popular or desirable.

The amount and closeness of contact required for bridging capital, which may provide the users with information but little support from "friends," can be minimal; thus, it may be available to the user even from online "friends" with whom the user has no offline relationship or recurring online contact. Nearly every user profile in this study's sample appeared to have at least one friend meeting this description; most appeared to have many more. So, even these more distant "friends" offer at least the potential for providing bridging social capital.

More complex is the relationship required for the accumulation of bonding social capital, which typically is provided by close friends and family. While it would not be impossible for a "friend" not geographically close to the user to provide such capital (a relative or offline friend now geographically distanced because of a move could, for example), a better potential would exist among "friends" living nearby, since proximity would facilitate a parallel offline relationship and perhaps a greater degree of interpersonal interaction. Frequent messages left at the user's page by these "friends" also may be an indicator. Given that on average at least half of user "friends" were close geographically and that some (though generally not the majority) left messages on the user's page, MySpace does appear to offer at least the potential for the accumulation of bonding social capital, though at most roughly equal in amount to the accumulation of bridging social capital.

The messages, left by between 10 percent and 31 percent of user "friends," seem to suggest maintained social capital as well. In many cases, these messages were left over a period of several months or even years, which is significant in light of the relative newness of the social networking sites and therefore the user profiles. A better indicator of the capacity of social networking website for maintained social capital will be if messages continue to be posted in coming years, when the novelty of the sites, and perhaps the relationships, wears off

References

Alexander, J. 2004. *In their own words: LGBT writing the world wide web*. New York: GLAAD Center for the Study of Media and Society.

Bourdieu, P. 1986. The forms of capital. In *Handbook of theory and research for the sociology of education*, edited by J. G. Richardson. New York: Greenwood Press.

Bourdieu, P., and Wacquant, L. 1992. *An invitation to reflexive sociology*. Chicago: University of Chicago.

Boxer, A. M., Cook, J. A., and Herdt, G. 1989. First homosexual and heterosexual experiences reported by gay and lesbian youth in an urban community. Paper presented at the Annual Meeting of the American Sociological Association, San Francisco, CA, August, Sociological Abstracts 1963–2005 #89S21331.

Bulik, B. S. 2008. Wait . . . isn't this the same as social networks? *Advertising Age*, 17 March, Available at: http://adage.com/digital/article?article_id=125708. [Accessed 18 March 2008]

Cass, V. C. 1979. Homosexual identity formation: A theoretical model. *Journal of Homosexuality*, 4(3): 219–235.

Egan, J. 2000. Lonely gay teen seeking same. *New York Times Magazine*, 10 December, 110–113.

Ellison, N. B., Steinfield, C., and Lampe, C. 2007. The benefits of Facebook "friends": Social capital and college students' use of online social network sites. *Journal of Computer-mediated Communication* 12(4): 1143–1168.

Gonsiorek, J. C., and Rudolph, J. R. 1991. Homosexual identity: Coming out and other developmental events. In *Homosexuality: Research Implications for Public Policy*, edited by J. C. Gonsiorek and J. D. Weinrich. Newbury Park, CA: Sage, 161–176.

Lam, S. 2006. Survey says. . . . *The Advocate*, 20 June, 83–97.

Markoff, J. 2007. Who found the bright idea? *New York Times*, 1 September, C-1.

Mcilroy, M. 2007. What's a smart way to advertise on social networks? Initiative's Joshua Sarpen did a study to find out. *Advertising Age*, 28 August, Available at: http://adage.com/print?article_id=120131. [Accessed 3 January 2008]

Parks, M. R., and Floyd, K. 1996. Making friends in cyberspace. *Journal of Computer-mediated Communication* 1(4). Available at: http://jcmc.indiana.edu/ vol1/issue4/parks.html. [Accessed 3 January 2008]

Putnam, R. 2000. *Bowling alone: The collapse and revival of American community*. New York: Simon and Schuster.

Rosenbloom, S. 2007. On Facebook, scholars link up with data. *New York Times*, 17 December, A-1.

Savin-Williams, R. C. 1990. *Gay and lesbian youth: Expressions of identity*. Washington, DC: Hemisphere.

Savin-Williams, R. C. 1995. Lesbian, gay male, and bisexual adolescents. In *Lesbian, gay and bisexual identities over the lifespan*, edited by A. R. Augelli and C. J. Patterson. New York: Oxford University Press, 165–189

U.S. Supreme Court. 2003. Lawrence v. Texas. *United States Reports*, vol. 539, 558.

Vary, A. B. 2006. Is gay over? *The Advocate*, 20 June, 98–102.

Wellman, B., Salaff, J., Dimitrova, D., Garton, L., Gulia, M., and Haythornthwaite, C. 1996. Computer networks as social networks: Collaborative work, telework, and virtual community. *Annual Review of Sociology* 22: 213–238.

Part II

Commodity Networks

Chapter 5

Lesbians Who Are Married to Men
Identity, Collective Stories, and the Internet Online Community

Margaret Cooper

For any woman who finds herself attracted to other women, many questions will arise. For women who are married to men, who may have children, and may be heavily invested in presenting a heterosexual identity within the community, extended family, and church or religious organizations, the realization that she is gay is never less than problematic. Those who are geographically isolated by residence have, in the past, faced an even more difficult situation. They may lack local resources for gays and lesbians, from which they could gain information and support. In addition, especially if they are living in very conservative regions, small towns or rural areas, not only are they isolated but also likely surrounded by homophobic mythology, possibly fundamentalist religion and often traditional gender roles and belief systems about marriage and family.

For those who have access to the internet, a wealth of information and support is only a mouse-click away. Many lesbian online communities have formed in which women can join to ask questions, gather advice and share experiences. The internet has revolutionized how the LGBT population can access one another for support, identity testing, and community. In this chapter, we will look at how married lesbians, in particular, are able to join online communities where they may have contact with other women who are, or have been, in their situation. We will see how this impacts the woman herself and examine the role the internet community plays in establishing an alternative narrative for the married woman, one that contrasts with the formula "coming out" stories (Plummer 1995) promoted in the gay and lesbian movements. Through interaction in the community, we will see how the women create a narrative (Davis 2002; Holstein and Gubrium 1999; Loseke 2007; Plummer 1995) which constructs a collective (Benford 2002; Davis 2005; Loseke 2003) story which addresses "it won't be easy" (Loseke 2003) but that there is "light at the end of the tunnel."

Most gays and lesbians have had to use caution in coming out. But for the married woman, the risks may even be higher. What situations will she face with her husband? What about her kids? How will they react? Will they be taken from her? Will they be used against her? Or even turned against her? Will her kids be teased at school?

In addition, there are issues which all lesbians and gay men face when they come out. Will they become victims of harassment within their communities? Or hate crimes? Will they lose their jobs or their mothers and fathers? All of these issues appear to be weighing on the minds of married lesbians when they turn to the online community with questions and requests for support and advice. Online communities utilize an essentially self-help model whereby individuals assist others with similar experiences, share details about what has worked for them and hasn't, suggest how to go about finding support in the community, and even how to come out to your kids, your husband, your parents, and others. Yet it is even more accessible than a typical support group and contains less risk because it is online.

Virtual communities offer the opportunity for identity testing, preparation for coming out, if one chooses to do so, and a support system throughout the entire process. This is especially essential for women who, in many cases, married because of a desire to have children and now risk the possibility of losing these same children, or have married because of the desire to please others in their lives, and now risk losing these same others as well. In this respect, the online community constructs an alternate family, friendship network, and community, where she may continue to come.

For this research, my essential questions were: How do lesbians who are in marriages with men tell stories (Plummer 1995) about their own lives? How has the internet changed the ways in which these women can access information and support from others in similar situations? And finally, what impact does this have on their lives?

Methods and Results

Many internet service providers, such as AOL and MSN, have chat rooms and message boards regarding a variety of topics. Both of these have included many online communities catering to various interests within the LGBT communities. One MSN room, Lesbian Town, became very active and attracted hundreds of members.[1] To conduct my research, I became a member of LT and a participant observer. I obtained message board transcripts dating back to 2005. Last year, however, MSN discontinued its online communities. My collected data, therefore, proved invaluable to me in this research.

Those who belonged to LT represented a range of ages and geographical locations. Many in the group identified themselves as lesbians and among these, most had been out for a number of years. Others had entered the group seeking advice regarding their sexual identities. Many of these women were married to men.

Although this online community also boasted a chat room, I focused my attention on the message board. There was a "general" board on which comments and questions are posted on various topics. There were also boards specifically

Lesbians Who Are Married to Men

designed to examine issues relating to "coming out," "venting," creative writing, fixing computer problems, as well as several others. The most posts were concentrated on the "general" board, although I looked at threads on all of the boards and isolated comments and questions to and about married women who were having romantic feelings for other women.

These communities assisted with everything from how to fix your car, how to fix your computer, or how to fix a great Thanksgiving dinner. Members posted pictures of themselves, their partners, their pets, and shared daily events of their own lives. Yet they delved deeper into what troubled individual members. Often conversations would begin by one member posting a message which begins a thread. After this, others would respond with their own experiences, advice, and commitment of support to the original poster.

The typical thread began with a member posting her situation and question and then asking for advice from others or comments. In most cases, women appeared to have responded quickly, most of them relating how they were currently in the same position or had been in the past and how they had resolved their issues. In some cases, women asked for specific advice on how to find out the nature of their feelings, asking questions like, "Is this normal?" "Has anyone ever felt this way?" and asking others for input on how to navigate the situation. Some specifically asked for help in "coming out" to their husbands, children or parents. In response, many women shared how they accomplished these feats, advising on what tactics worked well and others that didn't, and offered support throughout the process.

The following comments are representational of many posted on the boards regarding the realization of lesbian feelings while married to men:

> I have three kids and have been married for nine years … I live in Kentucky an in a very domestic suburban neighborhood I am the poster girl for straight to look at me … inside though knowing I long to be with a woman.

> We've just celebrated our eighth anniversary … We have a gorgeous daughter together. We have recently moved into a house we had built. … It looks so perfect … but then there is me. I am a lesbian, no doubt about it. 100% sure.

> I have married for seven years now and we have four kids. I am SOOOOOO unhappy with my life … I don't want to be with men any more but with a woman. But I am stuck. Trapped. I am a stay at home mom, live in a very small town in a very rural state. I am so unhappy. I can't just up and leave.

> I have no money there are no jobs around here. I am scared, scared, scared. …. I just want to be happy.

These comments are represented several issues confronting the women: 1) the realization of feelings for other women, 2) the acknowledgement of their virtual social identities as heterosexual women in marriages, 3) the presence of children which further complicated the situation, 4) isolation from gay and lesbian communities, and 5) the conflict inevitable in the reality of being married to a man while desiring a woman. Our first writer, Nancy, talked about how she appeared to others as the heterosexual wife and mother. Indeed, her life even appeared idyllic to others from the outside, yet she knew that inside of her, she possessed the feelings which could destroy, or at least irrevocably change, the apparent bliss of her suburban, Kentucky lifestyle. Our next writer, Cheryl, also reflects some of the same feelings and conflicts. She discusses her daughter and how "perfect" her life appears, and yet she now considers herself to be a lesbian, and she is "100% sure." Finally Michelle states the desperation of her situation. She has four children, no occupation or access even to a job to support herself, is isolated and, in her own words, "trapped." She poignantly describes her unhappiness and fear.

Prior to the age of the internet, these women would likely be suffering in silence. It is unlikely they would find other lesbians in their heterosexual social circles and even if they did, still might have feared taking the risk of coming out with their feelings. In these situations, what will happen if a woman is "outed" before she has worked out what she will do with regard to information management, the control of information, and its flow to others as well as the negotiation of her identity in specific life situations and to specific individuals? Thanks to the internet, she is now able to find other women who are in her situation. She is also able to locate others in cyberspace who have been in her position as well and are able to assist with information, resources, advice, and support. While her decisions are not necessarily easier ones due to this, they are often made to appear more manageable because other women in the group now serve as role models, those who have navigated through treacherous waters, have survived and in many cases, have become happier, freer, and more successful.

As women gather to construct and reinforce a collective story, a narrative emerges in which the woman is seen at some point in a process often beginning with her confusion about feelings for women and often ending in the successful accomplishment of a lesbian identity, often lived openly, with statements about one can now live with integrity. Women at the latter end of the process often remain to coach others through the process and assist in defining each experience as a natural part of the process culminating in the narrative. Therefore they serve as guides to the lesbian experience and in doing so, further influence the collective narrative and the interpretations of the process by women at various stages.

There can be little doubt that the women who begin writing the group for help are often feeling very desperate. Consider these messages left by Sherry:

> Going through the roughest time of life and can't seem to stop crying all the time. Can't even get a post together that does not sound really pathetic and I

am very must stuck in the negative at the moment ... Been married for fourteen years and have 3 kids.

[Another post by Sherry] Life is a mess and I have screwed up so much somedays I am not sure if I am coming or going. In my heart I want to do the right thing but in life it is hard. My kids deserve a family ...

[a note from Sherry about her kids] I know they deserve so much more than a messed up mom who no matter how hard I try I have time to be an egotistical wench. Can't go back in time though so all I do is the best I can for today and hope they can forgive me.

[about her lesbian feelings] Somedays I get so stuck in the past and questioning over and over again why I did not see or pay attention to the signs on me. All my life I have tried so hard not to hurt anyone but do what I could at the time to be a good person, good friend as much as I knew how. But here I am on the road to hurting so many people and some times I just feel evil for it.

On another occasion, Sherry wrote simply that she "felt lower than dirt." The pain and conflict is so evident in her posts that it is difficult for the reader not to be moved by her struggle. As someone who had always wanted to "do the right thing," be a "good person," and "not hurt anyone," Sherry now has to face the fear that by actualizing her own desires and dreams, she will do and become everything that she has feared. In fact, now she feels "evil."

Without the internet support group, one wonders what avenues would be open for Sherry in her path to self-discovery and the positive acceptance of her identity. However, within the online community, other women began to immediately respond to Sherry's plight.

In the following post, Connie empathizes with Sherry's desire to please others, yet, sharing her own experience, encourages Sherry to move forward:

Hey ... I know it's not easy, having been there myself it's very difficult.

You spend so much time during your life doing what you "think" will please others, doing what you "think" is the right thing to do. If I've learned nothing since my divorce I have learned one thing, doing all those things to please others isn't really what anyone that matters wanted in the first place, they want what will make you happy ...

Connie, along with other writers, often coach the women to think about themselves and what makes them happy, to transition from pleasing others to finally pleasing oneself. Connie continued in her post to say:

> I think we get caught up in trying to please everyone else before ourselves.
>
> I've learned to look at me first, if it pleases me then I'm doing it so long as it's not destructive to me or my children. ...You will get through this, and then you'll look back at what it took to get you where you are, happy that you made the journey to finding you. I think it's one of the greatest journeys we make.

While Connie establishes the end of the journey, or process, as attainable for Sherry, she also acknowledged that it's a difficult path. Again, sharing her own experience, Connie wrote:

> I remember the day my lawyer called to tell me she had been served with my divorce papers, I cried. When the final papers came through the mail, I cried again, then opened a bottle of wine and toasted me and my new life, whatever that would be. Wasn't easy but I made it and you will too, keep the faith!
> ...
> Here's to you and the journey ahead, may your road be paved with friendship, companionship and love.

By relating her own pain over the divorce, Connie is saying that Sherry's feelings are natural, and gives her permission to mourn. She frames the experience not as an obstacle which caused her to turn back, but instead a natural, even expected, part of the journey. As Connie wrote, it "wasn't easy," but she "made it," and tells Sherry that she will too.

Ellen contributed to this thread by assuring Sherry that she was not alone in her experience. She wrote:

> You are most certainly not the only person to have been in this situation—so don't feel as though you've done something terrible or anything. You are YOU and when you are not happy, it will show in all parts of your life ... Congrats on the big step forward, and keep your chin up—you're going to be ok.

Not only are reassurances accentuated by the respondents to this thread, but they are also actively coaching Sherry on reframing her actions not as "terrible" but as necessary to obtain integrity to oneself. They are also directing her to reinterpret her feelings and to not consider herself selfish, one of the apparent fears Sherry had experienced at the thought of meeting her own needs while disappointing others.

It is important to note that while the writers emphasize that Sherry ultimately can be successful in attaining her own life, fulfilling her own desires, and acquiring happiness, they do not gloss over the pain which they know Sherry is experiencing, nor do they pretend that there won't be heartaches along the way. Consider a few more posts from other community members to Sherry:

I've read this a few times, chewed on it awhile ... frankly I think you are being way to [sic] hard on yourself. Life is about taking chances, doing things for reasons that no one need know but us. Well make choices, yours have not been wrong, they were very right at the time you made them. None of us know things will turn out, we don't know the outcome, there is no crystal ball so you have to go with it. If mistakes were made, GREAT! That's how we move forward, it's how we live, it's how we learn and ultimately it's how we grow. Stop beating yourself up and CELEBRATE the wonderful person you are.

(Vicky)

I've learned two things for sure in my life. NOTHING LASTS FOREVER, and also, NO MATTER HOW BAD THINGS ARE, SOME GOOD WILL COME FROM IT. These two things have held me up many times ... You seem to have plateful in front of you right now, and I wish you strength and determination to persevere. Keep writing. Vent do whatever you feel like, and STAY IN TOUCH. We care and we are here to support you.

(Alice)

We all make choices that are hard and some of them are hard to live with. I stayed with my husband for 18 years so I could raise the kids in a stable environment. Boy was that a mistake! ... So hang in there and look at all you do right. You are a unique and special lady and have much to offer the world around you. Keep your head high and keep reaching for that dream.

(Susan)

Notice the direct attempts by others to speak of their support for Sherry, to raise her self-esteem and to assure her that obstacles will not prevent her from attaining self-sufficiency, identity acceptance, and ultimately, happiness. Faye wrote that although she had "lost" much, she still was in a much better place:

I went through a divorce a couple of years back. My entire life changed. I lost many material things, including two children we were about to adopt, a great job, my home, friends and his family. I lost all that, but gained freedom to be myself. I wish you the best.

Faye pulls no punches when describing her losses, and yet even with all she has been through, she still feels that her journey was a success. The goal of the "freedom to be myself" has been achieved. Vicky reiterated this when she wrote another post to Sherry of her own struggles regarding her children,

And now ... I am who I am, they (the children) accept that and love me when I don't think I can love myself. Children bounce back and sometimes understand more than we give them credit for.

Vicky concluded her note with, "Have faith, this to [sic] shall pass and when it does, you'll look back and say yeah, I made it!"

Mary described herself as being "scared and alone" since she left her husband, but added, "U know what? I am much happier this way." She wrote to Sherry that she must focus on herself, coaching as have others had done, that Sherry must be concerned with her own happiness. Mary wrote:

> My friend ... u just have to take control and plow through to what it is u really want. I just left my husband after 34 yrs of marriage. I have 3 adult kids. 2 small grandsons ... I just want happy ... I was failing to thrive and survive. I near ate myself to death ... and just dint [sic] want to liver [sic] anymore ... to hell about him ... focus on just u and the kids ... If u need a friend just contact me.

At one point, Sherry wrote, "Thank you all so much!!! Your support means more than I can say right now." At another time, she wrote, "I will be honest, if not for you ladies here and your support I am not sure where I would be today." After Sherry filed for divorce, she wrote of her pain. Others again were quick to respond, again assuring Sherry that what she was feeling was a normal part of the process:

> I found that I went through some grieving at the end of the marriage ... It is a loss just like any other ... You'll have good days and bad days but at the end I hope you're happier for it. I am.
>
> (Dana)

> You're in my thoughts ... It's an emotional rollercoaster, but given the chance, I wouldn't wave that magic wand to have things back the way they were.
>
> (Annie)

> Doing what is right for you doesn't make you bad or evil—it just means you're taking care of yourself. And yes, sometimes we hurt the people we love, but that can't always be avoided, and sometimes it does lead to better things—for everyone. You are still a good person, this won't change any of that.
>
> (Rosie)

Interestingly enough, later when a new member expressed her conflict about being in a marriage with a man yet falling in love with a woman, Sherry was one of the ones who wrote a response to her. She said, "It is what you make of it. And that is never easy. For me I have a lot to decide to move beyond the trap I have created for myself. But all things are difficult before they are easy." Even though Sherry was not at the same point in the journey as those who had written to her, her own note reflects a personal stake in and awareness of the collective narrative which she and others have constructed through their interactions and sharing of personal experiences.

Conclusion

The internet has provided us with unique opportunities to look at the stories of how women come to identify themselves, begin a process of self-discovery and acceptance and create a support system of others who are in, or have been in, similar situations. The woman who finds herself married to a man yet attracted to women often discovers that she is in for a difficult ride to self-awareness and self-acceptance. If she chooses to divorce, not only will she face all of the issues facing heterosexual women who also do so, but she may additionally encounter all of the social stigma attached to gays and lesbians. For these women, online communities have provided a safe haven in which they can discuss feelings, test identities, and gather support.

For many of them, the online community was extremely important in identity testing and working out issues before doing so in their families and community, where the consequences may be very high. Community members even assisted in aspects of negotiating identity in potentially unsafe areas. In this way, the community was a sounding board, but one which remained engaged by providing support throughout the process.

The internet community becomes an arena by which one can: 1) question her identity in a safe, risk-free environment, 2) construct alternate systems of support, family, and community, 3) gather advice from others on even the mechanics of how to write a coming out letter and how to conduct a conversation with others about her lesbian feelings so that when she does do this, she has not done it alone, 4) gather assistance on transitioning from one identity to another, and 5) obtain education about gay and lesbian identity categories and resources.

Throughout the process, members await her next post detailing how things went, and are there to cheer her on and provide the necessary emotional support and encouragement if things don't go well. While many rural women especially may know little about urban lesbian communities, lesbian lifestyles, etc., they may know even less about lesbians who are in marriages with men. The online communities create a space for those for whom the traditional narrative does not fit. The internet has provided the arena for a construction of a narrative which is quite dissimilar from the dominant collective story of the movements and sets up a narrative by which the identity trajectory is quite different than the ones typically promoted by movement coming out stories (Plummer 1995). This alternative narrative can now sit beside the more traditional movement narrative and, just by its existence and articulation, allows for the possibility of the inclusion of women who have often heretofore felt excluded, often both by the heterosexual communities and the lesbian communities.

The internet community also provides the opportunity for women to create and experience a transitional identity, one that will assist them in bridging the gap between the heterosexual world and "coming out" into a lesbian existence. While some may ask whether the women in the study expressed an interest in seeing themselves as somewhere along the "sexual continuum," I must note that most of the women saw a necessity of being either with a man or a woman. It was not that they necessarily only believed that one could be attracted to only one, but that due to concerns about fidelity, it was necessary to not be involved with both a man and a woman at the same time. Some had initially labeled themselves as "bisexual" and have moved into a lesbian identity through the process. While a few indicated that they wanted to remain with their husbands and also date women, they were typically discouraged from doing so by other community members. This usually related to concerns about monogamy, faithfulness overall, but also related to the difficulty the woman would add to her situation by trying to juggle two separate relationships, with managing two lovers' emotions and jealousies, and negotiating two potentially disparate identities. For the most part, the woman chose to claim an identity or category. There was little discussion about the validity of constructed categories and the women in the study seemed to feel the necessity of identity-claiming. Whether this was because it was perceived as more functional for their present lives, more research would be necessary to ascertain. Self-acceptance of one's self as a lesbian, for some, often appeared to be the ultimate goal and was supported by others in the community. For others, it was a matter of choosing one partner and creating a stable, monogamous relationship with her or him.

In my research, I have observed that the women have constructed an actual process through which they believe they pass, from confusion and alienation at the beginning to the feelings of integrity, happiness, and being true to one's self. While others acknowledged the trip would not be easy, they ultimately confirmed that that it could be successful and that goals could be attainable. Through the interaction of members of the online community, a narrative (Holstein and Gubrium 1999; Loseke 2007) was constructed which consisted of "war stories," "success stories," and promoted the establishment of an acceptable vocabulary of motives (Dunn 2005; Mills 1940). The collective stories had a discernible beginning as well as markers for its successful completion. The communities allowed for the creation of narrative which can exist alongside more traditional, LGBT "coming out" formula stories. As Benford (2002) noted, often movement narratives become social controls which limit the acceptance of others with dissimilar stories. By constructing an alternative narrative, these women created space for themselves within the greater LGBT collective story.

Due to the geographical isolation of many married lesbians and the fears regarding the risks and dire consequences of their situations, this constructed narrative would not likely have been possible in "real time" without the internet. While some women may have entered lesbian or feminist communities after coming out and thus constructed the narrative in hindsight, the internet provides the unique opportunity for women to enter into the story at earlier points and to be included in the narrative whether or not they later ever choose to come out into a lesbian community. In this case, the internet allows both for agency and community. As the woman often begins by seeking community, she obtains agency and often remains to coach others through the process, assisting with the reframing of events and the reinterpretation of feelings. Recall how women tried to show Sherry that she was not being selfish, but merely expressing the desire to be "true to one's self."

Finally, throughout the posts, the women affirm the importance of the online community by encouraging others to stay engaged, by offering continued support, and by confirming the role the community had in their own survival and success. In the twentiy-first century, the possibilities for gays and lesbians, especially those who are geographically isolated, have increased exponentially. For those of us who study the New Media, the opportunities are limitless as well.

Notes

1 Lesbian Town was a members-only community. Potential members had to request entrance from the community's site manager by emailing and stating why she wished to belong and how she could benefit from membership. Due to this membership-only status of the LT and the fact that MSN has since discontinued their online communities, no URLs are given for the comments presented in this chapter.

References

Benford, R. D. 2002. Controlling narratives and narratives as control within social movements. In *Stories of change: Narrative and social movements*, edited by J. E. Davis. Albany, NY: State University of New York Press, 53–78.

Davis, J. E. 2002. Narrative and social movements: The power of stories. In *Stories of change: Narrative and social movements*. Albany, NY: State University of New York Press, 3–30.

Davis, J. E. 2005. *Accounts of innocence: Sexual abuse, trauma, and the self*. Chicago: University of Chicago Press.

Dunn, J. L. 2005. Victims and survivors: Emerging vocabularies of motive for battered women who stay. *Sociological Inquiry* 75: 1–30.

Holstein, J. A. and Gubrium, J. F. 1999. *The self we live by: Narrative identity in a postmodern world*. London: Oxford University Press.

Loseke, D. R. 2003. Formula stories and support groups for battered women. In *Social problems: Constructionist readings*, edited by D. R. Loseke and J. Best. New York: Aldine de Gruyter, 241–250.

Loseke, D. R. 2007. The study of identity as cultural, institutional, organizational, and personal narratives: Theoretical and empirical integrations. *The Sociological Quarterly* 48: 661–688.

Mills, C. W. 1940. Situated actions and the vocabularies of motive. *American Sociological Review* 5(6): 904–913.

Plummer, K. 1995. *Telling sexual stories: Power, change and social worlds.* London and New York: Routledge Press.

Chapter 6
A Very Personal World
Advertisement and Identity of Trans-persons on Craigslist

Daniel Farr

Personal ads have been significantly transformed since their development online. Americans are increasingly engaging with the new opportunities and resources that the web can offer for their personal lives. Despite the growing number of people posting and responding to online personal ads, this continues to be regarded as a deviant form of intimacy or courtship initiation (Rajecki et al. 1991). Using the internet to locate romantic or intimate partners is considered by many to be a last resort—an option turned to only by the most desperate and undesirable. However, with ever-expanding access to the internet, either privately or in public venues, accompanied by demographic and cultural shifts, this stigma has begun to dissipate (Baker 2002, 2005). Regardless of the cultural ethos affiliated with online personal ads and meeting via the internet, this phenomenon is certain to continue to grow in acceptance. The increasing legitimacy is likely attributed to the larger numbers of people engaging in online personal ads, the mainstreaming of online "dating" sites (such as "eHarmony.com"), and number of people who have entered long-term relationships and marriages initiated via the web. While used by many, the internet offers particular opportunities for marginalized and disenfranchised populations (Koch and Schockman 1998), such as among the lesbian, gay, bisexual, and transgender (LGBT) community, to meet and make connections.

This research seeks to explore the personal ads of transgendered individuals, a population limited in size and often stigmatized, to examine how this gender and sexual minority population engages with online personal advertising. Informed by grounded and feminist methodologies, this research seeks to particularly address the gendered variations found among transgender personal ads, the types of relationships or interactions sought, and especially the variety of body and sexual descriptions employed.

The ads analyzed in this study were collected from the Craigslist website. Craigslist is an online website with pages dedicated to over 550 cities in the United States and 50 countries. Established in 1995, Craigslist has grown to be the eighth largest English-language website globally, with over 12 billion page views per month by over 50 million visitors, equating to 40 million in the United

States alone (Craigslist 2009). Visitors are able to post classified and personal ads, with most ads free of charge. The widespread use of Craigslist, the anonymity of online, and the free nature of its ads offers a particularly rich environment for the examination of trans- personal ads.

The examination of personal ads offers a breadth of information about the socio-cultural construction of beauty, intimacy, identity, and advertising ideologies. Not only do these ads expose individual desires and expectations, but they reveal underlying cultural ideologies informing the language and content. Other than direct methods such as interviews, social venue observations (for example, in a bar), and surveys, the personal ad is one of the few ways that partnership selection can be effectively observed and analyzed (Goode 1996a, 1996b). While personal ads are used by people of all types, gay men and lesbians have been particularly noted for employing this tool to locate intimate partners (Cockburn 1988; Harris 1997). The use of personal ads is exceptionally effective for sexual and gender minorities as it creates an opportunity to appeal to potential partners regardless of social situation and geography; perhaps a necessity given the limited size of the visible LGBT community in some locations. Certainly, many may prefer to locate a potential partner within a limited geographic region for convenience, but there are also those who are willing to expand their search nationally, even internationally, in pursuit of the ideal person.

Examinations of personal ads have explored their varying uses, associated gratifications of users and respondents, and communication tactics (Davidson 1991; Epel et al. 1996; Gibbs et al. 2006; Milewski et al. 1999), but have often centered upon heterosexual personal ads. Recent works have sought to explore the personal ads of gay men and lesbians (Bailey et al. 1997; Bartholome et al. 2000; Child et al. 1996; Deaux and Hanna 1984; Gonzales and Meyers 1993; Gudelunas 2005; Hatala and Predhodka 1996; Smith and Stillman 2002), men who have sex with men (Ward 2008), and bisexuals (George 2001), but little analysis of transgender populations has occurred (see Child et al. 1996 for exception) in part due to the limited number of advertisements. With such limited information available about transgender personal ads, an understanding of gay men's and lesbian's personal ads is the closest proxy to inform this work.

In an analysis of gay men's personal ads of a phone service in Ottowa, Canada, Barthalome, Tewksbury, and Bruzzone (2000) examined the manners of body description and sexual roles/acts sought. While racial-ethnic identities were only mentioned in 8 of the 167 ads analyzed, physical descriptions were included in approximately 80 percent of the ads with over a third specifically referencing genital characteristics and sexual acts. Among the genital references, 45 percent used explicit language, particularly describing size, with 75 percent discussing their own and 25 percent describing the characteristics of the phallus sought. Forty percent of respondents mention a sexual role and 38 percent describe the sexual act sought. Among sexual acts sought, oral sex was most common (79 percent), followed by anal sex (25 percent), masturbation (10 percent), fondling/licking (6.3 percent), kissing/cuddling (5 percent), and spanking (3 percent). With some of these acts, particularly oral and anal sex, explicit roles such as top, bottom, or versatile or give or receive, were common. The authors affirm that men seeking men are likely to emphasize physical characteristics and sexual relations.

Online interactions at large have demonstrated important socio-cultural meanings for gay men and lesbians (Woodland 2000) and trans-persons (Gauthier and Chaudoir 2004). While access to the internet, particularly from an early age, is mitigated by social class, the internet offers a safe space for LGBT persons (Woodland 2000), who were among some of the earliest to embrace cyber resources (Wakeford 2000). The internet offers a relatively safe space to explore one's identity and desires, as well as a location to make connections with other gay and lesbian individuals, both locally and at large. Indeed, online interactions may serve as a way of establishing a connection with another local person that can then transition into real world, face-to-face, interactions (Gibbs et al. 2006; Hardey 2002). Among the various reasons for seeking others online, a short-term sexual encounter is fairly common as the internet offers those of traditionally deviant sexual interests, which may include anonymous sexual encounters, one-night stands, swinging, and various fetish sex, access to each other (Quinn and Forsyth 2004; Rosenmann and Safir 2006). While sexual encounters with relative strangers brings considerable risk it is not uncommon, particularly for gay men, to seek sex online (Gudelunas 2005; Okie 2000). Meanwhile, heterosexual men seem to use personal ads more often to pursue long-term relationships and less often for casual sex (Child et al. 1996; Gonzales and Meyers 1993; Hatala and Prehodka 1996).

Gudelunas's (2005) analysis of 200 personal ads from PlanetOut, an online gay and lesbian community, accompanied by surveys of the advertisers, explores the uses and content of gay and lesbian online personals. Analysis of these ads revealed a sample with an average age of 32.8 for men from urban settings and 28.3 for smaller, suburban and rural settings; for women the average ages were 30.8 and 28.6 respectively. The inclusion of images within the ads was particularly addressed. Advertisers who included photos overwhelmingly reported they did so to increase the response rate. Additionally, the use of photos helped to assure one knew what they were getting into should they meet someone off-line. Those who chose to not include photos cited technical issues, morality, and privacy concerns as their primary reasons. However, those without pictures included higher levels of physical description to compensate. While most respondents recognized the national access to personal ads, nearly all reported searching by zip code. Clearly, those who are using personal ads are particularly interested in locating individuals who are in a reasonable geographic range, with the likely expectation or goal of meeting in person.

Research addressing transgender use of the internet has been limited despite the important role it plays for many seeking to find a community (Gauthier and

Chaudoir 2004). Given the significant risk of violence faced by many transgendered in our heterosexist culture (Lombardi et al. 2001), the internet offers a venue for information access and sharing that may feel anonymous and safe. While problematic to determine population size, estimates suggest that 1 in 33,000 men and 1 in 100,000 women are transsexual (DSM-IV 1994), with the number of transgender being higher given the cost of sex reassignment surgery and individual body-gender preferences. Despite increasing social visibility, the presence of trans-personal ads has received limited attention due to their small numbers.[1]

Superficially it may seem simple to post an advertisement on Craigslist,[2] but there are a myriad of factors to be considered including categories, descriptors, and photograph inclusion. Among the personals sections of Craigslist there are nine subject groupings: "strictly platonic," "women seeking women," "women seeking men," "men seeking women," "men seeking men," "misc. romance," "casual encounters," "missed connections," and "rants and raves." Given the especially obtuse nature of "missed connections" and "rants and raves" advertisements in these sections were not included in the sample. Informed by basic terminology use within trans- communities, searches were initially performed with the following terms: MTF, FTM, transgender, transexual, transsexual, trans, transwoman, transman, transguy, and transgirl. Through these initial searches additional terms were garnered and incorporated into the search protocol, including: genderqueer, tgirl, tranny, tman, transfag, m2f, and f2m. Advertisements that indicated part-time cross-dressers, partial cross-dressers (i.e. a statement from a man such as "I like to wear panties during sex play."), and those who appeared flippant, rude, or humorous in their deployment of a trans- identity were not included in the sample. For each advertisement all text was copied and coded. If an advertisement included imagery it was printed and digitally catalogued.

Given the tremendous size of Craigslist it would have been impractical to attempt to sample every city and location. Among the top 20 U.S. cities and metro regions 10 were selected for analysis with effort to spread these locations across the country. The cities addressed in this project included: Atlanta, Boston, Chicago, Dallas, Los Angeles, Miami, New York City, San Francisco, Seattle, and Washington, DC. For each city there were 100s of personals, among which only a small number were from trans-persons. In some cities the personal ads could be traced back as much as four to six weeks, however in New York City, Los Angeles, and San Francisco the high volume of incoming personals resulted in the loss of substantial ad history limiting the available data to within a few days of data collection sessions.

One particular obstacle to collecting online personal ads is the poster's ability to edit or delete their ad at anytime, resulting in a constantly changing pool of ads (Gudelunas 2005). Indeed, those who post on Craigslist may add, edit, or delete a personal ad at any given time making it impossible to obtain a complete data set. To increase sample validity, systematic data collection occurred during

December 2007 and January 2008.[3] As posting personal ads is free through this website, some posted multiple ads with nearly the same information in different sections, such as in "men seeking men" and "casual encounters." When multiple postings from, seemingly, the same advertiser occurred within a single day they were reduced to one for use in data analysis.

Given the binary nature of the American gender system the majority of trans-ads could be distinguished as born males living as women (MTF, to draw from transsexual terminology for male-to-female) or born females living as men (FTM, again, from transsexual terminology for female-to-male). Alternately, some were more gender queer, wherein a biological sex and social gender were indeterminable (for example, the advertiser simply employed an abbreviation t4m to indicate trans- for male) or muddled (for example, referring to oneself as a transman and also using the abbreviation MTF). The use of MTF and FTM are problematic when engaging with transgendered persons given the mélange of embodiment and social enactments, but were exceptionally common terms among the personal ads.

The data collection culminated in a sample of 195 advertisements (102 from December, and 93 from January). This sample demonstrates diversity in gender identity, age, racial-ethnic identity, and in types of relationships sought. This sample included 81 MTF (41.5 percent), 102 FTM (52.3 percent), and 12 Queer (6.2 percent) advertisements. Within the sample 47 (24.1 percent) ads did not report an age. Among reported ages there was a greater frequency among those aged 18–34, but ranged into the 50s. For MTF personal ads, self reported mean and median age was 29.7 and 29; for FTM 29.6 and 28, respectively. Among the queer advertisements it was uncommon to report age. Indeed, given the low number of queer ads in this sample the majority of statistical analysis will center upon the more prevalent personal ads that dichotomized their identities; occasional statistics from the queer personal ads will be incorporated as appropriate.

Only 47 (24 percent) of the sample included racial-ethnic self-identification in their advertising text. The language used to define racial-ethnic identity varied from terms such as black, white, and Latino to more specific identifications such as French and Cambodian, Puerto Rican and Italian, to racial and tone characteristic blends such as Asian/mocha/caramel and light skinned chocolate. While somewhat simplified, the general distribution of identity among these self-identified was: 34 percent black, 21 percent white, 15 percent Latino, 15 percent mixed/multi-, 13 percent Asian/Pacific Islander, and 2 percent East Indian. An additional facet of racial-ethnic identification is embedded within the use of photographs in the personal ads. Of all ads, 67 (34.4 percent) incorporated at least one, up to four, pictures or images. Of these 67 ads, 15 (22.4 percent) had images of cartoons, sexual toys, scenery, sports logos, and other non-person images. The remaining 52 (77.6 percent) included pictures of the person advertising, presumably. The majority of these photos included faces, but a significant proportion included body, erotic poses, and sexual body parts, especially among ads seeking casual sexual encounters. Interestingly, among these pictures approximately 43 percent of the advertisers deployed the photo to express their racial-ethnic identity without written confirmation in their description. While it is problematic to define another's identity based on the interpretation of physical characteristics, it is clear that a number of these ads portrayed those who would likely be culturally defined as white, black, Latino, and other racial-ethnic minorities. While they do not clearly state racial-ethnic identities, these ads do demonstrate them to the audience.

Since ads were located within different sections there was little interpretation necessary. The breakdown of percentage distributions among the different types of personal ads is presented as Table 6.1

Geographically, the number of ads collected from each city varied. San Francisco, by far, had the most ads (N = 48; 12 more than the second highest). This was likely mitigated by a strong LGBT community presence, but also longer community engagement with Craigslist, as it was founded there. The average number of responses per city was approximately 20, with a median number of approximately 15. The city with the fewest ads was Washington, DC, with only 2. While some cities, such as New York City had relatively equal MTF and FTM ads, other cities were more skewed, such as San Francisco with 33 FTM and 10 MTF.[4]

Self-description of one's body was a common feature among these personal ads with 61 percent of advertisers doing so. Most of the queer respondents did not describe their bodies. This is in part the reason that distinguishing their gender "identity," within the traditional gender constructs, was problematic. Among FTM respondents, it was equally divided to self-describe or not. Among MTF, there was a greater likelihood of description, with 77 percent doing so. Further, the type of description offers insight. Descriptions were coded as primarily quantitative in nature, for example, I am 5'10", 165lbs . . ., 36-26w-32h, qualitative in nature, for example, good looking . . . tall, attractive man, or as a combination of both characteristics. Among FTMs who described their physical attributes, 65.5 percent did so in qualitative terms, 11.5 percent in quantitative terms, and 23

Table 6.1 Percentage Distributions Among the Different Types of Personal Ads

Personal Ad Type	MTF	FTM	Queer
casual encounters	55%	52%	83%
women seeking women	11%	13%	9%
misc. romance	22%	10%	8%
men seeking men	5%	16%	
women seeking men	3%	3%	
men seeking women	2%	2%	
strictly platonic	2%	4%	

percent blended the two. Meanwhile, among MTFs who described their physical attributes, 39 percent did so in qualitative terms, 28 percent in quantitative terms, and 33 percent blended the two.

Health, disease, and drug use are common topics among the personal ads, but often in obtuse and imprecise manners. A significant number of ads, for example, use terms such as "drug and disease free" or "ddf" to describe themselves or partners sought, but few ads specifically spoke to the issue of HIV. Only 10 ads (5.1 percent) mention HIV/AIDS directly, primarily to indicate that they were HIV negative or sought only such. Despite the sexual health risks affiliated with casual sex, only two ads (~1 percent) explicate the advertiser as HIV+ or "pos."

While the study was unable to determine the number of trans-persons who advertise in personal ads without clarifying their trans- status, among those who do reveal this identity it is often clarified and specific in their ads. Terms such as FTM, MTF, and transguy were among the most common identity markers employed, but were often accompanied by clarification, such as "FtM (transitioning/-ed from female to male),"[5] "I am not a T-girl. I am a MW FTM (Female to Male)," or in more graphic manners such as "Lets make this clear and simple, I am an FTM (ie: a guy with a pie) . . . not a chick with a dick." This clarification and distinction of trans- types appears only among FTM ads. It would seem that cultural perceptions of trans-persons as only being MTF encourages some transmen to specify and distinguish their embodiment.

The idea of legitimacy and social passing was addressed across many ads with advertisers clearly stating they were of a particular gender or sex or even suggesting that they are "100% passing." Some clarify the distinction of their gender and physical embodiment, as with a 36-year old, "I'm a T-girl (although I prefer transwoman) . . . I am TS, but choose not to go any surgical route. I do look like a girl though, and I am adept at what I do." While she may not have made surgical changes to her body, she is clearly expressing her trans- identity and that she does so in a manner that is socially acceptable or passing. Across all ads, the importance of being seen as a "real" man or woman was clearly an important aspect of their identity construction and portrayal.

Despite the strong tendency of trans-persons to create personal ads that clearly indicate their identities as transmen or transwomen, with over 90 percent of the sample doing so, many also engage with the identity and gender fluidity that accompanies a trans- status. It is common to find reference the transformative process affiliated with transitioning, for example, "I am an MTF starting transition . . . you must be patient and understand with a tgurl 'under construction.'" Many also speak to being "pre-op." While several FTMs referenced not having had genital surgery, it was not necessarily regarded in a derogatory way. Indicative of their own body fluidity, a number engage with transformative language to symbolically confirm their gender or sex identity—some FTMs spoke of having "NO surgery down below but my 'clit' grew to about 2 inches hard (now my cock)" while others spoke of having a "big clit" instead of a penis. This form of figurative genital transformation among MTF, such as with the use of "pussycock," was found only rarely. Indeed, for these MTFs it seems that having a penis serves as a sexual or social resource. Many not only mention the size of their phallus, but its functionality as well, which serves to bridge sex-gender to create and perhaps eroticize the "chick with a dick." Near universally, the referencing of genitals was present only among those seeking casual encounters. Counter to the commonplace portrayal of gender fluidity some, particularly MTFs, seek to reinforce their identities with an essentialist focus on sex and body, as with one 40 year old "transsexual Pre-op woman" who describes herself as a "female." Others engage with the idea of naturalness, speaking of having "all-natural" or "real b-cup tits."

A variety of advertisers conveyed a sense of frustration with common culture and its lack of understanding of trans- identities. Some specify that "no beginners" or "curious" sought. One ad was even more specific in stating "FTM (if you don't know what that is then don't respond)." Frustration with respondents also emerges in language such as "real only" and "no fakes need apply." The culmination of respondents who don't understand who they are contacting and the common spamming and brief responses results in a culture of brief ads. Many of the personal ads were quite brief, two to four sentences in length, despite the ability to write ads more than a page in length. It may be that some do not wish to invest significant time in posting an ad for limited responses. Additionally, many specify a requirement of a photograph for more information (i.e. "your pic gets mine") or even a response (i.e. "no pic . . . no reply"). Ultimately, these general frustrations of email interaction and responses are not specific to trans- personal ads, but are found throughout Craigslist personal ads.

Among MTF personal ads the integration of femininity and maleness are synthesized into a nuanced image of trans- femininity. Many employed phrasing and terminology to reinforce their feminine personality characteristics, such as "playful," "sexy," and "caring." They also engage with a variety of feminine descriptors when describing their bodies, such as "petite, slim & slender." Similarly, among FTM descriptors such as "strong," "big guy," and "hairy" (facial hair was often specified) were deployed to affirm a masculine interpretation.

Hormone treatment is a common practice among trans-persons, fostering secondary sex characteristics that may help one pass. Indeed, among all types of personal ads the referencing of hormones was relatively common. Many used the specific term "hormones," but some used subcultural terminology such as being on "t" [testosterone]. In conjunction with the mention of being on hormones, the length of time in use was commonplace. It appears that the use of and length of time on hormone, regardless of surgical body transformations, serves as a significant marker for gender identity for many trans-persons.

The images used in these advertisements included a variety of normative face and body shots, as well as a variety of sexually explicit images. While no queer ads included an image, both FTM and MTF ads included normative (g-rated) pictures. However, both also included sexual images, especially when seeking casual encounters. Among MTFs these sexual images often took the form of posed, erotic images, reflective of those seen of women in heterosexual pornography, with only one image including genitals, but as secondary to buttocks. Most emphasized breasts and buttocks. Meanwhile, FTMs images were fewer, but included some of the most graphic images of sexual acts. The use of sexual imagery reinforces gender ideologies of women being erotic and seductive and men being performative and aggressive.

While the classifying of these personal ads as FTM, MTF, and queer may be reductionist and ultimately incongruent with the lived experiences of many trans-persons, the majority of advertisements clearly articulated their gender in dichotomizing manners. This suggests that for many trans-persons it is functional to explain or define their identity in a fashion that cisgendered[6] persons are likely to recognize and understand. These clarifications help reduce confusion and the manifestation of problems if an online interaction transitions into the real-world.

Craigslist has created a safe space for personal ads by creating category boxes that allow for the identification of a "T" [trans] identity—there is not the presumption that people are only men or women. While this system is relatively welcoming of trans- advertisers, it is limiting in that this is only an option under casual encounters, which may in part account for its bias among advertisement categories. Categories such as men seeking men create an androcentric environment, wherein female-born men may feel unwelcomed or be placed on the defensive. For trans-persons advertising in these clearly gendered arenas there must be a clear explanation of their identity and body to avoid misunderstandings and potential problems. A further nuance to this issue is the limited construct of relation types available: m4t, t4m, t4mw, and mw4t. There is no option for a woman to seek trans or vice versa. This suggests the heteronormative and gendered assumptions of trans as being only MTF and being primarily interested in men.

Surprisingly little regional variation was demonstrated by these ads. Occasional references to specific social clubs or bars aside, one would be unable to discern region of origin, let alone particular cities from these ads. This is suggestive of the universalizing and generic nature of a venue such as Craigslist and the cultural familiarity of personal ads. This lack of regional variation is also likely the manifestation of changing American ideologies and the influence of mass media. The eroticization and idealization of body and its linguistic descriptors are becoming mainstreamed and less regionally specific.

While it is impossible to know the number of personal ads on Craigslist from trans-persons that are not self-identifying their trans- status, those who are doing so are actively conveying the synthesis of their physical bodies and social identities. There is a clear cultural presence of trans-persons on Craigslist, but their cultural existence in America at large is brought into question. Given the prevalence of clear explanations of body and defining of identity, it would appear that the average American personal ad consumer is under-informed about trans-identities, especially for transmen. The presumption that all trans-persons are MTF not only limits the opportunities of transwomen, but also works to limit and constrain gender and sexuality at large.

While there is fluidity and variation, it appears that many trans-persons are posting personal ads in a manner similar to gay men, with an emphasis upon casual sexual encounters. This may be influenced by Craigslist system limitations, but may also be reflective of the loosening of sexual mores and increased use of the internet for the pursuit of casual sexual encounters among all types of people. Current research has yet to address Craigslist personal ads in any significant systematic fashion, making it impossible to determine the numbers and types of personal ads placed. Anecdotally however, when contrasting the heterosexual categories with homosexual categories, there is a clear distinction. Heterosexuals (both men seeking women and women seeking men) appear to be advertising less often for purely sexual purposes, more often advertising for dating and relationships, while homosexuals (men seeking men) frequently advertise explicitly for sex. Further research must be accomplished before a more significant understanding of these ads can be assessed. Perhaps the prevalence of trans- ads seeking casual sex is ultimately the manifestation of minority status and social marginalization. Given the socio-legal obstacles faced by sexual and gender minorities, perhaps long-term relationships are not regarded in the same manner as among heterosexuals. The influence of sexual mores among gay men and lesbians as portrayed in mainstream media and within subcultural communities may also be influencing this population often grouped to a similar minority status. Regardless, the implications for intimacies and sexual health are issues that ought to be addressed in further research on these personal ads.

This said, the personal ads of this sample speak to much more than the mere construction of body and the types of interactions sought. These ads speak strongly to the desires of trans-persons to be accepted and validated in their personal interactions and relationships. The use of language to resist negative stereotypes and to educate the consumer clearly demonstrates the desire to be regarded as "normal." These advertisers are not only seeking to connect physically or emotionally with others, but are seeking legitimization and acceptance. Their frequent highlighting of their ability to pass serves not only to attract, but also bolsters heteronormative ideologies of gender and sex. Certainly, many embrace queered gender ideologies in their presentations, but the majority are working to integrate their trans- identities within the social constraints of a binary gender system. While society may be increasingly accepting sexual diversity, gender diversity still faces significant prejudice and discrimination—this forces trans-persons to simultaneously flame and minimize their trans- statuses to assure mutual understanding and acceptability, while reducing the risk of violence and rejection.

Notes

1. George (2001) had intended to include trans-personals in her analysis of British print personal ads, but was unable to do so because of the small number of ads found in her sample.
2. Personal ads on Craigslist are accomplished by clicking "post," followed by the selection of subject grouping. You are then prompted to select who you are and who you seek from predetermined options, such as "a man," "a woman," "someone TG/TV/TS," etc. At this point you are taken to a form with boxes to list a posting title, age, specific location, and posting description. You also have the option to add images, such as pictures. After you have completed your ad you may proof and submit it to the system after agreeing to the terms of use and completing a visual text test to assure you are a person, not a spam computer program. You will then receive an email where you can confirm, edit, or cancel the posting of your ad. An ad will not post unless you confirm for it to do so; it may then be removed at any time per your direction. Ads on Craigslist employ an anonymous email identity system that routes email responses to you without revealing your email address to the responder. The responder only becomes aware of your email address if you choose to respond in kind. This system is efficient to navigate and effectively protects one's anonymity and privacy.
3. Ads were collected weekly, alternating between Fridays and Wednesdays. One data collection session occurred on a Sunday in an attempt to capture variation that may emerge during a weekend. No significant variation was demonstrated in the content regardless of data collection timing.
4. A complete breakdown of the numbers per city follows: Atlanta had a total of 36 ads (15 MTF, 19 FTM, 2 Queer); Boston had 25 ads (8 MTF, 16 FTM, and 1 Queer); Chicago had 14 ads (3 MTF, 11 FTM); Dallas had 17 ads (13 MTF, 2 FTM, 2 Queer); Los Angeles had 12 ads (10 MTF, 2 FTM); Miami had 11 ads (8 MTF, 2 FTM, 1 Queer); New York City had 20 ads (9 MTF, 10 FTM, 1 Queer); San Francisco had 48 ads (10 MTF, 33 FTM; 5 Queer); Seattle had 12 ads (5 MTF, 7 FTM); and Washington DC had 2 ads (2 FTM).
5. I have incorporated direct quotes from the data set to exemplify themes and meaning. If the complete context of a particular quote is desired a copy of the ad may be obtained by contacting the author at DFarr77@gmail.com.
6. Cisgendered persons are those whose gender and sex correlate in traditional manners, such as a man who was born male or a woman who was born female.

References

Bailey, J.M., Kim, P.Y., Hills, A., and Linsenmeier, J.A. 1997. Butch, femme, or straight acting? Partner preferences of gay men and lesbians. *Journal of Personality and Social Psychology* 73: 960–973.

Baker, A. 2002. What makes an online relationship successful? Clues from couples who met in cyberspace. *Cyberpsychology and Behavior* 5: 363–375.

Baker, A. 2005. *Double click: Romance and commitment among online couples*. Cresskil, NJ: Hampton.

Bartholome, A., Tewksbury, R., and Bruzzone, A. 2000. "I want a man": Patterns of attraction to all-male personal ads. *Journal of Men's Studies* 8(3): 309–321.

Child, M., Low, K. G., McCormick, C. M., and Cocciarella, A. 1996. Personal advertisements of male-to-female transsexuals, homosexuals, and heterosexuals. *Sex Roles* 34: 447–455.

Cockburn, J. 1988. *Lonely hearts: Looking for love among the small ads*. London: Simon & Schuster.

Craigslist. 2009. Fact Sheet. www.craigslist.org/about/factsheet. [Accessed February 2009]

Davidson, A. G. 1991. Looking for love in the age of AIDS: The language of gay personals, 1978–1988. *The Journal of Sex Research* 34(5/6): 125–137.

Deaux, K. and Hanna, R. 1984. Courtship in the personals column: The influence of gender and sexual orientation. *Sex Roles* 11: 363–375.

DSM-IV. 1994. *Diagnostic and statistical manual of mental disorder*, 4th ed. Washington, DC: American Psychiatric Association.

Epel, E. S., Spankos, S., Kasl-Godley, J., and Brownell, K. D. 1996. Body shape ideals across gender, sexual orientation, socioeconomic status, race, and age in personal advertisements. *International Journal of Eating Disorders* 19(3): 264–273.

Gauthier, D. K. and Chaudoir, N. K. 2004. Tranny boyz: Cyber community support in negotiating sex and gender mobility among female to male transsexuals. *Deviant Behavior* 25: 375–398.

George, S. 2001. Making sense of bisexual personal ads. *Journal of Bisexuality* 1(4): 35–57.

Gibbs, J.L., Ellison, N.B., and Heino, R.D. 2006. Self-presentation in online personals: The role of anticipated future interaction, self-disclosure, and perceived success in internet dating. *Communication Research* 33(2): 152–177.

Gonzales, M. and Meyers, S. 1993. Your mother would like me: Self-presentation in the personal ads of heterosexual and homosexual men and women. *Personality and Social Psychology Bulletin* 19: 131–142.

Goode, E. 1996a. Placing/answering personal ads as a form of courtship. *Sex Roles* 34: 141–169.

Goode, E. 1996b. The ethics of deception in social research: A case study. *Qualitative Sociology* 19: 11–33.

Gudelunas, D. 2005. Online personal ads: Community and sex, virtually. *Journal of Homosexuality* 49(1): 1–33.

Hardey, M. 2002. Life beyond the screen: Embodiment and identity through the internet. *The Sociological Review* 50(4): 571–585.

Harris, D. 1997. Personals. *Antioch Review* 55(1): 6–24.

Hatala, M. N. and Predhodka, J. 1996. Content analysis of gay male and lesbian personal advertisements. *Psychological Reports* 78: 371–374.

Koch, N. S. and Schockman, E. H. 1998. Democratizing internet access in the lesbian, gay and bisexual communities. In *Cyberghetto or cybertopia: Race, class and gender on the internet*, edited by B. Ebo. Westport, CT: Praeger, 171–184.

Lombardi, M., Wilchins, R., Priesing, D., and Malouf, D. 2001. Gender violence: Transgender experiences with violence and discrimination. *Journal of Homosexuality* 42(1): 89–101.

Milewski, K., Hatala, M. N., and Baack, D. W. 1999. Downloading love: A content analysis of internet personal advertisements placed by college students. *College Student Journal* 33(1): 124–130.

Okie, S. 2000. When virtual contact becomes real contact. *The Washington Post*, July 26, A2.

Quinn, J. F. and Forsyth, C. J. 2004. Describing sexual behavior in the era of the internet: A typology for empirical research. *Deviant Behavior* 26: 191–207.

Rajecki, D., Bledsoe, S., and Rasmussen, J. 1991. Successful personal ads: Gender differences and similarities in offers, stipulations, and outcomes. *Basic and Applied Social Psychology* 12: 457–469.

Rosenmann, A., and Safir, M.P. 2006. Forced online: Push factors of internet sexuality: A preliminary study of online paraphilic empowerment. *Journal of Homosexuality* 51(3): 74–83.

Smith, C.A. and Stillman, S. 2002. Butch/femme in the personal advertisements of lesbians. *Journal of Lesbian Studies* 6(1): 45–51.

Wakeford, N. 2000. Cyberqueer. In *The Cybercultures Reader*, edited by D. Bell and B. M. Kennedy. New York: Routledge, 403–415.

Ward, J. 2008. Dude-sex: White masculinities and 'authentic' heterosexuality among dudes who have sex with dudes. *Sexualities* 11(4): 414–434.

Woodland, R. 2000. Queer spaces, modern boys and pagan statues: Gay/lesbian identity and the construction of cyberspace. In *Lesbian and gay studies: A critical introduction*, edited by A. Medhurst and S. R. Munt. London: Cassell, 1997.

Chapter 7

The Facebook Revolution
LGBT Identity and Activism

Margaret Cooper and Kristina Dzara

Using Facebook (2009), a popular worldwide social networking site with millions of members, is just one way that people stay in touch with old friends and meet new ones. Although Facebook was originally created as a site for college students, it has since expanded so that anyone with a valid email address can join. There is one key difference between Facebook and other online social networks. Facebook is one of the few social network sites where those who are friends online are also friends or at least acquaintances in real life (Ellison et al. 2007; Ross et al. 2009). Thus, Facebook serves as an additional way that a user can interact with friends and loved ones.

In this article, we dissect Facebook as a tool that LGBT users employ to construct, maintain, and sometimes hide their identities. We do this because Facebook is an innovative social tool that enables users to attempt to reflect to their friends who they believe themselves to be. Although this sense of and management of identity begins with the individual, it may be encouraged or discouraged by other Facebook users, potentially creating conflict. Below, we draw on broad-ranging social psychological principles to explore, analyze, and explain the use of Facebook by those under the LGBT umbrella.

Methods and Analysis

In her work with rural lesbians, Cooper (1990, 2007, and forthcoming) recently discovered a change in the way these women could acquire information. Where formerly isolated by geography, rural lesbians were able now to go online and seek out communities where they could gain information and support from others in similar situations. Cooper then became interested in the internet, and was led to the topic of Facebook by her LGBT college students. She then joined Facebook herself and became a member of many LGBT groups. Her co-author had been a member of Facebook since 2006 and has joined a number of political and social Facebook groups. Together Cooper and Dzara explored the site as participant observers, analyzing profiles available to all users for constructions of identity and obtaining anecdotal information from users. In addition, we conducted an academic search of journal articles and books related to Facebook as well as a Lexis Nexis search on Facebook articles in the popular press. We also reviewed academic research conducted on the topics of Facebook, internet activism and issues of personality and identity (Ellison et al. 2007; Pempek et al. 2009; Raacke and Bonds-Raacke 2008; Ross et al. 2009; Seder and Oishi 2009; Valkenburg et al. 2006; Zhao et al. 2008).

Our observations led us to three areas of constructionist analysis. These are: 1) identity construction, 2) identity management and negotiation, and 3) collective identity, activism, and the construction of issues as social problems.

Identity Construction

> They (Facebook) allow people to display themselves not just as self-made individual persons, but as dividuals. In one way, they give everyone the chance to be individuals in the sense of being unique, because any person can be shown as being in the centre of a social universe—their own. No matter who you are, your Facebook website has *you* as the one in focus.
>
> (Dalsgaard 2008, p. 9)

Buhrmester and Prager (1995) developed a "model of self-disclosure" in which adolescents can achieve "identity development" and "intimacy development" both through the process of revealing their thoughts and feelings to their peers. Today's generation of youth possesses a new and different tool for self-revelation through Facebook. In fact, according to Pempek et al. (2009, p. 228), "such contacts (on Facebook) may foster the development of identity and intimate relationships, including friendships as well as romantic relationships." The internet, overall, has changed communication for most (Raacke and Bonds-Raacke 2008).

For the Facebook user, self-revelation is not merely an act of sharing personal details, but is also an active construction of one's perception of who one is. Through Facebook, the user creates a social artifact expressing one's self. This involves developing a profile which states basic information about the individual (however much he or she desires to reveal), possibly posting pictures, reporting a current "status" based upon what the user is doing at any selected time and posting music or news events on their "walls." In addition, users post messages on the walls of other members.

Users have the ability to limit views of their profiles to just "friends" or to anyone in all of their "networks." Networks represent typically a geographical region or a college or university to which the individual chooses. According to a study by Pempek et al. (2009, p. 233), "61.96% of respondents allowed their profile page to be seen by all of their networks and all of their 'friends . . .' Put simply, most students provide open access to personal information."

In Pempek et al.'s 2009 study, respondents were asked about the development of their profiles and the reasons for including information in various categories. "Interestingly," Pempek et al. (2009, p. 233) wrote, "students often posted media preferences—favorite books, music and movies—as a way to express identity." Often these selections were viewed as symbolic representations of how they wish others to perceive them. Pempek et al. (2009, p. 233) wrote that the "About Me" section "was also commonly chosen as an expression of their identity. In this section, college students sometimes write funny facts, clever statements, or provide links to pictures and websites that they like." Each of these entries by students can act as deliberate markers by which they present themselves (Goffman 1959).

Users also may provide information about their religious and political views (Dalsgaard 2009). According to Pempek et al. (2009), however, students more often presented their media favorites instead of these religious and political preferences. Some users, however, use their profiles to link to others with similar political views. LGBT users often join groups within the gay and lesbian virtual community which then become a part of the user's profile. In addition, LGBT users may actively seek to construct an "out" identity by presenting news on gay and lesbian events, information about social or political activities, or news stories relating to some topic of interest to the LGBT audience.

Facebook allows the opportunity for the user to choose his or her relationship status and to list the name of the individual whom he or she is seeing. An email is then sent to that individual to confirm the relationship and upon confirmation, the status of the relationship and the partner's name are posted on the user's Facebook website. Some users of the site have recently started a group to complain that Facebook does not allow "civil union" as a relationship status. This limits the LGBT individual in a civil union to choose "married to" or "in a relationship with," or simply, "it's complicated."

There have also been complaints by the transgendered and their allies that Facebook forces a choice between only "male" and "female" for one's sex. While Facebook now allows the option of not showing one's sex in the profile, a transgendered option is not available. In contrast to MySpace, another popular social networking site, Facebook does not ask nor present the user's sexual orientation but allows it to be ignored, implied, or directly presented by the user. While Facebook can be seen as multiplying options for networking among LGBT individuals, in other ways it may be seen as perpetuating the hegemonic discourse by its creation of a structure that does not permit total flexibility in self-identification.

Facebook allows users to invite "friends" to their page. Once someone is invited, they must confirm that they are indeed friends with the person who sent the invitation. When this is done, they appear on the user's page under the "friends" section and are allowed to post messages on their "wall." Ellison et al. (2007) and Steinfield et al. (2008) have studied the number of friends and how this often acts as an indicator of social capital or popularity. Not only does the friend list contribute to identity presentation of the user in this way, the individuals the one selects as friends often contribute to the identity construction. If a person is known to be gay and out, "friending" this individual also makes a statement to the others on the friend list. Thus some who are gay and out may discover a hesitance of others to "friend" them on Facebook, even when these individuals may interact in "real-life." Not only does your friend list contribute to your identity construction, but your presence on another's list contributes to the messages he or she wishes to present, or not present, based upon his or her own identity. As Goffman (1963) indicated, one may become stigmatized simply by association with one who bears a discredited identity.

Users may post photos of themselves as identity markers. In these photos, some may choose to display themselves with romantic partners, or in other situations. For example, one young man changed his profile picture to show himself participating at a recent drag event. Photos also allow for the presentation of gender identity. Users may also "tag," or identify other Facebook users, in his or her pictures as well. If one's picture is "tagged" by another user, a notice is posted that this individual is in the picture. A user has the option of "untagging" his or her own picture. However, this does not remove the picture from the other's website. According to Pempek et al., (2009, p. 233), "the most common reason for females to untag a photo was displeasure with their appearance in the photo (88.88% of females who untagged photos), indicating how they looked was an important part of their self-presentation to others." Males, according to Pempek et al. (2009), were likely to "untag" photos for this reason, but also "because the photos depicted them engaging in an act that they did not wish for others to see, such as underage drinking." For the LGBT community, there has been no specific research about how the "tagging" of pictures by others may influence the LGBT individual's identity construction, although it most certainly has the potential to influence the perception of one's identity by others. This issue could directly be linked to concern about disclosure of one's orientation and the difficulty of managing and negotiating stigmatized identity (Goffman 1963) in a virtual setting.

Identity Management and Negotiation

> To display or not to display; to tell or not to tell; to let on or not to let on; to lie or not to lie; and in each case, to whom, how, when and where.
> (Goffman 1963)

Erving Goffman wrote about the decision-making strategies which occur in daily interactions for those who possess potentially discrediting identities. In face-to-face interactions, an individual has the ability and power to discern the possible acceptance level of the other and choose what (and how much) information to reveal at any one time. This can be particularly crucial for those who reside in rural, conservative areas with a possibility of resultant discrimination and violence.

In contrast to the one-to-one interactions, Facebook represents a "one-to-many style of communication" (Pempek et al. 2009, p. 227). Facebook presents new opportunities for LGBT individuals in the possibility of finding networks, social support and information. It, however, also presents new challenges as well. For a gay individual, how much information does she or he present to others? How much of this is directly given and how much is implicit? What strategies does one develop to manage the data about oneself?

Many are often mistaken in the assumption that "coming out" is a simple event, completed totally and irrevocably. Instead, "coming out" is rather a process, and one by which a gay individual may choose to reveal bits of his or her identity and to manage the flow of this information. Goffman (1963) called this "information control." In this case, a gay person may choose how much information to give to any selected individual at one time, interpret the reaction of the individual, and then decide, based upon the other's response, whether to contribute more information about one's identity. In addition, a person may choose to give some information to one individual, much more to another, and still little or no information to someone else. In day-to-day interactions, this constitutes an active negotiation of identity (Goffman 1963) based upon management and control of information given. When someone chooses to post information about one's self on Facebook, a special challenge is presented. How much information does one present about one's sexual identity? And in what matter does one do so, knowing that this will be seen by a multitude of "friends," likely with varying degrees of comfort with the user's sexuality.

Each of us represents a multiplicity of identities, from those of a sibling, son or daughter, classmate, or employee, among others. Facebook can create a conflict about how to present oneself in a way that is not detrimental to oneself in any of these categories. Popular news stories have told of those who lost their jobs, were denied promotions, or were not hired due to their Facebook profiles. In addition, gay individuals may experience family members wanting them to "friend" them. Each of life's roles may be seen as having scripts, along with acceptable norms and guidelines. What is acceptable for one role is potentially not for another. These challenges are present for everyone. For an LGBT individual, the negotiation of these may be even more crucial, and even potentially hazardous.

The following scenarios are based upon anecdotal information given by LGBT Facebook users:

- Rob is "out" to friends in real-life. He is not out on Facebook, however, since not all of his family members know. He plans a secret trip with his new boyfriend, who posts how he can't wait for their romantic European vacation.
- Sarah is also "out" in everyday life but has not posted this, or any indicator of this, on Facebook, due to the fact that she may face discrimination at work. Several coworkers have added her to their friends list. She states in a status

update that she can't wait to go to a movie on Saturday night. One real-life friend posts, "Can't wait to meet your new lover!" Another friend posts, "You guys will like her! She's really nice!"
- Cary is out to friends and family. Yet some of his family members are conservative and uncomfortable with public displays of affection between Cary and a partner. A friend of Cary's posts pics of him and his boyfriend in an embrace at a party. Another pic posted shows Cary's boyfriend in drag at a fundraiser.

In scenario one, Rob may be able to delete the message from his new boyfriend so that it does not appear on his wall. However there is no guarantee that others have not seen it before Rob has. If this is the case, the information has already been revealed. If Rob does choose to delete it, he then must explain to his new boyfriend why he did so. While these are discussions that often enter into gay relationships, about who will know about the relationship, etc., in the case of the internet these conversations often arise before the individual is ready to have them. Simply because of the nature of "one-to-many" communication, everyone will know what you know, sometimes before you do.

In the second scenario, Sarah is out to her friends but not to her coworkers. This is not an unusual situation when someone fears discrimination at work. In these cases, an individual typically is able to decide in which coworker to confide, if any, and on what basis. Yet with the Facebook scenario, she has been outed to coworkers and has lost control over the information regarding her identity.

In our third case, Cary has been out to his family and friends. Yet his relationships with some had functioned best when little personal information was given regarding the romantic nature of his partnership. Some considered it a "don't ask, don't tell" situation. Cary was comfortable with this setup because it allowed him to share his basic identity with others important to them, yet did not risk losing them due to their personal unease with the issue of homosexuality. Now Cary is seen in a different light due to the romantic embrace with his partner and the picture of his partner in drag. While sexual identity may have been revealed to others, the individual may have had control over what kind of information was conveyed and in what manner the recipient could hear and accept. Now he must renegotiate identity with those concerned, not only about being gay, but what it means to be gay, how he lives his life, and the role gender identity plays with regard to his partner. Even if Cary "untags" these pictures from his profile, the photos will still be available on his friend's website, to which family and friends may have access. Another possible threat resulting from these postings would be the reaction of an employer who may be uncomfortable with such a presentation online.

In another case, Randy, who is married and not out to his wife, joined a gay sexual identity group on Facebook. A note appeared on his friends' pages, including his wife's, that he had joined this group. If he then chose to leave the group hoping to cover his tracks, a note would be sent that he had just left a gay group

(Facebook no longer typically sends these messages). The name of the group also appears on one's page.

The internet presents quite a unique opportunity for those who desire to "come out online." Facebook allows for the individual to post their revelation for all to see, and some young people may choose this option for "coming out."

Yet others may be out in their everyday lives and out on Facebook, and then face the decision of confirming friends who did not know of their orientation, perhaps an old friend from high school or a former teacher or pastor. If they don't confirm the friend based upon this, there will likely be hard feelings. If they do, the new information will be now thrown into the mix of their relationship, sometimes changing its nature.

Facebook users may choose to allow anyone in their "network" to view their pages, or to only allow friends to do so. Still most people have a diverse group of friends entailing many aspects and realms of their lives. Recalling the quote from Goffman (1963) at the beginning of this section, Facebook presents new and different challenges, some possibly even more complicated than those before.

Collective Identity, Activism, and the Construction of Social Problems

> The Internet has done more than simply change the distribution of information and reduce the cost of movement activity and development. Perhaps the most significant contribution the Internet offers social movements is the expansion of where activism happens. The Internet has developed into more than a tactic or tool social movements employ: it has become a space-albeit a virtual one-within which organizing and activism can happen.
>
> (Shapiro 2004, p. 172)

The ability to join LGBT groups on Facebook creates access to information and resources. For many, especially those in isolated, rural areas, these groups may be the individual's first contact with others who share similar identities. Many groups post pertinent information related to LGBT political issues and community social events. In addition, members may access message boards whereby they are able to read posts by others, ask questions, and gather information. Through online communities, not only may a personal identity be tested and accepted, but the connection between the individual identity and the collective identity develops (Hunt and Benford 2004; Melucci 1995; Taylor and Whittier 1992; Valocchi 2001). The young gay person can gain a sense of not being alone and of belonging to a community larger than oneself. Through online communities and through the social and political events and activities they promote, cultural markers of community can be learned by the individual. These may include the knowledge of the rainbow flag, the pink triangle, and other symbols and customs of a community.

In addition to advertising social events in the LGBT community, these online groups also serve as valuable transmitters for issues of concern within the community itself. Many Facebook groups have developed in tribute to those who have been victims of hate crimes or abuse due to their orientations. News regarding cases such as these is often posted and sent to group members. Messages also are sent directly, in many cases, to the member's Facebook message inbox, with an email to the person alerting him or her to the presence of this message. This system has been used effectively by those who seek to mobilize regarding a social issue.

Social constructionists' views of social problems (Benford and Hunt 2003; Davis 2005; Loseke 2007; Spector and Kitsuse 1987) focus on the process by which an issue becomes considered an actual problem. According to Loseke (2007, p. 20), "social problems work is the human activity needed to construct social problems and to do something about social problems." This is because "people create meaning because meaning is not inherent in objects" (Loseke 2007, p. 25). Just as identity is negotiated, so is the process of social problems identification. Consider that issues such as child abuse, domestic violence (Loseke 2007) and hate crimes (Jenness and Broad 1997) have always existed, but only lately have they been considered a recognizable kind of social problem. For this to have occurred, claims-makers (Loseke 2007; Spector and Kitsuse 1987) have developed the concepts which portray these issues as problems, engage in framing of information and messages (Snow and Benford 1988), and attempt to attach meaning to various events and ideas in a which will be culturally specific (Loseke 2007) and resonant (Snow and Benford 1988).

Through "causes," on Facebook, anyone may create a "cause" which is of concern. They engage in framing the message of this cause, promote it to potential sympathizers, and gather supporters or "members." These practices assist in legitimating an issue as a social problem to the Facebook membership. As users join the cause, the potential for change becomes even greater. In this way, Facebook "cause" creators and their adherents work to validate issues as social problems and often offer corrective measures (e.g. petitions, rallies, boycotts, etc.). Holstein and Miller (2003, p. 78) note that "social problems work is interactive as well as rhetorical." According to Loseke (2007, p. 20) "the goal of the social problems game is to persuade people to worry about a condition and to do something to resolve it."

Joel Best (1990) once wrote that for social claims to be taken seriously, there is a competition among those claims-makers to make their issues heard. Benford and Hunt (2003) also discussed how these issues become part of the "public problems marketplace," where "the point of most of this work is to use public arenas to persuade particular audiences to accept specific definitions of imputed problem conditions." (2003, p. 155) To Best, however, "there is nothing even-handed about this competition . . .

> In general, the advantage belongs to the insiders, the owners of well-established social problems, with ready access to the policymakers and the media. Outsiders are at a disadvantage. Their chances are particularly remote in some arenas; legislatures are far more likely to respond to the concerns of lobbyists and other insiders than to claims from outsiders. In comparison, the media, with their constant need for fresh material ("news"), are more receptive to outsiders' claims. But because the media offer the best hope for many outsider claims-makers, the competition for media attention can be fierce.
>
> (1990, p. 16)

Facebook goes a long way toward leveling these playing fields. With Facebook, the user does not have to have access to traditional means of communication or media, he or she can develop a cause for concern, market it to its potential audience, and direct interventions from behind his or her own computer. Users have established groups to support hate crime legislation, have organized protests to California's Proposition 8 and have supported rallies for gay marriage rights. In these ways, Facebook users have subverted the traditional structures which act as gatekeepers of dissent.

Yet while Facebook has greatly increased the ability of LGBT connections and the possibilities for collective identity, social problem construction, and activism, Michael Shernoff (2006, p. 21) worries the internet is:

> … lulling us into a false sense of security. Because if we're sitting at home, we can't be out in the street carrying signs or running the risk of getting gay-bashed outside a bar, or hearing someone yell "Faggot!" when we walk home with a lover. Are we forgetting about the realities of homophobia while we sit at home forwarding petitions or talking dirty with strangers? … At what point do we trade our slippers in for walking shoes and go back out into the physical gay world, which has been shrinking in recent years?
>
> (Shernoff 2006, p. 21)

Sally Kohn, a community organizer, concurs. In a June 8, 2008 article for the *Christian Science Monitor*, she wrote, "Internet activism is individualistic. It's great for a sense of interconnectedness, but the Internet does not bind individuals in shared struggle the same as the face-to-face activism of the 1960s and '70s did. It allows us to channel our individual power for good, but it stops there." Kohn added that the "real challenges in our society … won't politely go away with a few clicks of the mouse."

Are these writers identifying unique challenges presented by internet activism or are they simply nostalgic for a bygone era and underestimating the subversive impact of a new medium? Does Facebook create an entirely new way of being, complete with new norms for belonging and innovative tactics for activism?

While the arena of internet activism is certainly new and, to some degree, relatively untested, we can not deny its potential force and impact. Through its ability to connect those from geographically disparate or isolated areas, assist with the construction of a personal identity and an awareness of collective identity, its power can not be dismissed. Internet activism goes straight to the source: the potential audience. It does not have to court traditional sources of access for media-play or attention and basically subverts the hegemonic system of competition written of by Joel Best (1990).

As with anything new, there will be unforeseen challenges. The points raised by Shernoff and Kohn are valid ones. True success, while initiated in virtual space, will be measured by change in the world around us. Facebook, however, has created a place for activism to occur and has empowered those who seek to create a cause to do so, to promote it, educate about it, and enlist members. Eve Shapiro, writing of transgender activism on the internet, states that:

> There are two central ways in which the Internet has transformed transgender organizing. First, the Internet has become a *tool* for activists and organizations to use to reduce organizations' upstart and maintenance costs and to provide quick and efficient information distribution. Second, the Internet has become a *space* within which to facilitate networking and collective identity development and employ new tactics, leading to the further development, growth and success of the transgender movement.
>
> (Shapiro 2004, p. 171)

Conclusion

> ... with social networking sites, users are now the creators of content, and they view one another's profiles and information rather than viewing mass-produced content made by large corporations. They also became the stars of their own productions.
>
> (Pempek et al. 2009)

Facebook has created a new realm of interaction in our society. While research on internet social networking sites is still new, we can, without a doubt, assert that it has revolutionized our means of communication and our possibilities for connecting with others. Since it is such a new cultural fixture, those of us who are Facebook users create, learn, and modify norms of its use. We learn new forms of etiquette and find new ways to stay in touch with those who matter to us.

As we create our identities online, constructing ourselves as we wish others to perceive us, we clarify to ourselves who we are and what matters most to us. We ask ourselves the questions: Who do I want to be? How do I want others to see me? We create and transmit these images to others, as we interact with those which they have designed as well. Through Facebook, youth face an opportunity to construct themselves in a way unknown to prior generations of young.

For the gay individual, we see not only the opportunities for self-presentation and social networking. We also see the challenges of identity negotiation and information control. While gays and lesbians have faced these dilemmas for generations, Facebook presents an entirely new arena with no known or verifiable strategies for management. Each individual must test the waters for him- or herself. A fertile ground for future research will be on the topic of just how LGBT individuals negotiate and manage information in these new virtual settings.

As we've seen, the internet can present a huge potential for activism. Facebook offers exciting and unique ways in which to make social change. As we have seen in this chapter, Facebook members take part in "social problems work," creating and legitimating causes in our "public problems marketplace." In these ways, Facebook offers an unprecedented opportunity for networking and activism. Anyone can create a cause, market it, and educate others. By taking the issues directly to the audiences, Facebook subverts traditional paths to social change and eliminates the hegemonic gatekeepers.

While our chapter on Facebook is not meant to be exhaustive and comprehensive, we feel that we have raised some important topics for further discussion. We hope that others will continue to research Facebook to discover how LGBT groups grow and develop, how collective identities are acquired and how Facebook has changed the nature of social activism.

As Facebook grows and matures, we will undoubtedly continue to be fascinated by its opportunities and challenges. We have entered into a reflexive relationship whereby we will be influenced while we are indeed influencing others. The LGBT community will still negotiate identities, both personally and collectively. Facebook will offer new and exciting ways to learn about ourselves, others, and the issues which most affect those under the LGBT umbrella. Our world has been changed by Facebook. No doubt it will continue to be so.

References

Benford, R. D. and Hunt, S. A. 2003. Interactional dynamics in public problems marketplaces: Movements and the counterframing and reframing of public problems. In *Challenges and choices: Constructionist perspectives on social problems*, edited by J. A. Holstein and G. Miller. Hawthorne, NY: Aldine de Gruyter: 153–186.

Best, J. 1990. *Threatened children: Rhetoric and concern about child-victims*. Chicago: University of Chicago Press.

Buhrmester, D. and Prager, K. 1995. Patterns and functions of self-disclosure during childhood and adolescence. In *Disclosure processes in children and adolescents*, edited by K. J. Rotenberg. Cambridge: Cambridge University Press, 10–56.

Cooper, M. 1990. Rejecting femininity: Research notes on gender identity in lesbians. *Deviant Behavior* 11: 371–380.

Cooper, M. 2007. What is it like to be a rural lesbian? In *Readings in deviant behavior*, edited by A. Thio, T. Calhoun, and A. Conyers. Needham Heights, MA: Allyn and Bacon, 171–175.

Cooper, M. forthcoming. Rural popular culture and its impact on lesbian identity. In *Queer identities/political realities*, edited by K. German and B. Drushel. Oxford: Oxford Scholars Press.

Dalsgaard, S. 2008. Facework on Facebook: The presentation of self in virtual life and its role in the U.S. elections. *Anthropology Today* 24(6): 8–12.

Davis, J. E. 2005. *Accounts of innocence: Sexual abuse, trauma and the self*. Chicago: University of Chicago Press.

Ellison, N. B., Steinfield, C., and Lampe, C. 2007. The benefits of Facebook "friends": Social capital and college students' use of online social network sites. *Journal of Computer-Mediated Communication* 12(4): 1143–1168.

Facebook. 2009. http://www.facebook.com/ [Accessed August 24, 2009]

Goffman, E. 1959. *Presentation of self in everyday life*. Garden City, NY: Doubleday.

Goffman, E. 1963. *Stigma: Notes on the management of a spoiled identity*. London: Pelican Books.

Holstein, J. A. and Miller, G. 2003. Social constructionism and social problems work. In *Challenges and choices: Constructionist perspectives on social problems*, edited by J. A. Holstein and G. Miller. Hawthorne, NY: Aldine de Gruyter, 70–91.

Hunt, S. A. and Benford, R. D. 2004. Collective identity, solidarity, and commitment. In *The Blackwell companion to social movements*, edited by D. A. Snow, S. A. Soule, and H. Kriesi. Malden, MA: Blackwell, 433–457.

Jenness, V. and Broad, K. 1997. *Hate crimes: New social movements and the politics of violence*. Hawthorne, NY: Aldine de Gruyter.

Kohn, S. 2008. Real change happens off-line. *Christian Science Monitor*, June 30.

Loseke, D. R. 2007 *Thinking about social problems: An introduction to constructionist perspectives*. New Brunswick, NJ and London: Aldine Transaction.

Melucci, A. 1995. The process of collective identity. In *Social movements and culture*, edited by H. Johnston and B. Klandermans. Minneapolis: University of Minnesota Press, 41–63.

Pempek, T. A., Yermolayeva, Y. A., and Calvert, S. L. 2009. College students' social networking experiences on Facebook. *Journal of Applied Developmental Psychology* 30: 227–238.

Raacke, J. and Bonds-Raacke, J. 2008. MySpace and Facebook: Applying the uses and gratifications theory to exploring friend-networking sites. *Cyberpsychology and Behavior* 11(2): 169–174.

Ross, C., Orr, E. S., Arseneault, J. M., Simmering, M. G. and Orr, R. R. 2009. Personality and motivations associated with Facebook use. *Computers in Human Behavior* 25: 578–586.

Seder, J. P. and Oishi, S. 2009. Ethnic/racial homogeneity in college students' Facebook friendship networks and subjective well-being. *Journal of Research in Personality* 43: 438–443.

Shapiro, E. 2004. Trans-cending barriers: Transgender organizing on the internet. *Journal of Gay and Lesbian Social Services* 16(3/4): 165–179.

Shernoff, M. 2006. The heart of a virtual hunter. *Gay and Lesbian Review*. (January–February): 20–22.

Snow, D. A. and Benford, R. D. 1988. Ideology, frame resonance, and participant mobilization. *International Social Movement Research* 1: 197–217.

Spector, M. and Kitsuse, J. I. 1987. *Constructing social problems*. Hawthorne, NY: Aldine de Gruyter.

Steinfield, C., Ellison, N. B., and Lampe, C. 2008. Social capital, self-esteem, and use of online social network sites: A longitudinal analysis. *Journal of Applied Developmental Psychology* 29: 434–445.

Taylor, V. and Whittier, N. E. 1992. Collective identity in social movement communities: Lesbian feminist mobilization. In *Social movements: Perspectives and issues*, edited by S. M. Buechler and F. K. Cylke. Mountain View, CA: Mayfield Publishing, 505–519.

Valkenburg, P. M., Peter, J., and Schouten, A. P. 2006. Friend networking sites and their relationship to adolescents' well being and social self-esteem. *CyberPsychology* 9: 584–590.

Valocchi, S. 2001. Individual identities, collective identities, and organizational structure: The relationship of the political left and gay liberation in the United States. *Sociological Perspectives* 44(4): 445–467.

Zhao, S., Grasmuck, S., and Martin, J. 2008. Identity construction on Facebook: Digital empowerment in anchored relationships. *Computers in Human Behavior* 24: 1816–1836.

Chapter 8

PlanetOut and the Dichotomies of Queer Media Conglomeration

Ben Aslinger

My first encounter with PlanetOut (2009) came from watching a promo on a VHS copy of Brian Sloan's *I Think I Do* (1997), an independent film distributed by New York City-based Strand Releasing. In the ad, a car driven by a merry band of "queer" travelers breaks down in rural America. The travelers succeed in dragging the car to the nearest town, where a mechanic tells them that repairs will take two days. While most of the travelers are saddened, a savvy drag queen convinces a young mechanic to post a party invitation on PlanetOut, and soon, a dance party breaks out in a nearby barn. PlanetOut's promo illustrates two common 1990s attitudes towards the Internet: that Internet technology could overcome the tyranny of geography and that it would enable new forms of queer cultural flows. PlanetOut's marketing messages in the 1990s were more than simply pragmatic business moves. The company's messages epitomized the utopian visions of early Internet commerce, and the belief that new technologies, content forms, and structures of distribution would provide "better" representations of sexual alterity that would stimulate LGBT equality. As PlanetOut emerged as a major player in queer media, however, the company began to face charges that its role in queer media conglomeration was hastening the homogenization of queer culture and taking the charge out of queer politics (Gamson 2003). In this chapter, I examine PlanetOut's economic and industrial history and examples of web design in order to better understand how queer web users have been defined and targeted in the new economy.

Lisa Nakamura (2002, 2008) has critiqued techno-utopian discourses surrounding the web, arguing that race, class, gender, and sexuality matter on the web and have been made to matter by software/tech firms, the designers of interfaces, and web users themselves. Joshua Gamson (2003) echoes the concerns of political economists worried about the future of the Internet. Gamson analyzes the increasingly concentrated ownership of LGBT media outlets. He writes, "The dynamics and impact of media ownership in the media systems of marginalized or minority groups are not well understood.... The gay and lesbian 'monopoly' controversy points out how much remains to be understood about the dynamics and impact of ownership concentration in the media of marginalized groups"

(p. 257). Gamson's analysis of gay media conglomeration is posited as a counterpoint to research that analyzes "how new technologies have provided a breeding ground . . . for 'the evolving cybercultures of sexual dissidents'" (p. 258). He argues that economic events like PlanetOut's increasing size and clout point to the ways that "new media influence already-existing conservative trends in sexual identity politics" (p. 258).

While not disputing Gamson's findings, I argue that paying attention to the economic and representational histories of queer new media enterprises gives scholars and users a clearer perspective on dichotomies of queer media conglomeration such as citizen/consumer and commerce/politics. I work to update Gamson's findings by examining the history of PlanetOut's commercial ventures, to bring the ghost of web textuality into the picture, and to position constructions of queer identity on the Internet within historical contexts of the rise of ecommerce, "the dot.com bust," and the regrouping of the "tech" sector. Given the ephemerality of the web as a medium and the historical silences that render writing queer political, social, and cultural histories so difficult, it is important to not only examine the history of queer online identity, but to connect identity constructions to the economic practices of corporate America and the aesthetic practices of web design. In order to achieve these goals, I first sketch out PlanetOut's history—its emergence as an economically viable identity portal, the mergers and acquisitions that turned PlanetOut into a LGBT media conglomerate, and the ways that the "dot.com crash" and the rise of web 2.0 threatened PlanetOut and called into question what role it played for LGBT web users. I do this before briefly examining visual elements of web pages in order to find connections between industrial drives, the look of the web, and the potential experience of queer users. Paying attention to the industrial history of queer media conglomeration is necessary in order to examine the connections between Silicon Valley corporate cultures, the "California" ideologies of libertarianism and neoliberalism, and cultural practices of constructing, representing, and addressing LGBT communities and users.

Boom, Bust, and Regroup: PlanetOut's Corporate History

The roots of PlanetOut's media empire can be traced to when Mark Elderkin started Gay.com as a chat service and Tom Rielly launched PlanetOut as a way to provide gay content to the dominant portals of the 1990s—AOL, MSN, and Yahoo! (Shabelman 2008). By 1996, Tom Rielly and his twenty employees succeeded in making PlanetOut a part of AOL's services (Hopkins 2000, p. B7). PlanetOut's success can be seen from the amount of venture capital it obtained and from the level of attention that the financial community bestowed upon the new venture. In 1996, PlanetOut succeeded in obtaining $2.7 million of venture capital from Menlo Park, California based Sequoia Capital. In September 1998, PlanetOut obtained $16.4 million in funding from investors including America Online, Mayfield Fund, and Eden Capital (Stone 1999). By 1999, individual investors included RealNetworks founder and CEO Rob Glaser, E*Trade President Kathy Levinson, and former MIT Media Lab head Nicholas Negroponte (Fitzgerald 1999, p. S40). In 1999, investment firm Salomon Smith Barney chose PlanetOut to present at its annual conference, and CEO Megan Smith was quick to tell *Adweek* how impressive it was that PlanetOut was the first gay and lesbian company to receive venture capital funding and to be honored in this way by a major investment house (Adweek 2000). That a gay new media venture attracted major investors and the attention of respected investment bankers meant that members of the financial community perceived LGBT web users to be a viable demographic and believed that PlanetOut's leading executives were credible business leaders.

During 2000, PlanetOut merged with Gay.com, a site that had been started in 1996 by Mark Elderkin as a chat service for LGBT web users and that had been purchased by the firm Online Partners. Elderkin's Gay.com had primarily relied on the conversations that took place in the site's chat rooms, and the site's design in its earliest incarnations emphasized community over commerce. Together, PlanetOut.com and Gay.com reached 3.5 million gay and lesbian consumers (Kuczynski 2000, p. G4). The company was renamed PlanetOut Partners, although CEO Megan Smith, former Online Partners CEO Lowell Selvin, and corporate leadership decided to keep the two sites separate. Selvin told *Advertising Age* in 2002 that the merger was motivated by a desire to coordinate activities and not put in jeopardy either PlanetOut.com's or Gay.com's ability to attract advertisers and investors. Selvin stated, "There had been a lot of rivalry and competition for ad dollars, but we put that behind us, and today we're a different company with a different business model" (Fitzgerald 2002, p. 20).

In spring 2000, PlanetOut purchased Liberation Publications, owners of *Advocate* and *Out* magazine, for around $30 million in cash and stock (Advertising Age 2000, p. 60). While this allowed ad sales forces to pool resources, this attempt at synergy stoked fears about the homogenization of gay media content in the United States. At the same time, PlanetOut began to pursue new investors and partnerships with other online firms. Clifford Carlsen (2000) notes that PlanetOut Partners secured $10 million in new funding from repeat investors: America Online and the Mayfield Fund, and new investors BMG Entertainment, Creative Artists Agency, and EDventure Holdings. E*Trade agreed to provide financial news to PlanetOut along with a newsletter for PlanetOut's Money Channel (Bank Marketing International 2000).

And then the dot.com bubble burst. The crash led PlanetOut to re-evaluate audience measurements and to begin relying on subscription services in order to boost revenues. Early in the dot.com boom sites promoted themselves to investors with statistics regarding the number of eyeballs, the number of unique visitors, or the average number of minutes users spent on a certain site. In April 2000, PC Data Online reported that PlanetOut had 717,000 unique visitors (Gunn 2000). In September 2000, Clifford Carlsen noted the then common practice of measuring minutes users spent on each site, noting that users spent around 18.3 minutes per month on PlanetOut and 77.1 on Gay.com. New York Internet rating service Media Matrix released results for July 2000 that PlanetOut had 586,000 unique visitors while Gay.com had 522,000 (Carlsen 2000). While the number of users and their time spent online did not become completely irrelevant, these indices lost power as businesses and investors became increasingly aware that it was not how many users logged on or the duration of site visits that mattered; how much money users spent was the vital statistic. Fitzgerald quotes Selvin in 2002: "We've always had a huge community of people chatting online that could be leveraged into profitability" (Fitzgerald 2002, p. 20). The question was how.

In the immediate wake of the dot.com crash, PlanetOut began to charge for its *Out&About* travel newsletter and started developing a $5 per month personal ad service (Elgin 2000, p. 172). In 2003/2004, the personals quick search became a fixture on the PlanetOut home page. Users were able to search for potential connections and were able to see featured profiles on the home page—working to alternate between lesbians and gay men in the featured profile. As PlanetOut developed subscription-based services in order to remain financially solvent, it followed other identity portals that saw ad dollars dry up overnight. As Doug McCormick, the CEO of women's portal iVillage said, "The Internet ad business is being treated like the fire hydrant at the dog show" (Elgin 2000, p. 172). By 2001, PlanetOut laid off 12 of its employees (14 percent of its workforce), because of the dot.com crash and the subsequent reduction of original content production (Daily Deal 2001).

As PlanetOut re-negotiated its economic footing from the techno-utopian 1990s into the cold economic light of day of the early 2000s, the company engaged in a delicate balancing act. *New Media Age* reports in 2002 the delicate balancing act: "While more emphasis in now placed on maximizing revenues from its paid-for dating and ad sales, the portal still professes a not-for profit ethos and prides itself on its reputation as a trusted resource, serving both the gay community and the friends and families of gay people" (New Media Age 2002, p. 30). Fred Turner (2006) notes the odd mixture of counterculturalism, liberalism, and libertarianism that marks many firms in software, tech, and new media sectors. While new media firms may point to their anti-establishment origins in order to insulate themselves from activist, social, and academic critiques, recent work by John Caldwell (2008) and Mark Deuze (2007) points to the multivalent and ambivalent definitions of media labor and the goals of media work. Following Caldwell, I want to suggest that rather than treating firms such as PlanetOut as the devils responsible for the homogenization of LGBT culture and the villains to be blamed for alternative media distribution monopolies, we call attention to a central issue of new media labor: that new media workers and firms often engage in conservative activities underneath a liberal banner while believing that their activities help foster progressive ideas and agendas. Rather than a localized case of PlanetOut's suspect strategies, then, PlanetOut's economic history and its harnessing and potential co-optation of LGBT identity issues illustrates the need to better understand web histories and the discourses that work to define and channel new media work.

After PlanetOut's regroup, the conglomerate sought to become a publicly traded company. However, PlanetOut still faced tough economic times. In August 2004, PlanetOut slashed the share price for its initial public offering (IPO) from $12 to $14 to $9 to $11 (Daily Deal 2004), after which it succeeded as the first gay IPO. PlanetOut's successful IPO was nothing to sneeze out, even given all the bumps in the road. In 1999, Charlie Walker, a managing partner at Hambrecht & Quist, a San Francisco-based investment bank, said, "An openly-gay company can absolutely go public." But he adds, "You have venture capitalists openly questioning whether a gay company can go public, which tells you there are some residual concerns" (Bank 1999, p. B6).

PlanetOut sought more partnerships and tried to expand its holdings, with mixed results that contributed to declining share prices. In 2005, PlanetOut partnered with Boston-based m-Qube to provide wireless applications and content to gay mobile users. In hopes of launching a text-messaging service, PlanetOut secured the shortcode PRIDE (77433) (Gibbs 2005, p. 7). Much like its listing on the New York Stock Exchange as LGBT, PlanetOut commodified the signifiers of identity politics. In 2006, PlanetOut agreed to purchase the gay travel company RSVP Productions, Inc., shelling out $6.5 million in cash and agreeing an additional $3 million if performance targets were met in 2007 and 2008 (Daily Deal 2006). But in 2007, sluggish sales of gay-themed travel services and cruises signaled that PlanetOut's acquisition was a risky move (Dewson 2007). In October, 2007, Atlantis Events, a company specializing in gay and lesbian travel, agreed to purchase RSVP from PlanetOut (Daily Deal 2007). In 2006, PlanetOut's share price fell 27 percent after its third quarter reported earnings were 14 percent less than had been forecasted (Boston Globe 2006 p. E4).

In 2007, Dewson noted that declining numbers of personal ad subscriptions stemmed partially from the emergence of various other sites such at Match.com and Nerve.com. Selvin noted in 2002 that PlanetOut had a significant population of users that could be leveraged into profits; however, the rise of blogs, social networking sites, and the hype around web 2.0 made PlanetOut a less popular web destination. In January, 2008, *Corporate Financing Week* called PlanetOut a "beleaguered gay and lesbian media company" (Corporate Financing Week 2008).

Propagating Myths about Gay People @ PlanetOut

PlanetOut's need for several rounds of venture capital in the late 1990s in order to stay financially afloat paralleled the precarious economic situation faced by many new media ventures before the dot.com crash as investors helped fuel the hype surrounding Internet commerce even as many new ventures were overvalued and had failed to turn significant profits. What made PlanetOut so unique, however, was that executives took advantage of both the dot.com bubble and over-inflated and misrepresentative accounts of LGBT buying power in order to sell investors on a venture that was risky because of its technological and narrowcasted nature. PlanetOut's difficulties would in part spring from the challenges in defining, measuring, and targeting queer web users when both the category of the user and the nature of the queer audience were shifting signifiers.

Katherine Sender (2004), Rosemary Hennessy (2000), and Suzanna Danuta Walters (2001) have analyzed the ways in which queer visibility in the 1990s was predicated on the myth that LGBT populations (treated most often in advertising discourses as gay white men) were wealthier than average consumers. M.V. Lee Badgett (1997) argues that these constructions of the LGBT audience were often based on readership data garnered from subscription lists to gay and lesbian print publications—a sample size too small to be truly representative of gay and lesbian America. PlanetOut's efforts to gain advertising revenue helped solidify market constructions of the queer audience. By convincing advertisers to invest in banner ads that were less expensive than print advertising space, PlanetOut served as a stepping stone for advertisers getting used to addressing LGBT consumers—a market that would be further constructed and whose contours would be reinforced when advertisers transitioned into other gay media venues. While PlanetOut allowed users to contest dominant constructions of LGBT identities via users' online activities, comments, and site contributions, PlanetOut used LGBT users' activities to bolster and reinforce mythic constructions of the LGBT audience and worked to deliver LGBT users to national/mainstream advertisers, whose interests lay primarily in capturing pink dollars rather than in creating social change.

Unfortunately, when LGBT users as a market construction diverged from the material conditions in which many LGBT users lived, PlanetOut suffered. The buzz surrounding the buying potential of gay and lesbian consumers led to investors' hopes that could not be matched by the purchasing and consumption habits of actual gay and lesbian users/consumers. In some ways, PlanetOut needed to propagate the myth of gay wealth, since its initial pitches to investors occurred at a time when the web user himself/herself was a member of a privileged elite. As a gay media outlet, PlanetOut capitalized on and reinforced the myth of gay wealth endorsed by Madison Avenue and the national glossy gay and lesbian magazines. As a new media venture, PlanetOut needed the upscale user in order to curry investors' interest. As an identity portal, PlanetOut wrestled with the potential disconnect between marketing discourses and its attempted address to a target demographic that was both diverse and disenfranchised.

Not only did PlanetOut capitalize on the myth of gay affluence, it also capitalized on market constructions of LGBT populations as technophiles and netizens. John Schwartz writes,

> Since the very earliest days of the online revolution, gays have known that a modem could help them to reach out, even if they didn't come out. But these days, trying to bring that community under one online roof—and delivering the prosperous gay market to advertisers—is the name of the game.
>
> (1999, p. E1)

In 1998, Michael Wilke helped inflate the myth of the tech savvy queer web user: "A major gay-market study in 1997 by Simmons Market Research Bureau confirmed suspicions that gays are large online subscribers—51.5% usage for gays compared with 15.8% for the general population" (Wilke 1998, p. 30). Even if the myth of technophilia is true, it is surprising that no one anticipated the difficulty of courting gay web users and corralling them into specific online corporate spaces. On the one hand, gay men are posited as early adopters, a status that involves both trendsetting and migration to new services, platforms, and devices, while on the other hand, market constructions of gay men as brand loyal posited gay men's media uses as habitual and routine. While PlanetOut capitalized on and used statistics that might be hard to believe, the construction of the queer market would also affect content.

PlanetOut and Queer Representations

PlanetOut's success was in part a product of a social context in which televised gay images were rarely seen, and when an emerging communications medium allowed LGBT men and women to connect with "like-minded" souls without the fear of public reprisal, humiliation, or forced outing. The conglomerate's economic woes can be traced in part to the mainstreaming of queer images and increased cultural visibility that enabled advertisers to target queer audiences in other ways via print, television, and the web. PlanetOut promoted itself initially as the alternative to old media representations of queerness, including alternative "old" media sources such as gay newspapers and magazines. As PlanetOut placed magazines such as *Out* and *Advocate* under its corporate umbrella, however, it both mainstreamed itself as a gay media conglomerate and risked nullifying its own existence for being—its status as a new way to address queer audiences and its content as an alternative to other print and televisual messages. Ironically,

PlanetOut is a victim of its own success and the role it played in mainstreaming images of LGBT life in the 1990s and 2000s.

PlanetOut argued that, since it featured high-ranking gay and lesbian executives and was explicitly addressed to sexual minorities, it was inherently more democratic and progressive than the mass medium of television. New media companies saw the power of the web to address audiences who were rarely featured in broadcast television. Web services emphasized their ability to extend the potential of narrowcasting, and high-level executives often used television as a dramatic foil in order to suggest that their services could address underserved audiences, turn underserved audiences into users, and turn users into purchasers of advertised goods. New media executives reinforced the idea that the user was a more active and liberated subject position than the supposedly passive audience of television programming.

Looking back at the history of PlanetOut, I have thus far focused primarily on how the firm's economic evolution illustrates the uneven spread of LGBT media conglomeration, and the ways that PlanetOut created mythologies of the queer web user. In addition to these issues, PlanetOut's web content illustrates shifts in web aesthetics and design and difficulties in creating content for lesbian, bisexual, and transgender web users. Instead of looking back at early web sites as poor examples of web design, Megan Sapnar (2008) argues that definitions of quality web aesthetics are historically contingent propositions that designers and new media firms participate in constructing. Lisa Nakamura (2008) argues that the visual cultures of popular Internet sites have received little critical attention, with most attention given to online new media art objects that most closely resemble high culture texts. Revisiting the visual culture of PlanetOut's web sites allows us to examine the representation of queer identities on the popular and commercial web during a time of transition.

PlanetOut's home pages reflect many of the concerns regarding age and gender in queer communities. For example, on January 21, 2002, the site featured a news story about Bayard Rustin—a leading activist in the nonviolent civil rights movement, an openly gay man, and friend of Martin Luther King, Jr. This is noticeable because it was one of the few times any pictures on the front page were of gay men aged over 40. PlanetOut also had difficulties creating effective web content directed to lesbian users. Mark Watson, UK manager at PlanetOut, said,

> One area we are particularly poor at is targeting the lesbian community. It is a common thing (in gay media) that a lot of content is male-oriented and we need to change that. ... Lesbians also want to use the Internet and there are not that many good sources of lesbian content about, so we have a role to change the balance.
>
> (Hill 2003, p. 7)

Tabs such as Entertainment, Money and Careers, News and Politics, Families, Fitness, Health, Living, Pride, Popcorn Q Movies, Travel, and Video evidence a range of content areas that signal that PlanetOut sought to address LGBT users as both consumers and citizens, even if it did not always live up to its promise. The Entertainment, Popcorn Q Movies, and Video tabs also illustrate the ways that the site sought to evaluate and publicize LGBT films, television programs, and LGBT film festivals. (While the list of tabs initially were clustered at the bottom of the web page, designers placed them on the left hand side as the site became more visually rich.)

A quick comparison of PlanetOut's home page from February 19, 1998 and January 25, 1999 illustrates how quickly the look of the web changed. In 1998, the site emphasizes photographic and graphical representations of LGBT men and women including an African American man gesturing enthusiastically to the user, a drawing of two Hollywood vixens, and two men kissing. Images of LGBT men and women serve as icons stressing the diverse nature of PlanetOut as an online community and calling attention to the site's main content areas: People, Netqueery, PopcornQ, Newsplanet, Civic Center and Shop. However, the page is rather short on hyperlinks, and most of the hyperlinks occupy the bottom of the page in the list of Newsplanet Headlines and the day's offerings on Gloradio. By as early as 1999, PlanetOut began featuring banner ads. This page includes an ad for the Dinah Shore Weekend and a mention of an online music retailer. We see subject areas like before, but this time we see more tabs and more hyperlinks, meaning that users interested in viewing the message boards on coming out could link directly to that message board from the lead page. The page begins to play more with color, background images, and features the PlanetOut Poll. The page may not feature the enthusiasm of the 1998 page, but it does illustrate the growing use of hyperlinks, the segregation of web page spaces (bracketing off spaces with background colors and borders), the growing emphasis on membership with the log in prompt, and a shift to a more vertical page layout. The 1999 page illustrates the evolving nature of web design as PlanetOut became more commercial and as discourses of what constituted quality web design evolved. As the look of PlanetOut became more professionalized, the company sought to become the dominant LGBT identity portal.

Conclusion

In this chapter I have attempted to better historicize PlanetOut's activities by connecting new media industries, web textuality, the construction of LGBT users, and debates about queer media conglomeration. Recent events in LGBT media industries signal that concerns about queer media conglomeration remain important issues for LGBT media studies scholars and for scholars interested in exploring transformations of the web and emerging technologies. In April 2008 Regent

Entertainment Media, best known for the gay cable network Here! and its film distribution arm Regent Releasing, negotiated the purchase of PlanetOut's magazine and publishing business for a paltry $6 million (San Francisco Business Times 2008). By January 2009, Regent signed a merger agreement with PlanetOut (Advocate.Com. 2009). An unnamed staffer on the blog Queerty (2009) writes in the post titled "All of gay media are belong to Paul Colichman," "Score one for gay media—or score one for yet another media conglomerate gobbling everything up in some senseless stab at synergy while the people who suffer are the consumers?" (Queerty 2009). The Queerty post, whose title riffs on the 2000–2002 Internet meme "All your base are belong to us," highlights an ongoing concern with connecting economic shifts in LGBT media with what audiences are offered and what users can do.

I became interested in writing about PlanetOut while re-watching a cheesy 1990s indie gay film on VHS. Accidentally bumping into that historiographic trace made me curious about how PlanetOut evolved and how it addressed and constructed LGBT web users. In conducting this research, I have relied on trade press materials and archived web pages from the Wayback Machine (2009). In an era when we are surrounded by web content, it is easy to immerse ourselves in the content and forget about the ways that economic imperatives as well as marketing and design decisions shape our experiences. Additionally, with so much going on online all the time, it is easy to forget about the history of the web and difficult to think about how we might write web histories. The Wayback Machine, which does an admirable job of archiving web sites, primarily devotes its attention to home pages, meaning that even as home pages are being archived, our access to the deeper web remains limited. Also, as interest in web studies grows, how do we analyze texts that may be beyond our own linguistic capacities as users? How do we acknowledge the hegemony of English on the web, and how do we make sure that analyses of the American and UK web do not become hegemonic accounts of web history? PlanetOut is one case study of how LGBT identities and new media commerce have been articulated, but there are other stories to be told and more lessons to be learned about how to design online experiences for LGBT communities. What will the web archive be—and what role will queer web designers, new media executives, web users, and scholars have in shaping it?

References

Advertising Age. 2000. For the record. *Advertising Age*, March 27, 60.
Advocate.Com. 2009. Regent media assumes majority interest in PlanetOut. Advocate.com, January 13. http://www.advocate.com/news_detail_ektid70389.asp. [Accessed June 8, 2009]
Adweek. 2000. IQ interactive special report: Shock troops/the media—this way out. *Adweek*, May 1.

Badgett, M. V. L. 1997. Beyond biased samples: Challenging the myths on the economic status of lesbians and gay men. In *Homo economics: Capitalism, community, and lesbian and gay life*, edited by A. Gluckman and B. Reed. New York: Routledge.

Bank, D. 1999. Gay net firms' coming out party spoiled by wallflower investors: Strong fundamentals haven't brought IPO riches to Gay.com, others. *The Globe and Mail*, October 1, B6.

Bank Marketing International. 2000. E*Trade prepares to target gay market. *Bank Marketing International*, September 21, 5.

Boston Globe. 2006. PlanetOut inc. *The Boston Globe*, September 7, E4.

Caldwell, J. T. 2008. *Production culture: Industrial reflexivity and critical practice in film and television*. Durham, NC: Duke University Press.

Carlsen, C. 2000. PlanetOut wins $10 million. *Daily Deal*, September 21.

Corporate Financing Week. 2008. Gay and lesbian media company shares fall. *Corporate Financing Week*, January 21.

Daily Deal. 2001. PlanetOut partners. *Daily Deal*, July 23.

Daily Deal. 2004. IPO outlook. *Daily Deal*, August 5.

Daily Deal. 2006. On the smaller side. March 17.

Daily Deal. 2007. M&A briefly noted. *Daily Deal*, October 12.

Deuze, M. 2007. *Media work*. Cambridge: Polity Press.

Dewson, A. 2007. Gates invests in publisher PlanetOut. *The Independent*, July 5.

Elgin, B. 2000. What's a dot-com to do after the advertisers bolt? *Business Week*.

Fitzgerald, K. 1999. Coming out: New campaign, cash and talent among Smith's plans to grow PlanetOut's pull. *Advertising Age*, November 1, S40.

Fitzgerald, K. 2002. Gay media shakeout. *Advertising Age*, February 25, 20.

Gamson, J. 2003. Gay media, inc.: Media structures, the new gay conglomerates, and collective social identities. In *Cyberactivism: Online activism in theory and practice*, edited by M. A. McCaughey and M. D. Ayers. New York: Routledge.

Gibbs, C. 2005. PlanetOut teams with m-Qube for wireless offerings with gay themes: Games, online store part of offer. *RCR Wireless News*, February 28, 7.

Gunn, E. P. 2000. PlanetOut goes mainstream. *Advertising age*, June 19, 60.

Hennessy, R. 2000. *Profit and pleasure: Sexual identities in late capitalism*. New York: Routledge.

Hill, A. 2003. Gay.com targets women. *PR week*, June 6, 7.

Hopkins, J. 2000. PlanetOut CEO taps gay market exec, becomes power player in $450B industry. *USA Today*, June 21, B7.

Kuczynski, A. 2000. Technology: 2 companies in gay media plan to merge. *The New York Times*, November 16, C4.

Nakamura, L. 2002. *Cybertypes: Race, ethnicity, and identity on the Internet*. New York: Routledge.

Nakamura, L. 2008. *Digitizing race: Visual cultures of the internet*. Minneapolis: University of Minnesota Press.

New Media Age. 2002. Strategic play: gay.com. *New Media Age*, May 2, 30.

Planet Out. 2009. http://www.planetout.com/ [Accessed August 24, 2009]

Queerty. 2009. All of gay media are belong to Paul Colichman. Queerty: Free of an agenda, except that gay one, January 9. http://www.queerty.com/all-of-gay-media-are-belong-to-paul-colichman-20090109/. [Accessed June 8, 2009]

San Francisco Business Times. 2008. PlanetOut agrees to sell magazine business for $6 million. *San Francisco Business Times,* April 9. http://sanfrancisco.bizjournals.com/sanfrancisco/stories/2008/04/07/daily29.html?jst=b_ln_hl [Accessed June 8, 2009]

Sapnar, M. 2008. Designers as auteurs in the dot-com boom: Industry logics and the looks of the web. Paper presented at the Society for Cinema and Media Studies Conference, Philadelphia, March 7–9.

Schwartz, J. 1999. Online gays become a market for advertisers. *The Washington Post,* May 22, E1.

Sender, K. 2004. *Business, not politics: The making of the gay market.* New York: Columbia University Press.

Stone, M. 1999. PlanetOut gains heavy hitters in second-round financing. *Newsbytes,* September 28.

Turner, F. 2006. *From counterculture to cyberculture: Stewart Brand, the whole earth network, and the rise of digital utopianism.* Chicago: University of Chicago Press.

Walters, S. D. 2001. *All the rage: The story of gay visibility in the 1990s.* Chicago: University of Chicago Press.

Wayback Machine. 2009. About the Wayback Machine. http://www.archive.org/web/web.php [Accessed August 22, 2009]

Wilke, M. 1998. Burgeoning gay web sites spark advertiser interest: Saturn, IBM among those tapping, in. *Advertising Age,* June 22, 30.

Chapter 9

Commercial Closet Association

LGBT Identities in Mainstream Advertising

Ian Davies

> ... to sell, not offend.
> (Commercial Closet Association 2009a)

Advertising is essentially created to attract attention to and sell products widely, yet it is not a static medium: the quest for greater market share, the development of new market niches, and the building of positive brand image inspire ever more sophisticated targeting of the buying public in general and diverse consumer groups in particular. The way in which such groups or their perceived representatives are portrayed in all-pervasive commercial communications potentially exerts a powerful influence over how audiences see themselves and others and what they allow themselves to be and aspire to achieve. This is particularly so for "minorities" such as non-heterosexuals, who may not necessarily identify (or be identified) with the "mainstream" values or aspirations widely depicted. Yet how accurately might adverts hope to reflect their audience, and can they keep pace with the unprecedented social changes taking place in the current era? To approach these issues, a source or repository, a kind of collected history of the evolution of advertising (with a focus on non-heterosexual identified people) is required for the exploration of some emerging realizations around commercial advertising and the ways in which it may touch the lives of LGBT citizens.

The Commercial Closet Association was founded in 1996 by veteran advertising journalist Michael Wilke as an evolving educational and advisory body promoting awareness of and respect for diversity of identity and gender or sexual orientation in business. A fundamental principle of the Association is that "advertising seeks to sell, not offend." It acknowledges the need to attract attention and inspire interest in a product, and that this has often been achieved using humor, but mitigates this with the commercial and social reality that "a laugh must also translate into sales from a wide variety of people." It accepts that advertising has not necessarily kept pace with changes in social outlook and the developing awareness of diversity, and aims to offer guidance to companies who wish to improve brand image and sales by creating advertising that does not negatively exploit or defame the identity of non-heterosexual people.

To this end, the CCA has created an impressive historical library of advertisements, reflecting non-heterosexual identity in some form, gathered largely from television but also including print and posters. The work of more than 1000 corporations and 500 advertising agencies is already represented, in almost every conceivable product category. The database allows the user to search randomly or according to criteria such as theme, product, agency, sponsor, year, or intended audience. Each ad is rated to reflect the positivity of its portrayal. Users can post comments, link to related sites and contact the CCA. For the creative professional or the casually interested user alike, the site offers an opportunity to learn from this developing "canon" of established work.

With the CCA repository as a principal source and focus, I will explore the use of historically embedded stereotypes as an advertising technique and examine how such portrayals may limit the potential of non-heterosexual people to find and construct meaningful, productive identities. My discussion will consider whether this influence has evolved in parallel with wider awareness of non-heterosexual lives in society. I question the extent to which commercial advertising can yet be seen as an inclusive mirror of representation: although there is increasing acknowledgement of the equal participation of LGBT people in everyday life, how sophisticated is the focus?

That there has been unprecedented (if not universal) political progress in terms of freedom to express diverse sexual orientation and gender identities is indisputable. However, the question of whether (and why) particular non-heterosexual identities have come to be considered more *commercially* viable than others is more complex. I will consider the potential contradiction between an apparently developing commodification in representations of LGBT identity and a widening acknowledgement of diversity in contemporary society, drawing conclusions as to what this may predict for the future direction of LGBT representations, and how they may influence and reflect the future potential of diverse personal identity expression.

Advertising (particularly televisual) is inescapable wherever one lives in the twenty-first century, and might easily be interpreted as a mirror of how we live, how we "are" as individuals and who we aspire to be. Whether on a conscious or subliminal level, it would be difficult to entirely escape this enduring influence on our sense of self, our very identity. This is not to say that advertising entirely imposes identity models on consumers or delimits their choices, rendering them passive and conformist,[1] but that, as a widespread expression of popular culture, and one whose remit is to win and retain the loyalty of a large audience, it is likely to reflect the perceived values of the "mainstream" of that audience, and unlikely to take risks by including potentially uncomfortable issues. Conversely, it must also be acknowledged that, as posited by John Fiske (1989a, 1989b), the power of interpretation and choice is complex, individual, and lies with the audience, and the values of any human culture are by nature fluid.

Stereotypes and "Othering"

Joshua Gamson (1998), reflecting on how non-heterosexual people are portrayed in the media, (specifically in television "talk shows"), states: "Homosexuality has been integrated enough into the cultural fabric to be seen, at least sometimes, as a fact of life" (p. 146).

Perhaps beginning with the decriminalization of male homosexuality in the UK[2] in 1967 and the removal of homosexuality from the American Psychiatric Association's manual of mental disorders in 1973 (Sender 2004, p. 29), advertising in westernized societies has reflected this increasingly since the late 1980s, but as in talk shows, the images produced have seldom been direct and honest representations with which large numbers of LGBT people might readily identify. Before the relatively recent growth in advertising targeted specifically at non-heterosexuals, the rare LGBT content in ads tended to use stereotypes which might have been intended to appeal to a majority outlook at the time, often using humor and comic shock/surprise value.

Taking a relatively early example from the CCA library, the "Disguise" commercial screened in the US in 1984 for the Dunkin' Donuts brand: a character (straight-identified, mustachioed, middle-aged "Fred the Baker") familiar to and well liked by US viewers at the time, is used in a comic scenario: he assumes female attire and a glamorous wig as a disguise, posing as a "typical" customer while spying on rival grocery stores.

At first sight, the content of this ad is neither shocking nor overtly offensive to anyone. "Fred" is obviously a straight man in drag and comically raises a finger to hide his moustache as he (poorly) mimics a feminine persona. The presentation could be read as "carnivalesque," and is reminiscent of music hall/carnival tradition where established social order is overturned by performers who adopt the clothing and parody the characteristics of their perceived social opposites: this type of playfulness is familiar and unthreatening, even potentially empowering in some circumstances (Bakhtin 1994). However, the traditional reactions expressed by the "normative" foils in this comic vignette carry a subtly damaging message of re-enforcement of the dominant "patriarchal" culture: a shopper protectively turns her daughter's head away from the spectacle of "Fred" in his wig, store employees gape in exaggerated shock, another shopper appears repulsed and drops her bread.

The stereotypical non-heterosexual identity traits and "inappropriate" gender behavior displayed by "Fred" are publicly ridiculed and reviled here for the amusement of the majority: the suggestion of a "different" identity is formally rejected, with a connotation that it is to be feared (and therefore likely to attract widespread disapproval and potentially, violence[3]). A real person exhibiting similar traits (perhaps a teenage boy experimenting with flamboyant appearance, or a male child preferring artistic pursuits to sports) may also be seen as separated from the norm and distanced, his identity subjugated by the reactions of his peers and family.

Taking a later example from the archive ("Opportunities," screened in the US for Honda in 1996), to illustrate this argument from a different angle, a young man is depicted investigating a number of unpromising career opportunities, with the punchline "Lots of career opportunities, one car. Make it a good one." Ending on a "humorous" note, the final opportunity is working on a fishing boat. An older sailor encourages: "Twelve men, one boat. What could be better?" The young man looks fearful as the sailor tentatively touches his shoulder, implying an unwanted predatory advance (this final segment, according to the CCA site notes, was later edited out by Honda at the request of the Gay and Lesbian Alliance Against Defamation, GLAAD).

Reviewing a number of older (and some recent) mainstream ads, for example: "August" (Calvin Klein, US 1995); "Bedroom" (Clothestime, US 1996); "Ice Bucket" (MullerLight, UK 2001); "Run Wyclef Run" (VirginMobile, Europe/US 2002), the viewer receives a persistent impression that the only accepted "normal" identity is that of the heterosexual male. The non-heterosexual is portrayed (in the sub-text of comic presentation) as sex-obsessed, a predator, a freak, or an object of pity and ridicule. It is as if to exhibit traits associated with femininity (including an attraction to men, or adopting feminine apparel) somehow dehumanizes and diminishes the individual, marking them as inferior to the accepted group. Conversely, in adverts playing with gender confusion where an attractive female character is revealed to possess masculine attributes, this is more often portrayed as positively subversive, intriguing, or sophisticated (although duplicitous), for example: "Beatles Haircut" (Iceberg, US, year nk); "Bricklayer" (Foster's, Europe 1999); Le Rendezvous (Jean-Paul Gaultier, Europe/US 2000).

Michael Pickering (2001) states, ". . . stereotypes operate as a means of evaluatively placing, and attempting to fix in place, other people or cultures from a particular and privileged perspective" (p. 47). Such "typification" of difference into recognizable character traits or "types" serves a dual negative purpose: it fuels fear and misunderstanding of LGBT people among the straight-identified majority, and has the potential to further damage the already poor self image of those who are being continually rejected in this way. As Pickering also suggests, there is a deeper potential consequence: to define a person or group as "other" is a kind of labeling which enduringly marks them in reductive terms (p. 48). The "other" is distanced from belonging, participation, dialogue, and self-determination, and is likely to come to identify themselves as rejected and subjugated by the society in which they live. Michael Pickering (2001), citing African-American author W.E.B. DuBois (1996), tell us:

The indelible effect of [this] recognition of yourself as "other" ... allows you to see yourself only through the eyes of others, leaving your own, secret striving for a more independent sense of identity bereft in "a world that looks on in amused contempt and pity."

(Pickering 2001, p. 77)

Pickering sees the end-product of this as "an obstacle to change and transformation," diminishing the lives of both those in the dominant group with social power and those who are "othered," whereas a healthy society is ideally in a fluid state of continual development. Interestingly, a similar argument is developed by Richard Dyer (1993): ". . . poverty, harassment, self-hate and discrimination (in housing, jobs, educational opportunity . . .) are shored up and instituted by representation" (p. 1).

The question now, in supposedly enlightened and liberalized early twenty-first century westernized societies, after decades of social transformation, is whether commercial representation of non-heterosexual citizens has kept pace with social (and legal) changes in everyday life.

Groupings, Power, and Revelation

It is interesting that ads on the CCA website are organized in categories and subgroups including terms like "Trans Beauty," "She's a He," "Bears," and "Butches," which (necessarily) acknowledge a degree of stereotypical audience identification. Richard Dyer (1993) develops a convincing theory that these groups are in a constant (and healthy) state of flux and construction, and that the individual does not consistently identify with a single group to the exclusion of others (an argument reinforced by the fluid spectrum of user comments on the CCA site): ". . . we all belong in many groupings, often antagonistic to each other or at least implying very different accesses to power" (p. 4).

Dyer (pp. 2–4) suggests that although it is impossible to live outside of "the society, the network of representations in which one finds oneself," acknowledging that mainstream society tends to adopt a (sometimes negative) image of a striking member of a group as a "type" representing that group as a whole, it is also true that such images are not always interpreted negatively, and further, that many non-heterosexual people do not recognize themselves in the identities expressed (with positive intent) within gay or "queer" culture: self-perception is subjective, multi-faceted, and fluid.

It is difficult to discern with conviction whether the increasing visibility of non-heterosexual people in commercial media in recent decades has afforded them greater access to "power" (in terms of freedom to participate equally in society and to self-determine). The question is perhaps double-edged. Changes in perception (or at least, depiction) are evident, but it is uncertain whether these are principally motivated by a widening social awareness among advertisers, or by market forces. Perhaps in their growing visibility as they fought for civil rights in the 1960s and 1970s and for their very lives in the 1980s in the face of AIDS, non-heterosexuals (and gay men in particular, for reasons which I will further explore) have come to be acknowledged (if not welcomed in all quarters) as part of human society in diverse cultures worldwide. In westernized societies, this has also precipitated their identification as a new and growing market niche, particularly following changes in perception of the nature of HIV/AIDS (as a global, universal challenge) and of people living with it, and their life chances,[4] as medical advances and social awareness have developed in the last decade.

Early media coverage may have focused negatively on the gay men initially affected by HIV/AIDS in the US and Europe, yet in transmitting their stories worldwide it perhaps inadvertently confirmed that they were neither mentally ill nor outcasts to be feared, but individuals from every background, capable of love, courage, compassion, and self-sacrifice, who had families, lifelong partners, and friends who loved them, grieved for them, and believed it was worth fighting for their human rights.

From Stereotypes to Social Types

Advertising sponsors (with laudable exceptions such as Absolut Vodka (Sender 2004, p. 36)) may have avoided associations with non-heterosexuality as the AIDS epidemic took hold, but as the outlook thawed in the early 1990s (and with economic recession driving a quest for new market niches), advertisers demonstrated renewed interest in a fledgling "gay market," accessed principally through the predominantly male-oriented gay press. This evidence, as Katherine Sender (2004) describes, suggests that over a sustained period, a combination of visibility through intense social activism and economic market forces led to a situation where certain groups (traditionally "othered" by mainstream culture) such as gay men and, to a growing extent, lesbians, finally came to be acknowledged as a functioning (if contentious) element of the society in which they live.

Richard Dyer (1993) refers to a theory which encapsulates this concept:

> Social types are ... those who belong to society. They are the kind of people that one expects and is led to expect, to find in one's society, whereas stereotypes ... do not belong, ... are outside of one's society.
>
> (p. 14)[5]

There is evidence to suggest that LGBT people are increasingly portrayed as "social types" in advertising, reflecting a shift both in mainstream perceptions of their identities and in their own expectations (for example: the IKEA furniture group, the Subaru Motor Company, and the Ford Motor Company have created international advertising campaigns in televisual and print formats depicting gay men and lesbians positively in normative, family/domestic and aspirational settings, sometimes in the face of fierce criticism from conservative pressure groups[6]).

However, there remains a sense that certain non-heterosexual identities are more commercially viable in terms of representation than others: that wider LGBT identity is being distilled into a saleable "social type:" the affluent, youthful/trendsetting, and cultured gay male, personified in ads for luxury goods and services in the gay press or placed around gay-themed television programming. Some interesting examples include "When Friends are Family" (Mercedes Benz, print, US 2005), "Coffee Shop Date" (Nokia, TV, US/Europe/Asia/Australia-NZ/Middle East 2006), "Natural Beauty" (Hyatt Resorts, print, US 2007), and "Be Fabulous" (Moët & Chandon, print, US 2007).

As Katherine Sender (2004) posits:

> ... although marketers and journalists refer to ... "the GLBT market" to encompass ... this "class" of non-heterosexual people, their interest and investment are mainly focused on affluent gay men. ... Marketers occasionally acknowledge bisexuals and transgender people ... but most believe these groups too small to warrant marketing attention.
>
> (pp. 10–11)

Sender (2004, p. 10) cites the evolution of a "phantom normalcy" (Clarke 1999) in the commercial depiction of non-heterosexuals. The "less respectable" (i.e. marketable) members of LGBT communities: lesbians, bisexuals, people of color, poor and working-class gays, transgender people, and sex radicals (p. 15) are obscured, denied participation in favor of those who are likely to already be empowered (white, educated, and affluent gay men). Sender further suggests that "marketers have structured the gay niche from a history of invisibility and negative stereotyping to produce gay and lesbian 'socially recognizable persons' (Elliott 1992) in '... a vision of gay lives worth emulating'" (Sender 2004, p. 19), a kind of "model minority" which is also unthreatening to existing heterosexual social norms (Sender 2004, p. 237).

From another perspective, Joshua Gamson (1998) draws similar conclusions. He cites a recognized opposition in LGBT awareness between middle class, educated people whose approach to fighting for civil rights has focused broadly on assimilation into mainstream society, and "others favoring a transgressive, confrontational 'queer' politics that pushes the boundaries of normality" (p. 191).

Social Awareness and the Dawn of Wider Inclusion

For gay, lesbian, and bisexual identified people in particular, the growing international governmental/legal acknowledgement of such basic human rights as civil partnerships, adoption, workplace and school equality, and unprejudiced access to goods and services has transformed life expectations and effectively set in motion an unprecedented political process of positive inclusion and participation in mainstream society. Commercial representations have undeniably evolved into the twenty-first century to reflect this more honestly, and (in my opinion) there are encouraging signs of a general media progression toward a wider inclusion of LGBT diversity.

In 2004, Nadia Almada was the first transgender person to appear on UK "reality" television show *Big Brother* (Channel 4, 1999–date). Her history was disclosed to the audience from the outset, but not to housemates (Transgenderzone, 2008). She was accepted into the group as a woman and well received, winning the show with more than half of the total votes cast.[7] This was an important watershed in terms of popular, mass-media acknowledgement of identity diversity.

In 2008, transgender actress Candis Cayne appeared on mainstream television in the US and Europe in ABC's prime-time serial drama *Dirty Sexy Money*, as "Carmelita," the mistress of co-star William Baldwin's heterosexual character "Patrick" (Serano 2008). Transgender characters have been portrayed with increasing empathy, notably in well loved soap opera (*Coronation Street*, ITV, UK 1960–date) with the character of Hayley Patterson (introduced 1998); in drama (*The L Word*, Showtime US 2003–date) with the character of Max; and in successful film (*Transamerica*, Duncan Tucker, US 2005) with the character of Bree, but "Carmelita" is the first to be openly represented by a transgender performer. The character's role as a forceful, honest, shame-free, and moral person and the depth and integrity of her relationships in the storyline are also groundbreaking. This is a departure from historical fears around portrayal of transgender identity, and the international success of the series demonstrates a general shift in social perception (which is also likely to be reflected in future commercial representations).

A seed of this pluralistic outlook is discernible in ads already in the CCA repository, such as "Drag Show" (1-800 Contacts) US 2005, a mainstream commercial for contact lenses where "trans" identity is incidental to the storyline, positive, and honest. A refined search reveals a handful of other ads of similar spirit such as "Joe Namath" (Hanes Beautymist) US 1974 (perhaps the first of this kind); "The Appointment" (Boisvert Lingerie) Europe 1996; "The Secret" (Campari) Europe 2005, and "Proudly Brewed for the Human Race" (Coors Light) US 2003. The latter, displaying a joyfully diverse non-heterosexual gallery, is particularly interesting since Coors was widely criticized by LGBT groups for supporting organizations such as "Colorado for Family Values" politically opposed to social change, yet the ad, in its commercial effort to reach a pluralist customer base, is empowering regardless of origin. A small number of other extraordinary examples, particularly in print, such as "Macho Mint" (Altoids) US 1999 and "Not Quite Middle England" (Malvern Mineral Water) Europe 2003, although marketing popular brands, cheerfully abandon pretence to mainstream assimilation in an unabashed expression of non-idealized, uncommodified sexual identity.

In perusing the CCA repository and attempting to contextualise the stories it tells about historical depiction of LGBT identity (in terms of social changes taking place today), there is a powerful sense of interdependence and cross-fertilization between the political and personal struggles of real people for recognition, acceptance, and self-determination, and the commercial motivations inspiring the development of these advertisements, which are in effect, slices of popular culture; snapshots of a moment in the evolution of a society.

Katherine Sender (2004) states:

> [T]he gay community, on a national scale at least, is not a preexisting entity that marketers simply need to appeal to, but is a construction, an imagined community formed not only through political activism but through an increasingly sophisticated, commercially supported, national media.
>
> (p. 5)

Given that advertising exists primarily to generate and expand sales on all fronts in a competitive climate, it must demonstrate sensitivity to the flux of social change if the trust of fresh consumers is to be won, yet equally it must maintain an appreciation of the range of political and social standpoints held dear by its audience, if sales to existing loyal markets are also to be protected (as illustrated by recent industry responses to consumer controversies in the UK and US[8]). Therefore, a commercial representation cannot necessarily be expected to incisively reflect current social reality, as that is not its purpose.

However, if it is to sell, an advert must not defame or offend members of its potential audience (as the CCA website affirms in its educative mission statement). It is clear that advertisers have historically developed a deepening awareness of exactly who the members of their audience are today or might be in the future. Through an ill-starred history of stereotypical misrepresentation, some lessons have been learned and the emerging social visibility and broader acceptance of LGBT people has been acknowledged, explored, and widely supported and promoted, as a burgeoning market. There appears to be a fluid and delicately balanced, almost symbiotic relationship between advertiser and consumer, where concepts of social progress, identity politics, and the competitive commercial realities of international business are inextricably intertwined.

Interactivity and the Potential of New Media Forms

Comments posted on the CCA site reveal a startling spectrum of reaction and opinion, not least among LGBT-identified people. Such open debate is healthy, and the fact that it has become possible is a major step forward, but at a time when an image of two men kissing still carries a particularly provocative charge, it would perhaps be unwise to presume that the future direction of the commercial depiction of non-heterosexual people can be confidently predicted.

The rising popularity of internet social networking sites such as MySpace and Facebook and entertainment sites such as YouTube (which already features clips of controversial ads) suggests internet-based interactivity is likely to seep further into advertising (or vice versa). Is the recent advent of concepts like "viral marketing" (utilizing the "word of mouth" of social networks via internet and mobile phone to enhance brand awareness with market research games and questionnaires[9]), a clue to the possible future direction of advertising? A new generation has grown up with interactive technologies beyond the passively consumed mass-media of the twentieth century. When advertisers are able to address non-mainstream identified people (or any group) directly, without fear of offending the sensibilities of a mass audience, the issue of (mis)representation may potentially recede in the face of widening opportunity for self-expression. Where this may lead is open to interpretation, but it is evident that no future mode of expression or communication can flourish without respect for, understanding of, and reference to the past.

The CCA expresses no grand pretensions and acknowledges the contradictions and imperfections inherent in the very nature of advertising. It encourages dialogue regarding its content and interface, and presents itself simply as a kind of evolutionary information source with a positive social and business outlook. However, at the time of writing, it appears unique in its potential to provide an open-minded, honest historical context to the representation of LGBT identities in commercial media. The organic and highly interactive nature of the internet will no doubt inspire future projects with a similar or related mission. It is perhaps in the growth of this very interactivity that the future of the CCA and its potential influence may lie. It already attracts fluid, uncensored comment and debate both immediate and considered, from a diverse, global audience.

It may be idealistic to imagine that non-mainstream sexual orientation and gender identity might be considered an unremarkable aspect of everyday life in the near future. Yet however issues of identity may develop and refine, if the advertising of tomorrow is to inspire a deeper brand loyalty which will translate into enduring business growth beyond the mainstream, where better for creative professionals to begin than with such an unfettered, un-idealized research source, where lessons learned from a canon of past works might be contextualized through interactive exchanges with today's LGBT consumers?

Notes

1 As might be interpreted from Adorno, 1991.
2 Excepting Scotland.

3 Lawrence King, aged 15, bullied because of nonconformist dress and use of make-up, was shot and killed by a classmate in February 2008 in Oxnard, California (Broverman 2008). Michael Causer, aged 18, a happy and proud 'out' teenager with a penchant for frequently changing his hair color, was beaten to death in August 2008 in Liverpool, UK by persons yet unidentified, after attending a party (Pidd 2008). Just two of many recent real examples of the grave potential outcome of homophobia which received scant coverage in mainstream media.
4 Evidenced in part by the appearance of ads in the gay press for combination therapies such as Sustiva—e.g. "I have HIV but I'm making the grade" (Bristol Myers Squibb 2008).
5 Taken from O.E. Klapp (1962).
6 The American Family Association mounted a campaign of protest and boycott against Ford, because of content and placing of adverts and inclusive policy toward LGBT staff. The AFA also strongly criticized IKEA for depicting non-heterosexual families in normative settings (source: pinknews.co.uk; OneNewsNow.com, May 2008).
7 Source: Socialist Unity Network (2008).
8 A Heinz television advert for "Deli Mayo" mayonnaise was prematurely withdrawn after viewer complaints about a scene depicting two men kissing (source: Daily Mail Online 2008a).
A Mars Group advert for "'Snickers" was also withdrawn, this time following complaints from GLAAD that the ad was defamatory towards gay people (source: Daily Mail Online 2008b).
9 For example: UK Channel 4's Gay-O-Meter site (Channel 4 2008).

References

Adorno, T. W. 1991. *The culture industry: Selected essays on mass culture.* London Routledge.
Bakhtin, M. 1994. Selected writings. In *The Bakhtin reader: Selected writings of Bakhtin, Medvedev, and Voloshinov*, edited by P. Morris. London: Edward Arnold.
Broverman, N. 2008. Mixed messages. *The Advocate*, issue 1005: 28–33. April 8.
Channel 4. 2008. Gay-O-Meter. http://www.channel4.com/life/microsites/G/gay-ometer/gayometer.html. [Accessed August 25, 2008]
Clarke, E. 1999. Queer publicity and the limits of inclusion. *Gay and Lesbian Quarterly* 5(1): 84–89.
Commercial Closet Association. 2009. http://www.commercialcloset.org/common/news/reports/detail.cfm?Classification=report&QID=4141&ClientID=11064&TopicID=0&subnav=resources&subsection=resources [Accessed August 13, 2009]
Daily Mail Online. 2008a. http://www.dailymail.co.uk/news/article-1028794/Heinz-mayonnaise-advert. [Accessed July 7, 2008]
Daily Mail Online. 2008b. http://www.dailymail.co.uk/news/article-1039369/Mr-Ts-Snickers-advert. [Accessed August 23, 2008]
DuBois, W. E. B. 1996. *The souls of black folk.* London: Penguin (orig. pub. 1903).
Dyer, R. 1993. *The matter of images: Essays on representations.* London and New York: Routledge.

Elliott, S. 1992. *A market that's educated, affluent, and homosexual.* New York Times, September 23, D27.
Fiske, J. 1989a. *Understanding popular culture.* London: Unwin Hyman.
Fiske, J. 1989b. *Reading the popular.* London: Unwin Hyman.
Gamson, J. 1998. *Freaks talk back: Tabloid talk shows and sexual nonconformity.* Chicago: University of Chicago Press.
Klapp, O. E. 1962. *Heroes, villains and fools.* Englewood Cliffs, NJ: Prentice-Hall.
OneNews now.com/PinkNews. http://www.pinknews.co.uk/news/articles/2005-3679.html. [Accessed May 9, 2008]
Pickering, M. 2001. *Stereotyping: The politics of representation.* Basingstoke, UK: Palgrave.
Pidd, H. 2008. Liverpool's gay community pays tribute to killed teenager. *The Guardian*, August 11.
Sender, K. 2004. *Business, not politics: The making of the gay market.* New York: Columbia University Press.
Serano, J. 2008. First Lady. *OUT Transgender Issue*, 62–65, April 2008.
Socialist Unity Network. 2008. http://www.socialistunitynetwork.co.uk/counter/nadia.htm. [Accessed August 13, 2008]
Transgenderzone.com. http://www.transgenderzone.com/features/bigbrother.htm. [Accessed August 13, 2008]

Part III

Fan Cultures

Chapter 10

Queering Brad Pitt
The Struggle between Gay Fans and the Hollywood Machine to Control Star Discourse and Image on the Web[1]

Ronald Gregg

The emergence of the web with its astonishing number of celebrity websites, both authorized and unauthorized, has had a profound impact on the nature and management of star discourse. By destabilizing the boundaries between public and private speech and threatening the hegemony of the star discourse fostered by the film industry, it has produced a new and unprecedented politics of star management. The early history of the web has been marked by consistent skirmishes between Hollywood and its fans, a struggle which may never be resolved.

As theorists and historians such as Richard Dyer (1986), Constance Penley (1991), and Henry Jenkins (1992) have noted, the individual and collective predilections, identifications, desires, and fantasies of fans have long influenced star discourse. Far from being passive consumers, many fans collect filmic and extrafilmic material on stars, they construct images of cherished stars that depart from their authorized images, and they share their own star constructions with other fans. Many fans are savvy enough to know how to distinguish what is publicity hype, what is fantasy and speculation on star lives from the fan industry or from other fans, and what is unknown and worth speculating about for themselves. Fans influence the construction of the star, and they influence the public knowledge about stars. This is evident as star publicists measure, encourage (or may discourage) the sort of positive and negative fan responses that can shape a star's career. They follow fan interest through a number of tools, including fan letters, surveys, box office receipts and demographics, and recently, by charting the various layers of fan discourse on the web. Publicists are aware that a single star may appeal to distinct fan communities for different, sometimes antagonistic, reasons. Tom Cruise's heterosexual fans want to believe he is straight as much as his gay fans want to believe that he may be gay. Publicists strive to solicit both fan groups, although usually doing so in a way that will not antagonize the larger, more easily troubled heterosexual group.

This is not new. Throughout its history, Hollywood has devised legal and public relations strategies for controlling and containing illicit star images and discourse. A quick review of those earlier strategies highlights the novel character of the situation in which Hollywood now finds itself.

Even before 1921, when the studios saw the career of their megastar Fatty Arbuckle collapse due to a sex scandal, Hollywood had established strong connections with lawyers experienced in contract and defense law. After Arbuckle, the studios added morality clauses to star contracts. These contracts obligated stars to protect both the physical appearance and the persona that the studio constructed for them. For instance, as written into the contract, RKO Studios could fire actress Frances Dee if her physical appearance changed in any significant way and damaged her uniqueness as an actress (Dee 1933). The character actor Sydney Greenstreet was contractually obligated to maintain his weight at 250 pounds or above (Gaines 1991, p. 148). Thus anything that a star did to tarnish her or his body or public image could result in termination, although studios were more likely to take steps to punish and rein in a major star to salvage her or his image. Successful stars whose sexual peccadilloes ended up being discussed in fan magazines and the courts were defended by high-powered lawyers. Noted Los Angeles criminal defense attorney Jerry Geisler, for example, successfully defended Charlie Chaplin, Errol Flynn and other stars, salvaging their images and careers.

The studios also devised ways to control fan discourse. We can see the complicated ways this worked by looking at the early 1930s, near the end of Prohibition, a moment like our own when gender bending and gay and lesbian characters proliferated in fashion layouts, novels and short stories, stage plays, cartoons, and other venues of high art and popular culture alike (Chauncey 1994; Gregg 2003). Hollywood responded to this development by including homosexual characters and themes in film, and also by allowing some of its stars to project an ambiguous sexual and gender image (Gregg 2003; Weiss 1993). This momentary loosening was evident in stars as varied as Marlene Dietrich, Greta Garbo, Cary Grant, Gary Cooper, William Haines, and even Clark Gable in his alleged pre-macho, pre-hunter, pre-homophobe phase.

The most infamous of the male stars at the time was William Haines, whose star profile in the late 1920s and early 1930s hinted at his homosexuality by allusions to his effeminate tastes, narcissism, attachment to his mother, and other easily recognized homosexual signifiers. The repetition of specific biographical details in fan magazine profiles of Haines indicates that these details came from the MGM studio's star biography, a standard publicity document put together by studios for the use of print journalists.

MGM constructed a thread of heterosexuality for Haines by regularly publicizing Haines' supposed heterosexual romances and emphasizing his female fan appeal. But at the same time, they highlighted his very close relationship to his mother and let columnists label him "dreamy," "moody," "despondent," and "tempestuous." MGM also underscored Haines's interest in art, antique collecting, and interior decoration.

But MGM eventually found that it had gone too far, as discussion of Haines's unconventional gender behavior resulted in speculation about his imagined

Chapter 2

"A YouTube of One's Own?"
"Coming Out" Videos as Rhetorical Action

Jonathan Alexander and Elizabeth Losh

> Hey guys—um—I've been meaning to make this video for a long time now, and I—uh—finally got the courage to—uh—to do it. Um. I'm not going to make you guys wait a long time. I'm just going to come right out and say it. I am gay. I am a homosexual, and I'm very proud. Um. I've been keeping this from you for a long time now, and a lot of you have been asking about it. And so I really just thought, I really just thought I should—um—tell you guys. Uh. Oh. I feel so I feel so—you know—relieved that—you know—everyone knows, and I don't have to hide it anymore. Um. I am single, so—uh, you know—I don't have a boyfriend right now. That's all I really have to say in this video. Gosh, I feel so much better about myself. Um. Well guys, I'll see you—uh—in my next video, my Washington D.C. video. So, uh. See you later guys. Peace and love.
> April fool's . . . bitch!

A fake coming out video (x44jackal44x 2009), shot in black and white and set in the space of an anonymous kitchen, features a teenaged boy in a baseball cap, who is recorded solo by his webcam below, as he seems to engage in an act of radical personal disclosure, only later to retract his admission when the footage cuts to a wide shot of him shouting that it was all an April Fool's Day prank.

The very existence of this video indicates that its young YouTube star is clearly aware that he is parodying a specific genre readily available on the popular online video-sharing site, one with many potential audience members. He even ends the clip with a blanket disclaimer stating his intention to avoid alienating any segment of his audience with his hoax: "*** Note this video was not meant to offend any people of any sexual orientation it was just a joke***"Then he follows up with a second ending, which is an appeal for input from those watching on YouTube for feedback assessing the credibility of his performance: "Post a comment to let me know if I was actually believable! I thought I was pretty convincing!"

The "believability" of his video "Coming out" might be attributable to his deft handling of some of the commonplace rhetorical moves shared by many coming out narratives. For instance, his monologue is punctuated with familiar tropes that signal both his hesitance at going public and his sexual availability to like-minded others. At the same time, however, there are also clues that he is unaware that other parts of the prescribed scripts for such coming out videos are missing. For example, he seems unable to supply any narrative context for his act of disclosure or any normative instructions to others who might be contemplating imitating his course of rhetorical action—all somewhat standard moves in coming out narratives (Plummer 1994). Indeed, such moves compose a meta discourse that this chapter will argue is commonly invoked in this genre, if only because such coming out videos almost always consist of much more than a simple declaration of sexual orientation on camera.

Indeed, genuine coming out videos have become a distinctive YouTube form, one that appropriates the site's dominant modes of personal confession and mutual surveillance and yet also affirms the existence of separate online communities of potential resistance. In bedrooms, kitchens, living rooms, and dining rooms that demonstrate at least a temporary mastery of domestic space and control of the gaze of the viewing public looking in, "queers" using YouTube are sharing coming out stories and asserting their place in related and often contentious networked publics. A search with the terms "coming out" on YouTube reveals thousands of such videos, and users frequently create "playlists" to collect their favorite instances of the genre.[1] We might dismiss such disclosures as part of the "normative exhibitionism" that regulates other discourses of being "out" (in other, not specifically sexual ways) on the Internet, such as the dissemination of "public secrets" like the "five things you don't know about me" meme that swept the blogosphere in 2007 (boyd 2006). And yet, this robust rhetorical output often occurs through a variety of self-sponsored and commercial means of production and expresses various pressures put on video makers addressing the complex personal and social phenomenon of sexual orientation self-identification.

We argue in this chapter that the proliferation of coming out videos offers us a unique opportunity to consider the management of sexual identities in online spaces. This occurs particularly since the coming out video is often an intentionally broadcast statement that attempts to negotiate the boundary between intensely personal desires and public identities. It therefore shows us, through varied performances, the shaping of personal desire through public discourse about sex, sexuality, and sexual identity. Unlike the top-rated videos on YouTube that tend to celebrate hegemonic values from the mainstream media and reify standards of stereotypical masculinity or femininity, coming out videos offer alternative ways of understanding sex, sexuality, and gender. This occurs even as they create their own normative understanding of rhetorically effective coming out narratives. Alexandra Juhasz has described alternative communities sustained on this Google owned and operated site as "niche-tube" (Jenkins 2008), since online video can also subvert the logic of high-school popularity, conformity, status checking, and expected role playing and offer the possibility for genuine homosexuality. Haines's official but ambiguous image legitimized a more direct, unofficial questioning of his heterosexuality by the tabloids. In 1931, the tabloid *Broadway Brevities* directly suggested that Haines cruised for sailors and labeled him a member of the "third sex" (Martin 1931). Haines's imagined queerness became too explicit a subject of discussion, for the Hollywood industry.[2]

Haines's star persona would not be the only character affected by the more fluid sexual and gender conventions of the Prohibition era. Gary Cooper also projected an ambiguous erotic image that appealed to both homosexual men and heterosexual women. His publicity described him as a possessor of male "It,"[3] the code word for sex appeal, and closely followed his romantic liaisons with Clara Bow and Lupe Velez. By itself, "It" might have suggested male virility, but the studio presented Cooper in fan magazines and gossip columnists with a disarming beauty, which became the subject of caricature. In a 1933 cartoon depicting Hollywood stars at Malibu Beach, for instance, the artist portrayed Cooper with his hands on his hips, long eye lashes, and full, seemingly painted, lips (Anonymous 1933). At least in 1933, Paramount publicists must not have feared how this affected Cooper's standing with fans; they placed him in the starring role in director Ernst Lubitsch's 1933 subtle queer film version of Noel Coward's play *Design for Living*.[4]

In the early thirties, however, Hollywood was forced to respond to outside political and moral criticism of its films and the unconventional gender and sexual image of many of its stars. The industry was attacked by reformers who threatened it with federal censorship and boycotts, and it couldn't ignore the post-Prohibition crackdown on homosexuals in cabarets, theaters, nightclubs, and newly legalized bars (Chauncey 1994). The industry publicly joined in this broader crackdown on "queers." It gave the Hollywood Production Code more power, eliminated overt homosexuality from its films, and reined in the images of its stars. Studio publicity departments normalized the images of their stars by straightening up their clothing and behavior; making stars appear in public with female dates (known as "beards"); starting rumors of marriage and/or heterosexual romance for suspected stars; and orchestrating interviews with stars by compliant reporters and magazines. They also reined in the gossip and fan industry by cutting off their access to the studios and stars if they did not sustain the new emphasis on heterosexuality and monogamy in the studios' star discourse. Some stars could be made straight; Cooper, for one, married and settled down into a more conservative life. Others (like Haines) had developed too queer an image, and were fired. Publicists learned a valuable publicity lesson—not to *queer* their stars too much.

While Hollywood learned to manage the public sphere, an underground economy of queer salacious gossip and image-making continued. For instance, "Tijuana Bibles"—pornographic comics produced in the 1930s, 1940s, and 1950s—crudely fantasized about the sexual behavior of stars, developing both heterosexual and homosexual scenarios. One "Tijuana Bible" titled *Boys Will be*

Girls, for instance, portrayed Jimmy Cagney and his male friend "Pat" enjoying oral and anal sex with each other. In another, titled *Who's a Fairy?*, Cary Grant had to prove his heterosexuality (Adelman 1997, pp. 101–108). Such pornographic gossip was part of an underground economy, sold from the back of a car or under the counter of a bookstore. So long as it stayed in this underground, Hollywood had no desire to acknowledge it or draw public attention to it.

In the 1950s, however, Hollywood was forced to develop new strategies to deal with sensational gossip. Faced by the resurgence of tabloid journalism, which thrived by circulating salacious, uncontrollable gossip, the studios began trading in gossip, promising to provide some tantalization, but did this to keep the worst of this out of print. But when the tabloids came too close to the "truth," for instance, in *Confidential*'s 1957 exposé on Liberace's homosexuality in its infamous article "Why Liberace's Theme Song Should be 'Mad About the Boy,'" the industry began suing the newspapers, forcing them to spend large sums of money to defend themselves. These heavy-handed legal tactics helped contain rumors of stars' homosexuality in the underground.

However, in recent years the growing visibility and acceptability of gay life and the growth of new public spheres associated with the World Wide Web have had complex effects on Hollywood's efforts to control star discourse. In the 1990s, film roles, publicity photographs, and/or publicity material for stars Brad Pitt, Leonardo DiCaprio, Tom Cruise, Keanu Reeves, Ryan Phillippe, and others indicate that at various times their publicists were cultivating their erotic appeal to gay men as well as to straight women. Brad Pitt, for instance, played Louis, the intimate traveling companion of the bisexual vampire Lestat (played by Tom Cruise) in the "queer" film *Interview with the Vampire* (Neil Jordan 1994, USA). When he starred in the homoerotic film *Fight Club* (David Fincher 1999, USA), he posed for a series of erotic photographs in *W* magazine and posed in a dress for *Rolling Stone*. Similarly, Ryan Phillippe as a youth played the first gay teenage character in an American soap opera, Billy Douglas in *One Life to Live*. He later starred in the film *54* (Mark Christopher 1998, USA) and was featured in the erotically charged publicity campaign for the film. The initial publicity for *54* stressed that the film's depiction of the hedonism of Studio 54 during the sexually liberated 1970s would include an on-screen kiss between Phillippe and another young male star. The kiss was eventually cut from the film, but only after the publicity had established the actor Phillippe's comfort in kissing another man on screen.

As *Interview with the Vampire* and *54* suggest, by the 1990s, Hollywood was once again prepared to appeal to a gay fan base. But the web made it more difficult for the film industry to control the circulation and interpretation of such images and ideas. The emergence of fan-driven celebrity websites and pornographic sites in the 1990s dramatically destabilized the balance of power between studio- and star-controlled publicity and the circulation of gossip. The web began with a decentralized structure that facilitated unrestricted speech and an anti-corporate, outlaw stance. Despite its recent commercialization, the web still perpetuates some of its earlier unregulated character. There are still a remarkable number of personal web pages on which people describe their sexual fantasies about stars. The sort of gossip and musings that used to be private or contained within subcultural conversation have found a place in public on the web. Here web users post personal scrapbooks with confessions and photographic collages, friendly chat detailing sexual desire and fantasy for stars, and reports of star sightings in queer spaces. Equally striking is the commercial marketing of celebrity nudes and pornographic fantasy stories featuring celebrities. The innovation of the web has been to take what was underground, like "Tijuana Bibles," and put it above ground, or, rather, to put it in a virtual space that short circuits such distinctions.

Not so many years ago, for instance, gay and straight fans of Pitt or Phillippe could move without restriction through a virtual Dante's circle of websites concerning those stars. Spiraling down from the official websites and individual fan sites which were the equivalent of the romantic posters covering the bedroom walls of a teenage girl or boy, fans could enter chat rooms where other fans discussed sexually explicit fantasies and sites displaying celebrity nude photos or fake pornographic images. To an unprecedented degree, fans became active within the construction of sexual fantasy involving celebrities. This made the star publicity machines very nervous. While official depictions and subcultural readings of stars had always coexisted, the web enabled a democracy, placing them within the same arena.

Among the diverse websites available in the late 1990s and early 2000s were numerous official fan websites, where gossip and fan companies offered (amongst many other things) publicity photos, news, and merchandise. Then there were individual fan sites, where gay and straight fans shared their personal collages of images devoted either to one star or a number of idols, drawing upon official publicity photos. These sites were often open about gay desire, but offered no nudity or explicitly sexual comments. Then, there were chat rooms devoted to discussions of stars with romantic fantasies that included gay desire. For instance, in one ESL (English as a Second Language) chat room, women and men from different national, ethnic, racial, and sexual backgrounds discussed how much they loved Ryan Phillippe (ESL Discussion Center 1999).

At another level were sexually explicit chat rooms and fictional fantasy sites devoted to recounting both heterosexual and homosexual desire. One chat room discussion thread titled "Questionable Keanu," for instance, asked the question, "Is Keanu Gay?" Pseudonymous straight and queer contributors quoted Keanu Reeves, talked about his movies, posted Keanu sightings, and discussed whether they believed posted Keanu sightings. Many of the people on this site, most of whom seemed to be gay men, fantasized about meeting and having sex with Keanu in such places as back allies (Keanu Reeves Gossip 1999). On other sites, queer men (although gender cannot be assumed in this pseudonymous world) posted sexual fantasies about having sex with stars such as Leonardo DiCaprio, Brad Pitt, and Ryan Phillippe in the shower, gym, and other iconic gay cruising spaces. These pornographic fantasy stories had such quaint titles as "A Surprise From Leo" (Menonthenet 1998a) and "Rubbing Off On Ryan" (Menonthenet 1998).

Then there were the nude and pornographic sites designed both by individuals and pornography houses targeting gay men. If a star had ever appeared in a nude scene, or the paparazzi had surreptitiously captured the star in the nude (as in the case of Brad Pitt), those pictures could be found somewhere on the web. Such photos became a staple of nude celebrity websites, removing penis type and size and other attributes from the realm of individual fantasy. And if a paparazzo had never caught a star like Ryan Phillippe in the nude, he might still show up on a website posting fake pornographic celebrity nudes.

In the past, the industry used strategies of star access, denials, and lawsuits to censor the circulation of such images and ideas. However, initially, Hollywood publicists found the unregulated status of the web and the independent industry of desire it spawned much more difficult to control. There were too many websites and even if those in the USA were shut down, stars and their handlers had to contend with those in other countries. For a brief period, it seemed that the web had changed the rules of the game governing star discourse. But Hollywood has responded forcefully.

As we have seen, Hollywood has experience in protecting its investment in star images, and it still has the resources to overwhelm individual fans and commercial websites. Stars' lawyers now incorporate the impact of the web in star contracts, asking for the copyright to certain images or the right to police unauthorized use of images. Stars use the right of publicity—which prevents the commercial use of a star's image without permission—to target websites that try to profit from the use of the celebrity's name, likeness, voice, signature, and other forms of identity.[5] In the case of celebrity nudes, both real and fake, stars can use a combination of strategies, utilizing the right of publicity, the complaint that unauthorized nudes place the celebrity in a false light and inflict emotional distress, and the right to privacy for photographs that have never been published.

Stars have also threatened litigation against individuals who spread gossip that might damage a star's persona, and thus livelihood. When Tom Cruise sued "erotic wrestler" and gay porn actor Chad Slater (who claimed to have had a relationship with him), the case elicited astonishment and even amusement on the part of some observers. However, Cruise won the suit and a ten million dollar judgment (Anonymous 2003). The case served as a deterrent against those who might try to sell their stories—real or manufactured—to the press.

Still lawsuits have had uneven effects on the web, so the industry has come up with additional web-based strategies. Brad Pitt's lawyers, for instance, sent "Cease and desist" letters to individuals publishing a paparazzo's nude photos of him on the Internet. However, such threats don't always work. One website defiantly published not only the nude photos, but also the law firm's threatening letter

(American Photo Syndicate 1998). The uneven success of such threats led star management teams to adopt other web-based strategies such as expanding websites for stars and having their designers develop the necessary keywords, architecture, and other features that would ensure such websites came up first in search engines. They also maintain a constant surveillance of the web, acting immediately and if necessarily aggressively, against unwanted photos and stories. Corporate investment in the web has empowered Hollywood's leverage, since it has increased the stakes of lawsuits and introduced a more corporate sensibility on the web. For example, YouTube (owned by Google) charges its community to respect the copyright for Hollywood-owned material. Also it is difficult for a pornographic image to stay posted on YouTube for long. Such developments have enhanced Hollywood's ability to shape access to information on the web and to redirect surfer attention.

The proliferation of independent celebrity websites in the late 1990s seemed to suggest that the web would reconfigure the boundaries between public and private, between official and unofficial star discourse. Hollywood acted swiftly to try to reestablish those boundaries, but recent developments in web technology and culture have allowed fans to continue to subvert such efforts. Nude photos of Brad Pitt and other celebrities, fake photos, and fantasy gossip about stars' sexual adventures continue to circulate on the web. Twitter (2009), cell phone photography, and the increased speed of downloading images and clips have all made it easier for fans to produce and share their own images and celebrity gossip despite Hollywood's formidable efforts. It seems unlikely that Hollywood will ever be able to exert its old control over the images of its stars. Perhaps even more importantly, the rise of reality television, YouTube, and other amateur web production may be diminishing the centrality of Hollywood stars to viewer fantasies.

Notes

1 I would like to thank George Chauncey for his invaluable feedback and editing suggestions, in the formation of this work.
2 For a fuller account of Haines, see Mann (1998) and Gregg (2003).
3 The concept of "It" was coined by British novelist and screenwriter Elinor Glyn, to identity individuals who possessed sex appeal and was popularized by the Clara Bow feature film *It* (Clarence G. Badger, 1927, USA).
4 With his proven track record for adapting sophisticated comedies from stage to film, Ernst Lubitsch decided to adapt Noel Coward's notorious *Design for Living*, which opened on Broadway in 1933. Coward's play depicted the bohemian lives of its characters, which included promiscuity, a lack of respect for marriage, and implicitly homosexuality. The play, set in the worlds of art and theatre, follows the shifting sexual relationships of its main characters—Otto, Leo, and Gilda—and by the end of the play, the three bohemians finally reach the conclusion that only as a threesome can they find blissful fulfillment. Coward famously described the play as "three people who love each other very much." While downplaying—although not completely erasing—the homosexuality, Lubitsch's film version of *Design for Living* (1933, USA) still celebrates a bohemian lifestyle and the modern choice of living as a threesome instead of traditional marriage.

5 For an explanation of the "right of publicity" and its use by entertainment lawyers, see Artsandbusinessphilia (2009).

References

Adelman, B. 1997. *Tijuana bibles: Art and wit in America's forbidden funnies, 1930s–1950s.* New York: Simon & Schuster.
American Photo Syndicate. 1998. Brad Pitt Photos. http://www.american-photo.com/celebrity/brad_pitt/pittthreat.htm. [Accessed February 23, 1998] This website is no longer available.
Anonymous. 1933. Hollywood's Malibu Beach. *Vanity Fair*, August, p. 23–25.
Anonymous. 2003. Cruise wins "gay" claims legal battle. BBC. http://news.bbc.co.uk/2/hi/entertainment/2664159.stm. [Accessed January 16, 2003]
Artsandbusinessphilia. 2009. http://www.artsandbusinessphila.org/pvla/documents/RightofPublicity.pdf. [Accessed August 15, 2009]
Chauncey, G. 1994. *Gay New York: Gender, urban culture, and the making of the gay male world, 1890-1940.* New York: Basic Books.
Dee, F. 1933. Agreement dated May 18th 1933, between Francis Dee and RKO Studios.
Dyer, R. 1986. *Heavenly bodies.* New York: St. Martin's Press.
ESL Discussion Center. 1999. Pics of Ryan Philippe [sic], discussion group. http://www.eslcafe.com/discussion/wwwboard5/messages/1751.html. [Accessed March 22, 1999]
Gaines, J. 1991. *Contested culture: The image, the voice, and the law.* Chapel Hill, NC: University of North Carolina Press.
Gregg, R. 2003. Gay culture, studio publicity, and the management of star discourse: The homosexualization of William Haines in pre-code Hollywood. *Quarterly Review of Film and Video* 20(2): 81–98.
Jenkins, H. 1992. "Strangers no more, we sing": Filking and the social construction of the science fiction fan community. In *The adoring audience: Fan culture and popular media*, edited by L. A. Lewis. London: Routledge, 208–236.
Keanu Reeves Gossip. 1999. "Questionable Keanu" discussion group, *HWG (Hollywood Gossip)*, http://www.jtj.net/jtj/gossip_keanu.shtml [Accessed November 15, 1999]
Mann, W. J. 1998. *Wisecracker: The life and times of William Haines: Hollywood's first openly gay star.* New York: Penguin.
Martin, J. S. 1931. Third sex plague spreads anew! *Broadway Brevities*, November 2, 12, 16.
Menonthenet. 1998a. A surprise from Leo, by A Fan. http://www.menonthenet.com/EroticStories/index.cfm?m=article&ArticleRecId=288143 [Accessed March 22, 1998]
Menonthenet. 1998b. Rubbing off on Ryan, by BW. http://www.menonthenet.com/EroticStories/index.cfm?m=article&ArticleRecId=294683 [Accessed October 29, 1998]
Penley, C. 1991. Brownian motion: Women, tactics, and technology. In *Technoculture*, edited by C. Penley and A. Ross. Minneapolis: University of Minnesota Press, 135–161.
Twitter. 2009. http://twitter.com/ [Accessed August 15, 2009]
Weiss, A. 1993. *Vampires and violets: Lesbians in film.* New York: Penguin.

Chapter 11

Internet Fandom, Queer Discourse, and Identities

Rosalind Hanmer

Introduction

Ken Plummer (2003) tells us that:

> People increasingly have come to live their sexualities through, and with the aid of television, press, film and most recently, cyberspace ... As such it is a part of a growing concern amongst scholars of sexualities to "read" the ways in which the sexual is coded in our daily lives.
>
> (p. 275)

Personal readings and identifications of media texts potentially offer audiences new understandings of self and sexual identity. New media fan sites construct discursive arenas, where audiences not only investigate the text but also senses of self may be revealed and explored, potentially re-coding everyday sexual life. An example of this is how certain fans belonging to an online fandom left their marriages to live with women they met online while others travelled to other states or countries, taking their children with them to join other fans with their families. Some fans dealt with past negative experiences through their online fan performances and activities, whether on an individual or collective basis: "The discursive power of these performances creates the potential for the transgression of identity constructs" (Pullen 2006, p. 161).

This chapter captures such potential through discussing the performativity of a small number of fans that view *Xena: Warrior Princess* (MCA-TV, U.S. 1995–2001), and contribute to an online community called *Xenasubtextalk* (1998) (XSTT).[1] I suggest the XSTT interactive online lesbian fandom in the nineties is one of the forerunners to new media game narratives such as "Second Life"[2] that enables virtual sexual identities and "real life" identities to exist simultaneously in two different autonomous worlds. The implications of the imagined virtual world of XSTT, in contrast to the actual world that the fans live in, provoke tensions that carry over into the evolution of new media, as some of the snapshot extracts from the fans will illustrate.

Xena: Warrior Princess (XWP) was a popular and innovative television programme (Goodman 2009), as Sharon Ross states "Xena was one of the first television shows to promote website use, advertising its website via Universal Pictures at the end of every episode" (2008, p. 38). Although no overt sexual diversity is displayed in XWP, XSTT often capitalizes on a potential lesbian reading of characters and storylines. This chapter focuses on a "queer" discourse. My understanding of queer discourse, in this context, is a shared meaning, in the broadest sense of the word "queer," that developed through queer theory in relation to how sexual practices construct their own reality of meaning and identity. This XSTT discourse is a result of a queer reading that does not reflect a biological or predetermined reality, and is constructed and performed online in relation to fluid sexuality and identity, and questions the lived experiences and fan practices of six fans.

The XSTT fans are viewers of a mainstream adventure/fantasy genre that enables a plurality of readings including what has been interpreted as a queer reading by many media and cultural theorists; these include Morreale (1998), Innes (1999), Bennett (1999), Helford (2000), Pullen (2000), Hamming (2001), Gwenllian-Jones (2000, 2003), and Mendelsohn (2002). According to Morreale, "Xena and Gabrielle's ambiguous sexuality is a constant subject of speculation both in the press and among Xenites" (1998, p. 79).[3] The television series and its online fandom prompted many queer discussions on radio, television, and in the press. These discussions are carried over to the bulletin boards, newsgroups, and fan sites.

This chapter is part of a larger doctoral case study that involved twenty-three fans from the XSTT fandom. I selected fans for this study who I suggest through their interviews and queer discourse are able to express as a heterogeneous group the sociological and cultural changes that take place when they move from the local to the global in terms of their online fandom. The fans produce a queer[4] discourse that empowers them through their online fan practices.

Virtual queer fandom assists individuals to resist the hold of the local, in respect of a queer virtual online identity. What began for the six fans I interviewed as a localized habit of television viewing and discussions between close friends develops as the self becoming an "agent of culture in process" (Fiske 1990, p. 86). My understanding of Alexander Doty's process of agency, through the use of mass culture, is something that "comes to influence and reinforce the process of queer identity formation" (1993, p. 6). For these fans an online fan identity, and later a sexual or cultural identity, becomes something they can relate to as an evolving work in progress. This work in progress is the combination of the local and the global.

I suggest that the destabilization of the local is best described by Anthony Giddens in his book *The Consequences of Modernity* (1990) as "[the] disembedding mechanisms [that] lift social relations and the exchange of information out of specific time-space contexts, but at the same time provide new opportunities for their insertion" (p. 141). This is part of the development of the Internet and its online globally provided performance that the fans explore. This immediacy articulates the interactions between the fans and the text of XWP that "support[s] a reading hospitable to desire between women" (Bennett 1999, p. 1). The XSTT fandom was able to support and empower the fans to make sense of their everyday lives, through engaging online in a queer discourse.

The data investigation gathered through IRC (Internet Relay Chat)[5] interviews suggests that XWP and the online fan club sustain some of the fans' coming out narratives. Fan activities can shape identities on the Internet both individually and collectively. The conversations took place in real time synchronously, and the data during analysis revealed a queer discourse running through first, the television text, second, through the lesbian Internet fan site dedicated to the series and, third, through the fans' conversations and discussions during the interview procedures.

The collection of my doctorial research data was extracted from the XSTT fan site and emails over a twelve-month period from 2001 to 2002. All the fans' conversations in this chapter remain unaltered apart from the fact that the font has been changed to Perpetua for easier reading. The spelling and grammatical errors will remain as part of the fans' online personas. As a heterogeneous group the alleged identities of these six individuals were as married, single, bisexual, heterosexual, lesbian, and potentially lesbian, biological mothers and co-parents. Ages range from eighteen to mid forties at the time of interviews. Class and cultural backgrounds were mixed and they were geographically positioned between Europe and America. I suggest alleged identities because the Internet virtual environment can suggest no identities are authentic or lacking. Therefore it contests heteronormative dominant representations that imply everything else is deficient or incomplete.

The fans' employment status at the time of the interviews were High School Math Teacher, Press Printing Technician, Accountant, Unemployed, Hospital Laboratory Technician, and one fan whose status was unknown. The diversity of the fan base reflects my position as a queer, feminist, lesbian poststructuralist reader who positioned herself as a bricoleur[6] using an interdisciplinary hybrid methodology, as part of the process of research and as an interested party.

Ken Plummer's proposal that "story telling may come very close to the life as experienced" is borne out by the analysis of the fans' conversations and discussions (1995, p. 168). His understanding that we are now in the era of a "post-modern new age queer" identity or representations challenges the necessity for a new discourse (1995, p. 81). Although the lesbian identity has and continues to discuss stories that evoke images of "Amazons, or Sappho's" as does the text of XWP, the representations of same sex relationships through online discourse can be seen as supporting the rites of passage for the modern lesbian. However, the progressive world of the lesbian story needs a new discourse and for the XSTT fans, their online fandom provided this discourse in its newest form.

The discussions online were very intimate and go towards the understanding of how a virtual fan subject can communicate in real time, heightening their awareness of the fluidity of identity. Online fandom offers potential lesbian or queer fans a form of life writing that opens up electronic queer and real transgressive radical identities. While I do not suggest that the fans interviewed use their fan practices as a strategy for their coming out narratives, the on line conversations certainly provided such a space for a queer discourse to be articulated.

Queer Reading

I argue that the fans use their queer reading of XWP's female protagonists' relationship to reshape, rethink, and rewrite their own changing and challenging sexual and cultural identities. John Fiske (1989) argues that television has the "ability to empower the subordinate by providing the opportunity of making resisting meanings of text, society and subjectivity" in its representations, and to engage with disenfranchised groups (p. 59). Linking this with Alan Sinfield's (2005 [originally 1994]) notion of cultural politics and queer readings, my understanding is that both authors challenge and question the stability of normative cultural practices while engaging with real life experiences. The cultural positioning of fandom and its practices can adhere to a queer reading in terms of cultural capital and agency and the cultural production of fandom. Certain fans gained confidence, self-esteem, and a form of agency by being able to discuss each episode in a friendly respectful environment. Agency for these fans means to have a socially determined capability to act on their own, to be aware of their ever-evolving identities that help form their lived experiences. Moreover, I argue that their online fan practices can be beneficial in a therapeutic way that can enhance the outcome of their life narratives.

The XSTT fan site enables fans to share their feelings of anxiety, isolation, and incompleteness, experiencing this negativity before entering into the online fan practices. These fans do not necessarily self-identify as queer, but for the purpose of this study are positioned as queer in terms of their ever-evolving economic, social, political, cultural, and geographical identities. I argue that fans can transgress previous sexual identity categories by responding to the representations of the characters of Xena and Gabrielle in the XWP text by engaging and challenging normative readings. They do this through their online queer discussions on both an individual and collective basis, as their life stories are interpreted as existing "in a space of possibility" (Bennett 1999, p. 5). Some of the fans have created, through their written online conversations, new sexual identities. The fans' interactive performance as an imagined virtual community "is imagined because even the members of the smallest nation will never know most of the fellow-members or meet them, or even hear of them, yet in the minds of each lives the image of their communion" (Anderson 2006, p. 6). In terms of fandom it allows individuals around the world to communicate and share similar interests and not be limited by geographical, spatial, and physical boundaries. Although they may never get to meet each other face-to-face (some do) they are linked as a community through their online discourse.

Xena: Warrior Princess and **Xenasubtextalk Fans**

During its six-year run from 1995 to 2001, the television series of XWP and the growth and development of the Internet ran parallel. Both the fans and the creators and crew of XWP became aware of the possibilities of online fandom and its capacity to inform a rapidly expanding audience. According to Sara Gwenllian-Jones (2000):

> From the outset, XWP fan culture has been predominantly Net-based. Online XWP fandom constitutes a vast conceptual territory that fans refer to as "the Xenaverse", a multimedia "environment" that encompasses everything relating to the series, from its production to its diegesis to fan-produced tests. ... In general, online fan cultures are bigger, better looking, easier to access, and much cooler than their offline equivalents.
>
> (p. 407)

I am suggesting that the lesbian or queer subject can define their desires, fantasies, readings, writings, and experiences as possessing a queer sensibility. Queer in this context is defined as a "coming out" narrative journey or as an acknowledgement of the transient notion of identity or sexuality and what it holds in terms of possibilities. The representation of Xena and Gabrielle's sexuality in XWP is the main theme of the discussions on the bulletin boards of the XSTT fan site.

Although the XSTT fan club is designated and marketed on the Internet as a lesbian site, therefore reiterating the articulation of lesbian identity, its format and public space becomes part of a subversive tool that destabilizes the constructed nature of a lesbian stereotypical fan identity. As a subversive tool the site does not exclude any form of transgressive identity, while still hailing the lesbian fan in terms of its repetition. In this instance the subversive potential overrides the performance, becoming part of a political queer discourse. Fans visiting this site interact with other fans in transgressing and breaking the codes of dominant cultural inscriptions of stereotypical identity.

The Fans' Interviews

An example of subversion can be seen in the queer discourse of a fan whose online pseudonym is "malki_35." All the fans interviewed are from the XSTT fan club (2001). This fan has friends on various sites and frequently engages in fan practices that include postings on the bulletin boards, joining the chat room discussions, and purchasing fan artifacts. This fan's self-identification of "I'm straight," in response to a question from me, is complex and interesting. When she was asked during the interview: "Do you think lesbians explore their identity through the series of XWP?" her reply was: "I don't know if explore is the right word maybe identify is better." When asked: "what are your favorite episodes?" malki_35 replied from what could be argued a queer sensibility:

> That is a tough one I have a few episodes I consider my favourites. *One Against An Army: Bitter Suite* and *Many Happy* Returns - What is the most memorable thing that happened on the show? Well for one "The Bite" in "Girls Just Wanna Have Fun", the first hot tub scene in " A Day in the Life", Gabrielle dying and Xena trying to do CPR on her in "Is There a Doctor In The House" there really is quite a few.

All these episodes are considered to contain strong lesbian or queer connotations in the plotline and have many scenes with Xena and Gabrielle hugging, kissing and enacting the role of lovers. The XSTT fan site provides the space for fans like malki_35 to converse with other fans regardless of the complexity of their political, social or cultural circumstances.

Support for this argument can be found in Shelley Correll's (1995) "Ethnography of an Electronic Bar" in which she interprets an interview given by a woman visiting an online virtual lesbian café/bar. The woman explains the reasons why she frequents this virtual space and community:

> Because of the pressures from family and friends, I lead a very straight life. The LC is the only place I can really feel "at home". For me the LC is an outlet. Somewhere I can go to get out of my reality.
> (Cited in Correll 1995, p. 283)

I would argue that the virtual space of XSTT could also be a place for intimate communications if requested, but hasten to add that it is a space that is mostly self-regulating even though there are gatekeepers[7] of the site. It is assumed that there are some levels or expectations of some levels of safety, so the risk factor is minimal. For people who do not identify as lesbian or queer, a virtual space enables them to still explore and experience a lesbian or queer community without fear of recognition or judgment. This fan's self-identification as straight was not requested during my interview and is not required in order to join the XSTT fan club; but the need to express a normative position in terms of sexual identity was obviously important. In the virtual community of XSTT, discrimination or exclusion is not part of the sphere of activity, and anyone can share a lesbian or queer experience without having to state that they may be questioning their own identity. XSTT as a part of new media online fandom has this potential function.

One fan expresses her identification and empathy with the television series's main protagonists; identifying with Xena's displeasures and Gabrielle's naivety, magmor writes:

> I identify strongly with *Xena's* terrible emotional repression – I managed to repress my lesbianism for over 18 years – and how she can flip into those rages. However, I also identify with Gabrielle a baby starting off on a great adventure, as I'm only three years out to myself, two and a half out on the scene.

The investment this fan has in Xena/Gabrielle's relationship and their television adventures suggests awareness that the show is not real, and yet she can conceive that embedded in the plot's superficiality and fantasy is an important moral tale. The tale is one of "being true to yourself." This fan has struggled with the repression of her sexual identity for a number of years, but through her online fan activities she has come to terms with her identity gaining empowerment. According to Gwenllian-Jones "fans recruit and interpret XWP so that they may further react to the text of the world ... by producing other texts" (2000, p. 406). Queer discourse is what informs their production of other texts online.

Empowerment

As Kirsten Pullen (2000) tells us, fans such as those who identity with Xena "are not fringe extremists with an unhealthy and unrealistic interest in particular media text, but savvy consumers who are able to use popular culture to fulfill their desires and needs, often explicitly rearticulating that culture in unique and empowering ways" (p. 53). The queer text of XWP and my interpretation of the online fandom proposes that some fans can gain a sense of agency and empowerment by reflecting on their internalized homophobic past that may have restricted their sexual autonomy. One fan called texArd had this to say about her identity:

> I knew when I was in high school that I was gay, but I was raised in a very strict Southern Baptist home. Being gay was a sin and definitely NOT an option. I was supposed to grow up, go to college, get married and have children. So that's what I did ... 2 husbands and 3 kids.

This fan's early life of residing in the South Coast of the U.S., in a state commonly known to be part of the "Bible belt" where many people hold conservative traditional family values, contributed to a belief system that anything other than a normative heterosexual lifestyle is aberrant. Part of the interview statement supports the language of oppression this fan lived under. Continuing the coming out experience, and understanding that there were now different choices available in terms of sexual identities, this fan discovered a new identity, a new home, and a new family:

> TexArd: After nearly a year, I sold my house, quit my teaching job, and moved me and my kids 1000 miles away to be with her. We have been together now for nearly 3 years, and I couldn't be happier.

What became more palpable as the interviews continued was the fans' desire for Xena and Gabrielle's love/sexual relationship to be fulfilled on screen, but they also wanted their own sexual/love desire to become a reality. Some fans had repressed these desires due to fear of being labeled as deviant, or through simply not having the opportunity before.

Mary Anne Doane's (1989) work uses the departmental store window as a metaphor for the gaze of the audience in a cinema, suggesting that the gaze can be likened to window-shopping. Gaines (1989, p. 50) develops this metaphor by suggesting that the holder of the gaze has no obligation to purchase anything but gains pleasure from their spectatorship. Adopting this allegory of erotic window-shopping as part of queer fan online practices, I suggest the XSTT online fandom takes this one stage further: some of the fans decide to cross the boundaries between "looking" and "having" in relation to window-shopping during their fan performances. Fans such as Critter 69_78 realize the magnitude of their desires and decided to take action.

To demonstrate this window-shopping experience, one of the fans interviewed – Critter 69_78 – states:

> i was married for about 22 years when all the while i always felt more drawn to women ..... i divorced last year and ever since have been coming to terms that i am a lesbian and i also have a girlfriend helping me as well ...

Online fan practice and fandom can provide a variety of life-changing situations for fans. My conversations revealed that some fans began as just viewers who enjoyed the XWP series but then decided to surf the Internet looking for information on XWP. Others using the Internet decided to delve more into the fan sub cultural practices online. Some fans decided to move house, or leave their jobs and start new lives with their new friends or lovers found through their online fan activities. Others started to write and publish fan fiction stories about their lives that ran parallel to the protagonists' development within the series.

Reneeg33, who suffered from domestic violence for over a decade, provides a good illustration of this. The friends she made through her fandom helped her leave the relationship after a very bad beating that left her hospitalized. She now felt sufficiently confident to discuss with other fans the domestic violence and her potentially dangerous, and at times life-threatening, situation. Reneeg33 began to surf the net looking for fan material, and came across a fan fiction writer's site. Her journey is one of courage and at the same time compassion for the person who treated her so badly. During her visits to the fan sites to have discussions with other fans, Reneeg 33's sexual identity evolved, moving towards an identity that felt more comfortable, and one that brought empowerment and happiness.

> Reneeg 33: you see i was married. it was bad. it was an abusive marriage and well when it was reruns for the summer for xena … my need for new xena stuff i started searching the web for stuff on her i had about 5 friends from the list that made sure they were there on line every night. realised that I was gay … now days I'm much happier …

XWP and its online fan site potentially offer diverse possibility. As Elyce Rae Helford (2000) tells us, feminists and LGBT "activists applaud the series for its strong woman-identified and ambiguously sexualized female hero constantly discussing the characters' representation and its cultural phenomenon" (p. 135). However I would argue that XSTT fans who questioned their sexual and cultural identity through their queer readings are the true heroes of the XWP narrative. Queer reading of a text is important for the outcast and dispossessed. A cultural politics of resistance and lesbian and queer subculture can be understood in the use of a quote by Teresa de Lauretis taken from Elizabeth Ellsworth's findings on the film *Personal Best* (1982) in which she tells us:

> Lesbian feminist reviewers adjusted the meanings proposed in conventional (Hollywood) codes of representations. They redefined the protagonist; ignored sections focused on heterosexual romance, disregarded the actual ending, and discovered apparently unintended erotic moments.
> (Sinfield 2005, p. 66)

The Internet and online fandom supports and sustains an oppositional reading towards dominant systems. Billenomates18: is a young unemployed XSTT fan who lives in a poor social area of the North East in Britain and whose schooling was very minimal. She is an avid fan who gained self-esteem and personal empowerment from XWP online fandom. At school, this young fan underwent a traumatic time. She became unemployed after working for a while, training to be a nursery nurse, and she felt let down by the system. She interpreted Xena's characteristics and adventures in a positive way in order to support her emotional stability.

Two questions I put to this fan during our conversations were: "I want to know if the television show has helped women to deal with their identity?" And, "Do you think you have changed since watching the show?"

billienomates18: replied:

> Some have changed a lot I know I've changed a lot and I'm bisexual. ... I feel stronger in myself when I was at school I wasn't strong I was bullied then I started to watch xena I started to ignore the bullies ... I think young girls watch it cos there fighting and action in it and adults women watch it cos they proble been hit by there husbands or boyfriends and they might feel strong in them self thinking they could be strong like xena.

The benefit gained through Internet fandom for this particular young fan helped her construct her cultural and sexual identity in a society where she is deemed an outsider. I would argue that for this fan, online fandom offers a therapeutic experience in that billionomates18: was able to "triumph over the past" (Plummer 2001, 193). Her choice of pseudonym is indicative of the isolation and low self-esteem, yet simultaneously reveals a confidence in self through her intimate disclosure.

Conclusion

Many of the fans' stories involve revelation and the challenging of identities; their heroic gestures to change their life histories have run parallel to their objects of fandom Xena and Gabrielle. These gestures are political in every detail, and the participation of these fans in developing a queerer discursive networking fandom removes the marginalized notion of traditional fandom and suggests a more democratic online "coming out" narrative. Arguably the XSTT fan site supports lesbians, but as Alexander Doty (1993) argues "the queer often operates within the nonqueer, as the nonqueer does within the queer" (p. xv), indicating ambivalence and the blurring of distinctions with regard to identity. Consequently online fandom itself engenders the potential for queer discourse in its focus on transience and fluidity in identity, and means that various readings may be possible. To this end XSTT as an online fandom offers both the opportunity for agency, and the stimulation of identification. In some instances this may result in action, as evident in the case studies above where fans were encouraged to announce their concealed sexual identity. However what must also be apparent is the potential to read a queer identity in isolation, publicly unannounced, and its therapeutic benefits. In this way the site is multivalent in identity potential, offering move to action, besides consolation and reassurances to senses of self.

As Ken Plummer (1995) tell us with regards to coming to terms with sexual identity: "the most common strategy for doing this is to gain access to new social worlds—an access to storytellers open to coaxing and coaching into the tales of gay and lesbian life" (p. 89). The fans of *Xena: Warrior Princess* discover these tales through reinvention and intense identification within the textual exchanges in

Xenasubtextalk. These may not be literal or immediately transferable narratives; however through queer pleasure and personal reading, these shared stories stimulate contexts of empowerment offering personal, social, and political change.

Notes

1 Three self-identified lesbians set up an online fan club called Xenasubtexttalk in October 1998.
2 "Second Life" is a virtual narrative game that involves a 3D world where users socialize, create and connect by voice and by using text.
3 Xenite is the name given to the fans of the television series of *Xena: Warrior Princess*.
4 Queer in this sense is a non-heteronormative online dialogue between the fans that came about through viewing the television text of XWP and its narrative then going online and discussing the programme and highlighting how it affected the fans individually and collectively.
5 Computer-mediated communications now allow the interviewer to use a web cam (small camera), and the video and audio facilities of new media have developed immensely since the time of my interviews when these resources where still in their infancy.
6 "The bricoleur produces a bricolage[,] that is pieced together, a close knit set of practices that provides solutions to problems in a concrete situation" (Weinstein and Weinstein 1991, p. 161).
7 Gatekeeper is a term that refers to people who set up the online fine site club and they are responsible for the updating of information and the scrutiny of the site; however, this term has changed since the search engines have increased, as they seem to be doing the job of the gatekeepers now.

References

Anderson, B. 2006. *Imagined communities: Reflections on the origin and spread of nationalism*. London: Verso.
Bennett, K. 1999. Xena Warrior Princess, desire between women, and interpretive response. http://www.drizzle.com/~kathleen/xena-p5 [Accessed in November 2003]
Butler, J. 1993. *Bodies that matter: On the discursive limits of "sex."* New York: Routledge.
Correll, S. 1995. The ethnography of an electronic bar: The Lesbian Café. *Journal of Contemporary Ethnography* 24(3): 270–298.
Doane, M. A. 1989. The economy of desire, the commodity form in/of the cinema. *Quarterly Review of Film* 11(1): 27.
Doty, A. 1993. *Making things perfectly queer: Interpreting mass culture*. Minneapolis: University of Minnesota Press.
Fiske, J. 1989. *Understanding popular culture*. Boston, MA: Unwin Hyman.
Fiske, J. 1990. Ethnosemiotics: Some personal and theoretical reflections. *Cultural Studies* 4(1): 85–99.
Gaines, J. 1989. The Queen Christina tie ups: Convergence of show window and screen. *Quarterly Review of Film and Video* 11(1): 35–60.

Giddens, A. 1990. *Consequences of Modernity*. Stanford: Stanford University Press.

Goodman, T. 2009. The Xena-philes: TV's warrior princess draws a mighty following. *Contra Costa Times* (US), November 17, 1996. http://www.ausxip.com/articles/1996/contracosta1196.php [Accessed December 20, 2009]

Gwenllian-Jones, S. 2000. Histories, fictions and Xena: Warrior princess. *Television and new media* 4: 403–418.

Gwenllian-Jones, S. 2003. Starring Lucy Lawless. *Continuum: Journal of Media and Cultural Studies* 14(1): 9–22.

Hamming, J. 2001. Whatever turns you on: Becoming-lesbian and the production of desire in the Xenaverse. Genders. http://www/genders.org/g34/g34_hamming.txt [Accessed October 20, 2001]

Helford, E. R. 2000. *Fantasy girls: Gender in the new universe of science fiction and fantasy television*. Lanham, MD: Rowman & Littlefield.

Hills, M. 2002. *Fan culture*. London: Routledge.

Innes, S. 1999. *Tough girls, women warriors and wonder women in popular culture*. Philadelphia: University of Pennsylvania Press.

Mendelsohn, F. 2002. Surpassing the love of vampires: Or why and (how) a queer reading of the Buffy/Willow relationship is denied in fighting the forces. In *What's at stake in Buffy the Vampire Slayer*, edited by R. Wilcox and D. Lavery. Lanham, MD: Rowman & Littlefield, 45–60.

Morreale, J. 1998. Xena Warrior Princess as feminist camp. *Journal of Popular Culture* (Autumn): 79.

Plummer, K. 1995. *Telling sexual stories: Power, change and social worlds*. London and New York: Routledge.

Plummer, K. 2001. *Documents of life. An invitation to a critical humanism*. London: Sage.

Plummer, K. 2003. Re-presenting sexualities in the media. *Sexualities* 6 (3/4): 275–276.

Pullen, C. 2006. Gay performativity and reality television: Alliances, competition and discourse. In *The new queer aesthetic on television: Essays on recent programming*, edited by J. Keller and L. Strayner. Jefferson, NC: McFarland.

Pullen, K. 2000. I-love-Xena.com: Creating online fan communities. In *Web studies: Rewiring media studies for the digital age*, edited by D. Gauntlett. London: Arnold, 53.

Ross, S. 2008. *Beyond the box: Television and the internet*. Oxford: Blackwell.

Sinfield, A. 2005 [1994]. *Cultural politics—Queer reading*, rep. London: Routledge.

Weinstein, D. and Weinstein, M. A. 1991. George Simmel: Sociological flaneur bricoleur. In *Theory, culture and society, Vol. 8*. London: Sage, 151–168.

XSTT Fan Club. 2001. http://messages.clubs.yahoocom/clubs/xe . . . d=xeansubtextalk&sid=13013546&mid=6417 [Accessed October 20, 2001]

Chapter 12

Transconversations
New Media, Community, and Identity

Monica Edwards

Introduction

A significant tradition in studies of media, in both cultural studies and sociology, has been to explore texts, and how audiences read them. Often, these works explore hegemonic and counter-hegemonic discourse, and inquire how attitudes are shaped by these discourses. Of the scholarship that focuses on the increasing representation of gays and lesbians in the media, some discussions center on negative versus positive stereotypes, and how these stereotypes affect gay and lesbian identities, such as Larry Gross's work that looks at "symbolic annihilation" and how media shapes the closet (Gross and Woods 1999). Other scholars, such as Evan Cooper (2003), are interested in whether this changing media landscape improves heterosexual audiences' attitudes about gays and lesbians. However, this chapter does not directly address explorations of texts and attitudes, but instead aims to articulate the ways that these cultural products get taken up by audiences, as resources in negotiating interactions and identities in their everyday lives. Furthermore, this chapter examines how representations become key factors in how lesbians talk about, and experience, their and others' place in the larger (imagined) lesbian community. The progressive television drama series *The L Word* is taken up as a key frame in conversations about lesbians in everyday life.

New to the scene of television, and noticeably underexplored within academic work, are such groundbreaking shows as *Queer as Folk* and *The L Word*, shows (both produced by Showtime) that revolve around the lives of gay men, and lesbian, bisexual, and transgender women. These shows move beyond the confines of "stereotypical" gay characters on shows such as *Will & Grace* and *Friends*, as critiqued in earlier research (Ingraham 2008; Raymond 2002) of the solitary "gay best friend," or other isolated and asexual character tropes. *Queer as Folk*, a show that depicts the lives of gay men, was important, and while there was a lesbian couple as part of the cast, the show's main focus was on men. Thus, awaiting *The L Word*'s 2004 premiere, I knew as an academic, a lesbian, and a television watcher that this was an important transition in media representations—the first show that centered on lesbian sexuality and the lesbian community. As Candace Moore

(2007) notes, "lesbians have historically been a latent, ghostly figure in visual culture [and as a result] it might be argued that *The L Word*—by allowing the 'invisibility' of queer female communities to find televisibility—has instigated a significant paradigmatic rupture" (pp. 5–6). Conversations, and anticipations, about the show began immediately—in the media and everyday life. I began observing internet forum discussions centering on episode narratives, noticing that the audiences' conversations about this show transitioned through various dialogical tropes and turned into discussions about the lesbian community more generally.

First and foremost, conversations erupted regarding the lack of "butch"—masculine—gender representation; the women in the show looked as Hollywood chic, not that dissimilar to all the "straight" women on television. After only a few episodes aired in 2004, this (excerpt of a) letter to the editor appeared in *The Advocate*:

> Where is the representation? Most of us don't wear our pants below our navels and have our hair done regularly. Lots of us live in the country. Portray a REAL lifestyle, where making love at night is not our only pastime. This show is not a valid representation of who we are…
>
> (PlanetOut 2004)

By engaging with the literature and observing online discussion forums, I can see that many scholars and audience members are invested in the politics of representation. These conversations and debates have become the basis of this research on the complex dynamic between sexuality, media, and everyday life.

Methodology and Methods

Media audiences actively engage with media texts, as both consumers and producers (for example as fan fiction writers, bloggers, script writers, etc . . .). This study is an exploration of a *process* of interpretation, reaction, acceptance, rejection, incorporation; a process of exploration where media texts are understood as a starting point in a contextualized audience participation process. For this study I have engaged in what Ward (2008) calls "cyber-ethnography," which is "a way of taking seriously online interactions in their own right, exploring them through a reflexively sensitive process that includes active involvement in online settings and interviews with participants" (Hine 2009). I observed discussion forum conversations on three different websites—"L-Wordonline," "afterellen," and "ourchart" (see also Showtime 2009)—revolving around *The L Word*, and engaged in email interviews with users, doing this after making my presence as a researcher known. I selected these websites because their missions are to serve the lesbian community, and both had discussion forums solely dedicated to *The L Word*. Furthermore, it was evident on these sites that the majority of participants self-identified as lesbian, bisexual, or queer. All participants are given pseudonyms in the reporting of the data.

As Hillier and Harrison (2007) state, "... new information technologies such as the internet have the potential to fundamentally change the way we relate to self and others; the way we think, the nature of our sexuality, the form of our communities and our very identities" (p. 83). These online conversations are an important source of knowledge, given the frequency with which individuals participate, and given the direction these conversations take. Thousands of people go online to discuss *The L Word* (and other shows) ranging from critiques of writing and acting, to emotional reactions to storylines, to frustrations with stereotypes. This participation illuminates the importance of queer media in individuals' lives, and exploring these conversations can shed light on *why* this is so. In such a location, we can map the intersection of pop culture, sexuality, and identity within the lesbian community, where a television show about lesbians is the starting point of an expansive online community worthy of sociological attention.

This chapter uses a queer lens in exploring the relationship between media and sexuality in everyday life, where queer represents disruption and change. As a result, my focus is on how sexuality is changing, or rather, shifting; how sexualities, as expressed in everyday life, are being transformed. Sasha Roseneil (2008) states, "speaking of sexual differences is vital, but we must be aware that pinning them down and delineating membership of sexual categories is impossible," while Gamson and Moon theorize that sexual identities are a product of historical and social negotiations (2004). Scholars frame sexuality as a social product rather than a natural fact; sociologists of sexualities understand sexual identities and consider behaviors to be shifting and permeable.

It is my belief that media texts such as *The L Word* are playing a significant role in instigating such a conversation in everyday life. Using a queer lens does not mean interviewing queer identified individuals, but rather looks at how life is being *queered* through changing approaches to, and ideas about, sex(uality). Halperin argues that "queer is by definition whatever is at odds with the normal, the legitimate, the dominant" (cited in Moore 2007, p. 9). I regard queer as anything that challenges heteronormativity, binary structures of sex/gender/sexuality, universalizing explanations of sexuality, and/or discourses of essentialism.

The focus of this chapter is the queer challenge facing the lesbian community through the text of *The L Word*. This queer challenge comes in the form of storylines that are engaging lesbian audiences around the idea of fluid—not static or essential—expressions of lesbian sexuality and gender. My approach follows the trajectory of Sally Hines's queer sociology that "examines how power is discursively produced and materially produced and resisted at the macro level, alongside analyzing subjective experience at a micro level" (2006, p. 52). Within this framework, I will explore how macro level institutions such as the media, and the cultural discourses that emerge from media texts, are incorporated into the micro level of everyday life. I agree with Sasha Roseneil (2008) who writes, "... the ideas and images of the sexual which permeate our every day world through popular culture are of considerable importance in framing the cultural imaginaries within which people lead their lives and construct their identities and relationships." Media texts such as *The L Word* should be taken seriously, not as static cultural objects, but as dynamic components of a larger process of meaning-making and a primary location through which individuals insert and situate themselves into their culture.

Representations

This chapter is, in part, a study of representations. This is a politically informed approach to *The L Word* that connects the television show to the everyday lives of viewers. As Richard Dyer (1993) argues, "how social groups are treated in cultural representation is part and parcel of how they are treated in life" (p. 1). This is not a macro-ideological textual analysis, but rather an exploration of how media texts become embedded in everyday life and become implicated in queer transformations of sexual and social life. Kathleen Farrell (2006) points out that, "as sociologists, we must explore the ways in which these media institutions interact with individuals and the ways that media viewers actively make sense of these powerful systems and the representations they impart" (p. 195). This chapter continues this conversation of exploring the ways that audiences are interacting with the media. The issue of representation is clearly a driving force in the online community's discussion of the show.

Representation on *The L Word* becomes a mirror for lesbians to look into to assess their community; the show is making the community look back at itself in a new way. The issue of representation, then, becomes important not in and of itself, but because the *visual* becomes a conversation about the *material*. Audiences are talking fervently about whether they "see themselves" in the show, all the while describing what they "look like" in a way that expands the community's understanding of itself and its diversity.

For example, one forum participant states that, "as a young, anorexic city girl (call me a lipstick lesbian if you will) I realize that I do not represent the entirety of the dyke community," while another writes, "then again, I'm somewhere between femme and soft butch, gothic and Native American, so I didn't expect to see myself represented on the show." Another poster writes that, "I think it's definitely an important question, but the issue that I have, is that it's impossible to represent all lesbians. We're all vastly different—with different styles, ethnicity, levels of affluence or poverty," while still another writes that, "I just find it extremely forced and pandering to stereotypes." It becomes immediately clear that those audience members who are active online deeply care about representation, though each from her own contextual location. We also learn about the range of individuals who claim belongingness to the lesbian community—white girls, Native Americans, anorexics, poor lesbians, etc. As a result, through this debate about representation, we learn more about a diverse community. What *The L Word* does, then, is make visible—through the show itself and conversations about it—stories of lesbian life in the twenty-first century on the screen, on the internet, at bars, and in homes, as audiences watch and talk about the show. I argue it is through audiences' engagement with representations that these stories of lesbians' everyday life get told. In the context of lesbian invisibility, *The L Word* is both telling these stories in the text, and instigating these stories from audiences as they experience the show.

A queer discourse has emerged at times on the television show and in the audience community's lexicon. For example, Shane, a character on the show, is quoted as saying, "sexuality is fluid, whether you're gay, you're straight, or you're bisexual, you just go with the flow." While Alice, in the same conversation says, "most girls are straight until they're not, and sometimes they are gay until they're not." Not only do we see the usage of the word "fluid" to describe sexuality, we see, written into the script, a conversation framed around unstable sexualities. Similarly, one discussion board participant stated (in response to a sex scene including Max, a transgender character):

> The fact that they're willing to take what little precious time Max has and show us that he's the queerest of the queer is awesome…This show has supposedly stressed the fluidity of gender and sexuality, but the only one we really see any of that in is Max…
>
> (Tina, Our Chart Forum 2008)

This comment is centered on the notion of fluid sexuality illustrating how this has been incorporated, both inside the show's script and outside, addressing the everyday world. In addition, this audience member is potentially engaged in what Stuart Hall (1997) refers to as a "counter-strategy" that works to "intervene in representation" (p. 277). That is, this conversation is part of the "'politics of representation' [that is] a struggle over meaning which continues and is unfinished" (Hall 1997, p. 277). The following quotes are part of the same conversation that the character of Tina (above) participated in:

> OOOKKKKK I'm sorry but can I just say … that whole thing with max and the translator was not hot at all!!! Lol it was more just disturbing … the translator was just a bystander, not really a character anyways and max … just let him like girls already!! Stop making things too complicated. I'm getting frustrated!!!" (Mary, Our Chart Forum 2008)

> Who really cares?? I, for one and maybe the only one, was pleased to see the Max character happy with someone. Good for him/her and most of all good

for IC to allow the "border" characters some form of pleasure. Most people, in real life, have people that they enjoy spending time with. Why should Max be any different? Max has long been confused and tormented. I was happy to see him smile and appear as if there is, indeed, some type of pot at the end of his rainbow. Kudos to you, Ilene.

(Julie, Our Chart Forum 2008).

This displays evidence of a continuing conversation, which might be related to Stuart Hall's ideas, where meanings and ideas are debated, rendered complicated and contradictory.

It is my belief that this dialogue produces discourse, stimulating estimations as to what the community looks like, and potentially influences how it should be represented visually. These conversations weave back and forth between the T.V. show and the forum, potentially relating the participants' (auto)biographies as becoming one larger conversation about sexuality, gender and the negotiation of everyday lives. We can see through these conversations how difference is handled; the extent to which difference is used as a bridge or a wall, illuminating an on-going process of meaning-making, and of defining the borders of the community.

As part of the dialogue about borders, two topics that pervade the discussion forums of afterellen.com (2008a, 2008b, 2008c) and ourchart.com (2008) are "bisexuality" and "transgender"—issues that emerge via *The L Word* characters Alice, Tina, and Moira/Max. Discussions about these topics deal with the question of "who belongs" to the lesbian community and makes clear what expectations the lesbian community has in terms of representations. These representations are seen as reflections of the "reality" of lesbian life; however, on the issues of bisexuality and transgender, it becomes clear that "reality" is a point of contestation. Gamson et al. (1992) write that "television imagery is a site of struggle" and that "the undetermined nature of media discourse allows plenty of room for challengers . . . to offer competing constructions of reality and to find support for them from readers whose daily lives may lead them to construct meaning in ways that go beyond media imagery" (p. 373). Audiences of *The L Word* are engaged with the show in such a way as to make such contestations visible.

Anti-bisexual and transgender sentiments are often framed by posters as an issue addressing stereotypical plot trajectory, and as a concern about representation (how it will be viewed by non-lesbian others), rather than as a personal bias against bisexuals or transgender people. For example, one poster writes, "I can't believe the Tina storyline. Let's just perpetuate the idea that what all lesbians really need to solve their lifes problem is a nice hard cock. Who wrote that crap and why?" (Gina, After Ellen Forum 2008a), while another writes, "I don't understand why, when we finally get a butch-identified lesbian [Moira/Max] on the show, she has to be transgender. I think it gives a really incorrect idea of what being butch really means . . ." (Rochelle, After Ellen Forum 2008b). Clearly these posters frame the issue as one of representation—of how this one character's story can be seen as reflective of *all* lesbians, thus perpetuating problematic stereotypes. At the same time, these statements and discussions can also be read as very protective of the lesbian community as a woman-only space, as directly against or negative towards bi and trans-women in the lesbian community; of deciding who we are and who we are not (Gamson 1997, 179).

Many of these critiques are brought into a group discussion, and the trajectories of conversations are always grounded within a personal context, as well as situated within a plot-line of the show. For example, forum conversations concerning Max (the transgender character) are predominantly connected to personal examples, situating Max within a larger community rather than isolating him as a "story," thus connecting his character to the lesbian community at large. He is understood to have a potential real-life impact. The discourse that emerges from audiences' conversations attempts to connect Max's story to the imagined real world. And, as Cohen (1996) points out, "contestation of identity has tangible effects, influencing the distribution of resources . . ." (p. 6). One poster writes that in her opinion,

> "this show is an embarrassment to our community and serves as an injustice to all that we are fighting for. It is a dangerous threat to the civil rights we seek to portray us as pathological, irresponsible, non-working, non-committed, freaks who 'choose' this 'lifestyle' ..."
>
> (Diana, L-Word.com 2006).

This poster's concern illuminates audiences' concerns over these "tangible effects," as cultivation theory argues that audiences use television as a source of information about the "real" world (Good 2007). Cultural representations serve as points of location to negotiate boundaries and collective identity as it connects to the political landscape (e.g. the gay rights movement). An online forum about television representation transforms into a discussion of material, everyday experiences as seen through the lens of representation on *The L Word*.

Transconversations

For the remainder of this chapter I will focus on one character in the show—Moira/Max—addressing the issue of transgender representation in the lesbian community. To be clear, this is not general analysis of transgender representation; rather, it is a specific conversation about transgender presence on *The L Word* and in the lesbian community. I argue that Max's character is a clear example of the shared process of defining the terms of the lesbian community—what Judith Halberstam calls the "butch/FTM border wars" (Coogan 2006, p. 18). According to

Coogan, these wars are "intense, yet sometimes subtly articulated, political battles waged by differing marginal subjects for visibility and inclusion within, as well as affiliation with, lesbian communities" (2006, p. 18). *The L Word* creators, then, are serving to facilitate discussion about these boundaries by writing Max into the story. The ensuing conversations are both part of the border wars, and analysis of them.

Max's character was introduced during the third season (2006) as "Moira," a butch lesbian dating Jenny, a main character on the show. Moira's entrance was well publicized, and seems to have emerged as a direct consequence of the fans' critiques of the lack of butch representation in the show. Afterellen.com quotes Ilene Chaiken, the show's creator, as saying of Moira, "She's our first real butch on the show—a fabulously attractive butch, but nonetheless a real butch" (Lo 2006). It became immediately clear that Moira was a gender bender, and after a few episodes it was evident that this gender bending included passing as a man. By mid-season, Moira began the transformation to Max.

This transformation has been complex: at first playing with clothes and "packing" (creating the appearance of a penis), then taking testosterone. He contemplated "top" surgery alongside a friend with breast cancer, he has been "in the closet" passing as a heterosexual man at work, and he latterly appears as an out non-operative trans-man. His self-presentation and identity has shifted across the various contexts of his relationships. Just before he began using testosterone, he presented as, and was interpreted as, a butch lesbian in the context of his relationship with Jenny. Later, he presented as male, and was accepted as male, in his place of work, where he began to date a woman. In this context, he was not out as a transgender person. He experienced himself, and was read, as a straight man. His character and his character's intimate relationships illuminate the complexities of gender and sexuality. Raine Dozier's research on trans-men documents this dynamic, as she writes that trans-men

> ... illustrate the relativity of sexual orientation. Sexual orientation is based not exclusively on object attraction but also on the gendered meanings created in sexual and romantic interaction. Sexual orientation can be seen as fluid, depending on both the perceived sex of the individual[s] and the gender organization of the relationship.
>
> (2005, p. 314)

Dozier argues that sexuality is shifting and context specific, challenging notions of essential and permanent sexual orientation. Like the trans-men in Dozier's study, Max can occupy different identity statuses, and experience sexuality differently across his relationships. How we understand, name, and experience our sexualities is not static but can change, on the basis of many factors including self-identity, perceived sex category, gender dynamics, and partner identity. This shifting creates the space for a queer understanding of sexuality to emerge. A character such as Max challenges the boundaries of a sex(uality) and gender binary system, and renders both the categories and the system itself a problematic. This problematic becomes evident in *The L Word* fans' online discussions.

Coogan (2006) argues that the butch/trans discussion in the lesbian community is in part about the usage of biological sex as the determinant for being "a lesbian," for entrance rights into the community. This determinant is not fixed; rather it is an on-going dialogue, a continued contestation. As Gamson (1997) writes, "Scholars now routinely note that social movements depend on the active, ongoing construction of collective identity, and that deciding who *we* are requires deciding who we are not" (p. 179). Max's character enters into this *conversation*, challenging biological sex as the marker of access to the lesbian community, about who belongs to the community, and we can see this process play out in discussion forums. As Max has transitioned across three seasons, the talk has also shifted in focus; Max was in season 4 a pre-operative trans-man. However, in season 5, he is a non-operative trans-man. What we see then, is a shift in the border conversation from Max's genitalia—is he a lesbian if he has top and/or bottom surgery?—to that of his sex partners. Latterly the question of his potential to belong to the lesbian community seemed to center around his having had sex with a gay man, thus shifting the question away from biological sex, and towards connectedness to men. As Coogan (2006) stated, summarizing Halberstam, these negotiation strategies are subtle—they are often framed as forum discussions focused on the character, and yet, through various dialogical tropes they become conversations about the lesbian community at large, and trans participation in the lesbian community. This conversation queers sexual identity categories, as they illuminate the social construction of sexual identity while challenging the essentialism of sex, gender and sexual binaries.

Here, *The L Word*—a television show—becomes a part of the process of meaning-making; of what the lesbian community is, of who belongs, of who has sex with whom and how. As people write about and process their reaction to what they've just watched on television (such as Max and Tom having sex, for example), they are determining for themselves what they think and feel about these issues, both on-screen and off-screen, and are engaging in a public dialogue where they are participating in (re)defining the terms of both lesbian and trans sex, and trans participation in the lesbian community.

Henry Jenkins (2006) writes extensively on fan communities, and their abilities to theorize for themselves. He writes that, "all I had was the impulse that fans were important theorists of their own practices" (p. 62). In these online forums, we can observe the community's desire to claim their ability to define their own terms, rather than be defined through the terms of (heterosexual) others. One poster gets at this when she writes that, "thing is, we want the show to represent our community in as many ways as possible" (Holly, After Ellen Forum 2008a). Here, posters on the forum work to take control over how their community is represented, to define the terms of their community's representation. *The L Word* butch/FTM border conversation is a definitive part of this process. As one poster writes a critique, another writes in praise, leaving the topic always open for continued dialogue and (re)interpretation; leaving the borders both policed and under negotiation:

> Also, L word STILL has no butch characters. Moira/Max does not count because he's a transgendered man which isn't the same thing! L word is making it look as if the natural progression for butch women is to eventually become transgender.
>
> (Georgianne, After Ellen Forum 2008b)

> And Finally. Max. I hated that he was away for three episodes but DAMN did he come back with a freakin vengeance! And had a hell of a sex scene! It probably bothered 97% of the people watching, but I loved it! I loved the fact that they showed that part of the gay community…. I was excited for the representation, excited for the character, just excited!
>
> (Patricia, After Ellen Forum 2008c)

All the while negotiating; however, fans enact and highlight their agency with each other, with the writers and producers of the show, and with the general public. These deliberations have an important public reach. Thus, those who may live their lives outside the lesbian community are still privy to—and potentially impacted by—these discussion forums. The stories in the show come to frame conversations about issues such as transgender sexuality, and trans-phobia in the lesbian community, issues that impact life in the real world.

Furthermore, we can see how participants use the online forum as a location to process their reaction, their thoughts and opinions, which are not fixed, but rather are open and mutable:

> Max—Woooooow. I'm a little speechless. I don't know how to really feel about the Max doin' it! I mean….wow. It was so unexpected!! I ain't seen the dude in like…5 episodes! Then. WhAM!!! He's getting' it with the interpreter. I gotta think about this one.
>
> (Emily, After Ellen Forum 2008c)

> I actually liked Tom and Max. Man that was a lot of sex….alot. A bit too much for me. Some just wasn't necessary.
>
> (Sarah, After Ellen Forum 2008c)

> Sex scenes were good except for the nasty Max one. Maybe I just don't understand it. I guess she's a gay boy now ha.
>
> (Brianna, After Ellen Forum 2008c)

In addition to responses that are more ambivalent, like the ones quoted above, there are also more direct conversations, where people with strong opinions discuss the issue with each other. These conversations, importantly, shift between the television show and participants' lives, weaving the show into the realm of everyday. For example, one forum participant writes,

> MAX HAS LOST HIS MIND~WHY DID THEY DO THAT TO HIS CHARACTER? NOW WHAT IS HE GONNA BE STRAIGHT>>>??? I'M SO CONFUSED>. NOT TO MENTION I ALMOST THREW UP~
> (Rhianna, After Ellen Forum 2008c)

A reader of this comment can interpret the capitalisation (of the font) to illuminate heightened expression on the poster's part. Another forum participant engages directly with this comment by writing the following reaction:

> Almost threw up? That's not nice. I know plenty of transpeople who have very fluid sexuality—one of my closet friends used to be a goldstar lesbian, then she transitioned, and now is a gay man. It's quite natural for these things to happen. … Just as we lesbians like to be accepted, so would transpeople. Maybe vomit's not the way to promote love and acceptance. I give Max, and the writers of the L word, a thumbs up for this episode.
> (Anne, After Ellen Forum 2008c)

This conversation illuminates the ways that these communities use *The L Word* to frame conversations that are much more personal for audiences—this is not just about a character on a show, but it is also about people's identities, friends, partners, crushes, and family members.

Conclusion

The functional benefit of Max's character, as a representation, is the stimulus it provides for conversation between audience members. These online audience members are talking to each other in ways that I would describe as queer. I argue they are talking *queerly* because the conversation is inconclusive; it is on-going and changing; thus it is not of an essentialist focus. The outcome of the conversation as a whole is a sexual discourse that is fluid and contextualized. Essentialist notions of lesbian identity still permeate the discussion boards; however, they are sitting side by side with queer notions; which often force us to ask questions about essentialist understandings of lesbian sexuality.

The L Word online community is conversing about Max in ways that challenge our traditional understandings of sex and gender. "Lesbian" identity is grounded in a binary sex category system (female/male). Discussions about Max, and trans-men in general, cause a rethinking of sex categories that disrupt more than a definition of lesbian, but also a normative heterosexuality that depends upon a sexed binary. In a review of Judith Butler's work, Gill Jagger (2008) writes that "it is not that sex and gender produce heterosexuality but that heterosexuality produces sex and gender in a binary form" (p. 1). Thus, a system of compulsory heterosexuality (Rich 1980) and the dynamics of inequality emerges, and it relies upon sex and gender binaries. I argue that the way that trans-men (such as Max) blur the binary of sex and gender results in a disruption of heterosexism; it is a queer representation and conversation precisely because it challenges the center.

We can see through these dialogues how reactions are taken from the show into the real world through discussions of trans-men in the real world. This is a queer conversation because it is asking questions about sexual binaries; disrupting categories just enough to leave them open for negotiation. In these forums, lesbian sexuality starts as the privileged status, and furthermore, "homosexuality ceases to be the exclusive site of sexual difference" (Stein and Plummer 1996, p. 135). Heterosexism relies upon the assumption and normalcy of heterosexuality. In the online forums included in this study, the assumption to be made in this space is centered on lesbian identity.

Through the course of the conversation, any kind of stable sexuality begins to be less certain. Discussions such as those which revolve around bisexuality question the notion of a permanent sexuality and support contextualized experiences. All the while, it is evidenced that transgender and bisexuality still remain marginalized in some locations, highlighting the dialectic of hegemonic dominance. As John Storey (2003) writes, "popular culture is one of the principal sites where these divisions are established and contested; that is, popular culture is an arena of struggle and negotiation between the interests of dominant groups and the interests of subordinate groups" (p. 51). In this particular location heterosexuality is not normatively invisible, but specifically pushed to the margins. The hegemonic struggle at the forefront is taken up by lesbians, and foregrounds bisexuality and transgender identity as subordinate statuses in the lesbian community.

That there is public space for this struggle and that *The L Word* contributes to this is a clear sign of the "queer tendencies" considered by Sasha Roseneil (2000). Gender and sexual binaries and the inequalities embedded within them rely upon stability. These conversations, even as they are subjective and incomplete, illuminate that in the media and everyday life people are shifting the discourse in queer directions.

References

After Ellen Forum. 2008a. www.afterellen.com/node/4611. [Accessed February 7, 2008]

After Ellen Forum. 2008b. www.afterellen.com/node/856. [Accessed March 21, 2008]

After Ellen Forum. 2008c. www.afterellen.com/node/29928. [Accessed March 17, 2008]

Cohen, C. 1996. Contested membership: Black gay identities and the politics of AIDS. In *Queer theory/sociology*, edited by S. Seidman. Oxford and Blackwood, NJ: Blackwell, 362–391.

Coogan, K. 2006. Fleshy specificity: (Re)considering transsexual subjects in lesbian communities. *Journal of Lesbian Studies* 10(1/2): 17–41.

Cooper, E. 2003. Decoding Will and Grace: Mass audience reception of a popular network situation comedy. *Sociological Perspectives* 46(4).

Dozier, R. 2005. Beards, breasts, and bodies: Doing sex in a gendered world. *Gender and Society* 19(3): 297–316.

Dyer, R. 1993. *The matter of images: Essays on representation*. London and New York: Routledge.

Farrell, K. 2006. HIV on tv: Conversations with young gay men. *Sexualities* 9(2): 193–213.

Gamson, J. 1997. Messages of exclusion: Gender, movements, and symbolic boundaries. *Gender and Society* 11: 178–199.

Gamson, J., and Moon, D. 2004. The sociology of sexualities: Queer and beyond. *Annual Review of Sociology* 30: 47–64.

Gamson, W. A., Croteau, D., Hoynes, W., and Sasson, T. 1992. Media images and the social construction of reality. *Annual Review of Sociology* 18: 373–393.

Good, J. 2007. Shop til' we drop: Television, materialism, and attitudes about the natural environment. *Mass Communication and Society* 10(3): 365–383.

Gross, L. and Woods, J. 1999. Up from invisibility: Film and television. In *The Columbia reader on lesbians and gay men in media, society and politics*, edited by L. Gross and J. Woods. New York: Columbia University Press.

Hall, S. 1997. *Representation: Cultural representations and signifying practice*. Newbury Park, CA and London: Sage.

Hillier, L., and Harrison, L. 2007. Building realities less limited than their own: Young people practicing same-sex attraction on the internet. *Sexualities* 10(1): 82–100.

Hine, C. 2009. Social research methods and the internet: A thematic review. Sociological Research Online, 2004, 9(2). http://www.socresonline.org.uk/912/nine.html [Accessed December 24, 2009]

Hines, S. 2006. What's the difference? Bringing particularity to queer studies of transgender. *Journal of Gender Studies* 15(1): 49–66.

Ingraham, C. 2008. *White weddings: Romancing heterosexuality in popular culture*, 2nd ed. New York and London: Routledge.

Jagger, G. 2008. *Judith Butler: Sexual politics, social change, and the power of the performative*. New York and London: Routledge.

Jenkins, H. 2006. *Fans, bloggers and gamers: Exploring participatory culture*. New York: New York University Press.

L-Word Online Forum. 2006. http://discussion.l-word.com/viewtopic.php?t=11053. [Accessed March 28, 2006]

Lo, M. 2006. Gender trouble on The L Word. Afterellen.com. www.afterellen.com/archive/ellen/TV/2006/4/butches/html.

Moore, C. 2007. Having it all ways: The tourist, the traveler, and the local. *The L Word. Cinema Journal* 46(4): 3–22.

Our Chart Forum. 2008. http://www.sho.com/site/message/thread.do?topicid=243857&boardid=4917&groupid=12. [Accessed August 6, 2009]

PlanetOut. 2008. www.planetout.com/news/letters/splash.html?id=142 [Accessed April 16, 2008]

Raymond, D. 2002. Popular culture and queer representations: A critical perspective. In *Gender, race and class in media: A text-reader*, 2nd ed., edited by G. Dines and J. Humez. Thousand Oaks, CA: Sage.

Rich, A. 1980. Compulsory heterosexuality and lesbian existence. *Signs* 5(4): 631–660.

Roseneil, S. 2008 [2000]. Queer frameworks and queer tendencies: Toward an understanding of postmodern transformations of sexuality. *Sociological Research Online* 5(3). http://www.socresonline.org.uk/5/3/roseneil.html. [Accessed February 15, 2008]

Showtime. 2009. Community: Our chart. http://www.sho.com/site/lword/community.do [Accessed August 15, 2009]

Stein, A., and Plummer, K. 1996. I can't even think straight. In *Queer theory/sociology*, edited by S. Seidman. Oxford: Blackwell.

Storey, J. 2003. *Inventing popular culture*. Oxford: Blackwell.

Ward, K. 2008. The cyber-ethnographic (re)construction of two feminist online communities. *Sociological Research Online* 4(1). http://www.socresonline.org.uk/4/1/ward.html [Accessed February 15, 2008]

Chapter 13

Out and About
Slash Fic, Re-imagined Texts, and Queer Commentaries

Richard Berger

In the 1960s, a highly sexual and transgressive form of fan fiction (fanfic), termed "slash fic," would subvert and make homoerotic the heterosexual relationships depicted in the TV series, *Star Trek*. Later, in the 1990s, the internet would facilitate a boom in these slash writings, as the web provided anonymity coupled with a potentially global audience. Slash communities started to form online, and new queer canons have emerged. This chapter will explore this new dialog between an established media text, its transgressive slash fic potential, and the dynamics of community members. I will argue that this can facilitate a queer space online as writers reflect on their own sexual identity.

Slash fic then can be conceived of as a subversive form of appropriation where the source text is opened up for the purposes of a "carnivalesque" sexual and political agenda, and allows for a critical reception of mainstream television texts, in the queering of such texts by online communities. Interactive media offered fan and slash writing far more participatory potential. It further blurred the barriers between the writers and readers, as Mikhail Bakhtin suggests the "carnival . . . does not acknowledge any distinction between actors and spectators" (1994, p. 198). The instantaneity of responses and reaction to online fan writing can be seen to heighten the excitement for readers and writers, becoming something akin to sexual tension and erotic foreplay. However it also offers what Aaron Ben-Ze'ev calls a "detached attachment"—an intimate closeness at a distance (2004, p. 26). Fan writing on the web is never ending, so any climax is deferred. The pleasure then for online fan writers and readers is in the *process*, and that is what I shall examine here.

Fanfic writers will often provide sequels/prequels to major literary, filmic or televisual works. Some writers go on to write "profic"—officially sanctioned stories. However, it is rare for fanfic, or profic, to become part of any "canon," so traditionally such texts sit outside and beyond the reach of "official" source materials. Even fairly prestige works—such as Jean Rhys's *Jane Eyre* prequel, *Wide Sargasso Sea*—are an adjunct to, rather than a part of the Bronte canon. Often such works play on a reader's desire to revisit favorite characters and diegesis. These works can be subversive, as Rhys's novel is far more sexually explicit than anything in the Bronte canon, and there have been fanfic stories exploring a perceived homoerotic attraction between Frodo Baggins and Samwise Gamgee in J. R. R. Tolkien's *The Lord of the Rings*.

As such, fanfic is a very durable form and has been in existence for many decades—the comic book genre was thrillingly subverted by the "Tijuana Bibles" of the 1920s and 1930s, where mainstream comic book characters were reimagined and recast in pornographic tableaux by amateur artists (see Adelman 2006). Today many writers encourage fanfic, while others deplore it; the author E. Annie Proulx commenting on the fans of her 1997 short story, *Brokeback Mountain*, complained that: "[The fans] constantly send ghastly manuscripts and pornish rewrites of the story to me, expecting me to reply with praise and applause" (cited in Shoard 2008).

When television became a mass medium in the 1950s, fanfic followed this, and a new generation of fanfic writers began to provide episodes of their favorite TV shows. So, fan writing is synonymous with fan culture and fanfic acts as a type of cultural virus in the way it can mutate and evolve to suit new media. Fanfic can refashion television into what Roland Barthes (1974) would call a "writerly" text. However, most fanfic adhered to broadly canonical structures and rules were quickly established whereby writers had to adhere to canonical aspects of a series, character or setting. Fanfic that synchronically departed from the rules of the diachronic source text were generally considered to be poor. The trick was to maintain a significant level of fidelity while at the same time exploring new plots and developments. In this way, minor characters in a canon would become popular with fanfic writers because they offered more scope for exploration, but still within the recognizable diegesis of a TV series.

The 1960s saw a boom in fanfic, generally in the science fiction genre. This decade also saw the emergence of a splinter-genre of fanfic which would deliberately frame itself as non-canonical—this was its virtue. Slash Fiction—so called because of its denotative "slash" in advertising a transgressive non-canonical coupling—was a more aggressive, and carnivalesque, form of sexually explicit fan writing. Slash fic writers would imagine sexual relationships between characters in largely mainstream television programs which weren't portrayed or explored in the original text. So, these texts sketched an ambivalence whereby well-known mainstream characters were often depicted as sexually transgressive. These rewritings were often inversions where "straights" were queered by slash writers, as Linda Hutcheon notes: "Parody, therefore, is a form of imitation characterised by iconic inversion, not always at the expense of the parodied text" (1989, p. 88). This highly sexual and transgressive form would seek to subvert and make homoerotic heterosexual relationships on television, for political purposes.

Decades later the popularity of the web would extend slash's landscape and would create a vibrant fan community where readers could discuss stories with like-minded audiences. As Susan Clerc suggests: "the most primal instinct a fan has is to talk to other fans about their common interest" (2001, p. 216). Since the 1960s, fan culture has become increasingly participatory as John Fiske observes: "Fans produce and circulate among themselves texts which are often crafted with production values as high as any in the official culture" (1992, p. 39).

However, these spheres of cultural reproduction are increasingly dialogical, as fans enter into a communion with an array of media texts. Dan McKee argues that the internet has allowed fan communities to form more quickly and these fans therefore display "agency in their everyday media consumption" (2003, p. 67). Again, for Henry Jenkins:

> ...an alternative conception of fans as readers who appropriate popular texts and re-read them in a fashion that serves different interests, as spectators who transform the experience of watching television into a rich and complex participatory culture.
>
> (1992, p. 23)

Clerc further suggests that:

> Fans, whether online or off, discuss characterisation [and] speculate about what would have happened if some feature of a story had been different...Fans try and fill in the gaps left by writers and form connections between episodes.
>
> (2001, pp. 216–217)

In pre-web mainstream television, one of the biggest "gaps" in texts was sexuality. So, fanfic writers had a rich ground to explore and develop in any number of non-canonical reconfigurations, because: "Fanfic happens in the gaps between canon. The unexplored or insufficiently explored territory" (Pugh 2005, p. 92). Alexander Doty (1997) makes a case for all texts having a queer aspect and he rejects any heterocentric notions of queerness as sub-textual: "Queer positions queer readings and queer pleasures are part of a reception space that stands simultaneously beside and within that created by heterosexual and straight positions" (1997, p. 15). So, the term "queer" here is far more complex and encompassing, and the post-web slash fic of the 1990s certainly reflected that.

This dialogue between an established media text, its transgressive slash/fanfic and the comments of community members can therefore facilitate the type of space Doty describes, as many writers dealt with their own sexuality through providing alternative storylines to established media texts from *Star Trek* in the 1960s to *Buffy the Vampire Slayer* in the 1990s. I want to map here how this genre moved from one of subversion and transgression to a more dialogical and "playful" mode. As many have noted, there has been a change in the representation of gay men and women: what Steven Seidman (2004) calls a "slow and uneven but steady march toward social acceptance and equality" (p. 2). Both Seidman and Richard Dyer (1995) reflect that homosexuality has been defined by heterosexuality. For Hutcheon: "The recognition of the inverted world still requires a knowledge of the order of the world which it inverts and, in a sense, incorporates" (1989, p. 99).

So, the "inverted" queer world of slash writing still depended on the "straight" world it was commenting on, certainly up until the late 1980s. Earlier, in the 1950s and 1960s, gay men were often portrayed as sad, lonely figures in media representation. It is no coincidence that the first slash stories started to emerge at this time. As Michael Warner puts it, "queers do a kind of practical social reflection just in finding ways of being queer" (2000, p. xiii), so slash in some ways asserts the queer nature of the world, moving from the sub-textual level where Doty (1997) argues it has always existed. Slash can be read here then as a queer commentary on popular culture, and this commentary—just as with the texts it seeks to comment on—has changed a great deal.

Adaptation theorists such as Geoffrey Wagner (1975) have often cited a text's re-purposing as having the potential for commentary, but this dialogue is little more than a conversation between an adaptor and an adapted work. Fanfic, and its sub-genres, is a far more interactive, visible, and therefore plural process. However, as I shall show, slash has shifted from the politically subversive—a reaction to the "queerlessness" of mainstream media and the "normal gay"—to the more carnivalesque and playful. Simon Dentith suggests that Bakhtin's carnival is: "An aesthetic which celebrates the anarchic body-based and grotesque elements of popular culture, and seeks to mobilise them against the humourless seriousness of official culture" (2003, p. 66).

So, slash fic certainly contains the ambivalence of the carnival, and juxtaposes the grotesque body of slash against the classical body of its source. However for Bakhtin the carnival was always temporary, and fan and slash writing has gained a type of permanence online, which makes this process far more participatory and open-ended. This then opens up the possibilities for a critical examination of the reception of mainstream television texts by online queer communities.

So, I am suggesting that fanfic is a genre and, like any such genre, it is by no means a fixed or closed system. Rather it undergoes fundamental change and development in its life-cycle; in this case a hegemonic cycle whereby the subversive elements of slash are reworked, albeit in a neutered way, back into mainstream culture. Now slash communities have formed online and new queer fanfic canons have emerged. These communities have provided nurturing spaces where a contributor's work is commented on and feedback is given. In short, slash can be conceived of as a subversive form of appropriation, where the source text is opened up to subversion for the purposes of a sexual and often political agenda.

Slash: The "Fanfic of Duty"

Interestingly, slash has provided problems for literary and cultural studies scholars, particularly when attempting to define the term. As Mark McLelland notes: "Slash . . . is an underground fandom and many English-speaking people, including academics working in cultural studies, seem unaware of the extent of the genre or its longevity" (2001, p. 9).

Hutcheon (2006) argues that fanfic is certainly not a type of adaptation and I would agree. Rather, fanfic, and slash, is more of a conversation, where fans are in communion with an array of texts which they already find a great deal of pleasure in. Furthermore some argue that fanfic is the preserve of largely female contributors: "Almost all fan fiction is written by women" (Clerc 2001, p. 218). Sonia K. Katyal agrees, but with further insight: ". . . it is widely held that the largest number of slash writers are heterosexual or lesbian/bisexual women who write not for profit, but for their own artistic pleasure and creativity" (Katyal 2006, p. 486).

At first glance this is surprising but "The crudeness and brashness of women in cyberspace often surprises men who encounter them there" (Ben-Ze'ev 2004, p. 196). Indeed, the first *Star Trek* slash story, published in the fanzine *Grup* in 1974, was written by a woman: "A Fragment out of Time" by Diane Marchant imagined a sexual relationship between the two principal male characters Kirk and Spock: "Like Western slash fiction writers, the authors took heterosexual, heteronormative narratives and 'queered' them by imagining sexual relationships between the male characters" (McLelland 2001, p. 6).

Right up until the late 1960s, gay men were usually portrayed as lonely, pitiful figures, even in such ground-breaking works as *Victim* (Basil Dearden 1961) (which discussed the illegal status of male homosexuality in the UK at that time, and issues of blackmail). So, this new emerging fanfic dutifully rectified in an instant what Dyer calls a representation of someone "physically less than a man" (1995, p. 42). Also, as McLelland argues: "Western women have had a long-standing interest in male sexuality" (2001, p. 90). Similarly Jenkins notes this more plural nurturing environment for exploring female desire: "Slash breaks . . . with the commodification of pornography, offering erotic images that originate in a social context of intimacy and sharing" (1992, p. 190).

The mainstream television of the 1960s and 1970s offered little in the way of representations of homosexual characters or storylines. In this period slash was a transgressive commentary on the mainstream portrayals of heterosexuality and the later crude stereotyping of homosexuality. Slash writers subverted storylines and characterizations of such popular shows as *Starsky and Hutch*, *Blakes* [sic] 7, *The Professionals*, and *The Man from Uncle*. All of these texts are notable for their foregrounding of heterosexual masculinity and male relationships. For Pugh: "Gay writers, or those concerned with gay issues, have used [slash] to establish a gay presence in a straight universe" (2005, p. 107).

I would argue that it is more than that, as slash writing provides a space where writers can explore and articulate their own sexualities and desires. It provides a forum for expression, offering anonymity. Slash is therefore performative as well as subversive—and therefore carnivalesque—where writers can explore their own sexual desires and sexualities in dialogue with a favorite show or character. This involves the reading of these stories, which ultimately results in the "writing" of them, and is a pleasurable activity, as Wolfgang Iser notes: "The reader's enjoyment begins when he himself becomes productive" (1978, p. 108).

The 1970s and 1980s period of significant slash writing I will call here the "fanfic of duty" as writers seemed determined to right the seeming wrongs of the mainstream television output of the time. The slash of this period was at its most political and was largely a reaction against the marginalization of homosexual representation in popular culture. This is by no means insignificant as Section 28 of the Local Government Act in the UK (in 1988) outlawed homosexual representation, promotion, and practices, and historically measures such as the Proposition 6 legislation in California, US (1978) stimulated similar potential oppression.

Slash: New Dialogues

The web of the early 1990s shaped fanfic in a number of ways: it provided a new space far beyond the reach of fanzines and conventions; it facilitated more sophisticated routes of anonymity; it made fanfic more visible; it allowed fanfic writers to form online communities and slash would join with other forms of sexually explicit content online. This period was a far more dialogical era for fanfic and their writers. Gay (or "queer") writers could now be far more open in queering the texts they were commenting on, offering more visibility generally. Some sites, such as Slashfanfiction.net (2009), began to archive material from the 1960s and 1970s, introducing the genre to a new audience who would go on to write their own stories. Slash sites still maintained a veneer of political duty however: slashfic.co.uk has the disclaimer:

> I'm not going to argue about it; the world is a grown-up place where guys can marry other guys and if you don't like it find another website.
> (Slashfic.co.uk 2009)

Some television shows gained a new type of longevity online, as fanfic often outlived their progeny source texts, particularly *Lois and Clark* (subtitled "The New Adventures of Superman" in the UK) (1993–1997) and *Buffy the Vampire Slayer* (1997–2003). The fanfic site slayerfanfic.com has been in existence since 1997, the year of *Buffy the Vampire Slayer's* initial exhibition on television, highlighting an emerging dialogical relay between fanfic and television. These types of sites were not exclusively confined to the sci-fi/fantasy genre, or "cult" television shows, for example Britslash (2009) contains links to more "mainstream" fanfic based on UK television shows such as *Goodnight Sweetheart* and *The Bill*, as well as soaps such as *EastEnders*.

It seems that narratives with the longest history were the most popular. *Lois and Clark* fanfic had many decades of comic books, films, and TV serials to plunder, and was not immune to slash writing either. Many slash sites imagined sexual relationships between Clark and Lex, or Clark and Jimmy. Often, it was the attraction of actors such as Dean Cain which motivated such fan authors. At Fictionresource.com (2009) Rositamia2 has written stories where "Superman gets amnesia. Jimmy finds him. Things happen" and one of his/her stories opens with the line, "Oh my God, I'm fucking Superman!"

Some sites such as xenite.org boasted that their fanfic was the place "where Xena and Gabrielle are more than just friends!" At the time of writing, Fanfiction.net (2009) had 1,624 *Xena: Warrior Princess* (1995–2001) stories. Some writers specialized in writing fanfic for just one series, such as Twilight who only writes *Buffy*- or "Whedonverse"-related stories at Twilightfic.tripod.com (2009). Others adopt pseudonyms which both highlight their affiliations as well as their sexualities such as sapphicslayer at Spacetart.tripod.com (2009). Again, these enactments of desire and fantasy online, in communion with a mainstream text, further entrenches the ambivalence inherent in much fan writing, as Bakhtin presciently put it: "Carnival is the people's second life" (1994, p. 198). *Xena: Warrior Princess* and *Buffy the Vampire Slayer* both had strong proactive female leads in otherwise previously male dominated genres: fantasy and the supernatural respectively. In a sense, mainstream television was beginning to enact fanfic strategies and the dialogue between the two forms became heightened as fanfic writers, "simply saw an unexplored gay subtext in the writing" (Pugh 2005, p. 95). As Seidman argues, in the 1990s, "the closet [had] less of a role in shaping gay life" (2004, p. 11).

Satellite, cable, and then digital television meant that there was now a great deal more televisual content. Also from the late 1990s, "quality" television drama was undergoing something of a renaissance. In addition representations of homosexuality were moving from virtually nothing and crude stereotyping to more plural types of expression. The whole idea of "mainstream" television was now in question as many subscription channels, such as HBO, got large audiences and critical plaudits for a raft of television dramas. Warner Bros' *The West Wing* (1999–2006) had no openly gay principal characters, but that didn't stop the slash community queering relationships between Sam Seaborn and Josh Lyman at sites like westwingstories.com.

In the UK, *Queer As Folk* (1999–2000) broke new ground in its portrayal of gay relationships and characters, and pushed the boundaries of what could be shown on television. *Queer as Folk* was remade in the US and exhibited on the Showtime network to great acclaim and had both gay and straight fans. The series was written by Russell T. Davies, himself a former fanfic author of some renown, who spent his early career writing *Doctor Who* fanfic, before going on to revive the British sci-fi series. Other fanfic writers would also join Davies on this project, such as Mark Gatiss, legitimizing fanfic as a form and a way of breaking into television and film writing. *Doctor Who* spin-off, *Torchwood* (2006–) would neatly encapsulate this by almost acting as its own queer commentary on its progeny text.

Torchword's central character is Captain Jack Harkness, a bisexual alien, who also appears in *Doctor Who*. So, *Torchwood* serves to develop a character in a similar fashion to fanfic in enacting almost slash-like strategies, and like slash, in a far more sexually explicit way. In a sense, from the late 1990s, fanfic had "remediated" (Bolter and Grusin 2000) television drama and this new dialogue legitimized slash to an extent, but also neutered its political power and subversion. *Torchwood* then, continues the conversation with *Doctor Who*.

The dialogue continued in the new millennium, as it had done in the 1990s, with some television dramas containing openly gay characters in traditionally "high-octane" testosterone genres. This shows that the era of what Seidman terms the "normal gay"—"a good citizen" (2004, p. 17)—was over. In fact, these overly positive images of gay men and women were as unrealistic as the negative representations in the 1960s and 1970s, as I would argue they were nearly always a middle-class representation of unthreatening sexuality. *Oz* (1997–2003) was a gritty prison drama, with very few female characters. It featured gay relationships and explicitly and brutally portrayed male rape in a way not seen before on television.

The most acclaimed drama of recent years, *The Wire* (2002–2008) was set on the mean streets of Baltimore and was concerned with the exploits of a number of street gangs and drug dealers, and their relationship with the police. The series was praised for its epic, novel-like qualities, but what was most significant here is that the most ruthless character, the "stick-up man" Omar Little, was gay. In *The Wire*, Omar's sexuality is not made an issue of—except perhaps when he avenges the murder of his partner, Brandon. Omar is exactly the kind of character a fanfic writer would create (or queer) in the decades previously. Omar was a canonically gay character. It is clear then that slashwriters had to now compete with canonically gay (and authentically queer) characters in television drama.

In response slash writers produced ever more explicit and transgressive stories:

> Implicit in many site owners' defence of their fantasies is the right to imagine sex which is not "politically correct": that is, sex which derives its interest from imagining power differentials, not equality.
>
> (McLelland 2001, p. 11)

The most unlikely of texts were subverted in this way. For example a great deal of slash was produced around the *Harry Potter* novels and films, perhaps to deliberately antagonize J. K. Rowling's sanctioning of fanfic that obeyed the diachronic rules of her novels.

The web in a way had "pornographied" slash, and slash itself was now competing with other forms of online porn. But largely, slash stories and communities became far more playful. These communities were not just supportive of slash fiction, but of the writers themselves. Young men and women could explore their sexualities in, paradoxically perhaps, a more anonymous and *more* visible way than they had ever been able before. Slash had moved from the intimate sphere of "duty" in corners of science fiction conventions and in small circulation 'zines, to the public sphere of a global computer network.

Slash became a way of recasting a favorite television program in the slash writer's own terms; a way of expressing their own desires in a fairly safe, but also an increasingly credible arena. For many writers, commenting on and having a conversation with a television character through slash writing is a safer and potentially more fulfilling way of exploring sexual fantasies than with a "real" person you don't know. For many, slash is a way of bypassing the explicit content in chatrooms and forums, but in a way that still allows for a sexually explicit exploration of desire.

In the last decade, fanfic communities have flourished online, and some sites have become very sophisticated. Many offer searchable databases and archives; others provide forums where readers and writers can discuss stories. Others even deploy classification systems and encourage feedback and reader reviews. Some sites, including Fanfiction.net (2009), have adopted a universal ratings system, rather like the BBFC in the UK and the MPAA in the USA. Here a story rated "K" is "Content suitable for all ages" and this system takes in "K+"; "T,""M" right up to "MA" which is the most explicit content. Squidge.org (2009) uses the MPAA's film ratings to classify fanfic, with the most sexually explicated receiving an "NC-17" certificate. Such sites then can be a repository for general fanfic, as well as slash, as the latter form is no longer confined to specialist sites.

So, fanfic now has at least the veneer of authenticity, mirroring the forms it seeks to comment on. It is no longer just a commentary on a text but it is a commentary on the medium of television itself. Slash merely takes this into a more playful realm of sexual desire.

Slash fiction and fan writing in general has evolved a great deal in the last 50 years. It has almost abandoned its original form, to find a new one online. In addition the texts it seeks to provide a commentary on have also undergone change: there are now far more gay characters in mainstream television, than there were in the 1960s, 1970s, and 1980s. In the US, legislation such as Proposition 8 (effectively cancelling gay marriage in November 2008) leave Californian constituents see-sawing between a recognition and re-statement of gay rights and the money and power of the religious right. However in the UK Section 28 has been finally repealed and civil partnerships are an increasingly common aspect of society.

Television has followed and to an extent appropriated fanfic conventions, providing its own spin-offs and commentaries such as *Torchwood* and *Angel* (1999–2004) which was a commentary on aspects of *Buffy the Vampire Slayer*. The UK "teen" drama *Skins* for example has many gay characters and storylines, as well as a significant online aspect requiring participation by the audience, including writing plotlines. So, I would argue that fanfic has remediated television drama.

The web has acted as a repository for the fanfic of the 1960s, 1970s, and 1980s, giving it permanence that Bakhtin's definition of carnival never had, and has been the engineer of a new era of fanfic writing. Therefore, slash is not just a response to television drama, but also to decades of fanfic too. Some fanfic writers produce sequels to the work of other fan authors. Slash can now be read as a commentary on its own progeny form, as fanfic has become a very popular activity online as online fanfic communities create their own canons. Some fanfic writers are now being recognized for their work and are gaining some semblance of status and cachet in cyberspace for their output. Slash then has responded by furthering the playful nature of its transgression in aping the "mash-up" practices of cyberculture.

Sites such as Crossoverfic (2009) encourage writers to move further away from perceived canons by cross-pollinating source material for subversive ends. This particular site contains a great deal of *Lost/West Wing* slash writing where characters from both shows meet and form relationships. In "The Witch and the Warrior" by daviderl, the eponymous hero from *Xena: Warrior Princess* forms a relationship with Willow from *Buffy the Vampire Slayer*; in "Through the Rift" Beatrice Otter provides a rebirth for Buffy as she survives falling into Sunnydale's rift, by appearing in modern day Cardiff having emerged from *Torchwood's* rift; in Azar's "Five Couples Jack Harkness Never Slept With" the bisexual promiscuous time-traveller from *Torchwood* is teamed up with characters from *Doctor Who*, *Stargate SG-1* and *Stargate Atlantis*—furthering slash's playful nature and removal from political agency.

A lesbian sub-genre has emerged: known as "femslash" or "femmeslash" it has its origins in the 1980s, but is only recently flourishing online. This may be in part as a reaction to the lack of gay women in television drama, as opposed to gay men, and such writing does seem to cluster around those texts which feature lesbian relationships, such as *The L Word* (2004–). Otherwise, femslash focuses on the same texts and characters that mainstream fanfic and slash has done, namely *Buffy the Vampire Slayer's* Willow and the young 20-something "good" witches in *Charmed* (1998–2006).

More television and print media is now devoted to celebrity, and the fanfic and slash communities have not been immune to the charms of reality television. Another emergent sub-genre is "Real Person Slash" or RPS. These slash writers began in the 1990s, and were a small community who wrote about imagined relationships between the members of boy bands, or between boy bands, such as New Kids on the Block, Take That, Boyzone, and Westlife. More "credible" pop artists were also "slashed," with Morrissey having his already ambiguous sexuality re-imagined and developed by RPS writers. So, it seems that anyone who circulates in celebrity culture is fair game. For example Fiction.fandomish.net (2009) exhibits an RPS story "The Birthday Boy" which has Justin Timberlake and the actor Hayden Christensen involved in a relationship. Some elements of the slash community have turned their backs on the fictional work of television drama, to the "real" world of celebrity. It seems then that slash writers have as much of an appetite for a constructed reality as have television viewers.

It is not really reasonable, however, to make a distinction between slash writers and television viewers or as Doty suggests between straight and queer audiences, because slash writers are almost exclusively television viewers and slash, therefore, is one of the best phenomenological commentaries on television there is. Television has appropriated, absorbed and re-purposed many of the properties of the world wide web, but this has been a relationship of mutual exchange, which any appreciation of online fan writing will reveal. Television audiences and "web users" are the same people, and therefore expect certain things from their media consumption. Fanfic is now closer than ever perhaps, to television, as well as many decades of fan writing. Fanfic is situated in the same arena as the media it seeks to comment on, but has now been joined by other types of commentary: "spin-off" television series; film/television prequels; sequels; fan sites; discussion forums, celebrity magazines etc. It is now perhaps more visible and less subversive, but it still acts as a community for lesbian, gay, and bisexual people; a community that often enacts its transgression and subversion through play, rather than necessarily direct politics. For Bakhtin, the carnival must be liberating, and slash, to an extent, has liberated many LGBT writers by allowing them a space to explore their identities and desires in a creative way, which is also in communion with an array of media texts, writers, and readers, as far from the wretched portrayals of lonely and bleak homosexuality in the decades before the web.

References

Adelman, B. 2006. *Tijuana bibles: Art and wit in America's forbidden funnies, 1930s–1950s*. London: The Erotic Print Society.

Bakhtin, M. 1993. Folk humour and carnival laughter. In *The Bakhtin reader: Selected writings of Bakhtin, Medvedev, Voloshinov*, edited by P. Morris. London: Arnold, 194–206.

Barthes, R. 1974. *S/Z*. Oxford: Blackwell.

Ben-Ze'ev, A. 2004. *Love online: Emotions on the internet*. Cambridge: Cambridge University Press.

Bolter, J. D., and Grusin, R. 2000. *Remediation: Understanding new media*. Cambridge, MA: MIT Press.

Britslash. 2009. http://www.britslash.co.uk/fictionlinks.htm [Accessed August 22, 2009]

Clerc, S. 2001. Estrogen brigades and "big tits" threads: Media fandom on-line and off. In *The Cybercultures Reader*, edited by D. Bell and B. Kennedy. London: Routledge.
Crossoverfic. 2009. http://crossoverfic.com/ [Accessed August 22, 2009]
Dentith, S. 2003. *Bakhtinian thought: An introductory reader*. London: Routledge.
Doty, A. 1997. *Making things perfectly queer*. Minneapolis: University of Minnesota Press.
Dyer, R. 1995. *The matter of images: Essays on representations*. London: Routledge.
Fanfiction.net. 2009. http://www.fanfiction.net/ [Accessed August 22, 2009]
Fiction.fandomish.net. 2009. http://fiction.fandomish.net/ [Accessed June 15, 2009]
Fictionresource.com. 2009. http://fictionresource.com/slash/ [Accessed August, 2009]
Fiske, J. 1992. The cultural economy of fandom. In *The adoring audience*, edited by L. A. Lewis. London: Routledge, 30–49.
Hutcheon, L. 1989. Modern parody and Bakhtin. In *Rethinking Bakhtin: Extensions and challenges*, edited by G. S. Morson and C. Emerson. Evanston, IL: Northwestern University Press.
Hutcheon, L. 2006. *A theory of adaptation*. London: Routledge.
Iser, W. 1978. *The art of reading: A theory of aesthetic response*. Baltimore: Johns Hopkins University Press.
Jenkins, H. 1992. *Textual poachers: Television fans and participatory culture*. London: Routledge.
Katyal, S. K. 2006. Performance, property, and the slashing of gender in fan fiction. *The Journal of Gender, Social Policy and the Law* 14(3): 462–518.
McKee, A. 2003. Fandom. In *Television studies*, edited by T. Miller. London: BFI, 66–69.
McLelland, M. 2001. Local meanings in global space: A case study of women's "boy love" web sites in Japanese and English. *Mots pluriels* 19 (October). http://motspluriels.arts.uwa.edu.au/MP1901mcl [Accessed May 8, 2009]
Pugh, S. 2005. *The democratic genre: Fan fiction in a literary context*. Bridgend: Seren Books.
Seidman, S. 2004. *Beyond the closet: The transformation of gay and lesbian life*. New York: Routledge.
Shoard, C. 2008. Annie Proulx bemoans torrent of "pornish" brokeback fan fiction. *The Guardian*, September 17.
Slashfanfiction.com. 2009. http://slashfanfiction.com/ [Accessed August 22, 2009]
Slashfic.co.uk. 2009. http://www.slashfic.co.uk/ [Accessed August 22, 2009]
Spacetart Tripod. 2009. http://spacetart.tripod.com/ [Accessed August 22, 2009]
Squidge.org. 2009. http://squidge.org/Squidge.org/Welcome.html [Accessed August 22, 2009]
Twilightfictripod.com. 2009. http://twilightfic.tripod.com/ [Accessed August 22, 2009]
Wagner, G. 1975. *The novel and the cinema*. Cranbury, NJ: Associated University Press.
Warner, M. 2000. *Fear of a queer planet: Queer politics and social theory*. Minneapolis: University of Minnesota Press.

Chapter 14

Identity Unmoored
Yaoi in the West[1]

Mark McHarry

I dedicate this chapter to the memory of Eve Sedgwick, whose work has been for me not only academically productive but also liberatory.

In most world regions, more women than men publish erotica about male–male sexuality. The stories and drawings they create are usually about media characters. The relationships in which sex takes place may be among multiple partners, between a minor and an older person, among siblings, or with authority figures or foes.[2] Often the sex acts are nonconsensual, violent and/or performed in public spaces. Although these representations may lie beyond real-world cultural boundaries, the theme of almost all of these works is the characters' surmounting of obstacles in order to connect or bond.

Called *yaoi*, *shōnen-ai*, boys' love, and slash, the first three of these genres originated in Japan, the fourth in the West. Of them yaoi is the largest and perhaps fastest-growing worldwide. It describes homoerotic literature and artwork based on young male characters in Japanese *manga* (comics) and *anime* (animation). In Japan, yaoi is comprised of noncommercial, fan created *dōjinshi* (manga) and artwork, and in the West, of fan stories and artwork. *Shōnen-ai* (lit., boys' love) and boys' love describe similarly themed works that are based on original characters and disseminated in English- and Japanese-language markets. All of these products also may be commercial and take the form of anime, video games, audio CDs and other forms in addition to manga. Slash describes the homoerotic works Western women and some men create about male characters from TV programs, movies and books. Although all four forms are consumed by a much smaller number of men in the West and Asia, most participants are women, many of them young, who identify themselves as straight or as someone whose sexuality is not nameable.[3]

Yaoi, on which I focus here, is a type of play, as its sardonic name implies, the acronym for *yamanashi, ochinashi, iminashi*, or "no climax, no point, no meaning." It and the two other Japanese-derived forms play at the intersections of identity and gender. Bodies in yaoi move fluidly past constructions of identity, gender, and sex, seemingly ignorant of cultural boundaries set around them. Judith Butler's work in gender theory, Elizabeth Grosz's on corporeality, and Eve Kosofsky Sedgwick's on homosociality over the last twenty years have become influential for conceptualizing gender and sexual identity in English. I will use some of their ideas as a frame of reference in reading a Western yaoi story and to show how yaoi troubles conventional notions of identity and gender to the point where it may be considered a form of resistance to them.

Popularity and Presence

In Japan, the popularity of boys' love and yaoi gives them a presence in mainstream culture, visible in manga and other products sold in bookstores and on magazine racks in small towns as well as cities. Tokyo's largest bookstore, Kinokuniya, held a boys' love manga fair on its main floor in March 2002. Wim Lunsing estimates there are 500,000 "core" Japanese yaoi readers.[4] In the West, yaoi is an activity seen on the Internet and in commercial bookstores such as Borders. Authors post stories to Web sites and LiveJournals, as well as to fan-fiction archives. One archive, FanFiction.Net, had more than 1.3 million works in May 2006, many of them yaoi stories, up from more than 997,000 in February 2005 and 200,000 in July 2002. Yaoi stories and artwork are the object of reviews on archive sites, commentary on LiveJournals, posts to discussion groups, and comments to Web sites' guest books. A work in one form, such as a story, can stimulate works in another, such as illustration.

A Google search on 7 June 2009 returned 17,400,000 Web pages with the word "yaoi," up from approximately 770,000 on 16 November 2003 and 135,000 on 4 May 2003.[5] Google searches for an anime title plus a neutral word such as "description" may return yaoi pages in the first ten results. To a much smaller extent English translations of commercial *shōnen-ai* works are sold in stores in United States cities. In early to mid 2006, *shōnen-ai* titles were visible in the window of Tower Records in San Francisco's gay-lesbian oriented Castro district and prominently displayed at the front counter or in the young-adult section in bookstores in other cities, such as Borders and Barnes and Noble in Washington DC's Dupont Circle neighborhood and in Honolulu.

Those unaware of yaoi may encounter it when searching the Web for anime or manga. An example is a young male's e-mail to the English-language yaoi Web site *Gundam Wing Addiction*. Daniel described himself as "an avid fan" of the popular anime *Gundam Wing*, whose protagonists are a quintet of fifteen-year-old male space pilots.[6] He wrote that he was "quite disturbed" upon being told by people in his school that the *Gundam Wing* characters depicted on a shirt he wore were gay: "So my question for you is- if any characters were actually gay in the original story line, and if so- who?" (Tyr 2000).

The site owner, Tyr, an adult, responded that none of the characters were, and then qualified this with, "or if they are, it is not explicitly stated in the show itself"

Figure 14.1 Endless Waltz. Duo Maxwell (left) and Heero Yuy. A Nippon Telegraph and Telephone Corporation telephone card offered to readers by the magazine アニメージュ (*Animēju*; in English, *Animage*) (Tokyo) in 1998 to mark its twentieth anniversary. That year the movie *Endless Waltz* featuring Duo, Heero, and other characters from the 1995–1996 TV series *Gundam Wing* was released in Japan.

(ibid). She reproduced a canonical illustration from the Japanese monthly anime/manga magazine *Animage* showing one of the pilots, Duo, in an embrace with another, Heero (see Figure 14.1). Even as she noted that "all [other] official GW illustrations have no yaoi content whatsoever," she wrote that "Japanese producers are very open-minded about the idea of yaoi" and that the owners of the anime encouraged fans to interpret their work in ways other than those promulgated canonically (ibid.). Tyr's response and its ambiguity to a question demanding a "yes" or "no" answer mark a discourse between the young and adults around same-sex erotics in the young.

Identity: Controversy and Contestation

Some same-sex attracted men have welcomed yaoi's representations as potentially liberatory. Others have expressed opposition to their sexuality's representational custody being in the hands of those who are neither homosexual nor male. From 1992 to 1997, a debate about yaoi took place in the Japanese feminist magazine *Choisir*. Satō Masaki, whom Lunsing (2006) identifies as "a gay activist/civil servant/drag queen," complained that yaoi's characters had nothing to do with "real gay men" (ibid.). Satō touched off a yaoi *ronsō* (controversy). For Satō, writes Keith Vincent (2002), "yaoi and its readers were violently co-opting the reality of gay men and transforming it into their own masturbatory fantasy." According to Satō:

> The more confused images of gay men circulate among the general public the harder it is for gay men to reconcile these images with their own lives and the more extreme their oppression becomes.... When you're spying on gay sex, girls, take a look at yourself in the mirror. Just look at the expression on your faces! [You look just like those dirty old men salivating over images of lesbian sex.] You can all go to hell for all I care.

In the United States, some gay-identified men have expressed unease about or opposition to yaoi. The widely published gay male porn writer Simon Sheppard (2002), speaking on a Yaoi-Con panel, called yaoi "a minstrel show" that "puts gay male sex out there for straight people." A yaoi artist told me that some gay-identified men have complained to her that males portrayed in yaoi are not representative of them or of gay males in general, and that they felt uneasy at being objectified by women (personal communication, Feb. 9, 2006). Matt Thorn reports that some slash fans "seem to feel the need to justify slash to the gay community, or even to reform slash in such a way as to make it more palatable or 'politically correct'" (2004, p. 173). Other men, some gay-identified, create and consume yaoi. They attend events such as Yaoi-Con, held annually in the United States since 2001, for similar reasons to those of women: to socialize with other fans, purchase *dōjinshi* and commercial products, engage in *kospure* (costumed play, abbreviated in English as "cosplay"), exhibit artwork, find out more about fandoms, share knowledge and meet prominent yaoi and boys' love artists.[7]

Identity is essential to our conception of self and it is at the center of the trouble some have with yaoi. Although a personal identity denotes one's sameness to some thing(s) over time, it implies his or her difference from others. A subject's identity is not his or hers alone. Constellations of attributes comprising an identity may become contestable, as they have for identities characterized by "race" or as "queer."[8]

Notions of identity posited by Judith Butler's gender theory maintain that an identity becomes linked to a subject by being interpellated by another and iterated time and again by the subject and others. Identity categories are unstable and elastic, needing continual reinforcement in order to maintain their integrity. Like the imitative effect of gay identities that "works ... to expose heterosexuality as an incessant and *panicked* imitation of its own naturalized idealization" (2004a, p. 129), yaoi works to destabilize not only anime and manga's canonical primacy but also fixed conceptions of gay identity.

Yaoi's expression engages gender at what Butler terms the "lived experience" of gender differentiation: the body's boundaries (2004b, p. 150). In a view that has gained currency in the critical theory community, Butler characterizes gender as performative, "produc[ing] on the skin, through the gesture, the move, the gait (that array of corporeal theatrics understood as gender presentation), the illusion of an inner depth" (2004a, p. 134).[9] The desires of the subject as well as others are imprinted as signs on the subject's body for others to see as presumed easily readable identities. Yaoi creators, by publishing works depicting nominally heterosexual characters engaging in non-homonormative scenarios and acts, blur the signs that signify contemporary hetero/homosexual identity. One way in which the fluidity of yaoi may be seen is in how the characters in yaoi stories look at one another.

Framing Desire

In *Chasing the Crown*, a story in the series *Mission: Arcadia and Beyond*,[10] based on characters and events in the commercial anime *Gundam Wing*, Duo Maxwell introduces his lover Heero Yuy to the idea of a ménage à trois with fellow pilot Wufei Chang:

> Heero's Prussian blue eyes widened momentarily then blinked at the sudden pictures in his mind. "I . . . Is that . . . Have you talked to him about this?" he finally managed. . . .
>
> (*Chasing the Crown*, 2006b)

Later, walking a few paces behind Duo, Wufei asks Heero,

> "Why is your lover flirting with me? He is doing that, correct?"
> "Wufei, have you ever looked into a mirror?" Heero asked. "And yes, Duo is flirting with you. He thinks you're handsome and so do I, but have you done the mirror thing? [...] [Y]ou stand naked in front of the mirror and Duo points out your good points. The objective is to get yourself looking at you in a different way." [...]
>
> (*Chasing the Crown*, 2006c)

> Wufei watched [Duo's] face intently, noting the momentary hesitance, and the glance. The Chinese pilot found that he was breathing very deeply. He turned, leaning his shoulder against the wall to face Duo more directly. "So you want to make up new rules, Duo?" he said softly, his dark eyes focused on Duo's face.
> "Why have rules at all?" Duo asked quietly before turning his head to peer at Wufei from under his bangs. "Why not just live, Wufei?" [...]
> "Just... live..." Wufei repeated, as if the idea was just beyond the edge of his comprehension. Suddenly he reached up, and placed his hand alongside Duo's cheek, leaned forward and pressed his lips to the other boy's.
>
> (*Chasing the Crown*, 2006d)

There may be no more fundamental way to show the presence of eros in desire than the gaze. Erotic desire is at the heart of yaoi and accordingly the gaze is probably the most common device in Western yaoi fiction. *Chasing the Crown*'s authors use the mirror to stress the link between erotic desire and the gaze.

In psychoanalytic theory, Jacques Lacan's idea of the infant's first seeing a reflection of itself in a mirror signifies the beginning of notions of corporeal self-awareness and hence the possibility for a subject's symbolic and linguistic exchange with others. In her discussion of Lacan, Elizabeth Grosz theorizes that the mirror is key to the infant's learning to place his or her body in space. An adult's notion of his or her surroundings, dominated as it is by "a spatiality of hierarchized perspective" (1994, p. 44), is only gradually realized by the child, who learns to "understand perspectives or the relations between figure and ground, which require oppositions that the child has not yet acquired" (p. 219).

Duo uses the mirror to frame the three pilots' bodies in the same space, collapsing the distance between them, and to show Heero and Wufei that they exist as erotic objects. In this, Duo's technique echoes the idea of the infant's learning from the specular image of itself that others can take a viewpoint on him (p. 93).

A theme common in *Gundam Wing* yaoi stories is portraying Duo with an intense need for love because of his fending for himself on the streets of a space colony slum during childhood. The authors' use in *Chasing the Crown* of a device prominent in psychoanalytic theory indicates the great importance they place on the gaze as a way to stress the urgency of Duo's desire.

Seeing also connotes apprehension of the seen. It is about the seer's autonomy and self-affirmation. The action in *Chasing the Crown* and other yaoi stories frequently brings the characters together in ways that facilitate their looking at one another. Several times in *Chasing the Crown* we watch characters interrogate each other's gaze as they talk or shift their gazes from one to the other during sex, in the latter case, a character framing what he sees as if it were a tableau to be committed to memory. In another story, Maldoror's *Freeport*, in several scenes, Wufei watches Duo's retreating form, seeing it as a challenge and an invitation to follow. In these and many Western yaoi stories, as the narrative moves between characters' points of view, our gaze moves with it. The effect of this constantly shifting gazing fits with the fluidity of yaoi's bodies and it produces a power equilibrium among the characters.

Resisting Identity

Central to *Chasing the Crown* and to Western yaoi fiction in general is a discursive frame that allows little in the way of conceptions of sexuality that operate to force an either/or identity division. Although most or all of the male characters in a yaoi story prefer sex with males, in almost all of the several hundred yaoi stories I have read, there is little or no sense of a homonormative environment established in opposition to a prevailing heteronormative one, little or no need for same-sex desiring males to form an identity or, in support of it, to allow or prohibit conduct and viewpoints. This is in contrast with the representations of "queer" in English-language comic strips, where, according to Edward Sewell (2006), queer cartoonists focus "on the creation of a thoroughly queer culture that often is in opposition, if not direct conflict, with the dominant heterosexual culture."[11]

The bodies of the three principal protagonists in *Chasing the Crown* move freely between being subject and object, fucking and being fucked, narcissistic identification and voyeuristic objectification, sometimes encompassing all of these states simultaneously. This is a characteristic of many yaoi stories and it is enhanced by yaoi's being a form that recreates canonical texts. Media characters seen first in canon, inscribed therein with a relatively fixed set of traits, are seen again and again in each new yaoi work, each time with their needs reimagined and their desires newly enacted. These continually evolving representations occur in a field of free-floating homoeroticism that lacks an oppositional context that might obstruct them. This fluidity is unlike the real-world construction of gender qualities into a state of opposing masculine and feminine sexual identities.

Eve Kosofsky Sedgwick describes the calculus of sexual identity in the West on a scale of masculine to feminine. She enumerates sixteen paired traits for sexual

Figure 14.2 Mite, mite! Heero Yuy carrying a younger Duo Maxwell. April 2000 http://www.silvertales.com.

© Kitsune, *Mite, mite!* April 2000 http://www.silvertales.com.

identity, showing how the elements of each masculine-feminine pair are constructed as binary opposites. They form a set shielding Western masculinity from things deemed nonmasculine (1993b, p. 7). Yaoi disrupts this panoply. It does so acutely in works featuring young children.

Chasing the Crown has five six-year-old boys living with Duo and Heero, mirror images, as it were, of the older characters in terms of both appearance and personalities (see Figure 14.2). The pilots took in two of the children, Kenny and

Duan, when they destroyed the base on which the two boys were living. The authors portray them in ways that maintain some stereotypically male attributes for fighters, such as their ability with explosives to destroy military targets, while more often showing them tenderly touching each other, holding on to one another, as Kenny holds on to Duan's braid—this sign of their intense friendship and mutual need a nonsexual echo of the relationship between Heero and Duo. The young boys' deep affection for each other is validated in their minds by that between the older pilots. The protection and love that the boys derive from the pilots' custody contrast starkly with Western culture, where, writes Sedgwick, not-masculine-enough boys and youth are effaced from the discourse of same-sex attracted adults, leaving them more vulnerable to homophobic predation than they might otherwise be.[12]

Yaoi recalls Sedgwick's conception of queer as "a continuing moment, movement, motive—recurrent, eddying, *troublant*" (1993a, p. xii). Western yaoi may have elements of queer, but as a genre it is not queer, if for no other reason than most of the yaoi creators with whom I have talked expressed disparate motives for their activities. Most refused to label what they did under any one rubric, including "queer." But yaoi fits Sedgwick's notion of movement.

New online media in general are independent of location and disruptive of a sequential flow of time. They tend to blur distinctions and attributes of things seen at first hand in the real world, and, as such, may give freer play to the unconscious in imagining subjects and objects.

One example of this blurring is in the Yaoi-Con Forums, a bulletin board open to anyone and frequented by those interested in or attending Yaoi-Con. Approximately fifteen to twenty percent of the attendees at this female created and run event are males. Many are young and dress themselves as the embodiment of boys' love, the *bishōnen* (beautiful boy)—*bishōnen* being a uniquely Japanese erotic topos dating from at least the tenth century CE and still part of the vernacular. They pose for photographs, help out at events and compete in Yaoi-Con's most popular event, the Bishonen Auction.

Their presence has become the number-one topic in the Forums. The dozens-to-hundreds of female and male visitors each day are producing discourses about males participating in yaoi. The dominant quality in posts that mention sexual identity and/or maleness is a resistance to definition and a blurring of and movement among categories. In response to being asked about "sexual orientation" in the topic "Single and Looking? Find other single yaoi fans here~!", some replied:

> Bi but trysexual works too (SeekingKnight)
> Gay… bi, no- gay?! (Omnithomas)
> sex: male… physically. Some would question my mental sex, though… (dunno001)
> Bi (or, I suppose perhaps, Pansexual) (loptr) (Yaoi-Con, 2009a)

Questions about maleness were often answered as questions or with humor, making the replies contingent on factors outside the discursive frame of what had been asked:

> Does a guy who is sort of like a girl count as a guy? (LordSora) (Yaoi-Con 2009b)
> What if I'm a fanboy who's okay (and fully supportive) of the listed fangirl philosophy? I can't decide!:o *'splodes* (Gothkitti) (Yaoi-Con 2009c)

These and other participants are creating an épistémè about what it is to be a *bishōnen* in a real-world event and what it could be like for males in the world outside of Yaoi-Con's liminal space to use *bishōnen* attributes and yaoi ideas with other males and females.

This might be part of what accounts for the intensity of the criticism of yaoi by some males who identify as gay. Accustomed to seeing real-life gay identified males and to participating in real-life discourses about them, they may construct some of their conceptions of gender and identity from these experiences. The multiplicity of imagined homoerotic acts and activities represented in yaoi discourses may work not to affirm but to unmoor an individual's sexual interests linking him to his conceptions of a gay identity. Yaoi's images may appear "confused" to Satō because they refuse a position beyond that of a wide-ranging homoeroticism, one which may not fit his or others' conceptions of "gay."

Yaoi, *shōnen-ai*, boys' love and slash are widespread. Yaoi allows the imagination free rein to queer the idea that gender boundaries should be fixed or that they should exist at all. It not only troubles culturally dominant notions of identity and gender, it empowers people—notably youth, who have little power—to resist them. As such it represents a critical nexus in the theory and praxis of gender.

Notes

1 This chapter is a revised version of a work of the same name published in Thomas Peele (2007), with the permission of the original publishers Palgrave.
2 For an example of a story with sexual relationships among multiple partners, see *Chasing the Crown* in this chapter. For a story describing a relationship between a minor and an older male, see *Pet Project* by Talya Firedancer (2009). For a story involving two brothers, see *Truth at the Bottom of a Sake Cup* by Alyssa Tay Tanoko (2009). For a story involving an authority figure (a university professor), see *The Discipline of Self* by Kai Foster (2009). For a story involving former wartime foes, see *After the Fire* by RazorQueen (2009).
3 For Japanese yaoi and boys' love generally, see McLelland (2000) and Suzuki (1998). For a description of Western fans reading a Japanese boys' love text, see Sabucco (2003). For slash, see Decarnin (2006, pp. 1233–1235). For Western yaoi, see McHarry (2003 and 2006, pp. 1445–1447).
4 Lunsing (2006). In August of 2007 more than 550,000 people attended Comiket, a

twice yearly fan-organized event in Tokyo (the largest of several held in Japanese cities), to buy or sell *dōjinshi*, much of it yaoi-themed, created by "circles," i.e., small groups of friends or individual artists. Over the last thirty years, women comprised fifty-seven percent of attendees and seventy-one percent of circle members; they were on average a little more than twenty-eight years old (Comic Market 2008, p. 21).

5 The search criterion for the Google searches was "yaoi." Returns were Web pages with the word in roman characters. Google searches are subject to large fluctuations for searches with a high number of returns, but the trend of steady and rapid growth between 2003 and 2009 is clear.

6 *Gundam* (War Story) began as an anime on Japanese TV in 1979 (Simmons 2004, p. 7). It follows a genre of super-robot anime popular in the 1970s, the story lines of which typically describe a male child or youth put in charge of a giant robot that must defend the world under threat from an external menace (Snyder 2000). *Gundam* was unsuccessful in its only season on Japanese TV, but gained popularity in re-runs, spawning a large number of follow-on products. *Gundam Wing*, the anime canonical for the yaoi story discussed in this chapter, was first shown on Japanese TV in 1995 and in North America via the Cartoon Network in 2000 (Simmons 2004, p. 8).

7 In talking with yaoi fans in Canada, Mexico, the United Kingdom and the United States, the only common denominator I found as to why they like yaoi is because it is fun.

8 John Russell (2006) discusses the effects of racialization in Japanese constructions of blackness, which he terms "simulations," that have been contested by some living in Japan who identify as black (pp. 6, 12). Jagose (1996, pp. 101–126) and Sullivan (2003, pp. 43–52) provide several examples of the contestation of "queer," including antithetical definitions by those publishing for a non-heterosexual audience: the editors of the Toronto queerzine *Bimbox* and the editor-in-chief of the gay and lesbian magazine *OutWeek* (pp. 44–45).

9 Performativity and repetition in attempting to stabilize a contested identity are also seen at the level of community. Paul Connerton (1989 cited by Featherstone, 1993) writes that a sense of place is "sustained by collective memory, which itself depends on ritual performances [and] bodily practices . . ." (p. 177). Mike Featherstone goes on to observe that these operate "in the countless little rituals, rites and ceremonies which take place in the embodied practices between friends, neighbours and associates. . . taken-for-granted routines [and] the co-ordination of bodily gestures and movements. . . ." (pp. 177–178).

10 The series, by RavynFyre and others (See *Chasing the Crown*, 2006a), is comprised of six stories totaling 116 chapters. The age given for the Gundam Wing pilots in *Mission: Arcadia and Beyond* is seventeen, not fifteen as it is canonically.

11 Sewell is writing about publications such as *XY Magazine*. Queer characters in comic strips drawn by heterosexual cartoonists for mainstream newspapers, on the other hand, do "not have any clear distinguishing characteristics to differentiate [them] from the dominant culture" (p. 268). Sewell defines "queer" in part as "a sexual orientation different from heterosexual or straight" (p. 271).

12 In her examination of the "apparently burgeoning epidemic of suicides and suicide attempts by children and adolescents in the United States" (1991, p. 18), Sedgwick quotes from the American Psychiatric Association's *Diagnostic and Statistical Manual III*, which identifies boys "display[ing] a 'preoccupation with female stereotypical

activities as manifested by a preference for either cross-dressing or simulating female attire, or by a compelling desire to participate in the games and pastimes of girls'" as meeting the diagnostic criteria of "Gender Identity Disorder of Childhood" (p. 20). Noting that the monographic literature about this condition since DSM-III's publication " is . . . as far as I can tell exclusively about boys" (p. 19), she cites representative examples which characterize male effeminacy as a global character pathology. Together with a male effemiphobia in the gay movement, which, she points out, has meant that the movement "has never been quick to attend to issues concerning effeminate boys" (p. 20), she reasons that the "great advance in recent gay and lesbian thought" of "theoriz[ing] gender and sexuality as distinct though intimately entangled . . . . may leave the effeminate boy once more in the position of the haunting abject— this time the haunting abject of gay thought itself" (ibid). Having written at the outset that "[i]t's always open season on gay kids" (p. 18), she concludes that "the eclipse of the effeminate boy from adult gay discourse would represent more than a damaging theoretical gap; it would represent a node of annihilating homophobic, gynephobic, and pedophobic hatred internalized and made central to gay-affirmative analysis" (p. 21).

Piontek extends Sedgwick's discussion in arguing that the rationale presented by the American Psychiatric Association for its pathologization of effeminacy in male children is paradoxical (2006, p. 60).

References

Butler, J. 2004a. Imitation and gender insubordination. In *The Judith Butler reader*, edited by S. Salih. Malden, MA: Blackwell, 119–137.

Butler, J. 2004b. The lesbian phallus and the morphological imaginary. In *The Judith Butler reader*, edited by S. Salih. Malden, MA: Blackwell, 138–180.

Chasing the Crown. 2006a. 21-June-2000 to 26-Jan-2002: *Chasing the Crown*. The Extended Family Fics Index. Gundam Wing Addiction. http://www.gwaddiction.com/bonnevon/exfam.htm [Accessed August 15, 2006]

Chasing the Crown. 2006b. 20-Sept-2000: *Mission: Arcadia* by RavynFyre, Kateri Marie, von and Bonnejeanne Part 25. http://www.gwaddiction.com/bonnevon/arcadia25.htm [Accessed August 21, 2006]

Chasing the Crown. 2006c. 15-July-2001. *Chasing the Crown*, An Extended Family Fic by RavynFyre, Nixer-chan, von and Bonnejeanne and guests Part, 32—Faux Pas. http://www.gwaddiction.com/bonnevon/crown32.htm [Accessed August 21, 2006]

Chasing the Crown. 2006d. 19-July-200: *Chasing the Crown*, An Extended Family Fic by RavynFyre, Nixer-chan, von and Bonnejeanne and guests Part 33—To Die For. http://www.gwaddiction.com/bonnevon/crown33.htm [Accessed August 21, 2006]

Comic Market. 2008. What is the comic market? A presentation by the Comic Market preparations committee. http://www.comiket.co.jp/info-a/WhatIsEng080225.pdf [Accessed August 15, 2009]

Decarnin, C.M. 2006. Slash fiction. In *Encyclopedia of erotic literature*, edited by G. Brulotte and John Phillips. New York: Routledge, 1233–1235.

FanFiction.Net. 2009. http://www.fanfiction.net [Accessed August 15, 2009]

Featherstone, M. 1993. Global and local cultures. In *Mapping the futures: Local cultures, global change*, edited by J. Bird, B. Curtis, T. Putnam, G. Robertson, and L. Tickner. London: Routledge, 169–187.

Firedancer, T. 2009. http://www.fyredancer.net/wk/WKpet01.html [Accessed August 15, 2009]

Foster, K. 2009. http://www.steelsong.com/fanfiction/feature/self.html [Accessed August 15, 2009]

Grosz, E. 1994. *Volatile bodies: Toward a corporeal feminism*. Bloomington: Indiana University Press.

Jagose, A. 1996. *Queer theory: An introduction*. New York: New York University Press.

Lunsing, W. 2006. Yaoi Ronsō: Discussing depictions of male homosexuality in Japanese girls' comics, gay comics and gay pornography. *Intersections: Gender, history and culture in the Asian context* (January 12). http://intersections.anu.edu.au/issue12_contents.html [Accessed August 16, 2009]

Maldoror. 2004–2006. *Freeport. Gundam Wing Addiction*. http://www.gwaddiction.com/Maldoror.shtml [Accessed August 15, 2009]

McHarry, M. 2003. Yaoi: Redrawing male love. *The Guide* 23(11) (November): 29–34. www.guidemag.com/content/index.cfm?id=225 [Accessed August 15, 2009]

McHarry, M. 2006. Yaoi. *Encyclopedia of erotic literature*, 1445–1447.

McLelland, M. 2000. No climax, no point, no meaning? Japanese women's boy-love sites on the internet. *Journal of Communication Inquiry* 24 (July): 274–291.

Peele, T. ed. 2007. *Queer popular culture: Literature, media, film, and television*. Basingstoke: Palgrave.

Piontek, T. 2006., *Queering gay and lesbian studies*. Urbana: University of Illinois Press.

Sabucco, V. 2003. Guided Fan Fiction: Western "readings" of Japanese homosexual themed texts. In *Mobile cultures: New media in queer Asia*, edited by C. Berry, F. Martin, and A. Yue.

Sedgwick, E. K. 1991. How to bring your kids up gay. *Social text* 29: 18–27.

Sedgwick, E. K. 1993a. Forward: t times. In *Tendencies*, edited by E. K. Sedgwick. Durham, NC: Duke University Press, xi–xvi.

Sedgwick, E. K. 1993b. Queer and now. In *Tendencies*, edited by E. K. Sedgwick. Durham, NC: Duke University Press, 1–20.

Sewell, E. H. Jr. 2006. Queer characters in comic strips. In *Comics and ideology*, edited by M. P. McAllister, E. H. Sewell, Jr., and I. Gordon. New York: Lang, 251–274.

Sheppard, S. 2002. Gay porn vs. Yaoi panel. *Yaoi-Con*, San Francisco, October 18.

Simmons, M. 2004. Introduction. In *Mobile suit Gundam: Awakening, escalation, confrontation*, edited by Tomino Yoshiyoki, trans. Frederik L. Schodt. Berkeley: Stone Bridge Press, 7–11.

Snyder, S. B. 2000. Giant robots/distant fathers: Size and anxiety in Japanese animation. Session: Entertaining passions: amusement and obsession in Japanese popular culture. Association for Asian Studies Annual Meeting, San Diego, March 9–12.

Sullivan, N. 2003. *A critical introduction to queer theory*. New York: New York University Press.

Suzuki, K. 1998. Pornography or therapy? Japanese girls creating the Yaoi phenomenon. In *Millennium girls: Today's girls around the world*, edited by S. A. Inness. Lanham, MD: Rowman & Littlefield, 243–267.

Tanoko, A. 2009. http://www.pacifier.com/~rebeccar/Ksake.html [Accessed August 15, 2009]

Thorn, M. 2004. Girls and women getting out of hand: The pleasure and politics of Japan's amateur comics community. In *Fanning the flames: Fans and consumer culture in contemporary Japan*, edited by W. W. Kelly. Albany: State University of New York Press, 169–187.

Tyr. 2000. Why Yaoi? *Gundam Wing Addiction.* http://gwaddiction.com/yaoi1.shtml [Accessed August 15, 2009]

Vincent, K. J. 2002. Envisioning the homosexual in Yaoi. Paper presented at Conceptualising Gender in Different Cultural Contexts Conference at the School of Oriental and African Studies, University of London, May 2–3.

Yaoi-Con. 2009a. Yaoi-Con Forums. Topic: "Single and Looking? Find other single yaoi fans here~!" 22 June 2007. http://www.yaoicon.com/component/option,com_fireboard/Itemid,258/func,view/catid,10/id,4131/ [Accessed August 15, 2009]

Yaoi-Con. 2009b. Yaoi-Con Forums. Topic: "guys going not for the yaoi but the fan girls." 29 August 2007. http://www.yaoicon.com/component/option,com_fireboard/ Itemid,258/func,view/catid,10/id,5091/ [Accessed August 15, 2009]

Yaoi-Con. 2009c. Yaoi-Con Forums. Topic: "How about a head count. Fangirls left, fanboys right." 22 April 2006. http://www.yaoicon.com/component/option,com_fireboard/Itemid,258/func,view/id,288/catid,10/#288 [Accessed August 15, 2009]

Part IV

Body Discourses

Chapter 15

Look at Me!
Images, Validation, and Cultural Currency on Gaydar

Sharif Mowlabocus

> [A]s a dimension of political practice, it abets the reshaping reformulation, and rethinking of gay male culture and its role in society. In short, pornography makes gay men visible.
>
> (Burger 1995, p. 4)

In this chapter I consider the role that images play in gay men's digital culture, exploring the meanings inscribed in such images. Principally I identify the assorted diverse knowledge produced by and through digital images of the (gay) self. I take as my focus the profile images found on Gaydar, Britain's most popular gay male dating website.[1] While my discussion is located within one specific gay male web space it should become clear that the discussion may equally apply to a range of similar websites and communities, such as Manhunt, Gay.com, Fitlads, and ManD8 to name just a few. Similarly, I am not arguing that these practices are confined to gay male culture, heterosexual dating sites may also serve as a rich site for a similar discussion. However, in locating my study within a gay male online space I acknowledge the specific political, cultural, and social implications that gay self-representation carries, which are not perhaps as prominent in straight/mainstream culture.

Digital images abound on Gaydar, varying greatly in terms of quality, size, content, sexual explicitness, and relationship to the user. My chief concern here is with two popular types of images, those that feature the user's face (known in Gaydar parlance as a "face-pic") and those of the user's body, or parts of his body. In both cases I will argue that such images operate as culturally important resources within "gay life" online and can be understood as confirming an investment in gay online culture. Also digital images such as this appear as a stabilizing force for identity formation and cultural legibility, offering a structuring device for the proliferation of specific ideas as to what it is to be a gay man in contemporary Western culture. Central to this understanding of cultural legibility is the relationship between profile images and gay pornography. I argue here for recognition of this relationship, and of the politics that such an investment in commercial sexual representation entails.

I aim to provide a foundational examination of how digital images (as discussed above) function on Gaydar. In doing so I seek to interrogate the profile image relevant to the culture that has produced it, and within which it circulates and has currency. This "embedding" of the image into wider gay male culture is essential if we are to fully understand the motivations behind such images and their functions in the space under investigation. This is important not least because the theme of visibility permeates gay men's history. It is therefore necessary to briefly consider this historical relationship in order to comprehend the "politics" of the profile image.

A History of (In)visibility

Visibility, as a theme, dominates the history of homosexual politics and culture, and many have identified gay male culture's investment in the visual (Hennessy 1995; Horne and Lewis 1997a; Medhurst 1998; Mercer 2000; Radel 2001; Weeks 1990). This is unsurprising given the fact that identifying as gay involves a conscious and (dis)continuous sequence of acts and performances. "Coming out" is about making one's self visible; throwing one's queerness into relief against a heteronormative background that would render it *invisible*. This invisibility has historically been a cause of tension and mistrust, not only for heteropatriarchy but also for other minority groups. As Bersani (1995) writes "[g]ay men are an oppressed group not only sexually drawn to the power-holding sex but also belonging to it themselves [. . .] we are in fact pariahs among minorities and oppressed groups." (p. 66). Commenting on the tensions between gay political groups and other civil rights movements he notes that "a middle-class white gay man can hardly claim to know the sort of oppression suffered by black men and women (p. 62) and that "our feminist sympathies [. . .] can't help being complicated by an inevitable narcissistic investment in the objects of our desire" (Ibid., 63)

While other minority groups distrust us, the dominant group fear us, for our uncanny ability is to "pass" and to move among them. However, the invisibility of the male homosexual has provided the motivation behind a raft of legal, medical, and social projects that have sought to identify and render him visible. Through such interventions, the homosexual has in fact been brought into being—he is, and has been, a product of such discourses. As Michel Foucault (1998 [originally 1976]) tells us:

> Discourses on sex did not multiply apart from or against power, but in the very space and as the means of its exercise. Incitements to speak were orchestrated from all quarters, apparatuses everywhere for listening and recording, procedures for observing, questioning, and formulating. Sex was driven out of hiding and constrained to lead a discursive existence.
>
> (pp. 32–33)

Rose (1996) talks of the discourse of genetics, which has sought to identify the homosexual, seeking to render the "gay brain" both visible and controllable. Meanwhile Grau (1995) and Plant (1987) detail the horrific experiments gay prisoners of the Nazi regime underwent as doctors sought to eradicate homosexuality through the identification of supposed hormonal imbalances. Such endeavors repeatedly underscore the notion of "queer invisibility."

Acts of identification and visibility are not only the project of external forces; throughout history the homosexual himself has undertaken projects of sexual signification, though arguably for radically different reasons, and often in more covert and sub-cultural ways,

> Given that sexuality is not as visible as race or gender, clothing styles and behavior become significant in signaling sexual identity, authenticity and belonging.
>
> (Holt and Griffin 2003, p. 412)

From carnations, to handkerchiefs, to (reappropriated) pink triangles, homosexual men have been signaling to anyone "in the know" for centuries. Such apparel and accessories have been deployed in an ongoing (though often fractured and fragmentary) process by which men can announce their sexuality to others without verbal affirmation (See Urbach 1996). These acts of visibility became politicized in the 1970s as gay activism urged men and women to battle their internalized homophobia and claim their "true" identity (Power 1995). This prioritizing of the visible continues to frame gay culture in the West today, where 'a sense of a recognizable identity may be variously signified by the wearing of certain clothes and the consumption of certain magazines, films, posters, and the visual packaging of music. (Horne and Lewis 1997b, pp. 99–100). In opposition to "mainstream" space, being seen in a gay venue confers a queer status upon the subject without further verbal or non-verbal queues. The space itself acts as a form of "outing," where the crushing and oppressive presumption of heterosexuality that gay men and women continue to suffer under is momentarily suspended, and where straight people have to "come out" as being the "different" members in the bar—the outsiders in such a space.

As Horne and Lewis note, it is "not just [. . .] forms of material culture that registers a queer identity, but the very act of being part of the village as spectacle in itself" (1997b, pp. 104–105). They go on to argue that:

> … for many urban gays (or those who visit the city) the activity of seeing and being seen in a clearly gay-coded space (be it a bar, a Pride march, a café or a sex shop) is part of affirming and asserting an identity.
>
> (Horne and Lewis 1997b, pp. 104–105)

Thus being seen in a queer-coded space serves to render homosexuality visible, making the subject "part of the scene" as it were—a member of the club:

> At the same time that we are repulsed by the non-Queer communities, we are attracted to and by the existing Queer community. We are drawn closer to spaces where Queers are known to safely and comfortably congregate.
>
> (Dishman 1995, p. 3)

Geographers (Sibalis 2004; Skeggs et al. 2004) have noted how devalued sites within cities have been appropriated by "devalued" queer communities. Examples such as New York's Meatpacking district or London's Vauxhall Arches demonstrate how, when repelled by non-queer society, queer communities utilize run-down, derelict or otherwise "low-status" spaces in order to (re)group, congregate, and create new zones of sexual, social, and personal safety. Commenting on the gay "ghetto" of West Hollywood, LeVay and Nonas write that while gay men may be "drawn together by sexual desire" they "find that more than sex unites them":

> Style, sleaze, and all, West Hollywood exudes a civic pride, a togetherness, an exuberance, based on the conviction that gayness is the central attribute of gay people's nature, an attribute that reaches into every corner of their daily lives.
>
> (LeVay and Nonas 1995, p. 136)

Non-physical space can also be seen to operate in similar ways. While many Internet sites are read as heterosexual by default (Kendall 2000), being "seen" on Gaydar can offer a sense of "place" while also operating as a marker of queerness. Maintaining a profile on a "regular" social networking website may say relatively little about one's sexuality[2], but having a Gaydar profile instantly marks the user as gay, or at the very least invested in same-sex desire. This is an important point to remember when considering the role of images within gay dating websites, as the maintenance of a user profile on a site such as Gaydar inevitably involves some degree of investment—both in the space created by the website, and the identity (or rather identities) that it supports.

My Face is my Passport: "Face-pics" and the Politics of Membership

As images that clearly show the user's face, sometimes in close up, face-pics are prevalent on Gaydar, though this is not to suggest that all members include them on their profiles. Indeed, many users choose not to include a face-pic, offering instead to send an image to browsers who contact them, "my face-pic in return for yours" being a common statement of intention. Others prefer not to use face-pics at all and there is a degree of tension on Gaydar surrounding this. It is not uncommon, for example, to come across users who refuse to respond to "faceless" browsers, the phrase "No Pic? No Dick!" being a regular utterance on profiles.

Refusals to show one's face, to communicate with a "faceless" user, and to volunteer one's face-pic without contact all point to the value of face images on Gaydar. It highlights the levels of investment made in presenting the face-pic, not that dissimilar to unashamed visibility in the gay bar. The face-pic demonstrates the user's investment in and identification with a queer identity. This drive to be "seen" on Gaydar—to allow one's self to be recognized—responds to the historical invisibility of gay men identified above, and is contiguous with the ensuing problems that such invisibility brings. Practices of visibility within gay male digital space must be compared to offline contexts and considering the *lack* of visibility afforded gay men within other spheres of their lives. Visibility in this way is inherently political. The history of gay male culture is not separated from the Gaydar profile; it forms part of its *constitution*.

For example, historically, just as being "in the closet" proved incompatible with the emerging gay consciousness (Power 1995, p. 35), today, authoring a text-only profile on Gaydar is, for many, not considered adequate. Honesty, integrity, and authenticity are key concerns within profiles as browsers need to feel that they are communicating with a "genuine" person who is closely aligned to their profile. In textual descriptions, claims of personal honesty are occasionally married with slightly self-deprecating remarks (similar to Coupland's study (1996) on contact adverts) often demonstrating a level of self-awareness and a lack of arrogance. Visually, the face-pic in particular serves to validate the user in this space. Chiefly the face-pic confirms that the user is willing to self-identify. It confirms his willingness, however limited and contingent, to be *seen* as gay. However the process is two-fold; the face-pic declares that the subject is gay, and also this allows the browsers to identify the user as gay. There may be no apparent difference in these terms; however, I argue that there is an important distinction. The face-pic *empowers* the user to self-identify but at the same time it *exposes* him, namely to identification by all who view his profile.

During the course of research conducted on the website some users explained why they had chosen *not* to include a face-pic on their profile, stating that "[I] chose not to have photos in my profile for the simple reason i prefer to choose who sees my pic." Another user who had included only body images replied that "I would rather only send that [face-pic] to people who are willing to show me there [sic] face-pics." He went on to argue that, "if I did put my facepic up, I would not know who is looking at my profile (maybe a friend), whilst they may know who I am." Thus, while a comparison between Horne and Lewis's gay-coded (offline) space and digital gay space can offer some insight, there are points at which the comparison must diverge (Horne and Lewis 1997b). For although the same form of self/identification occurs when entering a gay bar, the number of potential "spectators" is vastly greater on Gaydar. In a bar, 50 or 100 others can identify me at any one time; online I can potentially be viewed by millions (although the physical proximity is entirely different).

For users who *did* include a face-pic on their profile, the investment in the image as a signifier of authenticity, honesty, and "pride" was clearly evident. For example, one user stated that "[I] a[i]m to be proud of who I am" and wanted to "let other users see me." Other users stated that they chose to include a face-pic "in the interests of my own integrity" and that "a photo implies that I am open and honest about who I am." Still others chose to reveal their faces online stating that "I have nothing to hide."

This discourse of "pride" in being seen and being gay can be understood on two levels. Firstly, such a discourse taps into wider discourses of coming out that have prevailed within gay culture and politics since the 1970s (Weeks 1990). Regardless of the reason, "remaining" in the closet continues to be a stigmatized position within LGBT culture. Secondly, such a discourse serves to counter the disembodied facet of the Internet. Since the story of the "crossdressing psychiatrist" (Stone 1998, p. 65), fears of online deceptions and scams have circulated within scholarly and popular writing about the Internet. Gaydar culture is not immune to such anxieties and concerns over veracity, honesty and integrity often translate into a fear of being duped into meeting someone who bears little resemblance to the description on their profile. While such deceptions may not cost Gaydar users (the fraud not being a material one), they are seen as both a nuisance and a waste of time and energy. Coté and Pybus (2007) highlight the levels of immaterial labor that users invest in spaces such as MySpace, and one might see a similar level of labor going into the development and negotiation of contacts on Gaydar. Acknowledging the investment that users make, not only in their profiles but in contacting other users, means that such deceptions are not only a nuisance, but render the user's labor unproductive and without exchange value.

For many users face-pics are considered a form of insurance against such deception, acting as a promise of what they can expect in real life.[3] And this insurance is intimately tied into the process of self-identification and "outing" on Gaydar. The user responses highlighted above suggest that being *seen* as an out gay man is an important facet of their identity, and that being seen for who they really are is a marker of authenticity, and may be seen as a guard against deception in others (for failure to provide this). On Gaydar users ascribe a great deal of value to face-pics. These images serve to represent and thereby embody the self: acting as a visual declaration that authenticates both the profile and the user. In a sense, the face-pic—and by extension, the user's own face becomes a form of membership card, providing proof of legitimacy at the same time as it marks the user as *visibly* queer.

Of course "membership" has its limits and costs and there is also transactional facet to profile images. I mentioned above the comments from users who chose *not* to include face-pics in their profiles and such responses suggest that while acting as a membership card, the face-pic is not without economic value on Gaydar. Slater identifies "a concern [. . .] with reciprocity" (Slater 1998, p. 111) in online environments where images are swapped and "traded":

> Despite the fact that the supply of sexually explicit pictures on IRC is entirely free and apparently inexhaustible—beyond either scarcity or value—being ripped off or "leeched" is a matter of constant, obsessive anger and regulation.
> (Slater 1998, p. 111)

The responses of Gaydar users identified above suggest that a similar system of trade operates on the website and that similar concerns with reciprocity pervade the user profile and interactions between users. Thus the user who does not include a face-pic may be asked for an image prior to further interaction. This establishes a transactional relationship with the intended contact, and reveals the possibility that they may be shunned if they are perceived to be unwilling to "trade" identities.

Decisions behind such choices demonstrate the central role this type of image plays within what we might identify as the *Gaydar economy*. Like Slater's moral economy this economy is not financially based but functions on the level of subjectivity. Respondents who had chosen to include a face-pic often spoke derisively of those who remained hidden, for example, "I chose to include photos because many [people] are false and closets" or "I wouldn't reply to a message without photo's attached" and "I will not respond to any profile without a picture and don't expect others to—it makes it look as if you have something to hide." If this economy deals in subjectivity—be it the trading of images and messages, or an acknowledged investment in the space (through profile updates, detailed profile contents, or membership status and recent activity)—then what is also being traded simultaneously is *trust*. Thus, being seen to not invest in this space (for example through not including a face-pic), serves to dislocate the individual from this circuit of trust and place him in a zone of ambivalence. The "faceless" user is the sub-prime investment—unknown, unseen, and uncertain.

Jones observes that "[t]he self-portrait photograph is an example [. . .] of this way in which technology not only *mediates* but *produces* subjectivities in the contemporary world" (Jones 2002, p. 950) and recognizes the connection between the self-consciously radical photographers of her study and more mainstream self-representations,

> The point [. . .] is to engage with such images [. . .] in such a way as to open out the question of how subjectivity is established and how meaning is made in relation to *all* representations.
> (Jones 2002, p. 949)

Jones's argument is that the exaggerated performances of artists such as Claude Cahun, Cindy Sherman, and Lyle Ashton Harris serve to destabilize modernist assumptions regarding the "truth" not only of the photograph but also of a pre-given identity (Jones 2002, p. 948). The average Gaydar face-pic may not be as explicitly involved in staging such an assault on conventional notions of identity but Jones's comments are nonetheless relevant:

> The subject performs herself or himself within the purview of an apparatus of perspectival looking that freezes the body as representation and so—as absence, as always already dead—in intimate relation to lack and loss [...] At the same time [...] these works foreground the fact that *the self-portrait photograph is eminently performative and so life giving*.
>
> (Jones 2002, p. 949) (Author's emphasis)

On Gaydar face-pics not only validate the subject of the image, they also provide a sense of presence: a sense of "being there" and of embodiment. For example where users discussed their image in relation to other browsers the general consensus was that such images allowed a level of identification between user and browser; "I like to know who I'm talking too [sic] and vice versa." Unlike the cinematic gaze of narrative film (Mulvey 1975), users do not consider themselves as objectified by their profile images but instead embodied through this visual representation, "[I want to] let people c who they r chatting 2." Face-pics, it seems, act as conduits between those pictured and those looking and play an important role in "affirming and asserting an identity" in a specific online environment (Horne and Lewis 1997b, pp. 104–105).

Bodies on Display

Like many gay dating websites, images of users' bodies and body parts are commonly found on Gaydar. This focus on the body pre-dates the advent of an image-based Internet experience with Campbell (2004) identifying a heavy investment in representations of the (gay) male body in text-based gay forums. Likewise the work of Mercer (2000), Dyer (1989, 1992), and O'Toole (1999) demonstrates the focus on representing the male body that has been present within queer subcultures since before the Gay Rights movement.

Gaydar demonstrates this continuing interest in the male body, and users often self-present in a variety of ways, varying from fully clothed full-body shots, through to naked "poses," to close-ups of specific areas of the body. Images of the body in action (often sexual) are also commonly found. On one level such images serve to "sell" the user to the community of browsers, identifying not only the type, size, pertness, muscularity, skin tone, and age of the user but also his preferred sexual roles, acts, practices, and fetishes. This notion of "selling" and advertising is given another dimension when we recognize the fact that in many images, the tight framing, aesthetics, and pose chosen by the user echo the well-established conventions of commercial gay pornography. Similarly, the penis continues to operate as the principal signifier of sexual prowess, sexual desire, and sexual attractiveness in this space and the regular depiction of oral and anal sex echoes the conventions of commercial gay pornography where such acts are prioritized (the latter often being considered the "goal" or climactic act).

Feminist work may provide us with a critical framework for understanding these images. While the focus has historically been on the content and/or effect of sexual representation (Attwood 2007; Dworkin 2000; Paasonen 2006; Strossen 1995; Williams 1992) the *structure* of such material has been addressed by Suzanne Kappeler (1986). By comparing images of pornographic "fictions" with images of "real" torture, Kappeler is able to identify both the similarities between such images, and the divisions established between the victim/object of each representation and the audience/author of the representation:

> The host and his guests mingle and merge in the audience, they become one as the audience, but the host is the author of the party and they are "celebrating." The victim does not come out of the picture, the victim is dead. In this case [of murder] literally, in the general case of representation virtually, or functionally, as there is no designated role in the world, and in the continued existence of the representation, for the victim to take up. [sic] If the person filling the role of victim is not actually dead, s/he should be.
> (Kappeler 1986, p. 9)

Kappeler's argument recognizes both the *potential* for men and women to become objects of representation, and also the power imbued in the audience/author of such representations. Of course, this subject-object dyad blurs when we remember that profile images are often self-produced—the "victim" of Kappeler's logic is here also the author of his own victimhood—profile images are often user-generated and are always posted by the user himself. However, just as it matters little to Kappeler that more and more women are entering public life and attaining positions of power (Kappeler 1986, p. 6), so it is of little consequence that gay men are "choosing" to represent themselves online in this way. For in each instance, the power ostensibly "won" is ultimately obtained via, and in the service of, structures that are controlled by "a capitalist elite" (p. 78). Such an argument suggests that profile creation is tied to wider systems of commercial representation, whether directly (through imitation or simulation) or indirectly (through comparison with other profiles in a specific "genre" or of a specific "type").

D'Emilio (1992) argues that material capitalism has provided an opportunity for gay men to form identities and lifestyles based around their sexual object-choice. In doing so, it has also constituted them as "good" consumers, whose identities and sub-cultures are overwhelmingly centered around practices of consumption. Note the spaces identified above in which gay people feel validated. Bars, clubs, cafes, bookstores: acts of gay identification regularly occur within commercial spaces. The creation of a gay scene (commercial or otherwise) is invariably a politically, economically, and culturally powerful achievement. However, it is not without its costs and within the context of representation one of these costs is the overreliance on commercial representations of homosexuality in the production of gay subjectivity in digital space.

I have argued elsewhere (Mowlabocus 2007) that the amalgamation of ICT's with the structures of gay porn has proven to be a shaping force within contemporary urban gay culture, providing a cultural framework through which sexual identity is produced, negotiated, and maintained online. This is evident in the categorizing processes that are invoked via the website and through the user profile. Users are asked to identify according to a "type" (bear, skin, twink, cub, leather/rubber) that renders them legible but also knowable: the identification process is simultaneously a process of knowledge and of discipline (Foucault 1995 [originally 1975]). This knowledge is a sexual knowledge that draws heavily on the aesthetics, codes, and conventions of gay pornography. Thus a "bear" is expected to represent himself as hirsute, and larger in size than a "twink." He is also expected to identify with a different performance of masculinity to that of a twink and to invest in a different range of sexual practices and roles to the twink. Meanwhile, in identifying as a "twink" a user aligns himself with a particular body type (slim and relatively hairless), a particular age bracket (18–25) and presents a particular *performance* of age. Identifying with the "twink" type does perhaps not suggest specific sexual practices, but the twink aesthetic tends to lean towards more "mainstream" sexual acts (as opposed to BDSM, "watersports" or "fisting").

I am not however suggesting that the all men who identify as bears are hairy, or big, or butch, or into rough sex, or indeed that all men who identify as twinks are waif-like or that young. Rather, my assertion is that in identifying as a bear or a twink, the user positions himself *in relation* to sub-cultural understandings of what a bear or a twink should look like, revealing how he should act and what kinds of sex he prefers. Invariably the user is measured against an ideal, and that ideal is constructed and disseminated via commercial pornography. Western gay male sub-culture has a composite relationship with pornography, and many men have formed complex and subtle bonds with this form of representation (see Dyer 1989; Edwards 1994; Watney 1996). In this respect it is unsurprising to see gay men drawing from the representational constructs of gay porn, in their self-representation. However, such representation also inherits the problematic politics of gay porn. And while pornography may have the potential to break down sexual boundaries (Williams 1992) the exact opposite is occurring online. Thus the "body shots" that users post to represent themselves on Gaydar must be read within the context of this relationship with pornography, whether that be manifest in the pose, action, attitude, setting or content of the image.

Conclusion

In this chapter I have only been able to provide a thumbnail sketch of the role that profile images play within contemporary gay male digital culture. Different images clearly engender different questions regarding the identification and validation of the self, the relationship between the self and gay culture and the power of pornography to shape understandings of gay male representation. Stone refers to a "legible body" that subjects must inhabit in cyberspace, asserting that such a requirement is not unique to digital culture but is in fact part of wider society. Bodies, she argues, must always be understood as "culturally intelligible" and should be regarded as being articulated, regulated, and therefore subverted through the "textual productions" that "each society uses to produce physical bodies that it recognizes as members" (Stone 1998, p. 524).

In this respect the images that appear on the user profile not only represent the gay male body in cyberspace, but also operate as a medium through which that body is both (re)produced and understood in that space. Likewise, as the quotation at the beginning of this chapter illustrates, a more sympathetic reading of pornography than that offered by Kappeler may help us to identify the affirmative power of such images of the body.

While the Feminist critique of body images must be acknowledged, so must the specificity of the profile image as a sub-cultural artefact. Mercer (2000) articulates the ambivalent position he finds himself in when encountering Mapplethorpe's racially coded photography and perhaps we should be similarly ambivalent in our attitude toward the user profile, not least because this may prove to be a productive position from which to critique this ubiquitous sub-cultural form. Such a position allows us to recognize the paradoxical nature of the profile image. Operating within the confines of gay space, the profile image seeks to resolve long-standing questions pertaining to the visibility, identification, and validation of homosexuality (Macnair 1996) in Western culture, providing a means of authentic articulation through which the gay subject can come into being. At the same time however, it may also serve to fix, fasten and "discipline" an otherwise diverse gay male sexuality according to the conventions and structures of looking that have been established within the commercial arena of gay male pornography. I do not claim to have provided an answer as to the role of the profile image in gay male cyberculture, but hopefully this chapter has opened up a line of critical enquiry, and provided the context for further investigations of this multi-faceted form of digital self-representation and its popularity within Western gay male digital culture.

Notes

1 At the time of writing this, Hitwise UK ranked Gaydar the most popular dating website (irrespective of sexual orientation) in the UK.
2 Or, following Bell et al.'s assertion (1994), one could argue that such spaces are coded as heterosexual unless otherwise identified.
3 Though of course there are always cases where the picture is either out of date, particularly flattering or indeed, false.

References

Attwood, F. 2007. No money shot? Commerce, pornography and new sex taste cultures. *Sexualities* 10(4): 441–456.
Bell, D. J., Binnie, J., Cream, J., and Valentine, G. 1994. All hyped up and no place to go. *Gender, place and culture* 1(1): 31–47.
Bersani, L. 1995. *Homos*. Cambridge, MA: Harvard University Press.
Burger, J. R. 1995. *One-handed histories: The eroto-politics of gay male video pornography*. New York: Harrington Park Press.
Campbell, J. E. 2004. *Getting it on online: Cyberspace, gay male sexuality and embodied identity*. New York: Harrington Park Press.
Coté, M., and Pybus, J. 2007. Learning to immaterial labour 2.0. *Ephemera* 7(1): 88–106.
Coupland, J. 1996. Dating advertisements: Discourses of the commodified self. *Discourse and Society* 7(2): 187–207.
D'Emilio, J. 1992. *Making trouble: Essays on gay history, politics and the university*. New York: Routledge.
Dishman, D. J. 1995. Digital divas: Defining queer space on the information superhighway. http://www.usc.edu/isd/archives/queerfrontiers/queer/papers/dishman.html [Accessed July 15, 2002]
Dworkin, A. 2000. Pornography and grief. In *Feminism and pornography*, edited by D. Cornell. Oxford: Oxford University Press, 39–44.
Dyer, R. 1989. A conversation about pornography. In *Coming on strong: Gay politics and culture*, edited by S. Shepherd and M. Wallis. London: Unwin Hyman.
Dyer, R. 1992. *Only entertainment*. London: Routledge.
Edwards, T. 1994. *Erotics and politics: Gay male sexuality, masculinity and feminism*. London: Routledge.
Foucault, M. 1995 [1975]. *Discipline and punish: The birth of the prison*, 2nd ed. New York: Vintage Books.
Foucault, M. 1998 [1976]. *The history of sexuality: 1 The will to knowledge*. London: Penguin.
Gaydar. 2008. http://www.gaydar.co.uk [Accessed December 2, 2008]
Grau, G. 1995. *Hidden holocaust? Gay and lesbian persecution in Germany 1933–45*. London: Cassell.
Hennessy, R. 1995. Queer visibility in commodity culture. In *Social postmodernism: Beyond identity politics*, edited by L. Nicholson and S. Seidman. Cambridge: Cambridge University Press, 142–184.

Hitwise UK. Competitive real time intelligence. http://www.hitwise.co.uk/datacenter/industrysearchterms/dating.php. [Accessed December 2, 2008]

Holt, M., and Griffin, C. 2003. Being gay, being straight and being yourself: Local and global reflections on identity, authenticity and the lesbian and gay scene. *European Journal of Cultural Studies* 6(3): 404–425.

Horne, P., and Lewis, R. 1997a. Reframed: Inscribing lesbian, gay and queer presences in visual culture. In *Outlooks: Lesbian and gay sexualities and visual cultures*, edited by P. Horne and R. Lewis. London: Routledge, pp. 1–12.

Horne, P., and Lewis, R. 1997b. Visual culture. In *Lesbian and gay studies: A critical introduction*, edited by A. Medhurst and S. Munt. London: Continuum, pp. 99–112.

Jones, A. 2002. The 'eternal return': Self-portrait photography as a technology of embodiment. *Signs: Journal of Women in Culture and Society* 27(4): 947–978.

Kappeler, S. 1986. *The pornography of representation*. Cambridge: Polity Press.

Kendall, L. 2000. "Oh no! I'm a nerd!" Hegemonic masculinity on an online forum. *Gender and Society* 14(2): 256–274.

LeVay, S., and Nonas, E. 1995. *City of friends: A portrait of the gay and lesbian community in America*. Cambridge, MA: MIT Press.

Macnair, B. 1996. *Mediated sex: Pornography and postmodern culture*. London: Arnold.

Medhurst, A. 1998. Tracing desires: Sexuality in media texts. In *The media: A critical introduction*, edited by A. Briggs and P. Cobley. Harlow: Pearson Education, 283–294.

Mercer, K. 2000. Just looking for trouble: Robert Mapplethorpe and fantasies of race. In *Feminism and pornography*, edited by D. Cornell. Oxford: Oxford University Press, 460–476.

Mowlabocus, S. 2007. Gay men and the pornification of everyday life. In *Pornification: Sex and sexuality in media culture*, edited by S. Paasonen, K. Nikunen, and L. Saarenmaa. London: Berg, 61–72.

Mulvey, L. 1975. Visual pleasure and narrative cinema. *Screen* 16(3): 6–18.

O'Toole, L. 1999. *Pornocopia: Porn, sex, technology and desire*. London: Serpents Tail.

Paasonen, S. 2006. Email from Nancy Nutsucker. *European Journal of Cultural Studies* 9(4): 403–420.

Plant, R. 1987. *The pink triangle: The Nazi war against homosexuals*. Edinburgh: Mainstream Publishing.

Power, L. 1995. *No bath but plenty of bubbles: An oral history of the gay liberation front 1970–73*. London: Cassell.

Radel, N. R. 2001. The transnational ga(y)ze: Constructing the East European object of desire in gay film and pornography after the fall of the wall. *Cinema Journal* 41(1): 40–62.

Rose, H. 1996. Gay brains, gay genes and feminist science theory. In *Sexual cultures: Community, values, intimacy*, edited by J. Weeks, and J. Holland. London: Macmillan Press, 53–72.

Sibalis, M. 2004. Urban space and homosexuality: The example of the Marais, Paris' "gay ghetto." *Urban Studies* 41: 1739–1758.

Skeggs, B., Moran, L., Tyrer, P., and Binnie, J. 2004. Queer as folk: Producing the real of urban space. *Urban studies* 41: 1839–1856.

Slater, D. 1998. Trading sexpics on IRC: Embodiment and authenticity on the Internet. *Body and Society* 4(4): 91–117.

Stone, A. R. 1998. *The war of desire and technology at the close of the mechanical age.* Cambridge, MA: MIT Press.

Strossen, N. 1995 *Defending pornography: Free speech, sex and the fight for women's rights.* New York: Scribner.

Urbach, H. 1996. Closets, clothes, disclosure. *Assemblage* 30: 62–73.

Watney, S. 1996. *Policing desire: Pornography, AIDS and the media.* Minneapolis: University of Minnesota Press.

Weeks. J. 1990. *Coming out: Homosexual politics in Britain from the nineteenth century to the present.* London: Quartet.

Williams, L. 1992. Pornography on/scene or diff'rent strokes for diff'rent folks. In *Sex exposed: Sexuality and the pornography debate,* edited by L. Segal and M. McIntosh. London: Virago, 233–265.

Chapter 16

Gay Men's Use of Online Pictures in Fat-Affirming Groups[1]

Jason Whitesel

The Internet has occasioned a new relationship between gay identity and body symbolism, in reworked commercial images for men who are inadequately represented by advertising and other forms of media. Cyberspace offers fat gay men a forum where they can reconfigure imagery and text, to signal issues of personal, collective, and gender identity.[2] Though the counseling community has discussed how advertisements negatively affect gay consumers' perceptions of their bodies (Matthews 2005; Shernoff 2002), few have considered advertisements as part of an interactive process that provides an opportunity for gay men to re-evaluate their body images in virtual and actual experiences. To develop a larger model for understanding visibility politics and virtual body images, this chapter examines how the subject of fat gay men trying to gain a presence in existing advertising offers evidence of resistant cultural practices. Building on studies that unpack the complex semiotics of advertisements and media images (Bordo 1997; Goffman 1979), the chapter discusses how reworking the images can provide a site for both critique and reinstatement of conformity.

Two visual case studies—*Absolut Beefy* and the "fat morph"—provide physically inventive images that challenge conventional portrayals of fat in an effort to enhance fat's visibility to a number of supportive enthusiasts. The first is a remake of a vodka advertisement, and the second is a digital remake of an underwear advertisement, both introduce fat into advertising. Regarding semiotic structures, fat gay men emerge as "inveterate and promiscuous producers of signs" (Hawkes 1977, 134). Visual semiotics involves continuous dismantling and reassembling of visual texts, recognizing that visual communication represents "not the mere 'embroidery' of 'reality,' but a way of knowing it, of coping with it, and of changing it" (Hawkes 1977, p. 143). This chapter asks, "In what ways do emerging visual technologies reshape fat politics for gay men?"

This discussion focuses on work by an artist who recreates commercial images and another who digitally alters them, both doing something similar to "subvertisements" (a subversive form of re-appropriating advertising images (see Ironkite 2009)). Both artists mimic the "look and feel" of the originals while incorporating fat-affirming themes (Lasn 2000, p. 131). Both also "poach" basic visual elements from widely circulated ad campaigns, convert them into a vehicle for reclaiming a fat gay male identity, and recirculate the new images among members of online subcultures. Since these artists actively participate in online fat-friendly groups, their works "speak from a position of collective identity, to forge an alliance with a community of others in defense of tastes" (Jenkins 1992, p. 23).

Gay Bodies within the Bounds

Like heterosexual women, gay men experience conflict with their appearance, physique, and relationship to food more than heterosexual men do. Gay men do not retain the benefits of fatness that heterosexual men have historically. They also negatively associate fat with effeminacy. It is important therefore to identify boundaries, the role of advertising, and the historical context of fatness and body image, including its gendered implications for gay men. Folding in social history, this chapter situates the images in the context of developing gay social trends, referencing events like HIV/AIDS that influence gay men's current and everyday understandings of fatness and their bodies. Gay men revisit their relationships to fat subsequent to diseased bodies and recognize that their adherence to the norms and physicality of hegemonic masculinity remains under constant surveillance. Thus, gay men live in historically constituted and highly gendered communities. For the contemporary generation of gay men, loosening the restrictions on their waistlines signifies a reconfiguring of gay body concepts.

Body image influences boundary marking: "conceptions of bodily boundaries and social order" raise "consciousness about how fundamental body imagery is to worldview and so to political language" (Haraway 1986, p. 520). Commercialized images reify body boundaries. Most gay personals, for instance, reflect these persistent images and separate bodies with the usual seeker's request that one should be in shape and "please, *NO* fats or femmes!" Following the personal ad lingo, failure to be "height-weight proportionate" exceeds the bounds of how a gay body "ought to *look*" (Goode 2005, p. 328). Gay men marginalize those who don't conform to strict bodily standards and use these boundaries to create inequality, the most salient of which is gender (Giles 1998). Heterosexism perpetuates the myth that gay men are effeminate and that effeminate men must be gay; simultaneously, it assumes that same-sex relationships include a masculine role and feminine complement. Fat produces stereotypical feminized features that threaten masculinity and its archetype of the disciplined, muscular body (Bell and McNaughton 2007; Durgadas 1998). It reinforces the effeminate label when men develop breasts or hips and diminishes the visibility of their genitals (Millman 1980). To gain acceptance, gay men often adopt rigid gender roles, such as the straight-acting, masculine male, to create a border between themselves and the stigma surrounding the "fats" and the "femmes" (Bergling 2001; Connell 1992). Thus, gay men use gendered dimensions of the body to make in- and out-group distinctions.

Advertising plays an irresponsible role in the construction of boundaries, seducing gay men to subordinate their bodies to systems of commercial oppression. Similar to female beauty standards, gay men feel compelled to purchase products and procedures that market physical "perfection" (Signorile 1997). Thus, advertising as a boundary-ordering device implicates gay men in financing industries that contribute to their body dissatisfaction. Like other body aesthetics, the gay male aesthetic rewards those with a lean, taut, and muscular upper body, and visual elements of gay culture such as clubs and commercial representations reinforce this standard. The oppressive content of gay visual culture centers on body worship of male models in homoerotic media like pornography and magazines about physique and fashion. Because many gay men prioritize personal appearance, they spend an inordinate amount of time and resources trying to change their appearance through gyms, cosmetic surgery, tanning, and hair restoration and removal (Blotcher 1998; Drummond 2005; Feraios 1998; Padva 2002). Commercial images exclude imperfect gay bodies, namely fat, old, or disabled, and divide men along these lines.

Online Audiences for Gay- and Fat-Affirming Images

Web transformation of commercialized images is a proliferating phenomenon defined by its instability. The image analysis in this chapter comes from two personal profile websites that cater exclusively to fat gay men and their admirers.[3] The first, targeted at young adults, is marketed by a young network administrator from Florida, who is stereotypically handsome and "well built" (over 6 feet tall, about 190 lbs, with an athletic build). Since the site was started from his standpoint as an outsider who admires big-and-beefy college gays, objectification was central to this site's inception. Started in early 2003 as a fraternity with international membership mostly from North America, the site invites members to post personal profile images that provide pleasure to members who largely assume them to be authentic.

Affirming fellow gay men of larger stature, the second site was started by an insider, a big man from Ohio, and his supportive partner, in 1996 when the Internet was taking off (Textor 1999). On the main page, there was a clickable link to galleries featuring members' fat-and-gay fantasy and erotic folkart (Wright cited in Campbell 2004). The gallery contained everything from sketches and animation to digital artwork. This site went down in 2006 with hopes of moving to a new server.

Gay- and fat-affirming images on these sites resurface as numerous moderated e-mail groups pick up where the websites leave off. For example, one of the largest storehouses of images displayed a series of nine *Yahoo!* groups inspired by homoerotic pictures of beer-drinking college men proudly showing off their guts. Here members posted individual photo albums, but the archives mostly contained images collected by the moderator for admirers to consume. Now there are videos on YouTube that evoke responses from enthusiasts such as "I wish I looked like that!" Cross-posting provides images with broader coverage. Furthermore, each site sorts and catalogues images differently, so the categorization of different "types" varies depending on the group's specialization (Hacking 1986; Textor 1999). The appeal of appropriated images online comes from giving them a new twist under a fat-affirming framework. Members of fat interest groups negotiate and transform meanings of mainstream images by reading them both with and "against the grain," (Benjamin 1968, p. 257) taking what the image-maker originally intended and then recasting it in a playful "key" (Goffman 1974, p. 44; Hall 1998 [originally 1981]). Groups organize around similar viewing habits, reinforcing alternative visual codes that eroticize the fat male body.

New Media: An Apparatus for Social Change

Online groups of fat gay men construct a sense of community based on asserting the visibility of the body and they rely heavily on the stylized repetition of images to build their communities.[4] Based on conceptual interest, two image exemplars from these communities are discussed here, and interpreted in close relation to the analytical and theoretical frameworks of semiotics and boundary work.

During HBO's final season of the series, *Sex and the City* (Home Box Office 1998–2004, USA), Samantha's love interest, Smith Jared, appears in a vodka campaign with the slogan *Absolut Hunk*. Peter Gehrke, who takes pictures for the real vodka company, produced the fake ad (Atkinson 2003). The simulation, inspired by 70s pinups, features Smith nude with a vodka bottle carefully positioned in front of his genitals. In this iconic sign, Smith, the object of the advertisement, boasts a smooth, tanned and muscled physique, a sprinkling of facial scruff and surfer hair, all signifying sexual desirability. The bottle's placement associates vodka with sexual opportunity: removing it would fully expose the model, supplying sex plus the goods (Schroeder 2002). The ad was such a highly successful product placement that several viewers, even men, requested copies of the image (Atkinson 2003).

The glorious image of *Absolut Hunk* soon took on a new meaning. Following the episode, "celebrity fat" became a theme in the press and popular imagination surrounding the ad, appealing to gay men in fat-affirming groups. Was Smith fat? Absolutely not: as he drew in his abdominal muscles, viewers could see his ribcage. However, ad executives reported having digitally airbrushed the original photo to remove Smith's "love handles" (Atkinson 2003). Then a week into the media hype over the advertisement and its production, a fat gay artist decided to remake the ad by visually substituting his own body for Smith's and naming it *Absolut Beefy* (See Figure 16.1). From his double vantage point of artist *and* model,

Online Pictures in Fat-Affirming Groups 219

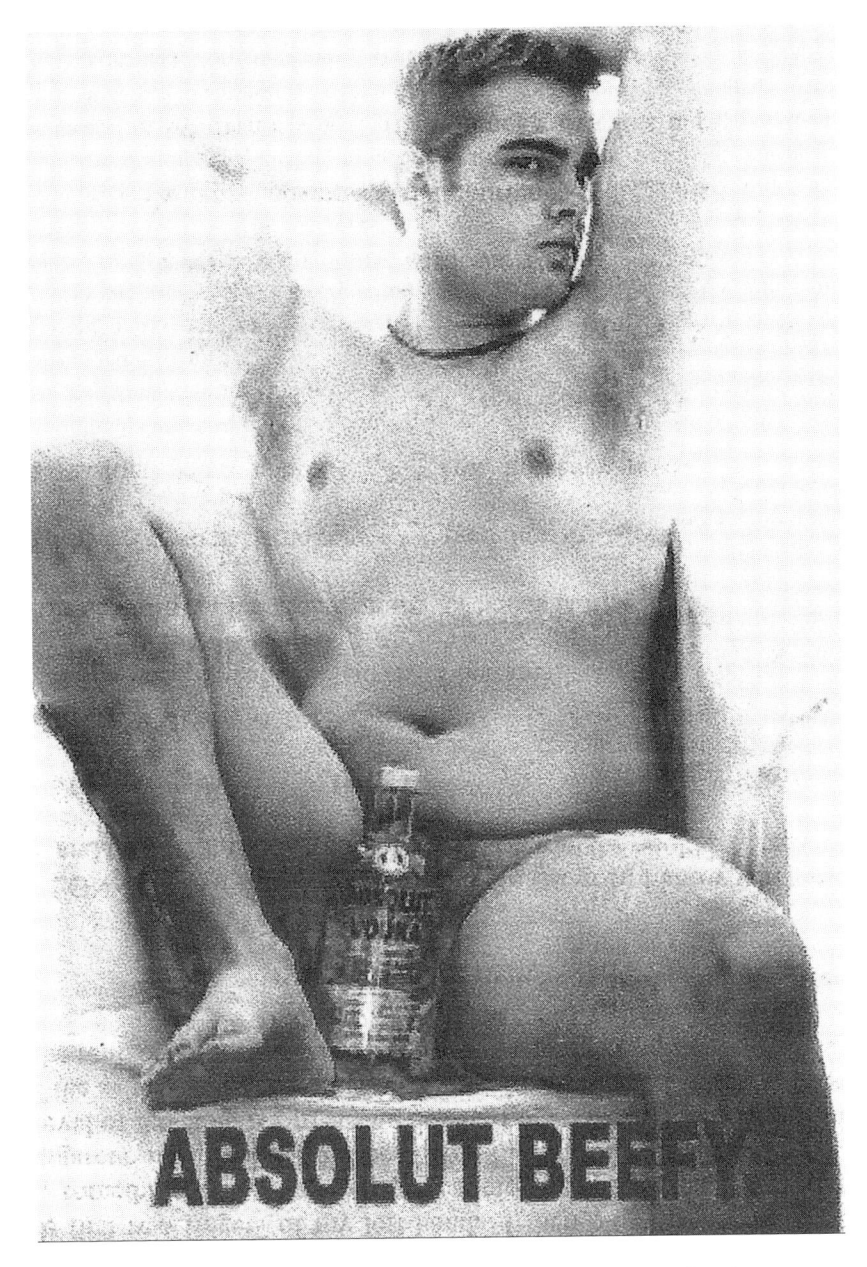

Figure 16.1 "Absolut Beefy." An appropriation of a commercialized image can be an online form of artistic and fat expression. (Author unknown: The publisher has made all efforts to trace the copyright owner of the image without success. Any information that would help identify and locate the owners would be greatly appreciated.)

the artist reflexively inserted himself into a narrow image of beauty, thereby redefining body politics through an alternative representation. This fatvertisement challenged the dominant one that the television producers had conveyed. Thus, in defense of fat identity, *Absolut Beefy* borrowed and changed the meaning of *Absolut Hunk* from that intended by its fat-phobic creators. The artist posted this subcultural image, with the similar slogan, on the first website mentioned above, where male spectators go to view profiles of fat men.

The fatvertisement appropriates the homoerotic content of the original, while imagining a popular culture inclusive of fat men. It resembles the original ad and demands that the beefy character be equivalent to the hunk. Even though elsewhere, the artist usually reveals body hair, he chose to mimic the original image in this fatvertisement, thereby commenting only on fat vs. thin. Had he left his body hairy in his fatvertisement, viewers might have missed his point about body size or been led to imagine a hairy *Absolut Bear*. Like the original, the parody retains a soft focus produced by the natural light and white bedding enveloping the model. However, the fat model's posture and gaze differ. The poached ad uses "self-flaunting" to re-signify Smith's languid posture and bedroom eyes used to entice the spectator (Joanisse and Synnott cited in Monaghan 2005, p. 101). It projects attitude: the model cocks his head and challenges the viewer with his dead-on stare, making no effort to "suck in" his stomach.[5] Nevertheless, the remake subtly pays "homage to the phallic power of masculinity" evident in the original, in which the positioning of the bottle substitutes for an erection (Hennen 2005, p. 35). In the remake, the artist/model intentionally positions the bottleneck to intersect the crease under his stomach and the cap directs the viewer to a cavernous navel surrounded by handfuls of flab. The fat model's swollen (which may be read as phallic) body contrasts with Smith's trim, muscular frame, shifting the sexual focus away from the penis and redirecting it across the entire upper body (Kulick 2005). Overall, *Absolut Beefy* sexualizes a body typically left out of both popular culture and gay men's media.

Similar to *Absolut*'s campaign, advertisements for Calvin Klein underwear accentuate the homoerotic aspects of the brand. It was in the early 1990s that icons modeling them became enormously popular: Mark Wahlberg began modeling underwear with Kate Moss in one of Klein's most widely distributed campaigns in 1992. Today, male models, who strike classically inspired poses in their contemporary boxer briefs, represent a mainstay of consumer culture. Such advertisements commodify (and sometimes domesticate) macho men like Wahlberg in order to persuade consumers to buy underwear.

One of the ads, taken by gay photographer Herb Ritts, features Wahlberg in his underwear against a vacant background, unaccompanied by models or props. In this mainstream underwear promotion, also cross-marketed to gay men, the hairless and ripped male body signifies an object to be consumed. The spatial organization of this three-quarter length, black-and-white portrait of Wahlberg standing and facing front creates a subordinate effect: the bad boy is now held captive for the viewer. The model's manner also communicates a related message: like a child, the model is clowning around naked, playfully tugging the hem of his underpants, euphorically throwing his head back, while appeasing the viewer with his irresistible smile, being vulnerable in a stereotypically feminine way (Bordo 1999; Goffman 1974).

Like the *Absolut Beefy* fatvertisement, a computer artist remade the Wahlberg image by morphing it (See Figure 16.2). The artist uses the process of "tweening" photographs, in which he morphs two images by computer, often stretching, distorting, and twisting them. Through this process he wreaks havoc on commercialized images of men, porn being the most popular (though male celebrities and sport stars come in close second) as targets of his use of transformative technology. The morph of the CK underwear ad parodies how advertisers signify a "real man's" body and appears on at least two fat-affirming websites and one moderated e-mail group. It disrupts the dominant visual system by distorting the original image and spoofing the written text of the ad. In the original, pleasure comes from imagining the genitals underneath the model's briefs, while the morph shifts the focus to another part of the body, that is, the bloated stomach now stretched tightly across the model's midsection with the help of computer technology.

The fat morph represents another way that gay men in fat-affirming groups can transform homoerotic commercial representations of the male body. Warping life-like images by computer, morphing plays upon notions of essential identity and confronts viewers with spectacles of unstable identity (Alcalay 1998). Such creative agency made possible by computers is especially popular among the youth culture whose members like to re-envision themselves by altering their appearance. It emphasizes the mutability of the body, corresponding with the "amodern" body concept put forth by cyberfeminists (Haraway 2004 [originally 1992]). In this way, morphs epitomize queer politics that mark the instability of identity.[6] Rather than completely overturning dominant images, they float between mainstream depictions and marginalized representations (Alcalay 1998). Morphs play with relationships between the body and technology, thus creating new virtual beings with no real human referent (Sturken and Cartwright 2001). For gay men in online fat communities, morphs superimpose fat onto idealized male bodies in homoerotic media.

The morph of the Wahlberg image recasts the masculine pursuit of "bodybuilding" signified in the original ad by the model's six-pack abs, and instead celebrates "bellybuilding," akin to belly worship. These images also symbolize an unfolding process of gay men "gaining," letting loose of their diet and exercise restrictions and putting on weight. Finally, they draw in the spectator with the new textual pun: *Underwear: Calvin Klein—Belly: Burger King.* This new slogan anchors the fatvertisement and focuses on pleasures of eating by relaying a category of male-identified cooking and food preference, grilling hamburgers and

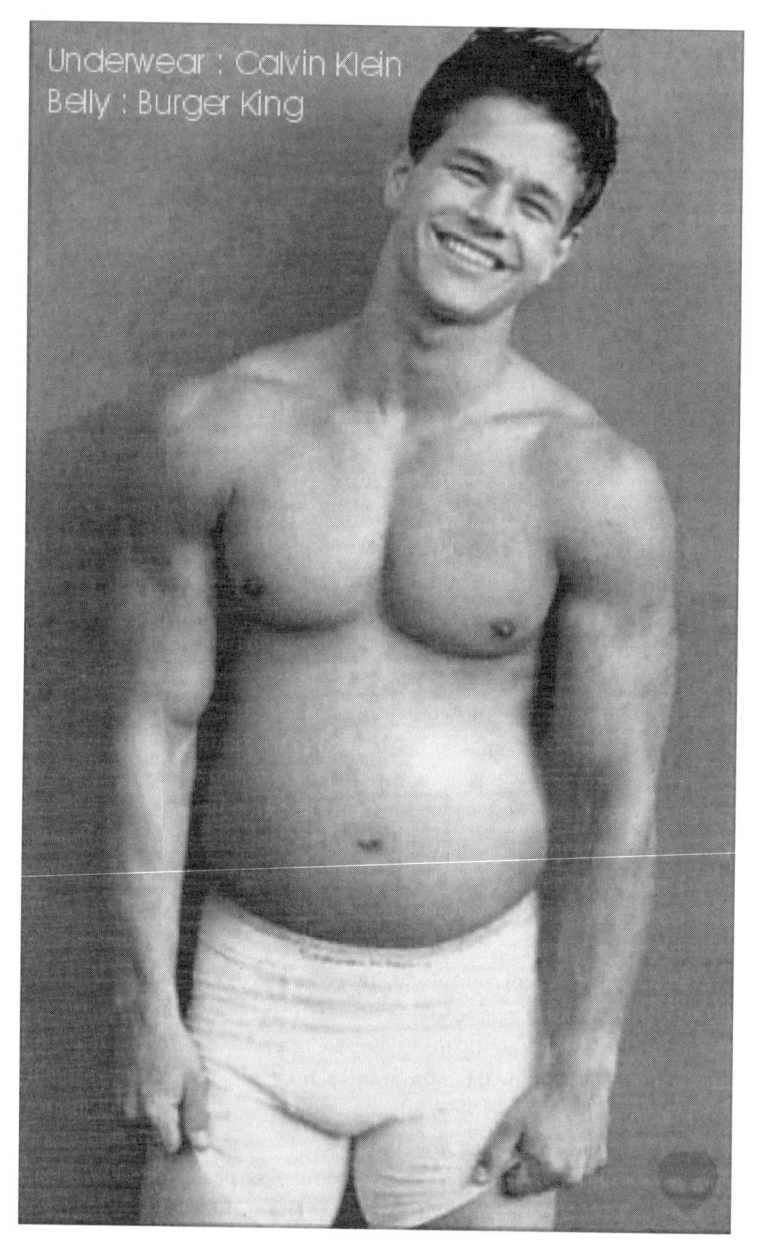

Figure 16.2 "Underwear: Calvin Klein—Belly: Burger King." Those proficient in computer generated imaging (CGI) techniques can take advantage of their transformative properties to rearrange the meaning of an existing commercial signifying system. (Morph courtesy of the producer, who wishes to retain anonymity.)

fast food, respectively (McGann 2002). If the dominant image displays the male body as a lean piece of meat, then the subcultural image displays a revised male body that has subsumed the original, in an effort to resist it (hooks 1992).

The morph also celebrates boyishness signified by the original bad boy. It reinforces this chubby-boy body that depicts gay men with youthful innocence, a body that dissociates them from the stigma of AIDS (Kruger 1998). As gay men attempt to compensate for the image of the wasting gay body, images of men with cherubic schoolboy looks emphasizing youth and health partially replace that of slim, gym-obsessed men thought to spread disease (Graham 2005). Ex-jocks-going-soft wearing backward-turned baseball caps symbolize healthy gay bodies that thrive on good food and beer. Gay boys are read as disease-free if they are not *too* thin, but just plump enough. Thus, boyish fat in the morph signifies good health.

A deconstructionist reading reveals disconnect: in the original, the face and upper body project an air of confidence. In the morph, this runs counter to how fat gay men are thought to carry themselves in a fat-phobic community, thereby making an implicit social commentary on how gay men typically define themselves and their happiness. The morph suggests that men who might otherwise be weight-conscious in private could come to pose self-confidently in public images, particularly those intended for fat admirers.

Finally, the disconnection between the upper body and the abdomen makes the morph look artificial, and not completely register as a "real" body. Unlike *Absolut Beefy* with its life-like softer fat distribution, the distended stomach in the morph invokes "hard fat" where the exaggerated midsection almost resembles another muscle, gendering it "masculine" (Moffet 2002). Members of fat-affirming groups often desire men with paunches because to them, it suggests masculinity. The morph signifies their attempt to reclaim beerguts and potbellies despite the gay community's aversion to them. Considering that many fat gay men feel denied gender prescriptions and relationship roles typically accorded to gay men with idealized physiques, this redeeming image is not surprising.

Mixed Modes of Resistance

In the context of shifting ideologies, these images highlight the opposition between the rejection of body fat and its acceptability. For instance, AIDS is not the cause of this shift, but rather, serves as an occasion for revisiting the "ideal" body type. Bodies are sites for negotiating ideologies, contradictions that can include the appeal and/or rejection of feminist critiques of heterosexual norms. Prevailing notions of physical perfection can become destabilized by AIDS as well as shifting sexual preferences, where the desire for health and new ideologies of fat coincide. Queer culture and queer bodies are often about destabilization in relation to a heterosexual dominant paradigm. On the Internet, they provide opportunities for innovation and rejection, and indeed reification of dominant paradigms. The tendency to reify restrictive boundaries describes most advertising; certainly, it is feminist criticism. These commercialized images also provide a site for critique and for bodies to exceed culturally bound ideals of beauty.

What do people do when the dominant sign systems do not represent them? Gay men in fat-affirming groups interpret dominant images differently, and some members actively rework them. The fat morph refigures what constitutes a pleasing body; in this way, visual technology affects fat politics. A fat stomach in both images discussed in this chapter no longer represents an undesirable feature, but symbolizes the "intimate experience of boundaries, their construction and deconstruction" (Haraway 1986, p. 525). The artists discussed in this chapter pattern their work after the social norms, aesthetic conventions, and interpretive practices of the larger online fat-affirming community. However, they do not avoid the trappings of the men's media or resolve the feminization of fat gay men without partially appealing to the hegemonic masculinity that works against them. *Absolut Beefy* is arguably the more powerful of the two images because it provides pleasure in its presumed authenticity and engages softer styles of masculinity. Nevertheless, the *Beefy* and *Burger King* slogans both serve to recoup masculinity and the morph still relies on idealized male qualities such as broad shoulders, strong arms, and a babyface.

For morphing to work, it has to keep some aspects of the sampled image recognizable. In the case of the fat morph, it alters the weight and size aspect of extreme body worship, while retaining the various idealized male qualities. This suggests that gay men in fat-affirming communities may still require other dominant drivers of ideal beauty. Men in these groups do occasionally marginalize other men for being too old or too thin, which implies that they may just exchange one rigid body ideal for another. There appears to be a conundrum if one explanation for concerns with body image focuses on social approval and acceptance in the gay community. Gay men in the "circuit" emphasize a desire for slender physiques, and leathermen prefer muscular bodies, while other gay subcultures emphasize alternatives. "Bears" admire larger hairy bodies, while "Chasers" prefer "Chubbies." Body type remains a significant criterion for inclusion in all of these subcultures.

Buying into conformity (or the rejection of it) often represents a mixed mode of resistance. Gay men in online fat-affirming groups seem to be involved in social protest, though not the same activities in which female fat activists engage. These may include scale-tossing/scale-smashing, ice cream socials in front of weight loss centers, or returning advertisements to magazines with decals that read, "Feed this woman!" (LeBesco 2004, p. 107). A *Jenny Craig* protest, for instance, tries to create fat visibility and sensitivity, but it is not necessarily about trying to evoke eroticism. The images in this chapter by fat men for fat men and their admirers try to remedy existing asexual depictions of fat people excluded from the commercial signifying system. Gay men's fat porn in Bigmen's media, for example (see Bulkmale 2009), is a response to fat as "sexy" and not simply a form of diversity. This is not to say that fat lesbians and fat women have not been erotically portrayed in their respective media outlets.

Fatvertisements provide a site for both conformity and resistance, ironically even at times when resistance is still conforming. Feminists face the same challenge in thinking about fat women who demanded stylish, sexy fashion only to embrace their consumer niche recognition as a feminist victory (LeBesco 2004). Should feminists recuperate fat-affirming beauty shows and pageants as "feminism"? Like fatvertisements, this is not an either/or proposition. Modes of resistance in commercialized contexts create strange bedfellows; they incorporate outcasts from the cult of beauty back into a questionable system, as does the question of eroticism, which leads to objectification sometimes as well. Perhaps a Foucaultian (see Foucault 1977) analysis can bring us closer to answering this question of eroticizing fat responsibly. Making this new set of associations with fat equating to sexy goes beyond fetishism, not eliminating sexual desirability as the system, but transforming its standards for what qualifies as "desirable." Then of course, one is obligated to consider the consequences of embracing sexual objectification.

Advertisers work in the business of creating conformity, an enterprise that is prone to failure. Under what conditions do people recognize this and do something about it? The perceived larger threat of AIDS-related death represents one cause for a reconfiguration. The categories of fat and thin reinscribe the binary, but together with the erotic, fat takes on new connotations like "healthy," and conversely "ill." This disrupts the binary and repositions it in a different discourse. Stereotypes of fat people characterize them as unhealthy or unfit. In gay men's fat-affirming subcultures, however, "fat" holds partial currency (admittedly alongside muscle) because "thin" suggests an inability to sustain life, where seriously ill or emaciated bodies complicate gay men's preoccupation with thinness. This definitional shift creates a new binary where some gay men switch signifying systems to accommodate an added signifier, that of healthiness. "Fats and femmes" persist as an out-group, even as they are gaining *some* acceptance, and it is important that they pick up some pieces of the signifying system in any way at all

This hybridization of digital images in semiotic cyberspace exemplifies the post-identity "*pleasure* in the confusion of boundaries" (Haraway 1986, 503). Fat gay men's online media challenges current cultural notions of identity and authorship, which contributes to our understanding of liminality by showing us two (or more) identities in one body. If cyborg imagery represents partial identities "of both imagination and material reality," then it follows that morphs share this uncertainty in their signification of "transformational identity" (Alcalay 1998, p. 136; Haraway 1986, p. 503). An imitation of an imitation, the *Absolut* replica, though it resembles the original, becomes a new cultural product with its own circulation. Morphing also creates this kind of simulacra (Baudrillard 2001 [originally 1988]): it turns the typical airbrushing for near perfection into a funhouse mirror, where unreal replicants can support a sense of connection or a "we-ness" of identity. These images provide a collective identity that people can join in on, and they can recognize themselves in the newfound category of proud fat gay men, which remains on the boundary. This liminal identity sustains fat gay men's precarious position by reinstantiating them in more familiar and accepted commercialized images. Morphs are liminal because they float between mainstream and subcultural images, creating assemblages of man and computer artifice. Likewise, the men discussed in this chapter negotiate their membership between their fat and gay identities.

What are some next steps and key questions in examining gay men's online negotiation of fat bodies? The thrust of most existing research is on obesity. Obesity researchers consider how subcultures influence their members' eating habits and body mass. However, their focus can lead one to believe that perhaps fat-affirming groups would increase the number of fat people. A more useful research approach would be not to confuse real bodies with the various negative appraisals of them and instead ask, what produces a new subjectivity from fat-hating to fat-admiring (Butler 1990)? While doctors both measure and calibrate body mass, Fat Studies scholars (such as LeBesco 2001 and 2004; Wann 1998) like me are interested in how some people can reconfigure negative perceptions and characterizations of fat, so that they can assume a livable fat identity. Most of the existing work along these lines, however, focuses on how women come to body acceptance.

Fat is a "spoiled identity"; yet, how do individuals reshuffle a stigma like this (Goffman 1963)? This is important to consider when one's sullied identity surrounding one's size becomes an object of desire. The point, therefore, would be to look at shifts from shame to pride. In the context of a society where bodies are subjected to intervention, even to surgery, tremendous self-consciousness surrounds fat bodies, especially gay bodies that are often held accountable to such an unforgiving standard (predominantly apparent within the "gay scene"). Unlike celebrities obsessed with perpetual youth, who therefore use concealment strategies, gay men in fat-affirming groups use fatvertisements to create visibility markers, having a field day with our body-conscious culture. If advertisements represent a paradigm that can be destabilized in multiple ways (e.g., AIDS or fatness destabilizing thin), then what would restabilization look like? My analysis of the two fatvertisements in this chapter identifies not only resistance to thin, but also the need to retain some semblance of recognizable features, such as a baby-faced boy with muscular shoulders and a smooth torso, juxtaposed against a fat belly. In cyberspace, these recognizable features, coupled with the abject fatness, work to create and sustain new paradigms for the range of acceptable and desirable gay bodies.

Notes

1 This is a revised version of an earlier work (Whitesel 2007), permission granted by *Limina*. Thanks to M. Cooper, M. Galin, C. Pullen, and A. Shuman for editing advice.
2 "Fat," "big," "beefy," and "chubby" are terms used by men in these groups.
3 For ethical reasons, I have chosen not to reveal the names of these two "safe-sites" that restrict access only to those that agree to the terms and conditions. To give some indication of user context, new members must create a username and password to log on to these websites. Once authenticated, they have access to personals, stories, chat and messaging—most free, though some accounts can be "upgraded" for a nominal fee.
4 Similarly, see Ferreday 2001.
5 For discussion of "face-off masculinity," see Bordo 1999, pp. 186–188. For description of the sensuous pleasures of abandoning restraint on the abdominal muscles, see Stoltenberg 1998, p. 406.
6 On "queering" fatness, see LeBesco 2001.

References

Alcalay, R. 1998. Morphing out of identity politics: Black or white and terminator 2. In *Bad subjects: Political education for everyday life*, edited by Bad Subjects Production Team. New York: New York University Press, 136–142.
Atkinson, C. 2003. Absolut nabs sexy HBO role: "Sex and the city" features fake ad, *Ad Age*, http://www.oaaa.org/presscenter/release.asp?RELEASE_ID=1368 [Accessed September 25, 2008]
Baudrillard, J. 2001 [1988]. Simulacra and simulations. In *Jean Baudrillard: Selected writings*, edited by M. Poster. Palo Alto, CA: Stanford University Press.
Bell, K. and McNaughton, D. 2007. Feminism and the invisible fat man. *Body and Society* 13: 107–131.
Benjamin, W. 1968. *Illuminations*, translated by H. Zohn, edited by H. Arendt. New York: Schocken Books.
Bergling, T. 2001. *Sissyphobia: Gay men and effeminate behavior*. Binghamton, NY: Haworth Press.
Blotcher, J. 1998. Justify my love handles: How the queer community trims the fat. In *Looking queer: Body image and identity in lesbian, bisexual, gay and transgender communities*, edited by D. Atkins. Binghamton, NY: Haworth Press, 359–366.
Bordo, S. 1997. *Twilight zones: The hidden life of cultural images from Plato to O.J.* Berkeley: University of California Press.
Bordo, S. 1999. *The male body: A new look at men in public and private*. New York: Farrar, Straus & Giroux.
Bulkmale. 2009. http://www.bulkmale.com/store/ [Accessed August 23, 2009]
Butler, J. 1990. *Gender trouble: Feminism and the subversion of identity*. New York: Routledge.
Campbell, J. 2004. *Getting it on online: Cyberspace, gay male sexuality, and embodied identity*. New York: Harrington Park Press.
Connell, R. W. 1992. A very straight gay: Masculinity, homosexual experience, and the dynamics of gender. *American Sociological Review* 57: 735–751.

Drummond, M. 2005. Men's bodies: Listening to the voices of young gay men. *Men and Masculinities* 7: 270–290.

Durgadas, G. 1998. Fatness and the feminized man. In *Looking queer: Body image and identity in lesbian, bisexual, gay and transgender communities*, edited by D. Atkins. Binghamton, NY: Haworth Press, pp. 367–371.

Feraios, A. 1998. If only I were cute: Looksism and internalized homophobia in the gay male community. In *Looking queer: Body image and identity in lesbian, bisexual, gay and transgender communities*, edited by D. Atkins. Binghamton: Haworth Press, 415–429.

Ferreday, D. 2001. Unspeakable bodies: Erasure, embodiment and the pro-ana community. *International Journal of Cultural Studies* 6: 277–295.

Foucault, M. 1977. *The History of Sexuality Vol. 1.*, trans. Robert Hurley. London: Penguin.

Giles, P. 1998. A matter of size. In *Looking queer: Body image and identity in lesbian, bisexual, gay and transgender communities*, edited by D. Atkins. Binghamton, NY: Haworth Press, pp. 355–357.

Goffman, E. 1963. *Stigma: Notes on the management of spoiled identity*. Englewood Cliffs, NJ: Prentice-Hall.

Goffman, E. 1974. *Frame analysis: An essay on the organization of experience*. Cambridge, MA: Harvard University Press.

Goffman, E. 1979. *Gender advertisements*. Cambridge, MA: Harvard University Press.

Goode, E. 2005. *Deviant behavior*, 7th ed. Upper Saddle River, NJ: Pearson.

Graham, M. 2005. Chaos. In *Fat: The anthropology of an obsession*, edited by D. Kulick and A. Meneley. New York: Penguin Group, 169–184.

Hacking, I. 1986. Making up people. In *Reconstructing individualism: Autonomy, individuality, and the self in western thought*, edited by T. Heller, M. Sosna, and D. Wellbery. Palo Alto, CA: Stanford University Press, 222–236.

Hall, S. 1998 [1981]. Notes on deconstructing "the popular." In *Cultural theory and popular culture*, edited by J. Storey. Athens: University of Georgia Press, 442–453.

Haraway, D. 1986. A manifesto for cyborgs: Science, technology, and socialist feminism in the 1980s. In *Feminist Social Thought: A Reader* (1997), edited by D. Meyers. New York: Routledge, 502–531.

Haraway, D. 2004. [1992]. The promises of monsters: A regenerative politics for inappropriate/d others. In *The Haraway reader*, edited by D. Haraway. New York: Routledge.

Hawkes, T. 1977. *Structuralism and semiotics*. London: Methuen, 63–124.

Hennen, P. 2005. Bear bodies, bear masculinity: Recuperation, resistance or retreat? *Gender and Society* 19: 25–43.

hooks, b. 1992. *Black looks: Race and representation*. London: Turnaround Press, 21–39.

Ironkite, 2009. Subvertisements. http://ironkite.smugmug.com/gallery/1521_QfrTR#43235_JdGh3 [Accessed August 23, 2009]

Jenkins, H. 1992. *Textual poachers: Television fans and participatory culture*. New York: Routledge.

Kruger, S. 1998. Get fat, don't die!: Eating and AIDS in gay men's culture. In *Eating culture*, edited by R. Scapp and B. Seitz. New York: State University of New York Press, 36–59.

Kulick, D. 2005. Porn. In *Fat: The anthropology of an obsession*, edited by D. Kulick and A. Menely. New York: Penguin Group, 77–92.

Lasn, K. 2000. *Culture jam: The uncooling of America*. New York: William Morrow & Co.

LeBesco, K. 2001. Queering fat bodies/politics. In *Bodies out of bounds: Fatness and transgression*, edited by J. E. Braziel and K. LeBesco. Berkeley: University of California Press, 74–87.

LeBesco, K. 2004. *Revolting bodies: The struggle to redefine fat identity*. Amherst: University of Massachusetts Press.

Matthews, T. 2005. Video. *Do I look fat? Gay men, body image and eating disorders*. Blah Blah Blah Productions, USA.

McGann, P. 2002. Eating muscle: Material semiotics and a manly appetite. In *Revealing male bodies*, edited by N. Tuana, G. Johnson, M. Hamington, and W. Cowling. Bloomington: Indiana University Press, 83–99.

Millman, M. 1980. *Such a pretty face: Being fat in America*. New York: W. W. Norton.

Moffet, F. 2002. Video. *Hard fat: An exploration of desire, masculinity and size*. Vidéographe Production, Canada.

Monaghan, L. 2005. Big handsome men, bears and others: Virtual constructions of 'fat male embodiment'. *Body and Society* 11: 81–111.

Padva, G. 2002. Heavenly monsters: Politics of the male body in the naked issue of attitude magazine. *International Journal of Sexuality and Gender Studies* 7: 281–292.

Schroeder, J. 2002. *Visual consumption*. New York: Routledge.

Shernoff, M. 2002. Body image, working out and therapy. *Journal of Gay and Lesbian Social Services* 14: 89–94.

Signorile, M. 1997. *Life outside—The Signorile report on gay men: Sex, drugs, muscles, and the passages of life*. New York: HarperCollins.

Stoltenberg, J. 1998. Learning the F words. In *Looking queer: Body image and identity in lesbian, bisexual, gay and transgender communities*, edited by D. Atkins. Binghamton, NY: Haworth Press, 393–411.

Sturken, M. and Cartwright, L. 2001. *Practices of looking: An introduction to visual culture*. New York: Oxford University Press.

Textor, A. 1999. Organization, specialization, and desires in the big men's movement: Preliminary research in the study of subculture-formation. *Journal of Gay, Lesbian, and Bisexual Identity* 4: 217–239.

Wann, M. 1998. *Fat! So?: Because you don't have to apologize for your size*. Berkeley: Ten Speed Press.

Whitesel, J. 2007. Fatvertising: Refiguring fat gay men in cyberspace. *Limina* 13: 92–102.

Chapter 17

"Compartmentalize Your Life"

Advising Army Men on RealJock.com

Noah Tsika

It is perhaps axiomatic that the U.S. military both attracts and angers gay men. Emboldened by mass-media depictions of elegant, domineering officers and their burly, compliant subordinates, gay American men are also conditioned to recognize (and asked to respect) the U.S. military's openly homophobic, discriminatory policies. The ambivalence that so often results can have a deeply distressing, disorienting effect. Even a cursory survey of recent military hate crimes confirms the violent coexistence of homoerotic attraction and homophobic repulsion in service environments.[1]

In a less ominous mode, one might rightly cite the media cynicism and opportunism that often simultaneously flatters and condescends to gay men, making them out to be both self-absorbed and self-loathing. According to cliché, the gay man's potentially autoerotic interest in the well-built male body makes him especially susceptible to army iconography, a longstanding source for gay porn and, lately, a structuring influence on the fitness routines and design schemes of de facto gay gyms (in the U.S. context, Barry's Boot Camp (2009) comes most readily to mind). Beyond combating stereotypes of effeminacy, however, gay male "muscle culture" has come to address the role of the U.S. military in shaping masculinity, and a wide range of writers have focused on the longstanding efforts of gay men to eroticize the armed forces through photography (Bronski 2001; Tyler 1972; Waugh 1996). Eschewing an allegedly outmoded social and sexual attachment to the "camp" carefully constructed soldier-stud (a figure popular in gay parades and famously celebrated in the music—and visuals—of The Village People), gay male bloggers have increasingly considered the value of military service and expressed their support for the U.S. Armed Forces, if not for the war in Iraq, and the sustained military presence there (in the early part of the twenty-first century).

This chapter considers the significance of a particular gay networking site, RealJock.com, in facilitating communication between civilians and soldiers. A survey of user-generated responses to "Don't Ask, Don't Tell" and other issues of pertinence to the gay serviceman suggest the centrality of soldiering to the philosophies of bodybuilding advocated by and through RealJock.com. Ultimately, while the website does index important information about military policy, and while its members do tend to communicate their support for the gay soldier, this study indicates that conflations of body pride and patriotism, operating under an emphatically masculine rubric of muscles and militarism, endorse the myth of the strictly celibate military and modify, even to the extent of consciously desexualizing, gay male identities.

In the case of RealJock.com, a vast number of the site's members are self-identified servicemen living and blogging abroad, in such "hot zones" as Iraq and Afghanistan. For the most part, these servicemen are posting pro-war comments not in order to incite debate or derision, but solely in response to civilians (typically young men between the ages of eighteen and twenty) who solicit information about military life. Understood to express a goal-oriented, positive pattern of behavior and upheld as a valid, even commendable career choice, soldiering signifies not only community but also physical and mental wellness in the postings of these inquisitive civilian men. Certain in their support for the U.S. military, such men tend rather tentatively to express their fear of its homophobic policies—particularly "Don't Ask, Don't Tell."

As much a topic of controversy today as when it was first introduced in 1993, "Don't Ask, Don't Tell" informs most, if not all, discussions of the U.S. military in online communities of gay men. As a point of reference, it seems to be de rigueur. RealJock.com, in particular, contains an abundance of threaded discussions of the policy, providing forums for debating its effectiveness, on the one hand, and its offensiveness, on the other. Generally, however, proponents of U.S. military policy (who tend to themselves be servicemen, and who post comments regularly) often write of their support for "Don't Ask, Don't Tell." One user, a self-identified Iraq War veteran, writes that the policy "does have a place":

> It protects gays from the persecution that was common . . . from the older and/or more closed-minded personnel in the service. It's nearly ended the gay witch-hunts and hazing that were common before the policy went into effect. It allows gays to keep their business to themselves and not have to worry about outside attention.
>
> ("Hidden Member," Real Jock 2009a)[2]

In any case, the relationship between gay men and the U.S. military seems even more contentious in the context of so infamous a compromise policy—one that was intended, as the above quotation indicates, to "protect" the closeted homosexual soldier while preventing him from openly identifying as gay. Although liberal critics of the policy point to its endorsement of an obviously offensive assumption—namely, that the presence of acknowledged gay men is fundamentally "disruptive" in a service environment (Halley 1999; Shawver 1996)—"Don't Ask, Don't Tell" does prohibit the military's previous use of "queerphobic" questionnaires designed to determine the level of "deviancy" of a recruit's sexual history. In its wholesale repudiation of what could be called "Kinseyesque" rhetoric (evoking Kinsey et al.'s (1948) findings on sexual behavior), in its refusal to permit open enunciations of gay identities, "Don't Ask, Don't Tell" also—purportedly—limits the use of actual and potential gay slurs. Nevertheless, as Janet Halley argues (1999, p. 50), military officials are still able to ask "a vast range of perfectly legitimate questions about sexual orientation identity," thus aligning the policy's semantic imprecision with that of its chief proponent, whose infamous, equivocal attempts to define "sexual relations" precipitated his impeachment. But beyond the ways in which the policy is understood semantically, a crucial question remains about how it is understood experientially, by actual gay soldiers. For obvious reasons, the opinions of active-duty servicemen are absent in much of the scholarship surrounding the policy, although recent polls addressing the experiences of straight-identified soldiers and assessing their collective understanding of human sexualities have been conducted (Shalikashvili 2007).

How, then, might one begin to approach the presence of self-identified gay soldiers in online communities? Does such visibility constitute a risk, or offer recognizable rewards? What happens when one gay man, not necessarily denying that he has ever "hooked up" with another, self-identifies as an active-duty soldier on a popular gay dating site? What does such a declaration reveal about the role of gay men in the U.S. military today? By making a case study of RealJock.com, this chapter considers the often contentious concurrence of military and civilian narratives that equally seek to read the meanings of muscles. As we shall see, the explicit centrality of sexual desire to civilian discussions of the male body and of militarism often provides a point of contention for servicemen. The latter tend to take an emphatically "anti-sexual" stance in an effort to combat stereotypes of gay men in the military—a stance that seems especially incongruous given its articulation within a gay dating site. Additionally, such responses have a tendency to duplicate the very totalizing approaches they purport to attack—to place one stereotype (that of the strictly celibate serviceman) atop another (that of the hyper-sexual gay soldier). Pivotal to the latter stereotype is the notion that gay men join the military out of desire for sexual activity, as opposed to what one user terms "patriotic intentions" (and the accompanying desire to "kick some muslim butt"). ("Hidden Member," Real Jock 2009b)

Tellingly, there is rarely an attempt to acknowledge potential subtleties or complexities in the conduct of gay servicemen: such subjects are either blind to eroticism, or bound to a salacious appreciation of the male body. Offering a way of reading these approaches, Richard Dyer has written of the social significance of stereotypes, arguing that the "content" of stereotypes matters less than "who controls and defines them, what interests they serve" (Dyer 2002, p. 12). In the case of civilian-authored stereotypes about lascivious servicemen, erroneous assumptions about the gender-segregated nature of the U.S. Armed Forces abound—indeed, seem to be frequent starting points. Such stereotypes therefore help to define some of the features of RealJock.com, a site that caters specifically to gay men rather than to a broader LGBT community.

In marked contrast to the countless lustful responses to civilian bodies that characterize this gay dating site, however, those postings that describe the military suitability of actual or would-be soldiers carefully sidestep sexual discourse, consciously combating eroticism at every turn. One asks, "What's so hard about not eyeing guys up or acting gay in public view for 5 years?" ("Hidden Member," Real Jock 2009c) In another, a recently retired soldier claims that "[sexuality] was never mentioned" during his eight years in the army ("Onetoughguy," Real Jock 2009d). All such responses motivate gay men to *temporarily* forsake a traditionally erotic gay male identity—to *temporarily* assume a celibate lifestyle—during their time in the service, and link such a forsaking to the feelings of transcendence that, it is argued, so often accompany training with weights. One soldier writes:

> I wanted to see how far I could push myself, and I wanted to prove to myself that I was tough enough to make it in the military. I...was reluctant at first because I knew that I'd have to go back in the closet. However...if I could do basic training all over again, I would.
>
> ("Hidden Member," Real Jock 2009e)

Another acknowledges that "giving up everything you know and love for the entire time you're in training is hard . . . but do-able," and goes on to describe the joy of "being able to do more than 60 push-ups and 55 sit-ups"("Hidden Member," Real Jock, 2009f). Still others confirm the presumed need for gay men to support the (gay) military, advising admiration for those who can "seriously sublimate" sexual desire:

> I would recommend serving to anyone with balls enough to do it.
>
> ("Hidden Member," Real Jock 2009g)

> You will have to learn to TOTALLY "compartmentalize" your life. You will also have to learn to live with hiding parts of who you are.
>
> ("ITJock," Real Jock 2009h)

> It is more of a mind game than anything else. You'll survive. I did! And you wouldn't believe how many people in the army are gay!
>
> ("Hidden Member," Real Jock 2009i)

The website's registrational mode of interactivity thus enables gay servicemen to maintain some ties to gay culture while providing a forum for expressions of their new, nonsexual service identities. Apparently "truly and contentedly celibate"—to borrow Janet Halley's phrasing (Halley 1999, p. 125)—these servicemen reject the centrality of erotic acts to the traditional self-definition of gay men, marking a clear distinction between one, celibate component of the Real Jock constituency and another, larger, openly sexual civilian one. Rather than "building a social consensus that homosexual erotic acts are good" (Halley 1999, p. 125)—a readily identifiable component of most pro-gay movements—a majority of these self-identified celibate gay soldiers declare their allegiance to country and aversion to any mixing of sex and service life, arguing for the impossibility of any integration of erotic identity and martial duty, not only "in this day and age"—and country—but "anytime, anywhere" ("Onetoughguy," Real Jock 2009j).

Given this mandate, it is hardly surprising that one self-identified celibate soldier assumed a scolding tone in response to a young man whose stated wish was to lose his virginity in a military setting, writing:

> I am disappointed about what you said about getting laid. If that's even one reason you want to join, then I'd be ashamed to have you protect and serve our country. The Military is not a hookup site. That is the exact reason I think gays should not be openly gay in the military. It's not a sex party. It's a job, it's a duty. Get your rocks off on your own time. Now while your [sic] protecting our amazing country. Go ARMY!
>
> ("Onetoughguy," Real Jock 2009k)

Predictably, other users were quick to endorse such a denunciatory stance, privileging a strictly desexualized conception of patriotism at the expense of an erotic gay male identity:

> I didn't join the military because I was gay, I joined to serve my country. To serve in the military is to sacrifice your personal needs for a greater good.
>
> ("Dclifterguy," Real Jock 2009l)

> Service to country rises above service to self.
>
> ("coolarmydude," Real Jock 2009m)

Such an injunction against sexualized, queer-political speech structures the majority of RealJock.com responses to the topic of gays in the military.

The next section will explore the impact of this injunction on the website's status as a dating service, showing the extent to which de-sexualized conceptions of gay men draw upon the very obsession with muscles that marks more lascivious, civilian-authored responses to the male body.

A Transit to Celibacy: Modifying Gay Male Identity through Registrational Interactivity

Described on its MySpace page as "a new web community for gay jocks and athletes," RealJock.com boasts over 25,000 members and offers "smart health and fitness advice from a gay perspective." Perhaps most importantly, its members can instant-message one another from "within" the website in a process that, potentially, facilitates actual physical contact between mutual "real jocks." Members post pictures (mostly so-called "body shots," showing heavily muscled torsos, arms, and legs) and list their hobbies and interests. In this way, RealJock.com closely resembles other such gay dating and "hookup" sites as DList.com (2009), ManHunt.net (2009), Gaydar.co.uk (2009) and Gay.com (2009). In its capacity as an "advice provider," however, RealJock.com is relatively unique, detailing various diets, fitness routines, and methods of self-motivation for the edification of its members. Additionally, threaded discussions—sequences of member-generated messages posted in the "forums" section—serve a community-building function by being open to all members and by purportedly addressing "all topics," except, of course, those deemed offensive by forum moderators. It is in the "forums" section that one discovers threaded discussions of a multitude of "gay issues," from the seemingly mundane ("Christmas music!" (Real Jock 2009n)), to the romantic ("Finding Him" (Real Jock 2009o)), to the indisputably political ("Gay Marriage Makes Cents" (Real Jock 2009p)). The latter postings in particular reveal an interest in consciousness-raising among members, and postings describing the experiences of gay men in the military proliferate.

Though avowedly a sport and fitness site, and obviously a dating and "hookup" one, RealJock.com also, perhaps inevitably, enables conversations between self-identified gay servicemen and civilians. Such conversations tend to confirm the central role of gay soldiers in international conflicts, including the War in Iraq (at the time of writing). Numerous gay servicemen, though pseudonymously, post pictures illustrating their Iraq War experiences: one depicts soldiers standing beside a tank and smiling, while another shows the same men asleep in their barracks at night. By showing soldier-subjects who self-identify as gay on the website, all such pictures serve the obvious purpose of "proving" the gay soldier's participation in the war. Given the frequency with which identities are contested online, particularly in the context of gay dating sites, such photographs function to both define and authenticate identity, and the fact that their captions contain pseudonyms seems less a comment on the gay soldier's closet than a condition of anonymity common to a range of websites. Presumably "authentic" (that is to say, not products of photo editing), these pictures depict the dust, white light, and general exoticism of Iraq at the same time that they show soldiers both at ease (sleeping, eating) and in action (operating tanks, transporting supplies). If some civilian members of the website discuss appropriating "authentic" markers of the

U.S. military, such as dog-tag necklaces, combat boots, and camouflage-print underwear, in order to appear simultaneously "butch" and fashion conscious within the RealJock.com community, their soldier peers use photographs of themselves in war zones in order, it seems, to strengthen their patriotic identities—and perhaps in order to solicit sex.

The latter possibility graphically highlights a central contradiction at work in those narratives that explicitly seek to suppress eroticism in relation to the U.S. armed forces: to post pictures on the website is to invite the subjective, sexualized responses of gay men. What's more, as Michael Bronski points out, photographs of soldiers tend to carry more semiotic weight as erotic, than instructional or strictly historical documents, especially for a gay male viewership. Bronski identifies the World War II years as epochal for the formation of (erotic) gay male reading strategies, implicating the U.S. Military and its relationship with mass media:

> The Second World War not only helped create recognizable gay communities, but also radically altered how the individual male body was viewed and understood. Photographs in such popular magazines as *Look* and *Life* of shirtless sailors and GIs on battleships and in trenches exposed the image of the nearly naked male body to a wider viewership than ever before.
> (Bronski 2001, p. 148)

In the context of a website whose members are almost uniformly fit and often appear "nearly naked," the eroticism implicit in photographs of soldiers may be taken for granted. But the fact that the self-identified soldiers themselves do little to ensure their eroticization is crucial to a consideration of the so-called status/conduct debate that has structured, and still renders controversial, "Don't Ask, Don't Tell."

According to Janet Halley (1999, p. 27), the U.S. Department of Defense's longstanding, pre-1993 policies placed a heavy emphasis upon status:

> The explicit terms of these regulations authorized military officials to determine not only what servicemembers did but what they desired and intended, all with the aim of determining who they were. It required the separation of any servicemember deemed to be "homosexual" and defined the excludable servicemember as "a person, regardless of sex, who engages in, desires to engage in, or intends to engage in homosexual acts."

By contrast, the purportedly less discriminatory "Don't Ask, Don't Tell" policy stipulates that, in the words of former Secretary of Defense Les Aspin, "homosexual conduct will continue to be the grounds for discharge from military service. On the other hand, sexual orientation is considered a personal and private matter" (quoted in Halley 1999, p. 28). In other words, what a service member does and not what he or she says is actionable, a distinction that, in the early days of the policy's public unveiling, "began to sound like a mantra" (Halley 1999, p. 27). It ought to follow that a self-identified gay soldier, in pseudonymously accessing a gay dating site, is not necessarily "announcing" his "intention to engage in homosexual acts." However the obfuscation built into the "Don't Ask, Don't Tell" policy, as Halley describes it, renders risky any such assumption. It is not surprising, then, that self-identified gay servicemen should tend to emphatically announce their celibacy—even, in some cases, claiming to avoid all physical contact with their soldier boyfriends. Such an announcement, clearly and persuasively expressed, can seem to counteract the common belief that membership in a gay dating site implies (in the parlance of Defense Department policy) "intention to engage" in sexual relationships, *in addition* to expressing individual or group identity. What complicates matters considerably is that, through their membership—and if only pseudonymously—such users are, in effect, "telling" of their homosexuality.

Like most gay dating sites, RealJock.com permits the user to reveal certain crucial aspects of his look and lifestyle, including his height and weight, his preferred sexual position, and even his HIV/AIDS status (all of which can be taken as indications of the website's central erotic—rather than chastely pedagogical—purpose). Unlike other sites, however, RealJock.com does not identify a space in which members can disclose and describe their "mannerisms," which the competing Gay.com (2009) divides into three broad categories: "masculine/butch," "feminine/femme," and "in the middle." This absence is most obviously attributable to the website's expectation of a uniformly "jock-like" base of users, though some variation in body type is certainly evident among them, as those who champion certain sports (an "athletic inclination" being but one suggested condition of membership) may themselves be skinny, or otherwise "out of shape." The website's principal, stated focus on bodybuilding—and on "bringing together" actual bodybuilders—isolates a specific body type as capable of giving and receiving pleasure, and users tend to "experience" that body type accordingly. A survey of member-generated responses to various "Men of the Day"—users deemed "delicious" by the website's content creators—indicates the influence of desire (as opposed to identification) and also exposes a willingness to openly eroticize (rather than simply emulate) the muscle-bound male body in these interactive communications. Many men, like the members quoted below, celebrate the gym-built body but expressly in the hopes of touching, "loving," or otherwise "consuming" it:

> You know, you see his big pecs, you see his big shoulders and probably drool over his big biceps…I would definitely welcome Mr. Ulisesfitness into my home anytime. WOOF!!! WOOF!!!!
> would you fuck me?
> can i eat u?[3]

Such "racy" responses expose the absurdity and superfluity of the website's main statements of purpose, its directing users to "build bigger, stronger muscles," "get lean and ripped," and engage in a coherent "muscle-building workout program"—all in the hopes of "getting healthy." As Michael Bronski (1998) notes in an important analysis of the 1950s physical culture magazine *Physique Pictorial*, which sought to sidestep charges that it was a "pornographic rag" by emphasizing the chaste healthfulness of the well-built male physiques depicted within:

> Such disclaimers might have been necessary in the fifties, but for the contemporary reader they verge on camp. Their emphasis on beauty, nature, and noble sentiments now reads as a naïve, middle-brow parody of the language and sentiments of the Victorian aesthetes.
>
> (Bronski 1998, p. 150)

Bronski makes clear that the discursive strategies employed by RealJock.com, wherein male muscles are made to reflect transcendently noble qualities, are not new. However, while the website's creators cannot conceivably fear "serious legal and social reprisal" (which, as Bronski points out, *were* prohibitive factors with gay-friendly physical culture magazines of the postwar period), some of its members—particularly servicemen—can. Consider, for instance, one user's caution that "the DOD [U.S. Department of Defense] could be reading this site now" ("yalemarine," Real Jock 2009q).

Viewed in this way, the equivocations of RealJock.com are not necessarily in the interests of the website itself but serve the (perhaps unintended) purpose of protecting its constituency of servicemen. The emphasis on "beauty, nature, and noble sentiments," that Bronski reads as camp in another context enables RealJock.com to contribute productively to the status/conduct debate—by, specifically, downplaying the centrality of sexual contact among the possibilities of self-improvement, it implicitly presents. By *explicitly* advocating physical fitness and the formation of a "body-conscious community," the website provides a readily observable alibi for its soldier members, even as the proliferation of passionate, sexualized user responses to "real jocks" (as indicated in the above quotations) overrides such a stated pedagogical mission.

However, such avowedly "sex-obsessed" responses are markedly absent from the more sanctimonious discourses surrounding the gay male soldier, which serve a decidedly "noble" function by foregrounding the serviceman's devotion to duty, and by demanding compliance with "Don't Ask, Don't Tell." It should come as no surprise that, given the popularity of bodybuilding among members of RealJock.com, actual military bodies are themselves the subject of much approbation in threaded discussions of weight training, though often at the explicit expense of "weak" civilians. These narratives serve most obviously as recruiting tools, tying the user's interest in the muscled male body to a nostalgic evocation of "brothers in arms." Such strategies, seamlessly woven into the fabric of the website itself, point to the formation of a radical and potentially contradictory gay male identity, in which the gay soldier, via his membership in a gay dating site, announces his celibacy and rephrases the "real jock's" injunction to celebrate the male body—this time, as a trainable, *nonsexual* machine.

To Serve, Without Lust

In the context of a gay dating site dependent upon photographic substantiation of one's jock status, the question "Can I serve?" clearly encourages responses that focus not on politics, and not on patriotism per se, but on the potential of the male body to become beautiful through weight training. If a man has not realized this potential (and the apparent self-portraits on his personal page are typically accepted as evidence), then it is quite likely that he will receive largely discouraging responses. For example one man is told that he is "too skinny" to serve; another is denounced as "manorexic," and promptly promises to "gain fifty pounds."[4] Such exchanges, in which the less-than-muscular are shamed and eventually agree to train with weights, would seem to endorse the U.S. military's own promotional rhetoric (such as "Be All That You Can Be," "There's Strong, and Then There's Army Strong," evident in recruiting commercials (see YouTube 2009a and 2009b)). The RealJock.com community can therefore seem to align a lack of muscles, or a lack of skill in the gym (what one user calls "gay laziness"), with more traditional, conservative charges of a lack of patriotism among potential soldiers who cannot, for whatever regretful reason, "get big." Those who post flippant, potentially offensive comments about the presumed effeminacy of most gay men ("too precious to send to war" ("Hidden Member," Real Jock 2009t)) rarely receive responses, and often, rather defensively, critique the Real Jock community *in advance* for its apparent humorlessness. One user explicitly links such solemnity to cultural myths about masculinity, arguing that in order to seem "butch," a man must dismiss his "inner bitch."[5]

Such statements seem at first glance to resist political outrage in favor of jocular banter, but in aggressively advocating the latter these postings also promote the use of humor as a political tool. Specifically, they argue for a return to the "glory days" of the gay wit and repartee, but theirs is a minority presence in an online community for which the stern masculinity of the "real jock" appears to be a given. If this community is largely interested in aggressively promoting its specific, muscle-conscious conception of patriotism against allegedly outmoded images of fey, apolitical, sex-obsessed gay men, then it is clear why the rare discouraging responses to "skinny" would-be soldiers are framed in terms of a failed masculinity: if a gay man shouldn't serve, it is not because he is gay but because he has failed to realize his masculine potential—as, specifically, excessively muscled.

It is, for instance, revealing that the young man who in his first few postings expressed a desire to favor fashion and "hair care" at the expense of direct political (and belligerent physical) action, is the very same man who later initiated a discussion of "Don't Ask, Don't Tell." From a position advocating "the precious and the pretty," this man moved rather suddenly to an endorsement of the "fighting potential" of "even hair stylists," writing, "Although I hate violence and am gay and out of the closet, I believe I could hide my true self within the military" ("Hidden Member," Real Jock 2009v). It is entirely plausible that, recognizing his initial anti-military position to be an unpopular and potentially quite offensive one (and observing also that no one seemed to be responding to it) he attempted to reintroduce himself to the RealJock.com community by complying with its wish to support the gay soldier, in the process nominating himself for active duty and soliciting comments about his potential suitability as a serviceman. It is scarcely surprising, then, that numerous responses to his later, pro-military postings cite the young man's physical attractiveness, describing his apparently "army-ready" body in references to the so-called "torso shots" available in the "photos" section of his personal page—comments that come dangerously close to sexualizing him but that ultimately fail to do so, for the simple reason that they explicitly accept physical beauty as a prerequisite not for sex but for service.

Such a stance can seem to span the blogosphere. Consider, for instance, the sober, thoroughgoing manner in which a former Marine responds to a lustful posting on the website TwitchFilm.net (2009a), decrying the carefully cultivated "sexiness" of the service life depicted in the 2005 Sam Mendes film *Jarhead* and emphasizing the extreme naïveté of those who would champion it:

> The only enjoyable portion of being enlisted is in boot camp where you are forced into the best shape of your life… You are so pleased with yourself that chillbumps rise at even being called a Marine. Then, reality hits… Excitement and thrill? It's more like hurry, now wait wait wait. Hurry, now wait wait wait. Clean weapon, clean this, clean that, now wait. No more chills, just constant complaining and bitching from all around without end.
>
> ("jarhead," Twitchfilm.net 2009b)

Note how this response reflects an intense admiration for the methods of bodybuilding presumably open only to soldiers, at the same time that it seeks to establish the far from erotic, routine-oriented nature of service life. Such statements demonstrate that efforts to deglamorize (and explicitly de-eroticize) the military are not unique to RealJock.com, where, as we have seen, celibacy and patriotism are indistinguishable and comprise at least one set of conditions for representing the gay serviceman online.

That a second set of conditions appears to require unconditional support for "Don't Ask, Don't Tell" is perhaps not surprising. Since the policy is in place for the alleged betterment of the U.S. Military, to attack or in any way oppose it would be to challenge the U.S. Department of Defense itself, and thus appear "unpatriotic." Like a range of laws affecting gay, lesbian, bisexual, and transgender identity, "Don't Ask, Don't Tell" is inextricably linked to insidious, longstanding, and totalizing cultural assumptions about what constitutes queer expression. However, unlike sodomy laws that explicitly seek to criminalize same-sex erotic acts among civilians, "Don't Ask, Don't Tell" has divided LGBT activists, most notably gay men.

As the above evidence indicates, and as the 2009 Congressional standstill confirms, the main problem with "Don't Ask, Don't Tell" may be its uniquely puzzling qualities, and the cultural contradictions it consistently faces. In the summer of 2009, the website Stripes.com (2009a), identified as "The Independent News Source for the U.S. Military Community," published an article detailing the reluctance of President Barack Obama to fulfill his campaign promise to repeal the then-sixteen-year-old law, even as he vociferously defended the extension of additional benefits to same-sex civilian partners of federal employees. As the article points out, Obama (whether deliberately or inadvertently through the temporary entanglements of timing) created a kind of catch-22, wherein Defense Department employees seeking benefits for enlisted partners risk violating the terms of "Don't Ask, Don't Tell" (Stripes.com 2009b).

That the law should continue to be embraced by so many members of RealJock.com reveals much about the construction of contemporary society, and about the generational and cultural distinctions separating active and retired servicemen. Reading Allan Bérubé's seminal book *Coming Out Under Fire: The History of Gay Men and Women in World War Two*, which was published in 1990, three years before the passing of "Don't Ask, Don't Tell," this evokes a strong sense of the courage of World War II veterans to, if not come out of the closet, then expand that closet to include same-sex romantic and erotic connections. Bérubé (1990) writes, "[T]he World War II generation slowly stretched their closet to its limits, not proclaiming or parading their homosexuality in public but not willing to live lonely, isolated lives" (p. 271). Considering the differences between such mid-twentieth-century narratives and those twenty-first-century online accounts that stress the sublimation of sexual desire (accounts that, as we have seen, are abundant on RealJock.com), one may be tempted to speculate about the narcissism of a generation raised on the web. Ironically, RealJock.com itself seems to mirror the confusions, and indeed the contradictions, embedded in "Don't Ask, Don't Tell." The website's potential to promote gay dating vies with a subset of users whose "personal pics" provide evidence of the "real reason" one serves in the U.S. Military: to simultaneously defend one's country and to "build up" one's body. The documentation of such muscle-building programs on a gay dating site seems less a defiance of "Don't Ask, Don't Tell," than a nod to that policy's imprecision, and its inability to integrate novel modes of expression, which may not be limited to online new media.

Notes

1 Perhaps the most notorious example of this ambivalence playing out and escalating to violence in a service environment, the rape and murder of Private Anthony Ray Jaurigui at an Army artillery training center in Fort Sill, Oklahoma, in 1975, is among the most horrific of military hate crimes. For an overview of the Jaurigui case and other related incidents up to 1993, see Randy Shilts (1993).
2 RealJock.com allows members to position their profiles in a private, "hidden" setting, so as to be accessible only to their online friends. In the notes below, the name "Hidden Member" does not refer to a single user but rather to a multitude of similarly private profile types.
3 These quotations were taken from a November 2007 forum discussion, titled "Rate Him," that has since been deleted.
4 See the forum discussions titled "Are there things you feel pressure to do just because your a gay man [sic]" (Real Jock 2009r) and "The United States Coast Guard" (Real Jock 2009s).
5 See the forum discussion titled "Being the jock" (Real Jock 2009u).

References

Barry's Boot Camp. 2009. http://www.barrysbootcamp.com/ [Accessed August 14, 2009]
Bérubé, A. 1990. *Coming out under fire: The history of gay men and women in world war two*. New York: Free Press.
Bronski, M. 1998. *The pleasure principle: Sex, backlash, and the struggle for gay freedom*. New York: St. Martin's Press.
Bronski, M. 2001. From Victorian parlor to *physique pictorial*: The male nude and homosexual identity. In *Passing: Identity and interpretation in sexuality, race, and religion*, edited by M. C. Sanchez and L. Schlossberg. New York and London: New York University Press, 135–159.
DList.com. 2009. http://www.dlist.com/welcome.do [Accessed August 23, 2009]
Dyer, R. 2002. *The matter of images: Essays on representation*. New York and London: Routledge.
Gay.com. 2009. http://www.gay.com/ [Accessed August 23, 2009]
Gaydar.co.uk. 2009. http://gaydar.co.uk/ [Accessed August 23, 2009]
Halley, J. 1999. *Don't: A reader's guide to the military's anti-gay policy*. Durham, NC: Duke University Press.
Kinsey, A. C., Pomeroy, W. B., and Martin, C. E. 1948. *Sexual behaviour in the human male*. Philadelphia: Saunders.
Manhunt.net. 2009. http://www.manhunt.net/ [Accessed August 23, 2009]
Real Jock. 2009a. Post by Hidden Member, 22 October 2007, 3:04 p.m., forum topic "Dont Ask Dont Tell [sic]": http://www.realjock.com/gayforums/46310/ [Accessed August 14, 2009]
Real Jock. 2009b. Post by Hidden Member, 8 November 2007, 3:36 p.m.: http://www.realjock.com/gayforums/46310/ [Accessed August 14, 2009]
Real Jock. 2009c. Post by Hidden Member, 23 October 2007, 3:24 a.m., forum topic

"Homosexuals in the Military": http://www.realjock.com/gayforums/46671/ [Accessed August 14, 2009]

Real Jock. 2009d. Post by Onetoughguy, 23 October 2007, 5:31 p.m., forum topic "Homosexuals in the Military": http://www.realjock.com/gayforums/46671/ [Accessed August 14, 2009]

Real Jock. 2009e. Post by Hidden Member, 3 February 2008, 11:43 p.m., forum topic "thinking of joining the army": http://www.realjock.com/gayforums/43276/ [Accessed August 14, 2009]

Real Jock. 2009f. Post by Hidden Member, 14 October 2007, 5:58 a.m., forum topic "thinking of joining the army": http://www.realjock.com/gayforums/43276/ [Accessed August 14, 2009]

Real Jock. 2009g. Post by Hidden Member, 13 October 2007, 8:37 p.m., forum topic "thinking of joining the army": http://www.realjock.com/gayforums/43276/ [Accessed August 14, 2009]

Real Jock. 2009h. Post by ITJock, 11 October 2007, 10:08 p.m., forum topic "thinking of joining the army": http://www.realjock.com/gayforums/43276/ [Accessed August 14, 2009]

Real Jock. 2009i. Post by Hidden Member, 12 October 2007, 5:46 a.m., forum topic "thinking of joining the army": http://www.realjock.com/gayforums/43276/ [Accessed August 14, 2009]

Real Jock. 2009j. Post by Onetoughguy, 13 October 2007, 8:40 p.m., forum topic "thinking of joining the army": http://www.realjock.com/gayforums/43276/ [Accessed August 14, 2009]

Real Jock. 2009k. Post by Onetoughguy, 13 October 2007, 8:40 p.m., forum topic "thinking of joining the army": http://www.realjock.com/gayforums/43276/ [Accessed August 14, 2009]

Real Jock. 2009l. Post by Dclifterguy, 18 December 2007, 12:25 p.m., forum topic "Ignoring 'Don't Ask, Don't Tell'": http://www.realjock.com/gayforums/68952/ [Accessed August 14, 2009]

Real Jock. 2009m. Posted by coolarmydude, 17 December 2007, 12:54 p.m., forum topic "Ignoring 'Don't Ask, Don't Tell'": http://www.realjock.com/gayforums/68952/ [Accessed August 14, 2009]

Real Jock. 2009n. http://www.realjock.com/gayforums/58572/ [Accessed August 14, 2009]

Real Jock. 2009o. http://www.realjock.com/gayforums/54565/ [Accessed August 14, 2009]

Real Jock. 2009p. http://www.realjock.com/gayforums/60109/ [Accessed August 14, 2009]

Real Jock. 2009q. Post by yalemarine, 12 May 2008, 7:04 p.m., forum discussion "Don't ask, Don't tell": http://www.realjock.com/gayforums/180729/ [Accessed August 14, 2009]

Real Jock. 2009r. http://www.realjock.com/gayforums/162678/ [Accessed August 14, 2009]

Real Jock. 2009s. http://www.realjock.com/gayforums/40350/ [Accessed August 14, 2009]

Real Jock. 2009t. Post by Hidden Member, 23 October 2007, 6:24 a.m., forum discussion "Homosexuals in the Military": http://www.realjock.com/gayforums/46671/ [Accessed August 14, 2009]

Real Jock. 2009u. http://www.realjock.com/gayforums/186327/ [Accessed August 14, 2009]

Real Jock. 2009v. Post by Hidden Member, 11 October 2007, 7:06 p.m., forum discussion "thinking of joining the army": http://www.realjock.com/gayforums/43276/ [Accessed August 14, 2009]

Shalikashvili, J. M. 2007. Second thoughts on gays in the military. *The New York Times*, January 2, op-ed.

Shawver, L. 1996. Sexual modesty, the etiquette of disregard, and the question of gays and lesbians in the military. In *Out in force: Sexual orientation and the military*, edited by G. M. Herek, J. B. Jobe, and R. Carney. Chicago: University of Chicago Press.

Shilts, R. 1993. *Conduct unbecoming: Lesbians and gays in the U.S. Military*. New York: St. Martins Press.

Stripes.com, 2009a. http://www.stripes.com/ [Accessed August 23, 2009]

Stripes.com, 2009b. "Don't ask, don't tell" in limbo for now. Posted by Leo Shane III, 22 June 2009: http://www.stripes.com/article.asp?section=104&article=63408 [Accessed August 14, 2009]

Twitchfilm.net. 2009a. http://twitchfilm.net/site/ [Accessed August 23, 2009]

Twitchfilm.net. 2009b. Post by jarhead, 14 November 2005, 10:48 a.m.: http://twitchfilm.net/archives/004036.html [Accessed August 14, 2009]

Tyler, P. 1972. *Screening the sexes: Homosexuality in the movies*. New York: Holt, Rinehart, and Winston.

Waugh, Thomas. 1996. *Hard to imagine: Gay male eroticism in photography and film from their beginnings to Stonewall*. New York: Columbia University Press.

YouTube. 2009a. Army commercial—Be all you can be (1986). http://www.youtube.com/watch?v=QplWbNg57h4 [Accessed August 23, 2009]

YouTube. 2009b. US Army—"Army strong"—Military recruitment commercial. http://www.youtube.com/watch?v=fznTfpDW33o [Accessed August 23, 2009]

Chapter 18

"Stephanie Is Wired: Who Shall Turn Him On?"

Trudy Barber

> Rather than conceiving of gender as fixed and existing independently of technology, the notion of performativity, or "gender as doing," sees the construction of gender identities as shaped together with the technology in the making.
>
> (Wajcman 2009)

In this chapter I hope to bring to light sexual interaction and "gender play and participation" by users of information and communication technologies (ICTs) such as the internet. I argue that there has and continues to be a silent minority of enthusiasts, amateurs and IT professionals who are getting together and customizing their ICTs, thus creating a modified and individually specified hybrid technology that allows for innovative play surrounding virtual sexuality and identity. This experimentation also includes a reconsideration of gender and identity in real-time offline life, thus providing some evidence in support of Wajcman's quotation above. Consequently this chapter discusses the pursuit of arousal within the context of new media debates; revealing how such communities develop their own user generated games of the online and offline body—with specific reference to current discourses of the virtual, of sexual identity, of transgender and of participation.

In order to do this I describe online and offline participation of informants who were active mainly from the UK Fetish community (the Fetish Scene) at around the turn of the millennium. I show that this specialist private group is embedded in a particular fetishism for information and communications gadgetry, consumerism, and transgender play; where the body is accessed through a multiplicity of customized and personally built servers and invasive devices; and where identity and the performance of gender are transformed by a select invited audience of those participating both offline and online in a "private" sexual game. In exploring this sexual game I aim to look at the pursuit of arousal as a focus influencing the passion for collecting technological objects that appear to enhance credibility and kudos for certain individual identities within the group setting. In this sense, I argue that the technology itself becomes both the object of desire and consequently also the "fetish tool" that enables the users and participants to explore notions of gender, identity, and intimacy. This is achieved through participating in what appears to be various degrees of physical separation in synchronous online and offline events that also appear to collapse time and space through instantaneous broadband connections. I will also suggest that developing communications technology has a large part to play in influencing our ever evolving sexual appetite, and that this is changing the way culture and society consumes sex and sexuality through converging media strategies; thus redefining our attitudes to contemporary notions of love and intimacy through the expression of online and offline identities experienced as actual physical sensation combined with notions of the virtual. This will contribute to what has been described in post-feminist discussion surrounding developing technologies "as fundamentally challenging traditional notions of gender identity" (Wajcman 2009).

Discussion surrounding gender and identity has been evident throughout the development of interactive ICTs (Danet 1998; Turkle 1995; Plant 1998; Spender 1995; Stone 1996, van Zoonen 2002; O'Riordan and Phillips 2007). The discussion surrounding the gendering of technology and cyberspace has had profound impact on communities of practice on the internet. The particular community of practice for this discussion has also undergone changes in identity attributions and transformation partially as a result of ICTs and is known (at this time of writing) as the BDSM community and subculture, and has been previously known as Leathersex, SM (Rambukkana 2007) and the "Fetish Scene" (Woodward 1983).

Firstly this chapter is a descriptive exploration and exposure of participants from a specific sexual grouping from the UK with a predominant interest in fetishism, sadomasochism and bondage (BDSM), with gender play; and secondly will reveal their innovative—and some may even consider deviant—use of new and old ICTs with other devices. This will include some concepts and notions of "subculture," that will be used to discuss the social grouping done with a view to inform and describe the cultural setting from which this study is taken. There will also be some detailed description of their devices and resulting interactions. To begin with, a discussion of notions of the "fetish" and of "fetishism" for this particular group will help to situate the reader in an understanding of how the combination of sexuality, sexual predilections and technology create a challenging mix of sensations. Such sensations also include activity, creativity, interactive behavior and a culture of spectacular innovation and participatory media with a purpose to enable participants to "feel" what they suppose might be sensations of other sexes and genders.

The Social Character and Cultural Practices of the "Fetish Scene"

The fetishist and sadomasochistic "subculture" in London came to my personal attention during the early 1980s and was generally described as the "Fetish

Scene." (Woodward 1983). Anarchic punk excesses of the 1970s combined with the atmosphere of capitalist greed during the 1980s appeared to have created a socio-cultural environment where people who worked hard also felt the need to show off their success by playing hard. This was a time in late modernity for popular clubbing, bohemian lifestyle, and creative subcultures to flourish in cities such as New York and London. Along with such excesses various forms of sexual expression came to the public sphere bringing into question notions of what Waites describes as the "fixity" of sexual orientation and sexual practices. He argues that in late modernity "transformations in biomedical knowledge for debates over sexuality," and an apparent "absence of consensus within the medical profession" was evident in understanding the "ways in which medical professionals have maintained a uniform and powerful public voice in public debates" (Waites 2005, p. 552).

Consequently gay, lesbian, transgender, transsexual, bisexual, and feminist sexual politics came to the notice of a larger public through the expansion of popular media, such as the impact of MTV (for example) and the emergence of contemporary and transgressive film and music video. This also foregrounded the exploration and revelations of fetishism, sadomasochism and hedonism. Popular music videos such as "Relax" by "Frankie Goes to Hollywood" from the vinyl album *Welcome to the Pleasure Dome* produced by Trevor Horn (1984), portrayed hedonistic, gay and sadomasochistic sexual displays. This popular exposure during the mid 1980s contributed to the public ostracizing of some sexual behavior which also became associated with the rise of the then recently discovered HIV and AIDs epidemic. The public ostracizing of specific sexual behavior also reached its sexual-political height a little later, in the early 1990s, by the "Spanner Case" (1991), where five men were jailed for enacting their sadomasochistic predilections. Sexual politics weighted with Waites notions of the "fixity" of sexual identities led to heated debates and the construction of fringe groups such as the *Sexual Freedom Coalition* by Tuppy Owens, and *Feminists Against Censorship* with Avedon Carole and Alison Assiter.

It is in this light of sensation, spectacle, and fear that the cultural practices of the Fetish Scene appeared to be surrounded with notions of danger, deviance, transgression, and an understanding of masochism that has been described as "being prepared to get into the disgusting and disgraceful side of yourself." (Phillips 1998, p. 15)

The explosion of new and convergent media towards the end of the twentieth century meant that such cultural practices of the Fetish Scene provided the general media audience with an emerging number of sensational television documentaries available to watch on satellite and cable and access to "cybersex" from home PCs via gaming and the internet. Nick Broomfield directed the documentary *Fetishes* (Lafayette Films, USA, 1996) where the practices of dominatrices were observed at "Pandora's Box", one of New York's most famous SM parlors.

The advent of the home PC saw computer games like Mike Saenz's *Virtual Valerie* (Reactor Oress, USA, 1994) on CD ROM in which the aim was to give protagonist Valerie an orgasm by clicking continuously on the mouse (leading to severe repetitive strain injury in some cases!). This was accompanied by the hype of interaction as "dangers of cybersex" were made known by new information and communication technologies, such as the internet which also contributed to the over sensationalizing of my own early work on immersive virtual reality sex environments (VR Sex Installation 1992). Thus, the development of cybersex was demonized and described by some sexologists as the "dark side of the force" (Cooper 2000). However, despite the hype of "cybersex" as being considered dangerous, some new media and cultural theorists and explorers such as me saw this as an opportunity to explore notions of pleasure, as "in contemporary academic literature, (it) is rarely interrogated" (Kerr et al. 2006, p. 64). In order to appease this lack Kerr et al. suggest the following:

> Drawing on the new media literature and our own experiences with the new media under study, we identified a small number of concepts that kept recurring and that we felt were seen as constitutive of, and central to, the pleasures offered by new media. These were: control, immersion, performance, intertextuality and narrative. Each of these concepts is quite complex and seems to offer a variety of positions along a continuum between, for example, as in play, being in control and not being in control, and, when combined, seem to produce more complex pleasures.
>
> (2006, p. 69)

However, I argue that for "cybersex" to be part of the "pleasures" offered by new media, one of the vital concepts that is also in need of interrogation is that of "arousal," and whether that arousal can be seen as having gendered attributes. I suggest it is, through the understanding and articulation of concepts of fetish that can also help explore concepts of arousal in terms of new media culture and its relationship to discourses of sexuality and performances of gender.

The generation of meanings given to the fetish object (such as in the case of rubber or leather clothing) by the fetishist locates its meaning with the implied activity expected whilst wearing the specific clothing. This involves the enactment of a specific scenario which includes gender attributes and behavior, such as "sissification" for example; where a male is forced to wear clothing more attributed to or associated with women. The expectation is sublimated by the cultural practice of sadomasochism that itself contains semiologically shared meanings for all interacting parties concerned. It is the intensity of specific cultural practice that includes such ritual, and enables the increase of gratification, sublimation, and pleasure for members in the Fetish Scene, who experiment with gender and identity. Consequently, ritual is a fundamental and essential part of the subculture's activity. For some it can take the form of extreme gender performance. For others, it is a form of ironic, exhibitionistic, or heterosexually stereotypical display, and for others, it may be forms of interactive play.

Hybrid Technologies: Hybrid Sexualities, Genders, and Identities

The fast expansion of ICTs enabled sex as entertainment to be easily available online for users. Initially it was recognized by Kibby and Costello (2001) that "sex entertainment both reflects and influences social attitudes and personal practices," and therefore redefined "the parameters of sex entertainment and potentially reshaping other aspects of lived experience" (2001, p. 354). Their observations are particularly resonant, as a small group of transgender, bisexual, and homosexual sadomasochistic transvestites did go on to re-shape their gendered aspects of lived experience through developing their notions of gender play with interactive ICTs. This group of about ten individuals, who were also participants in the fetish subculture, became part of my empirical study of arousal and computer fetishism.

The performative activity by this group appeared not only to reveal their arousal through experimentation with fetishism, SM and technology, but also it revealed in stark reality the "practices in both homosexual and heterosexual contexts that open surfaces and orifices to erotic signification or close down others [and that] effectively reinscribe the boundaries of the body along new cultural lines" (Butler 1999, p. 169). In this sense the enculturation of the participants in discussion here can be encapsulated in the processes of developing an "SM identity" (Rambukkana 2007). This was achieved through physically immersive online interaction which encompasses both public and private spheres, stimulating the internal psychological and envisioned fantasy and the external manifestation of the wished-for and performed gender identity of the participants.

This group deviated and customized their use of internet technologies by creating and building their own servers that also connected to vibrating devices and other sex toys. This was completed in tandem with their own body modifications (such as cross-dressing or surgery), and their social constructions and interactions. This converged with the notion of play with gender and constructions of sexual identity with ICTs. In this sense as they worked with their understanding of physical sexual orientation such as breast augmentation and full sex change surgery, for example, that would complement their "prosthetic communication" (Ross 2005, p. 342). They would also work on adding onto and developing their technological computer hardware and software. Consequently such users developed new approaches to sex as interactive entertainment along with creating and developing new hardware and software to enable their desires and instigate arousal and gender play. Not only were they modifying and customizing their bodies and sexual identities, but they were also connecting themselves to their

PCs through intimate attachments such as vibrators and mechanistic dildos. The PC and the body became unified for this specific group. The producer and the consumer of experience and immersive notions of telepresence merged with sense of place, gender construction, sensation and touch (haptic technologies). Something that was initially thought of as the stuff of science fiction narrative actually became real for this group. Sex and Science Fiction narratives have always been popular, however at this time films such as *The Lawn Mower Man* (Brett Leonard, USA, 1992)—where a computer scientist's experiment goes badly wrong, creating a "rape in cyberspace" sequence—added to the hype of immersive ICTs such as the dangers of cybersex as has already been mentioned. However, in turn, *real time* creative developments and experiments were also ongoing (along with my own work previously mentioned) such as *Cyber SM* by artists Kirk Woolford and Stahl Stenslie who worked on interconnected body suits that attempted to enable physical sexual pleasure through the internet. In this sense I argue that both the ICT and the body became fetish objects that mediated sex and gender play, and consequently remediated the perception and experience of self and identity.

There has been discussion that subcultures are mainly the concern of youth and/or consumerism based on a foundation of resistance and transgression; for example, Jervis suggests that "closet S/M mutates into bondage chic" (Jervis 1998, p. 318). However the Fetish Scene does maintain elements of resistance and transgression necessary for its inclusion in definitions of subculture, so comparisons can be drawn between definitions of "youth" and members of the specific group of my research, even though they are adults. In this sense the group transgresses notions of heterosexual relationships, by their very resistance in engaging in what may be considered as "normative" socio-sexual interaction, but appearing to identify more with "youth" or "nerds." The group interacts mainly from their own bedrooms and private "dungeon" constructions in their homes where they also connect online to each other. I argue that this is redolent of some youth behavior and game play and bears relation to Hodkinson and Lincoln's (2008) viewpoint in their research into youth and the use of the online journal:

> The bedroom is the first space young people are able to take ownership of and acts as a constant presence in their everyday lives throughout their teenage years and often well into their twenties. Whether in the context of a parental home or a shared house or flat, this is a space over which young people themselves regulate access, allowing who they wish to enter the space, and making boundaries clear to others.
> (Hodkinson and Lincoln 2008, p. 31)

Hodkinson and Lincoln also draw comparisons with youth and their use of online journals as metaphors for the "virtual bedroom."

> Like the bedroom, we argue, the interactive and multi-dimensional space of the online journal offers a safe, personally owned and controlled space which is used as part of the negotiation of youthful transitions via marking out of territory, the exploration and exhibition of identity and the generation and living out of personal social networks.
>
> (Hodkinson and Lincoln 2008, p. 28)

In this case, the specific Fetishists of my study exhibited such notions literally and in the physical world. They had their bedrooms set up with their new media technologies and other electronic toys, sex-toys, and gadgets. They would then hook themselves up physically and intimately to their PCs in order to enact what they perceived as specific gendered identities and/or sexual exhibitions of physical pleasure and/or pain whilst being connected online. The group would literally insert anal dildos into their bodies that would vibrate, have breast or nipple attachments that would suck/vibrate and various other forms of masturbatory devices that were connected to themselves, their PCs and, in some cases their mobile phones.

The personal social networks for this specific group were those interacting online with the body connected to the PC. They became the invited participants in an intimate form of play and interactive game via broadband. In this sense it is useful to consider the "uses and gratifications" approach to studying this form of new media interaction, as the study easily "focuses on the functions that individual people say particular genre or media play in their lives and within which media enjoyment and entertainment are seen as key" (Kerr et al. 2006, p. 65).

Once a member of this group is physically wired to the PC and has made their online connections, what are their sensations and what happens to them and the others in this complicated techno-sexological spectacle?

Online and Offline Participation

During such performances of attachment and belonging, branding, tattooing, and flagellation may take place, as well as the exchange of more traditional tokens of affection. Bloustein (2003) confirms that the importance of visual permanency made by marking the skin by a whip or brand is that the process is validated by physical sensation.

> The skin is injured by the lash in such a way as to reify its surface. Masochistic sexuality makes a fetish of the skin, infusing it with idolatrous power, and granting it an excess of visibility through tearing, bruising or piercing.
>
> (Bloustein 2003, p. 61)

In marking the flesh a form of "gifting" takes place between the dominant and the submissive. This creates the paradox of receiving pain given through the auspices of affection and attachment even though in this situation the people sharing the intimate moment may literally be oceans apart and living in entirely different time zones. The submissive thus "belongs" to the dominant, through online mediation and through subcultural ritual, and displays the interconnectedness between power and control with compliance and surrender.

The relationship between sexual deviation and technology can be revealed through a transgressive or alternative reading of technological determinism. Post modern ICTs, as used by the mass public, are a physical manifestation of the power of an autonomous sexuality. Sexual arousal is reified in computer technology. Upgrade culture (Lister et al. 2003) reveals spontaneous arousal over function leading to the transgressive use of technological artifacts.

The phenomenon of group activity within this type of intimate network is also a reminder of Tambiah's notions of participation, causality, and multiple orderings of reality (Tambiah 1990). With the development of mobile phones, the wireless computer and webcam connections then, the ability to penetrate the connected body and exchange sensations, or gender identity, for example, becomes ubiquitous along with surveillance and the gaze.

Koskela suggests that private non-commercial webcams, "promote nothing but the existence of the person presenting oneself—and perhaps her/his belonging to a certain (virtual, global) community" and therefore are different from surveillance cameras. But Koskela nevertheless agrees that webcams and surveillance can increase "our conceptual understanding of presenting and hiding, power and control, hegemonies and resistance" (2004, p. 204). For this group then, the individual is aroused whilst connected to the technology, and I argue that being observed by the others whilst responding to the connection is part of the arousal process and gender performance for the user. Observation and surveillance takes place by other members of the group who may be physically present to watch through their mediated or non-mediated eyes from within the realms of the virtual, the dream, the fantasy, and the real world. They are all simultaneously participating in both the public and private body. It is in this state that the individual who is connected experiences the immersion and transformation of the sexual self and gender identity.

In this particular case a physical "man" experiences what he thinks it is to be female. During his experience within this interaction this "male" member of the group shape-shifts and becomes "Stephanie," a "female." The blurring of boundaries and gender attributes is complete. Nonetheless, despite the blurring and fluidity of sexual identities and boundaries, it has been argued that situation and place are still important factors that ground the interactivity and notions of contemporary sexual citizenship. The sexual behavior may still be geographically located.

In this case, for "Stephanie," it begins in a bedroom dungeon, somewhere in London. Hearn (2006) confirms this notion:

> Place and space continue to matter, for both physical embodied sexual practice and organising around sexuality, sexualised violences, and sexual citizenships, even if place and practice appear more fragmented. ICTs and virtuality assist new socio-sexual possibilities, but their embodied sexual enactment is still likely to depend for most upon spatial proximity. The spatialised material bodily and the de-spatialising discursive representational are both separable and inseparable for sexual citizenships, with movements, contradictory, sometimes simultaneous, from private to public, and public to private.
>
> (Hearn 2006, p. 959)

Consequently Stephanie's cyber-gendered body becomes representational of time and place as invited members can connect to her body by internet and private server connections, as well as see her reactions and responses to their attentions via live and/or recorded streaming.

The participants were willing to discuss their interests with me, some of which they call E-Stim (electronic stimulation), in detail. During the research, one participant called "Master R" agreed to give an interview as well as allow me to observe his and the group's interactions over a specific period of time. His E-Stim sessions/parties would take place on a regular basis with specifically invited participants who also had similar inclinations and interests.

> Some might say E-Stim players are the "nerds" of the fetish scene—and it might well be true—most of the people I have played with over the years are in technology or engineering jobs where adding a new feature to a system is a thrill. E-Stim in particular is all about creating new physical sensations through changing wave forms or contact points. There is also a wide culture of shared experience and unlike many other forms of scene play it is easy to categorize and repeat sensations as they can be measured in well understood if rather clinical terms of Volts Hertz and wave formulae.
>
> (Master R)

At the time the group was also considering adapting, customizing, and modifying upgrades of their technology in order to expand on their sensations, interactions, and experiences of sex and gender between the virtual and the real. It was suggested:

> The next widely anticipated step is the use of broadband Internet for long distance remote control. My early experiments in this field have been somewhat patchy generally because of intermittent connections and low bandwidth.
>
> A webcam for feedback and good audio contact is essential. It should also be possible to use SMS messaging to drive a device such as a small ErosTek

box too—the main problem with this approach is that communication is typically one way—feedback as in all scene play is essential.

Technology is not the real obstacle at the moment—cost and battery life are the main hurdles.

(Master R)

The study was partially worked through the consideration of virtual ethnographic methodologies (Hine 2000). However, the geographical location of the experiences combined with the CU-C-Me feedback using web cams and/or mobile phones (and even on one or two occasions a television remote control!) made face-to-face interviews and personal observation more vital to teasing out the richness of these mediated sex and gender experiences.

The Pursuit of Arousal or the Convergence of Sex and Gendered Pleasures?

Seeing the practices first hand has provided a wealth of content for discussions surrounding issues of LGBT identity. The experiences certainly go some way to answering questions that have been posed in the past by Ault (1996). Those same questions surrounding bisexuality, identity, and agency still reveal the difficulties posed by the bi subjectivity of relationships and the "production of particular identity categories at different times and places." (Ault 1996, p. 451) In this case mediated bisexual activity in the form of "interactive Stephanie" may give us some answers.

However, does this also provide evidence of a fragmented and unstable understanding of postmodernism? Does this confirm Storr's argument that we are seeing the "rise of niche marketing and of minutely segmented and sophisticated patterns of consumption" (including the self reflexive creation of identity through consumption) (Storr 1999, p. 311)? In order to exchange the sex and gender attributes during such adult computer play, are we not exploring notions of what I metaphorically describe as "fractal" identity? The fractal is a mathematical axiom that continuously recreates itself and is often used in computing (Fractals and the Mandelbrot Set 2009). I suggest that in our pursuit of sexual pleasure and arousal our identity, gender and sexuality can be created from elements of a core sentience, for which the axiom is the metaphor that continuously modifies and duplicates itself (the fractal) through different technologically augmented environments, such as the ones created by this specific group for study. In this sense, "Stephanie" is a metaphorical fractal identity from the root identity of the male, who becomes her, whilst he is mediated by the technology. In this sense I am trying to use computer and mathematical language as a metaphor to describe the hybridity of human/computer interrelations in the pursuit of arousal and pleasure and the transformation of gendered experience. This is probably the language of the cyborg and the route to virtualization.

However, I do not wish to conclude by re-iterating notions of Haraway's (1991) ironic and classic Cyborg. I wish to consider the apparent malleability, and some would say sacrifice, of sex/gender for the sake of arousal and pleasure and the kudos of techno-fetishism. As we witness the blurring of boundaries and the convergence of communications, broadcast, mobile, and entertainment technologies, I argue that it is inevitable that we will see a "home-made" and even "hobbyist" approach to sex and gender. This approach will include a convergence of heterosexual and stereotypical gendered attributions with sexual inclinations associated with bio-medical interventions and a convergence of the physical body with technology in an implosion of amateurish and experimental hybridity. Like the protagonist Bob Arctor in Philip K. Dick's novel *A Scanner Darkly* (1977) which was also made into a film (Richard Linklater, USA, 2006), our notions of self and identity could become fluid, convergent, and interchangeable in time and space. In the animated film the protagonist wears a "scramble suit" a simulacrum that continuously changes the appearance, gender, and identity of the wearer, "thus rendering the description of the wearer as meaningless"(Dick 1977). If this is true, then I argue that sex and gender could become meaningless in real time, but that they have major arousal value in the virtual.

My extraordinary glimpse into a group's sex and gendered interaction with "new media" suggests trust and cohesion between the specific participants and a virtualization of self that is simply enabled at the click of a mouse. Their excitement and arousal during the sessions were evident not only in their dress, their bodies, and behavior and their interrelationship with each other, but also with their chosen technology of intimacy. This exposes and changes how we witness acts of arousal and what we mean by performative gender and sexuality. Hearn has argued that:

> Put together, LGBT, violence, ageing, environmental change, problematization of sex and biology, and ICTs and virtualization—are likely to produce significant changes in what is meant by sexuality, or sexualities. They exert effects on what sexuality *is*; the political economies of sexualities are likely to be reformulated, even within modernist resistances to change.
>
> (Hearn 2008, p 44)

It is hoped that this chapter gives a glimpse into such hybrid activity and arousal processes between sex, gender, interaction, and new media.

However there is some disappointment expressed by the participants once the party is over and there is a return to the mundane. Nonetheless some participants take elements of their "fractal" identity and develop them further, creating even more flamboyant experiences and characters for the next time around. This brings to mind extraordinary personalities such as the artist Leigh Bowery who created infinite versions of self as body and performance. In relationship to LGBT identity, the group at the center of this chapter took some breath-taking leaps into the exploration of the unknown and phantastical psyche and its relationship to the physical. By carefully and selectively engaging in this multiplicity of experience the group demonstrated concepts of identity, gender, and the sexual body that are entirely fluid and malleable. But at the same time they realize that in some senses they are also bound to their physical sexual bodies and daily selves after the play has taken place. For a short while, this group can be anybody, any gender, and any identity they wish to be.

Using new media and ICTs as the mask, there are many who are coming to see their gender and sexuality as truly virtual, (as in Second Life™ an online virtual environment for example) and submit to their physical real-life self as the mundane. The producer and consumer (the prosumers) of convergent new media technologies are also producing and consuming their own sexual identities and communities that may, in the future, negate contemporary notions of gender and sexuality. The outcome is that this is how the political economies of sexuality are being reformulated, re-represented, and re-mediated through interactivity, participation, innovation, and the ongoing search for arousal and gratification.

References

Ault, A. 1996. Ambiguous identity in an unambiguous sex/gender structure: The case of bisexual women. *The Sociological Quarterly* 37(3): 449–463.

Bloustein, D. 2003. 'Oh bondage, up yours!' Or here's three chords, now form a band: Punk, masochism, skin, anaclisis, defacement. In *The Post-Subcultures Reader*, edited by D. Muggleton and R. Weinzierl. Oxford: Berg, 51–64.

Butler, J. 1999. *Gender trouble: Tenth anniversary edition.* London: Routledge.

Cooper, A., ed. 2000. Cybersex: The dark side of the force. *The Journal of Sexual Addiction and Compulsivity.* Philadelphia: Brunner-Routledge.

Cyber SM. 2009. http://www.stenslie.net/stahl/ [Accessed August 24, 2009]

Danet, B. 1998. Text as mask: Gender, play, and performance on the internet. In *Cybersociety 2.0: Revisiting computer-mediated communication and community*, edited by S. G. Jones. London: Sage.

Dick, P. K. 1977. *A scanner darkly*. New York: Doubleday.

Feminists against censorship. 2009. http://www.fiawol.demon.co.uk/FAC/ [Accessed August 24, 2009]

Fractals and the Mandelbrot Set. 2009. http://en.wikipedia.org/wiki/Fractal [Accessed August 24, 2009]

Haraway, D. 1991. *Simians, cyborgs and women: The reinvention of nature.* New York: Routledge.

Hearn, J. 2006. The implications of information and communication technologies for sexualities and sexualised violences: Contradictions of sexual citizenships. *Political Geography* 25: 944–963.

Hearn, J. 2008. Sexualities future, present, past . . . towards transectionalities. *Sexualities* 11(37): 37–46.

Hine, C. 2000. *Virtual ethnography.* London: Sage.

Hodkinson, P. and Lincoln, S. 2008. Online journals as virtual bedrooms? Young people, identity and personal space. *Young* 16(1): 27–46.

Jervis, J. 1998. *Exploring the modern. Patterns of western culture and civilization.* Oxford: Blackwell.

Kerr, A., Kücklich, J., and Brereton, P. 2006. New media—new pleasures? *International Journal of Cultural Studies* 9(1): 63–82.

Kibby, M. and Costello, B. 2001. Between the image and the act: Sex entertainment on the internet. *Sexualities* 4(3): 353–369.

Koskela, H. 2004. Webcams, tv shows and mobile phones: Empowering exhibitionism. *Surveillance & Society* CCTV Special (Eds. Norris, McCahill, and Wood), 2(2/3).

Lister, M., Dovey, J., Giddings, S., Grant, I., and Kelly, K. 2003. *New media: A critical introduction.* London: Routledge.

O'Riordan, K. and Phillips, D. J. (eds.) 2007. *Queer Online. Media Technology and Sexuality.* Digital Formations series, Vol. 40. New York: Peter Lang.

Phillips, A. 1998. *A defence of masochism.* London: Faber and Faber.

Plant, S. 1998. *Zeros and ones: Digital women and the new technoculture.* London: Fourth Estate.

Rambukkana, N. 2007. Taking the leather out of leathersex: The internet, identity, and the sadomasochistic public sphere. In *Queer online: Media, technology and sexuality*, edited by K. O'Riordan and D. J. Phillips. New York: Peter Lang, 67–80.

Ross, M. W. 2005. Typing, doing, being: Sexuality and the internet. *The Journal of Sex Research* 42(4): 342–352.

Second Life. 2009. http://www.secondlife.com [Accessed August 24, 2009]

Sexual Freedom Coalition. 2009. http://www.sfc.org.uk/about.html [Accessed August 24, 2009]

Spender, D. 1995. *Nattering on the Net. Women, power and cyberspace.* Melbourne: Spinifex Press.

Stone, A. R. 1996. *The war of desire and technology.* Cambridge, MA: MIT Press.

Storr, M. 1999. Postmodern bisexuality. *Sexualities* 2(3): 309–325.

Tambiah, S. J. 1990. *Magic, science, religion, and the scope of rationality.* Cambridge: Cambridge University Press.

Turkle, S. 1995. *Life on the screen: Identity in the age of the internet.* New York: Simon and Schuster.

Van Zoonen, L. 2002. Gendering the internet: Claims, controversies and cultures. *European Journal of Communication* 17(1): 5–23.

VR Sex Installation. 1992. Trudy Barber. Central Saint Martins College of Art and Virtual "S." London.

Waites, M. 2005. The fixity of sexual identities in the public sphere: Biomedical knowledge, liberalism and the heterosexual/homosexual binary in late modernity. *Sexualities* 8(5): 539–569.

Wajcman, J. 2009. Feminist theories of technology. *Cambridge Journal of Economics.* http://cje.oxfordjournals.org/cgi/content/abstract/ben057 [Accessed August 18, 2009]

Woodward, T. 1983. *Skin two magazine.* London: Tim Woodward Publishing.

Chapter 19

Health Information, STDs, and the Internet
Implications for Gay Men

Joseph Clift

Introduction

In this chapter, I will argue that the use of online new media has become a mixed blessing. The Internet, at its most basic function, is an information source—including finding information pertaining to health. There is also another side to Internet use, and that is to find sex partners. Research suggests that a high percentage of gay men use the Internet to find sex partners and engage in high-risk behavior (e.g., unprotected sex) that puts them at risk for contracting and spreading sexually transmitted diseases (STDs) including HIV. This relates largely to the activities of MSM (men who have sex with men).

In public health discourse, the term MSM is used in lieu of gay or homosexual because not every man who has sex with other men identifies as gay. The gay liberation movement is often associated with the freedom of sexual liberty and, under some circumstances, the right to engage in carefree and unrestricted sexual behavior. Despite this, STDs are spreading though the Internet between MSM in a manner which reveals a threat to the democratic potentials of gay sexual freedom. In this chapter, I am using the term MSM to indicate a diverse group of individuals, including those that identify as gay and those who do not, who are engaging in unsafe sexual behavior. It is not my intention to suggest that this is widespread sexual behavior; however, as my data reveals, irresponsible sexual behavior is increasing among MSM. Researching and understanding why some MSM use the Internet is necessary to develop interventions to help stop the spread of STDs.

Men who have sex with men that have discomfort with their sexual identity are using the Internet to find sex partners because of the anonymity that the Internet provides. Homophobia and anti-gay politics create situations where MSM lead double lives (i.e., heterosexual in public and homosexual in private) and the Internet is often used by these individuals to find sex partners. Among all people, the spread of STDs and HIV is still highest among MSM, with the highest rates occurring within people of color. It is clear that curbing the spread of STDs among MSM needs our immediate attention.

This chapter begins with a brief description of the Internet and its role in health promotion; later I move on to a discussion of gay men's use of the Internet for sex, considering reasons for this, and what to do about it.

The Internet and its Role in Health Promotion

The new health care consumer is someone who uses the Internet to meet some of their health care needs, including finding information to understand a health condition or to inform a health-related decision. The Pew Internet and American Life project (Fox 2006) found that 80 percent of Americans use the Internet to find health information. According to the survey, on any given day, approximately 8 million Americans used the Internet to access health information; 66 percent began at a search engine while 27 percent began at a health-related site, and 53 percent said that the information they found had some kind of impact on them. These results point to the important role that the Internet has in health as more and more consumers are drawn to the Internet for health-related information. Internet use for health information is not limited to highly educated or affluent individuals; people of low socioeconomic status and less education also use the Internet for health-related reasons (Lizska et al. 2006).

The Internet also links people in health professions. Health educators in different community settings can use the Internet to communicate with each other and/or look up information specific to the community in which they are working in (see Community Tool Box (2009) for examples). This is especially helpful for health professionals in remote settings without access to libraries or other information sources.

The Internet, with respect to health information, is not restricted to text. Multimedia formats such as video, presentations, and sound recordings can enhance information use, especially those whose learning style takes an interactive approach.

The Internet, Sex, and Gay Men: A Look at the Literature

Most research on gay men's use of the Internet has focused on sexual behavior, including the spread of STDs. A renowned researcher who studies the Internet and sex, Cooper writing in 1998 (cited in Bowen 2005) stated that there are three reasons why individuals use the Internet for sex: access, affordability, and anonymity. No studies, to my knowledge, have looked extensively at the affordability aspect of MSM's use of the Internet. Many studies about gay men's use of the Internet have provided validity to access and anonymity. This section will discuss MSM's use of the Internet with respect to high-risk sexual behavior, including the spread of STDs.

According to the Centers for Disease Control and Prevention (2007a), some 19 million people in the United States become infected with any one of 25 known STD each year. Some people do not know they even have one. Others do not know that having one puts you at risk for contracting another. After the AIDS crisis in the 1980s, the spread of HIV among MSM started to decrease through the 1980s and 1990s. After the new millennium, however, the rate started to increase and continues to do so—especially among Black and Hispanic MSM. The Centers for Disease Control and Prevention (2008) recently released some alarming data: 46 percent of HIV/AIDS cases in the United States from 2001 to 2006 were among MSM, representing a 6 percent increase overall and a 12 percent increase among Black MSM.

A study conducted by Liau et al. (2006) attempted to find out how many MSM had used the Internet to look for sex and to study the prevalence of risky sex behavior among MSM who have and have not sought sexual partners online. They analyzed existing data and found that a substantial number of MSM used the Internet to look for sexual partners (range of Internet use in the studies was 23.3 percent to 98.5 percent). They also found that those who use the Internet were more likely to engage in high-risk unprotected sex. In studies where HIV status was reported, they found that HIV-positive MSM who used the Internet to look for sex were significantly more likely to engage in unprotected sex than HIV-positive MSM who did not use the Internet.

Using the Internet to find sex partners is not restricted to those living in urban areas. Rural MSM who often have few venues to meet other MSM, use the Internet to meet sex partners. In their study of rural MSM, Horvath et al. (2006) found that the Internet and bars were the most popular venues for seeking sex partners. Higher levels of risky sexual behavior (e.g., having unprotected sex) were reported among the Internet users in their study.

Disease outbreaks can be traced through Internet activity. Researchers were able to trace a syphilis outbreak in San Francisco through a chat room on the Internet (Klausner et al. 2000). They found that gay men with syphilis were significantly more likely to have met their sexual partners through the Internet.

In a study in the United Kingdom, Bolding et al. (2004) studied 4,974 MSM who completed an online questionnaire available at two popular Internet sites (Gaydar.co.uk (2009) and Gay.com (2009)). They found that 82 percent had looked for sexual partners online and about 75 percent had been doing so for more than a year. They also found that 47 percent indicated that the Internet was their preferred method of meeting partners; 40 percent said that finding sexual partners was their main reason for using the Internet. Also being HIV-positive, older, and having high-risk sexual behavior was associated with increased frequency of Internet use. In their study of Swedish gay men who use chat rooms, Tittanen and Ross (2000) found that the chat rooms attracted younger men, those who engage in high-risk behavior, and those living outside urban areas.

In a study of MSM who met their sexual partners online, Kim et al. (2001) found that MSM were more likely to use the Internet to find sexual partners than heterosexual men and women. Looking specifically at MSM, they found that survey respondents were more likely to report sex with an HIV-positive person and more likely to have causal sexual partners as compared to MSM who did not use the Internet to find sexual partners.

Among young men (aged 16 to 24) who completed an online survey, Garofalo et al. (2007) found that 48 percent had sexual relations with a partner they met online and only 53 percent used condoms consistently. They also found that the young MSM who sought sexual partners online also engaged in other behaviors that put them at risk for STDs (e.g., using drugs).

"Barebacking" (intentional unprotected anal intercourse) is resurfacing as a phenomenon in the gay community. Halkitis et al. (2003) found that of the men who knew what the term meant, almost half reported barebacking in the previous three months. Survey participants noted that use the Internet facilitated barebacking. Tomso (2004) reported on another phenomenon in the gay community called "bug chasing," which is where MSM are actively trying to become infected with HIV. The Internet has been shown to facilitate bug chasing by providing an outlet for bug chasers to find one another. Little qualitative information which might reveal the reasons why people voluntarily want to become HIV-positive, exists about this phenomenon (Grove and Parsons 2006).

The research presented here does not encompass the complete library of MSM's use of the Internet for seeking sex. Suffice it to say, concerns about gay men's use of the Internet for seeking sex are not unfounded. The next section discusses some reasons that gay men engage in high-risk sexual behavior.

Reasons for High-Risk Behavior

Men who have sex with men who engage in high-risk behavior do so for many reasons, such as identity issues, homophobia, inevitability and complacency (e.g., accepting the "fact" that MSM will inevitably become HIV- positive), drug and alcohol abuse, and psychosocial reasons. This section describes some of these reasons.

The link between high-risk behavior and one's identity is complex. Some MSM believe that freedom to have sex when and how they want it is a direct result of the gay liberation movement and a component of their sexual identity (Center for AIDS Prevention Studies 2000). Liberated sexual freedom and claiming [gay] identity was, in part, a response to increased homophobia after the AIDS epidemic (Jagose 1996). This is because some were tired of being closeted and wanted to counter the homophobia that arose from the AIDS epidemic (which was during the rise of the Religious Right during the Reagan Administration). This "freedom," however, has its negative consequences as it puts individuals at higher risk for STDs. Other issues with identity deal with hiding one's identity—either because of society's or one's own (internalized) homophobia. Individuals whose sexual behavior is discordant with their sexual identity engage in higher-risk behavior (Pathela et al. 2006).

Homophobia is a problem not only with respect to the mental health of the individual, but it also plays a part in their healthcare. Researchers have found that, especially for members of the gay community in rural settings, physicians and social workers will refuse to care for someone who is gay or if they have HIV/AIDS (e.g., Preston et al. 2004). In the Black community, Stokes and Peterson (1998) have noted that homophobia has contributed to the spread of STDs in the gay Black men's community and that African Americans routinely teach others that being gay is inconsistent with being Black. This homophobia, often with religion as the backdrop, has helped to create what we now know as the *down-low* community; that is, Black MSM, some who may in fact be gay, who lead their social lives as heterosexual and fulfill their sexual desires as homosexual. Similarly, in the Hispanic community, *machismo* keeps many in the closet. In rural communities, a lot of MSM will lead double lives as described above.

The reason that these identity issues and homophobia are of concern is that it puts the individual at increased risk. Those who think that having unfettered sex is part of their sexual identity are at an increased risk of having and transmitting STDs. Individuals who are hiding their identity are at risk for unprotected sex because they generally do not have a monogamous relationship, may be more inclined to be under the influence of drugs and/or alcohol, and are generally looking for sex when and where they will not get caught—thereby increasing chances they will engage in unprotected sex. Researchers have found that sexual risk taking is related to discomfort with one's identity (Robinson et al. 2000 as cited in Center for AIDS Prevention Studies 2000). The Internet has facilitated the anonymity that these individuals need when finding sex partners.

One could argue that the political arena has also contributed to high-risk behavior. In the United States, federal funding is provided to educate students about sex through the lens of hetero-exclusivity: generally advising "do not have sex until you are married." Since LGBT individuals cannot get married, this lens completely ignores LGBT youth, who go through their developmental years feeling ignored and unprepared to deal with safe sex from a lack of education on the topic.

Inevitability and complacency are resurfacing as reasons for high-risk behavior. The research points to gay men who have alluded to the notion that they are eventually going to get it (HIV) so why use protection? Others noted that they are not afraid to be HIV positive like they were in years past, especially because of the new medications that are out and the life expectancy of someone with AIDS has greatly increased (Demmer 2002).

Drug and alcohol use in the gay community is high and some studies have shown that gay youth are more likely to use drugs and alcohol than heterosexual youth (e.g., Blake et al. 2001). In addition, researchers have found that MSM who use the Internet to find sexual partners are also likely to use drugs (Garofalo et al. 2007). Club drugs, like crystal meth, are becoming problematic in the gay men's community (Reback et al. 2004). Gay men who use drugs and alcohol are at risk for engaging in high-risk sexual behavior (Reback et al. 2004). People under the influence of drugs and/or alcohol may forget to use protection during intercourse or forget to inquire about their sexual partner's STD status altogether.

Psychosocial issues, such as loneliness, are another reason why gay men engage in high-risk behavior; however, a word of caution is needed for the reader as more research into psychosocial aspects is greatly needed. Semple et al. (2000) found that gay men who engage in unprotected sex noted emotions such as loneliness and depression, and avoidance coping strategies.

Implications for Gay Men: The Internet as a Tool

While the Internet has been shown to be a facilitator of unsafe sexual behavior, it can also be used as a tool to help combat the spread of STDs among gay men who use the Internet to find sex partners. Researchers who have studied gay men who use the Internet to look for sex have found support for health-related outreach conducted in the venues that MSM use (e.g., Bolding et al. 2004). Using the Internet for health-related prevention work is a relatively new idea; few empirical studies about its effectiveness have been conducted. There are no Internet-based interventions on the Centers for Disease Control and Prevention's list of promising interventions that target MSM (Centers for Disease Control and Prevention 2007b).

One way the Internet can be used as a tool is through the use of personal risk assessment of sexual behavior. Individuals can go online and find a variety of personal assessment tools related to nutrition, heart disease, diabetes, and cancer. For example, a breast cancer tool (National Cancer Institute 2009) developed by scientists at the National Cancer Institute allows users to answer pre-defined questions in order to assess their individual risk level. Once users finish the online questionnaire and receive their individual results, they are usually taken to another Web page that provides more information. Users of such tools have immediate access to health information about their individual risk (Bensley 2001). Assessment tools can be created for MSM and provide links to obtain health-related information or provide information on how to obtain services (e.g., STD testing) in their area. Because research has suggested that gay men face hurdles in the health care system with respect to patient—provider interaction (Gay and Lesbian Medical Association 2001), assessment tools provide an anonymous way for individuals to assess their own risk level.

Health-related outreach conducted over the Internet has been growing over the past few years. For example, some health educators directly target chat rooms that are known meeting places for sexual activity by gay men and conduct health outreach in the chat room. Rhodes (2004) reported on the success of an interventionist who reached out to gay men in a chat room. Health educators can provide information to the chatters on a variety of topics, including STD prevention, "coming out" resources, general health information, and information about how to get tested. In the study conducted by Rhodes, 30 percent of the individuals (who provided demographic information via their bioline) were not "out" to anyone. This sub-group of gay men are at high risk for STDs (because they are not "out," they are more likely to engage in high-risk behaviors) and have little access to the health information they need (by not being "out" to their health care provider). Gay men who do not know where to obtain services can be provided with such information during the course of the online health education in the chat rooms.

Forums and discussions are another way that the Internet can be used as a tool. For example, the American Cancer Society has online forums and discussions about cancer-related topics where individuals can post questions and comments and engage other individuals, including health care providers. Forums and discussion sites can be created at university, government, non-profit, and for-profit organizations' Web sites for the specific purpose of allowing MSM to post their questions about health-related concerns. Sites may even provide opportunities for health professionals to answer questions.

The process of identity in stigmatized individuals is complex (Goffman 1986); gay men (and women) have used various strategies, such as withdrawal and coping, to deal with situations where they felt uncomfortable (Kaufman and Johnson 2004). This is one reason why the Internet is such an important factor because it enables gay men to obtain information without having to expose themselves until they are ready. In fact, gay youth have turned to the Internet to deal with identity issues (Hillier and Harrison 2007).

In sum the Internet can be used as a tool in a positive way to help combat the spread of STDs. Having unbiased, accurate, and gay-supportive information is imperative, especially for individuals who are not "out," whether to themselves, others, or their health care provider because they are, arguably, more in need of this information.

Future Directions for Research

More research must be directed towards the study of gay men and their use of the Internet. Specifically, studies on their general use of the Internet (not related to sexual behavior) and topics such health literacy are either scarce or do not exist at all. Below are some directions for research that I believe is of utmost importance if we are to fully understand the role that the Internet plays in the health of gay men.

More knowledge is needed about subgroups. We need to invest in research that investigates the role of the Internet in minority communities, especially Black and Hispanic MSM who are not open about their sexuality. In addition, more research that targets rural MSM also is needed. As Horvath et al. (2006) noted, the Internet is a source of finding sex partners for rural MSM. Without such knowledge, we cannot make any educated inferences about the differences between subgroups and understand who is at a higher risk and why.

Increasing the number of evidence-based, Internet-based interventions is of utmost importance. More research needs to be invested in studying Internet-based interventions so that a list of effective ones can be developed (Clift 2007).

Finally, but certainly not least, more research into the sociopolitical (e.g., homophobia, politics) issues that contribute to MSM using the Internet to look for sex is needed. By understanding the contributing factors, we can then work on a broader level to tackle the issue of STDs in the gay men's community.

Conclusion

The spread of STDs among MSM needs our immediate attention. Understanding, let alone trying to combat, the spread of STDs among MSM is difficult. There are far too many factors involved. We certainly cannot deal exclusively with identity in any one intervention or other targeted approach. If we target men who identify as gay, we may lose bisexual and straight-identified MSM. As researchers, health educators, and concerned individuals, we will undoubtedly have to have multiple approaches so that we can meet people where they are and deal with the total context of the situation.

Online new media is a mixed blessing. As described in this chapter, the Internet is both a source of beneficial information and a contributor to the spread of STDs. Gay men who use online new media to look for sex and gay men who use drugs and alcohol are at a higher risk of having unprotected sex and having sex with a person of unknown STD status. I have noted that sociopolitical factors, such as homophobia and politics, have contributed to this phenomenon. Until we combat homophobia, some people will continue to hide their identity behind the anonymity of the Internet when they look for sexual partners.

The Internet is also a tool that can be used to help combat the spread of STDs. Information can be posted online in various formats, including interactive multimedia formats that are fact-based, sensitive to the target community, and easy to understand. The Internet can be used to disseminate information to health care professionals including nurses, physicians, and public health workers, so that they can become aware of trends and issues in a particular community. Researchers have noted that the Internet can and does foster increased learning and increase openness among sexual minorities in the classroom, resulting in benefits for sexual minorities (e.g., Alexander 1997). There is no reason to believe that the Internet cannot provide the same outside of the classroom.

While the issues surrounding the spread of STDs are complex, the fact remains that the general health of the wider community is being adversely affected by the spread of STDs. Despite this, the Internet shows promise in dealing with some of the issues that contribute to the spread of STDs. However, it is not going to solve all of the problems. Nevertheless, we can use the Internet to reach out to people where they are, in whatever stage of identity, and educate them about the risks involved and help them get the information that they need to employ safe sex decision-making.

References

Alexander, J. 1997. Out of the closet and into the network: Sexual orientation and the computerized classroom. *Computers and Composition* 14: 207–216.

Bensley, R. J. 2001. Using technology. In *Community health education methods: A practitioner's guide*, edited by R. J. Bensley and J. Brookins-Fisher. Sudbury, MA: Jones and Bartlett, 223–244.

Blake, S. M., Ledsky, R., Lehman, T., Goodenow, C., Sawyer, R., and Hack, T. 2001. Preventing sexual risk behaviors among gay, lesbian, and bisexual adolescents: The benefits of gay-sensitive instruction in schools. *American Journal of Public Health* 91(6): 940–946.

Bolding, G., Davis, M., Sherr, L., Hart, G., and Elford, J. 2004. Use of gay internet sites and views about online health promotion among men who have sex with men. *AIDS Care* 16(8): 993–1001.

Bowen, A. 2005. Internet sexuality research with rural men who have sex with men: Can we recruit and retain them? *The Journal of Sex Research* 42(4): 317–323.

Center for AIDS Prevention Studies. 2000. What are men who have sex with men (MSM)'s HIV prevention needs? University of California San Francisco http://www.caps.ucsf.edu/pubs/FS/MSMrev.php#8 [Accessed September 28, 2008]

Centers for Disease Control and Prevention. 2007a. HIV/AIDS among men who have sex with men. http://www.cdc.gov/hiv/topics/MSM/resources/factsheets/msm.htm [Accessed September 28, 2008]

Centers for Disease Control and Prevention. 2007b. Subset of promising-evidence interventions, by characteristic. http://www.cdc.gov/hiv/topics/research/prs [Accessed March 5, 2008]

Centers for Disease Control and Prevention. 2008. Trends in HIV/AIDS diagnoses among men who have sex with men—33 states, 2001–2006. http://www.cdc.gov/mmwr/preview/mmwrhtml/mm5725a2.htm [Accessed June 27, 2008]

Clift, J. B. 2007. A sexually transmitted disease education and prevention curriculum, with implementation plan, developed for the gay men's community. *Dissertation Abstracts International* 68(1A): 98.

Community Tool Box. 2009. http://ctb.ku.edu/en/ [Accessed August 15, 2009]

Demmer, C. 2002. Impact of improved treatments on perceptions about HIV and safe sex among inner-city HIV-infected men and women. *Journal of Community Health* 27(1): 63–73.

Fox, S. 2006. Online health search 2006. http://www.pewinternet.org [Accessed August 3, 2008]

Garofalo, R., Herrick, A., Mustanski, B. S., and Donenberg, G. R. 2007. Tip of the iceberg: Young men who have sex with men, the internet, and HIV risk. *American Journal of Public Health* 97(6): 1111–1117.

Gay and Lesbian Medical Association. 2001. *Healthy people 2010: Companion document for lesbian, gay, bisexual, and transgender (LGBT) health.* San Francisco.

Gay.com. 2009. http://www.gay.com/ [Accessed August 23, 2009]

Gaydar.co.uk. 2009. http://gaydar.co.uk/ [Accessed August 23, 2009]

Goffman, E. 1986. *Stigma: Notes on the management of spoiled identity*, rep. London: Penguin.

Grove, C., and Parsons, J. T. 2006. Bug chasing and gift giving: The potential for HIV transmission among barebackers on the internet. *AIDS Education and Prevention* 18(6): 490–503.

Halkitis, P. N., Parsons, J. T., and Wilton, L. 2003. Barebacking among gay and bisexual men in New York City: Explanations for the emergence of intentional unsafe behavior. *Archives of Sexual Behavior* 32(4): 351–357.

Hillier, L., and Harrison, L. 2007. Building realities less limited than their own: Young people practicing same-sex attraction on the Internet. *Sexualities* 10(1): 82–100.

Horvath, K. J., Bowen, A. M., and Williams, M. L. 2006. Virtual and physical venues as contexts of HIV risk among rural men who have sex with men, *Health Psychology* 25(2): 237–242.

Jagose, A. 1996. *Queer theory: An introduction.* New York: New York University Press.

Kaufman, J. M., and Johnson, C. 2004. Stigmatized individuals and the process of identity. *The Sociological Quarterly* 45(4): 807–833.

Kim, A. A., Kent, C., McFarland, W., and Klausner, J. D. 2001. Cruising on the internet highway. *Journal of AIDS* 28(1): 89–93.

Klausner, J. D., Wolf, W., Fischer-Ponce, L., Zolt, I., and Katz, M. H. 2000. Tracing a syphilis outbreak through cyberspace. *JAMA* 284(4): 447–449.

Liau, A., Millett, G., and Marks, G. 2006. Meta-analytic examination of online sex-seeking and sexual risk behavior among men who have sex with men. *Sexually Transmitted Diseases* 33(3): 576–584.

Liszka, H. A., Steyer, T. E., and Hueston, W. J. 2006. Virtual medical care: How are our patients using online health information? *Journal of Community Health* 31(5): 368–378.

National Cancer Institute. 2009. http://www.cancer.gov/bcrisktool [Accessed August 15, 2009]

Pathela, P., Hajat, A., Schillinger, J., Blank, S., Sell, R., and Mostashari, F. 2006. Discordance between sexual behavior and self-reported sexual identity: A population-based survey of New York City men. *Annals of Internal Medicine* 145: 416–425.

Preston, D. B., D'Augelli, A. R., Kassab, C. D., Cain, R. E., Schulze, F. W., and Starks, M. T. 2004. The influence of stigma on the sexual behavior of rural men who have sex with men. *AIDS Education and Prevention* 16: 291–303.

Reback, C. J., Larkins, S., and Shoptaw, S. 2004. Changes in the meaning of sexual behaviors among gay and bisexual male methamphetamine abusers before and after drug treatment. *AIDS and Behavior* 8: 87–97.

Rhodes, S. D. 2004. Hookups or health promotion? An exploratory study of a chat room-based HIV prevention intervention for men who have sex with men. *AIDS Education and Prevention*, 16(4): 315–327.

Semple, S. J., Patterson, T. L., and Grant, I. 2000. Psychosocial predictors of unprotected anal intercourse in a sample of HIV positive gay men who volunteer for a sexual risk reduction intervention. *AIDS Education and Prevention* 12: 416–430.

Stokes, J. P., and Peterson, J. L. 1998. Homophobia, self-esteem, and risk for HIV among African American men who have sex with men. *AIDS Education and Prevention* 10: 278–292.

Tittanen, R., and Ross, M. W. 2000. Looking for sexual compatibility: Experiences among Swedish men in visiting internet gay chat rooms. *CyberPsychology and Behavior* 3(4): 605–616.

Tomso, G. 2004. Bug chasing, barebacking, and the risks of care. *Literature and Medicine* 23(1): 88–111.

Part V

Community Spaces

Chapter 20

The Demise of the Gay Enclave, Communication Infrastructure Theory, and the Transformation of Gay Public Space

Nikki Usher and Eleanor Morrison

Across America, former gay havens are making way for straights. As ever more straight women and then straight men come to party and ultimately to live in these areas, soaring property taxes and rents have driven many gays (especially young gays) out, if they were not already leaving to settle in newly gay-friendly straight neighborhoods. Families (both gay and straight) have also moved in, introducing the sound of tame baby rattles to a formerly pulsating and vibrant adult-only zone. As the "gay community" increasingly moves online, how much does this decline of a geographically based gay public space really matter?

We attempt to examine the decline of the gay enclave within the framework of communication studies. We proceed by viewing public spaces as contexts for communication and civic engagement, applying a theory that has previously been used to study neighborhood storytelling networks and geo-ethnic media infrastructures to gay enclaves and gay media. This theoretical orientation, Communication Infrastructure Theory, is concerned with the relationship between place, communication and action. We seek to investigate how it may be adapted to explore the decline of gay public space, and reveal the consequences of the move from local media infrastructure to an online media infrastructure.

First, we explain the relationship between public space and communication by explaining the central tenants of the Communication Infrastructure Theory, and draw on possible sites of investigation and parallels for the gay community. We then outline the formation and development of traditional gay neighborhoods as communicative spaces. Next, we outline some of the changes occurring in these physical gay neighborhoods, such as "straightening," or the movement of straight people into gay spaces, gentrification, and "gay sprawl," or the dispersal of gays from traditional gay neighborhoods into other geographic areas.[1] Finally, we discuss the new communication context for the gay neighborhood as imagined online and discuss some of the constraints and possibilities of this new space for civic engagement.

Communication Infrastructure Theory and Gay Public Space

Communication Infrastructure Theory (CIT) was developed by Ball-Rokeach and her colleagues (2001) to explain the relationship between neighborhoods, community organizations and ethnic media in diverse urban environments. The idea of the communication infrastructure is that it provides the information that individuals need to live their everyday lives. In this theory, individuals are viewed as agentic information seekers, who have the capacity to make choices and decisions that will influence their lives (Ball-Rokeach 1998). Ball-Rokeach and her colleagues are particularly interested in understanding the role of "geo-ethnic" media in communities, which they define as media that offers both "culturally relevant and locally vital information" to immigrants (Lin and Song 2006, p. 364).

There are two parts to the communication infrastructure: the storytelling network and the communication action context (Ball-Rokeach 1998; Ball-Rokeach et al. 2001; Wilkin and Ball-Rokeach 2006). The storytelling network reflects the interdependent relationship between geo-ethnic media, residents, and community organizations that use "mediated and interpersonal types of communication to build a discursive community for the identification and resolution of issues of concern to residents" (Wilkin and Ball-Rokeach 2006, p. 304). When these all interact to tell stories about the neighborhood, there is a marked increase in civic engagement and participation. The stronger this network, the more that members feel they will belong to this community and can solve its problems. A crucial link thus exists between telling local stories, community belongingness and civic action.

The second part of this multi-level theory is the communication action context, defined as the site where the communication in the neighborhood storytelling network actually takes place. In Ball-Rokeach et al.'s (2001) formulation, this includes the very basics of what makes a neighborhood tick and where people gather, such as what the supermarkets offer, what law enforcement is like, where there are streetlights, and so on. Significantly, for our purposes, the communication action context may range from open, one that "encourages communication amongst people," to closed, one that "discourages communication" (Ball-Rokeach et al. 2001; Wilkin and Ball-Rokeach 2006, p. 304). For gay spaces, the communication action context may not be supermarkets and coffee shops, but may be public parks, bars, and nightlife gathering spaces.

CIT also touches on issues of globalization (Kim and Ball-Rokeach 2006; Kim et al. 2006) that become relevant when we think about the concern over a concrete, physical "home community." Specifically, CIT offers a way to think about the relationships that immigrants have between home countries and the U.S., arguing that boundaries are increasingly nonexistent in a global world. CIT speaks of a large population of immigrants that have not left behind their point of origin but are actually migrant, able to communicate within both the "here" and "there" of the United States and their country of origin. In this way, CIT can help us to think about the way that gays might belong to a "real" gay neighborhood and tell stories about this neighborhood without actually "living there," offering understandings as the gay community transitions to an online existence.

Though CIT has traditionally been used to talk about immigrant populations, there are a few particular reasons to root our discussion of gay public space in CIT theory. First, the connection between gay enclaves and immigrant enclaves is well-founded. Both immigrants and gays have flocked to cities searching for new possibilities, settling in areas with people like themselves. Chauncey (1995) has written about the rise of a gay neighborhood in New York in close proximity to the immigrant enclaves in the Bowery, both communities developing at the margins of a more dominant society. Furthermore, the gay press and the ethnic media press have been historically subject to similar pressures and reasons for existence. As Carey (1997 [originally 1969]) points out, both gay and ethnic media are building blocks, "intermediate mechanisms linking local and partial milieus to the wider community" (p. 130).

Moreover, in their dislocation, gay communities and immigrant enclaves also find common ground; Japantowns in California have decreased from 40 to 3 and Little Tokyo in Los Angeles is under threat from yuppie condo-dwellers (Wanatabe 2007). While the immigrant/gay analogy can only go so far because of critiques of class, race and ethnicity, and visibility, the utility of CIT is nonetheless apparent: the theory enables us to ask significant questions about the relationship between public space, communication, and civic engagement. In this chapter, we are primarily concerned with the changes to the communication action context in the transformation of the gay neighborhood; while to a lesser degree specific links in the storytelling network are examined, through the rise and fall of this communication action context.

Traditional Gay Neighborhoods

Traditionally, gay neighborhoods have been physical spaces that have enabled sexual minorities to express themselves freely in a (relatively) safe space. Gay neighborhoods orient both individual and collective gay identity; individuals who share the common experience of sexual marginalization form an authentic community that is home to "residences, businesses, real estate, bars, restaurants, movie theaters, cultural centers, community based associations, street gathering and celebrations" which create a sense of "social life and cultural autonomy" (Castells 2004 [originally 1997], p. 271). The rise of gay neighborhoods is often attributed to the dislocation experienced during the mass urban mobilizations of World War II, where large numbers of single men were shipped to the port cities of Los Angeles, New York and San Francisco and an increasing number of women entered the workforce (Castells 2004; Gross 1997; Murray 1996). There, as Murray explains, "proto" gay bars existed in an era of wartime permissiveness. After the war, many of those who had come to enjoy the freedom of the city did not return home, and still others, dishonorably discharged, remained in the port cities.

Gay neighborhoods particularly flourished after the "gay liberation" movements of the late 1960s and 1970s, where there was an explosion of visibility in places that had always been gay but now were even more open, such as in New York's Christopher Street and San Francisco's Castro district. But tracing the rise of gay neighborhoods too closely to historical events may imply too much causation (Murray 1996); instead, we should think about the formation of gay neighborhoods as the more general product of the forces of urbanization and industrialization that made it possible for men and women who did not fit into the family structure to opt out of it (D'Emilio 1999).

Gay immigrants both depart from and share similarities with the formation of traditional immigrant communities. Like immigrant neighborhoods, gay neighborhoods were formed out of a sense of protection, offering safety in numbers and a collective affinity. This often meant moving to the least desirable, low-rent parts of a city where landlords were willing to rent to "undesirable" tenants. Gay neighborhoods were not formed in response to outright forms of enshrined legal discrimination (such as segregation) as many ethnic neighborhoods were, though legal prohibitions against sodomy did necessitate spaces of permissiveness where such sexual practices could exist without fear of reprisal (Murray 1996).

In contrast to most immigrant neighborhoods, gays slowly gentrify their neighborhoods, turning the previous low-rent neighborhood into a more economically viable one with their "sweat equity" (Gross 1997). This is not to say that immigrants do not attempt to improve their neighborhoods, but rather that gays have traditionally had more developed skills, greater resources, fewer family obligations, and a greater interest in staying in the minority neighborhood than those in immigrant communities (Gross 2009). This concentration and community development in turn creates a "social subsystem" that enriches the gay subculture with important institutions, such as newspapers, community associations and political organizations (Murray 1996).

For individuals, gay neighborhoods have traditionally been places of comfort and refuge for gays seeking those who are like themselves. For a young gay person who has recently acknowledged himself or herself as a sexual minority, a gay neighborhood is a place to find out how to dress, how to date, to how to "be" gay, and to shed his or her sense of isolation. On a more collective level, gay neighborhoods enable the possibility of political action through visibility and advocacy. Visibility happens in different ways through the claiming of spaces such as storefronts, sidewalks, and public parks as gay, as well as through the performance of gay or queer identity in these places (Polchin 1997). This traditional gay community has been a space of not only visibility but of open communication.

Spaces such as parks, bars and businesses where sexuality can be performed are also spaces for communication and collaboration, enabling possible collective action.

San Francisco's Castro district has traditionally been such a place that has embodied both an open communication context and a strong local storytelling network. The communication action context of Castro in the post-gay liberation era reflected an energized gay population dedicated to cultivating a livable neighborhood with a definable gay identity. One estimate suggests that over 90 percent of those involved in a Victorian restoration initiative by the city were gay men (Weightman, cited in Gross 1997). Though certainly not all bars were gay-owned, there were a variety of bars to appeal to the diverse gay subcultures, a network of community bathhouses, bookstores, cafes and a vibrant street life of gay spaces both during the day and during the evening. Bars were especially important to nourishing the storytelling network, as they served as places to distribute independent gay media that would not be stocked or printed in the mainstream (Meeker 2006).

Gay-specific businesses flourished, especially in light of post-liberation energy and visibility, creating other opportunities for meeting and greeting spaces. The Castro Theater in 1976 moved from showing second-run movies to presenting repertory theater tributes to Hollywood's yesteryear and enshrined itself as a gay gathering space and community center (Sawyer 2007). In a 1980 CBS Reports documentary on "Gay Power, Gay Politics," gay activist Cleve Jones spoke about the Castro, noting:

> Whenever there's a crisis, when something bad happens, we all know to come to Castro Street. It's our neighborhood. It's where we're strongest. I have to confess…when the police announce that they are leery of coming to our neighborhood, that gives me a certain amount of satisfaction.
> (CBS Reports 1980)

Bolstered by electoral reform that made the Castro a Board of Supervisors electoral district, gays in San Francisco were mobilized as political actors, pushing for a local gay rights ordinance and helping to defeat a statewide bill against gay teachers in public schools (Castells 2004). Gays were encouraged to "buy gay" by community leader Harvey Milk. A rich variety of local media, including San Francisco's gay newspapers, the *Bay Area Reporter* and the *San Francisco Sentinel*, provided comprehensive local political and entertainment coverage. Harvey Milk wrote a political column for the *Bay Area Reporter* before being famously elected to the Board of Supervisors (Streitmatter 1995). And as Streitmatter notes, it was around this time that gay newspapers were sophisticated enough to begin identifying "patterns of events" (pp. 232–233); the *Bay Area Reporter*, for example, took on gay bashing.

The trauma of the AIDS epidemic perhaps best illustrates the communication infrastructure of a traditional gay neighborhood like the Castro. Gay community-based advocacy groups and health organizations emerged from the social networks that were facilitated through the bars and other gay communication spaces. Locally produced media helped spread the activist messages through the community, and residents became engaged as activists. Public space became an activist space. As Castells (2004) notes, activists secured significant victories in San Francisco, including the establishment of an AIDS ward at San Francisco General Hospital, and the University of California at San Francisco Hospital becoming a center for AIDS research. The Castro at the height of the AIDS epidemic reveals a vibrant storytelling network; all of the nodes were activated, with community organizations, residents, and local media, facilitated by an open communication action context that encouraged the organizing of gay residents, producing action at a time when the community needed it most.

New Gay Neighborhoods

Traditional gay neighborhoods may be thought of as spaces where marginalized people came together in set geographic enclaves to live, shop, and socialize, providing a home for gay-owned and operated businesses, community organizations, and gay media. At present, however, gay neighborhoods are in a state of transition where many are losing their distinct identity as gay-specific enclaves. Gentrification has always been a pressure on gay neighborhoods, but now this gentrification is accompanied by increasing corporate commercialization, "straightening" (straights moving in), the rise of gay families, and "gay sprawl" (the dispersal of gays into increasingly accepting cities and suburbs at large). These forces have diminished the openness of the communication action context, which must be fostered by the existence of meeting and greeting spaces where gays can physically come together to form a sense of community, feel a sense of belonging, and spur collective efficacy.

The Castro of today is a radically different space than it was in the 1970s and 1980s. The Castro still looks like a gay space, perhaps even more visibly gay with giant gay flags marking its territory. But something has changed: the Castro no longer fills with throngs of cruising shirtless men at all hours of the day; instead, it is the rare man who walks shirtless along the main drag. Starbucks, the Sunglass Hut, Bank of America, Pottery Barn and Diesel have moved in (among others). The transition of the Castro away from the "seedy" underworld of gay bars to clean streetscapes and fancy bistros has prompted the movement of heterosexuals into the area, diluting the sense of the Castro as a gay-specific space (Brown 2007). Rising rents have made it more difficult for independent gay owners to keep their shops, making the area more prone to being taken over by commercial companies. The gentrification has also made it difficult for gay community-based organizations located in the neighborhood to afford their rents, and some have had to move out (Leff 2007).

The constituency of those living in the Castro has changed, as well, with single gay men making way for straight and gay families with children. Five hundred new condos planned for families have been planned (Leff 2007). Straights and gays are jointly challenging the neighborhood as a space for the performance of sexuality. For example, in 2005, a lesbian mother wrote to city officials to protest a S&M storefront in the Castro that showed a mannequin chained to a toilet, noting, "As an adult I find this disgusting…as a parent I find it unconscionable" (Bajko 2005). The era of sexual permissiveness and wholesale liberty may well be over, evident in the fact that one hotel has even installed security gates as part of an effort to discourage cruising (Leff 2007).

Some Castro residents are fighting back to counter a portion of these changes. Community organizers have created the Castro Coalition to address the new developments, and the city has promised $100,000 to bolster the neighborhood as a site of gay history (Buchanan 2007). But these attempts may be too little to address the demographic trends facing the Castro. Population shifts are diluting the neighborhood. According to UCLA demographer Gates, between 2000 and 2005 the number of same-sex couples in San Francisco dropped by 5 percent (Buchanan 2007). Even though many gays take a pilgrimage trip to the Mecca of San Francisco (Engle 2007), gays who move to town as residents often find the community is no longer the place that it was fabled to be, and many leave (Buchanan 2005).

The changes in San Francisco, then, represent a changed communication action context. The unique spaces for gays to meet and greet (such as bars and locally owned businesses) that represent distinct ties to gay-specific visibility have been replaced by generic chain stores. The presence of heterosexuals in the neighborhood has "straightened" it, diminishing the strength of interconnected communication that occurs informally when there is frequent incidental community exposure through population proximity and density. The dispersal of gay organizations away from the Castro has further severed ties that link residents to an integrated sense of neighborhood. Media from the Castro give a snapshot as to the potential (or lack thereof) for local storytelling. The *Bay Area Reporter* and the *San Francisco Bay Times*, the city's remaining gay newspapers, are notable because they are still locally produced. However, they are far from the hard-hitting local coverage of the 1980s exemplified during the AIDS crisis (Streitmatter 1995). The Castro, in short, is a shared commercial space home to a tamer gay population and a larger straight population, where gay people may no longer flock to settle, and where sexual performance and heightened political activism are mere shadows of years past.

This trend seems to be playing out in other cities across the U.S. Sex shops and obvious spaces of outward gay sexual performance around New York's

Christopher Street have been swept under cover, in part due to former Mayor Rudolph Giuliani's gentrification efforts and the protests of wealthier gay and straight locals who demand a tidier neighborhood (Warner 1999). In Oakland, lesbian book stores have shut down, lesbian magazines have closed down, and few lesbian bars remain (Buchanan 2006). In Dallas's Oak Lawn district, gays attribute both rising rents and increasing acceptance in surrounding neighborhoods to the visible decline in the once lively Cedar Springs strip (Flick 2007; Rodriguez 2007). In Toronto, condos are replacing the "Gay Village" as straights move in, and in DC, gay nightclubs were being demolished to build a new stadium (Buchanan 2007). In the mid 1990s, there were 16 gay bars in the Boston-Cambridge area; now, that number is down to seven (Sullivan 2007). Gates, the demographer, has noted declines in major gay urban populations in Philadelphia, Houston, Washington, New York, Houston, Detroit and Austin, while the population of gays in surrounding cities has risen. He argues that the shift is due to the increasing tolerance and acceptance of gays at large, suggesting that gays do not need the gay neighborhood for support and safety anymore because of the higher level of support and safety that now exists outside of these bubbles (Buchanan 2007; Gates 2007; Leff 2007).

Particularly relevant to the theoretical discussion at hand, local gay publications across the country (even those long held in regard by the community) are ceasing trading. *Update*, a weekly in San Diego, was the city's first gay publication and at the time of its recent closing had been in print for 27 years (Darce 2007). Both the *New York Native* and the *San Francisco Sentinel*, newspapers that were most active in agitating for AIDS patients (Streitmatter 1995), are now gone. Gross (2001) argues that the local papers are in part to blame for this trend, having taken increasingly more content from national wire services, cutting back on locally produced content, and thus rendering themselves less vital to the community.

The transformations that have happened in gay neighborhoods reflect a decline in the traditional storytelling network and communication action context. Gay physical space and the way that this space was invoked through communicative practices have changed. The tight network of residents living in gay neighborhoods patronizing gay bars and restaurants, reading local gay newspapers and relying on the resources of gay community organizations is no longer present. Gays have more and more freedom to choose where they want to live and socialize; the need to be all gay all the time simply does not have the same urgency. Gay news is covered more in mainstream newspapers now (Gross 2001), and gay bars are no longer needed as the distribution point for contraband gay pamphlets and newspapers. Community organizations built around serving the gay community still serve the gay community, but now community organizations outside the gay community address gay needs, too.

The coherent local storytelling network has been dissolved into something more amorphous as its anchor—the gay neighborhood—fades. The context for communication, a central place for gays to speak about gay community concerns and issues as well as to perform gay identity, has been de-localized away from the physical community. Gays no longer have the same ability to gather and to feel physically connected to the community they can call their own.

Decentering of Place and Identity?

But if gay neighborhoods and local gay media are on the decline, then where is gay community flourishing? What connections will foster civic engagement? And what do the storytelling network and the communication action context look like in a world where Castro businesses actively inhibit cruising? Perhaps predictably, the answer is that gays have gone online. The factors that enable and constrain community engagement and local storytelling (and ultimately create the conditions for civic engagement) are a distinct departure from those that existed in physical neighborhoods. The claims upon individuals, who now are located both globally and locally, have also shifted as they negotiate being members of a gay "community" that is unbounded by geography.

Gays have always looked for other channels of communication to create a sense of community and solidarity, typically being constrained by problems of distribution (Gross 2003; Meeker 2006). Gays were a natural fit for the Web, and were among the first populations to see its possibilities (Gross 2003). Cyberspace represented a response to a number of problems. First, gays (particularly young gays) could find resources about being gay online. The medium solved the distribution problems that had previously plagued gay publications and information efforts. Gays who could not be out in other contexts could seek community in online forums and discussion groups, finding friends from around the world who shared their experiences. Furthermore, gay sites online represented an alternative space for political engagement where gays regardless of location could come together to organize around common issues. In the early years of the Internet, the Associated Press found that more than one-third of all America Online discussion groups were gay (Gross 2003). And, of course, gays were quick to go online for sex, either for virtual pleasure or to solicit partners for real-world fun.

The online world has offered opportunities for de-localized storytelling that never could have happened without the Web. Consider, for instance, Joanne Fleisher's (2005) description of the plight of heterosexually married women who realize they are gay; for these women the Internet is a particularly important resource, as they do not feel part of the gay community but benefit from a non-intimidating, anonymous space in which they can explore their newfound identity. Gay fetish groups have been given new life online as those previously in the shadows are able to talk about their desires in an easily accessible safe space. Gay teens and transgender youth groups (with alarmingly high suicide rates) are coming out increasingly younger, thanks to the resources and the community available online (Quart 2008; Winerip 2007). An LGBT person no longer needs to escape to the world of the Castro or to Christopher Street to find people like himself or herself; instead, all the LGBT person has to do is go online. In other words, being tied to a specific neighborhood is no longer necessary for the gay experience. Campbell (2004), for example, has argued that online chatrooms can and do function as "virtual" gay bars, offering opportunities for socializing and for sex. The communication action context has moved, it now consists of online chatrooms, messageboards, dating sites, and for-profit and independently run sites that cater to the gay experience.

Significantly, this online gay communication action context does not have to exclude opportunities for storytelling within the local community. Now, online blogs and media outlets can help cement both local and global community relationships. In a recent and particularly visible example, openly gay director Gus Van Sant, working in cooperation with other openly gay producers, shot a star-studded biopic about Harvey Milk on location in the Castro. Special efforts were made to ensure the neighborhood played a vital role in the film, with the director and producers refusing pressure from financial backers to shoot in a cheaper out of town location. This correspondingly allowed them to visually return the Castro to its 1970s heyday, and to invite locals to appear as extras. By all media accounts, this inspired a very emotional shoot as the community became involved in telling its own story. In one of many such reported scenes, a 63-year-old extra broke down in tears on the set, explaining that the film "is an important thing for me because I want all the kids to know what Harvey did" (Stein 2008).

While this took place in the Castro and focused on a piece of Castro history, the film was widely discussed by members of the gay community outside of the Castro, with photos from the set and blurbs about the shoot frequently posted to gay blog sites such as Towleroad (2008) and AfterElton (2008). In this way, a localized community storytelling event was able to be accessed and shared by the larger gay community. Of course, while the Milk film biography provided the occasion for local and global storytelling through the online communication action context, such opportunities may be rare; a feature film starring Sean Penn will obviously attract more global interest and coverage than the typical local story.

Indeed, the newly developing gay communication action context at first appears extremely open with few boundaries limiting communication; but while there are indisputable benefits to the move online, the potential drawbacks must be acknowledged. One often cited concern, both of citizens and scholars, is whether the virtual can truly substitute for the real. John Newsome, co-founder of the group And Castro For All, believes "[t]here are a lot of really lonely gay people sitting in front of a computer" (Brown 2007), taking up the virtual-as-inferior position.

However, assumptions of technologically based communications functioning to isolate individuals must be questioned in the face of findings such as those of

Wellman et al. (2001), which state the Internet to be a supplement to social capital rather than a contributor or detractor, and of Flanagin and Metzger (2001) which evidence that communication has not changed that much, "even if the means of communicating have" (p. 173). Similarly, Baym et al. (2004) have argued that online interactions cannot be dismissed as less meaningful than face-to-face. For gays, as well as others using the Web for online interaction, social life online may supplement and or supplant offline engagement. Life online can be rich and rewarding, with physical space not quite as necessary for our social life as may have been thought.

An online communication action context also mandates a critical inquiry of Internet ownership and the commodification of the gay community (Clark 1993; Gamson 2003). The gay presence online must grapple with its largely commercialized domains, sites which offer the possibility of clear, cohesive community while simultaneously constituting gays as consumers (Clark 1993; Campbell 2005). For instance, Campbell (2007) has suggested that while gays do indeed talk about politics on these sites, they are more empowered as consumers than as citizens as their personal data is extracted for target marketing.

Local stories face difficulty being told online in the world of Gay.com (2009) and PlanetOut.com (2009). Overtures are made to local community coverage on these sites, but there is little specific knowledge to be gained about one's community from these sites. For example, during the first week in April 2008, PlanetOut featured a community calendar feature with sponsored weekly events at local bars. It had a few stories about the Los Angeles gay community written at three to five month intervals. At this time most recent stories were entertainment heavy, and included an interview with Mr. Gay Los Angeles and a story about a comedian. No community-specific West Hollywood news was featured in these highlighted articles, which instead preferred a generalized approach to the Los Angeles area. Some local community organizations were mentioned, and the site did link users to those organization sites, but the absence of geographically localized stories about the gay neighborhood suggests that the local storytelling network online is quite weak.

This lack of local information suggests that the sense of physical neighborhood belonging may continue to decline, underlining the changing attachment, evidenced earlier, that gays have to these neighborhoods, and raising a number of significant questions for further consideration. What is the motivation to tell local stories when the local geographic "community" is no longer the community it once was? What is the importance of the local in today's gay existence? Can gays still develop a sense of belonging to local neighborhoods if they have no local attachment? In what ways does an online storytelling network work that departs from a physically rooted one?

The transition of the communication action context from real to virtual perhaps can be seen as providing a safety net for a community that no longer feels the need to take a defensive stance against dominant social groups, and instead willingly moves out into the suburbs, feeling that a new degree of integration is possible. Indeed, gay culture and identity is increasingly mainstreamed and brought into the dominant culture in ways both overt and subtle (Trebay 2006, 2007). It may be that the most relevant storytelling for creating gay community may not be geo-ethnic media targeted to local communities but gays telling their stories in more mainstreamed contexts and even rallying allies through traditional media. Such a mainstreaming of gay storytelling may create identity and belonging amongst a broader group, although in another complicated twist, this larger "gay community" may no longer have as cohesive a gay identity to speak of, as Andrew Sullivan (2005) has discussed. In fact, it appears to be an earlier form of gay identity that has been mainstreamed, while current gay identity is so fractured, so multivalent and increasingly integrated into the larger population as to not even exist as a cohesive entity. Perhaps the gay neighborhood/media context is simply not needed anymore, or at least not in a way comparable to the ethnic minority neighborhood/media relationship.

With this in mind, we must consider how the transformation of gay identity into something more amorphous translates back into the CIT framework. Specifically, if we are to compare immigrant community communication networks with gay community communication networks, we must question whether this conceit still holds up as it once did, of a gay person feeling (like an immigrant) pulled between a native country and a country of residence. Does the recent dispersal of traditional gay neighborhoods, to a degree unseen in ethnic minority neighborhoods, make the comparison untenable? It is possible that this trajectory is unique to the developing history of gay acceptance and tolerance within the wider population. Alternatively, it is possible that all marginalized groups experience a similar transition, including the weakening of local ties and seeing their stories told globally. Communication Infrastructure Theory recognizes that ethnic neighborhoods are in states of flux, transitioning into the mainstream as new, U.S.-born generations move away and their stories become woven into the larger fabric of global community. The degree of similarity to or divergence from the gay community's trajectory thus presents itself as a subject worthy of further pursuit, yet unfortunately outside the scope of this present chapter.

Civic Engagement and the Future of Gay Community

Why does it matter if Castro Street has a Pottery Barn and gays have flocked to the conglomerate of PlanetOut/Gay.com or have found community online? It matters because these communication contexts set the conditions for civic engagement. We know that a traditional gay enclave created the conditions for successful civic engagement; the neighborhood had the kind of social spaces that enabled communication between residents and community organizations and local media to produce social change. But in this period of transition where the communication context has become increasingly decentralized from physical geography, it is difficult to anticipate how best to foster social change.

We should not forget that mainstreaming of gay culture does not translate into equal rights or freedom from discrimination for LGBT persons. There are still significant barriers to gays in the United States, both culturally and politically. Marriage, the standout issue of the day, is not the only important issue for LGBT people. Access to fair housing, equal employment, healthcare, and even something seemingly as benign as media representation all impact the daily quality of life for the gay community. All of these issues are national in scope, but play out on the local level. There is still plenty of activism left for gays.

Yet without having a stake in the physical gay enclave, do gays still feel a stake in their local gay community? Does the physical gay community just become a nighttime destination spot, home to a gay bar or two, an isolated sex shop, and possibly a bookstore? Will conversation about issues of significant civic important to a local gay community come up in this setting, and more importantly will such conversations, if they occur, lead to action? Or will local gays find no reason to coalesce around civic issues? In a declining gay neighborhood, it is unclear where the care for the physical community will be rooted. And when there is an urgent need for civic action, it is uncertain how gays can be mobilized without a strong local storytelling network, in a way that will enable them to be efficient advocates.

The transition to an online neighborhood creates other difficulties for civic engagement. With multiple claims upon gays to both global and local communities, it is uncertain where members of these online communities will feel the imperative for social action. Regarding issues facing the gay community, it is unclear how local and national community organizations can work together to harness energy online. The translation from online community to offline activism is still uncharted territory, developing terrain which the gay community should take note of with particular self-interest. Unfortunately, there lurks a suspicion that local activism will suffer in the face of a physically dispersed local storytelling network. As scholar Elizabeth Armstrong has argued, when the displeasing verdict was returned for the Harvey Milk assassination, "physical location mattered," with gays "able to assemble quickly, spilling out of the bars" in protest (Brown 2007).

We are not suggesting that the Castro or Christopher Street or South Beach have somehow vanished in the minds of gay people as gay spaces; however, these spaces have been dramatically reshaped in ways that are particularly notable given their configurations in the 1970s and 1980s. Similarly, it is important to remember that gay neighborhoods are still home to important community orienting features, such as gay nightlife, though in lesser capacity than before. Gay people do not need to live in these spaces any more if they want to live an out gay life. The threat to survival that community organizations were created to combat is no longer quite so urgent, diminishing the central place of gay organizations in gay civic life. And the opportunities for local storytelling and meeting and greeting have slowly been closed off as new ones with new contours have emerged online.

The challenge for gay activism will be to harness these new communication contexts. Local stories must continue to get told because gays still must be able to successfully organize themselves around local issues. National stories told to more people connecting in new ways may create the conditions for new forms of activism. The decline of physical spaces and the creation of new ones without boundaries suggest new possibilities for engagement, but it also reveals that an era of a particular form of gay mobilization rooted in the hyperlocal is behind us.

Note

1 It has been observed that lesbians already tend to be more dispersed through geographic areas, while gay men—particularly gay white men—have been more likely to congregate in gay enclaves (Buchanan 2006; Knopp 1997; Retter 1997). We thus acknowledge that this chaper deals primarily with the gay neighborhood as dominated by the gay man. At the same time, a diverse range of people, which includes lesbians and gay men of color, do live in these neighborhoods, neighborhoods which (regardless of precise content) form the geographical locus of gay visibility.

References

After Elton. 2008. http://www.afterelton.com [Accessed Mrch 28, 2008]

Bajko, M. 2005. Penis poses problem for Castro store. *Bay Area Reporter*, 10 November. http://ebar.com/news/article.php?sec=news&article=336 [Accessed April 2, 2008]

Ball-Rokeach, S. J. 1998. A theory of media power and a theory of media use. *Mass Communication and Society* 1(1/2): 5–40.

Ball-Rokeach, S. J., Kim, Y. C., and Matei, S. 2001. Storytelling neighborhood: Paths to belonging in diverse urban environments. *Communication Research* 28(4): 392–428.

Baym, N., Zhang, Y. B. and Lin, M. 2004. Social interactions across media. *New Media and Society*, 6(3): 299–318.

Brown, P. L. 2007. Gay enclaves face prospect of being passé. *New York Times*, 30 October. http://www.nytimes.com/2007/10/30/us/30gay.html [Accessed March 28, 2008]

Buchanan, W. 2005. Gay men find it's not easy being new in town. *San Francisco Chronicle*, September 2. http://www.sfgate.com/cgibin/article.cgi?f=/c/a/2005/09/02/WBGK5EF1PI1.DTL [Accessed March 28, 2008]

Buchanan, W. 2006. Marketplace finds lesbians an attractive, but elusive, niche. *San Francisco Chronicle*, September 7. http://www.sfgate.com/cgibin/article.cgi?f=/c/a/2006/09/07/BAG7FL0HUI1.DTL [Accessed March 28, 2008]

Buchanan, W. 2007. S.F.'s Castro district faces an identity crisis: As straights move in, some fear loss of the area's character. *San Francisco Chronicle*, February 25. http://www.sfgate.com/cgibin/article.cgi?file=/c/a/2007/02/25/MNG2DOATDK1.DTL [Accessed March 28, 2008]

Campbell, J. 2004. *Getting it on online: Cyberspace, gay male sexuality, and embodied identity*. Binghamton, NY: Harrington Park Press.

Campbell, J. 2005. Outing PlanetOut: Surveillance, gay marketing and internet portals. *New Media and Society* 7(5): 663–683.

Campbell, J. 2007. Virtual citizens or dream consumers: Looking for civic community on Gay.com. In *Queer online: Media, technology, and sexuality*, edited by K. O'Riordan and D. Phillips. New York: Peter Lang, 197–216.

Carey, J. W. 1997 [1969]. The communications revolution and the professional communicator. In *James Carey: A critical reader*, edited by E. S. Munson and C. Warren. Minneapolis: University of Minnesota Press, 128–143.

Castells, M. 2004 [1997]. *The power of identity*, 2nd ed. Oxford: Blackwell.

CBS Reports. 1980. Gay power, gay politics. Television, April 26. New York: CBS News.

Chauncey, G. 1995. *Gay New York: Gender, urban culture, and the making of the gay male world 1890–1940*. New York: Basic Books.

Clark, D. 1993. Commodity lesbianism. In *The lesbian and gay studies reader*, edited by H. Abelove, M. Barale, M. and D. Halperin. New York: Routledge, 186–201.

Darce, K. 2007. Gay newspapers face competition, but publishers remain optimistic. *San Diego Union Tribune*, April 4. http://www.signonsandiego.com/news/business/20070405-9999-1b5press.html [Accessed April 2, 2008]

D'Emilio, J. 1999. Capitalism and gay identity. In *The Columbia reader on lesbians and gay men in media, society and politics*, edited by L. Gross and J. D. Woods. New York: Columbia University Press, 467–476.

Engle, J. 2007. San Francisco works to lure gay travelers. *Los Angeles Times*, May 15. http://travel.latimes.com/articles/la-trw-gaynew14may14 [Accessed April 2, 2008]

Flanagin, A. J. and Metzger, M. J. 2001. Internet use in the contemporary media environment. *Human Communication Research* 27(1): 153–181.

Fleisher, J. 2005. *Living two lives: Married to a man and in love with a woman*. New York: Alyson Books.

Flick, D. 2007. Closing time for crossroads, center for gay activism. *Dallas Morning News*, December 1. http://www.dallasnews.com/sharedcontent/dws/news/localnews/stories/120107dnmetcrossroads.2b27686.html [Accessed April 2, 2008]

Gamson, J. 2003. Gay Media, Inc.: Media structures, the new gay conglomerates, and collective sexual identities. In *Cyberactivism: Online activism in theory and practice*, edited by M. McCaughey and M. D. Ayers. New York: Routledge, 255–278.

Gates, G. J. 2007. *Same-sex couples and the gay, lesbian, bisexual population: New estimates from the American Community Survey*. Los Angeles: The Williams Institute, UCLA.

Gay.com. 2009. http://www.gay.com/ [Accessed August 23, 2009]

Gross, L. 1997. From South Beach to Sobe. In *Voices in the street: Explorations in the gender, media, and public*, edited by S. Drucker and G. Gumpert. Cresskill, NJ: Hampton Press, 201–210.

Gross, L. 2001. *Up from invisibility*. New York: Columbia University Press.
Gross, L. 2003. The gay global village in cyberspace. In *Contesting media power: Alternative media in a networked world*, edited by N. Couldry and J. Curran. New York: Rowman & Littlefield, 259–272.
Gross, L. 2009. Personal communication, June 23, 2009.
Kim, Y. C. and Ball-Rokeach, S. J. 2006. Civic engagement from a communication infrastructure perspective. *Communication Theory* 16(2): 173–197.
Kim, Y. C., Jung, J. Y. and Ball-Rokeach, S. J. 2006. "Geo-ethnicity" and neighborhood engagement: A communication infrastructure perspective. *Political Communication* 23(4): 421–441.
Knopp, L. 1997. Gentrification and gay neighborhood formation in New Orleans: A case study. In *Homoeconomics: Capitalism, community and lesbian and gay life*, edited by A. Gluckman and B. Reed. New York: Routledge, 45–63.
Leff, L. 2007. Gay neighborhoods worry over identity. Associated Press, March 12. http://www.foxnews.com/wires/2007Mar12/0,4670,GayNeighborhood,00.html [Accessed April 2, 2008]
Lin, W. Y. and Song, H. 2006. Geo-ethnic storytelling: An examination of ethnic media content in contemporary immigrant communities. *Journalism* 7(3): 362–388.
Meeker, M. 2006. *Contacts desired: Gay and lesbian communications and community, 1940s–1970s*. Chicago: University of Chicago Press.
Murray, S. O. 1996. *American gay*. Chicago: University of Chicago Press.
PlanetOut.com. 2009. http://www.planetout.com/ [Accessed August 24, 2009]
Polchin, J. 1997. Having something to wear: The landscape of identity on Christopher Street. In *Queers in space: Communities, public places, sites of resistance*, edited by G. B. Ingram, A. M. Bouthillette, and Y. Retter. Seattle: Bay Press, 381–390.
Quart, A. 2008. When girls will be boys. *New York Times*, March 16. http://www.nytimes.com/2008/03/16/magazine/16students-t.html [Accessed April 9, 2008]
Retter, Y. 1997. Lesbian spaces in Los Angeles, 1970–90. In *Queers in space: Communities, public places, sites of resistance*, edited by G. B. Ingram, A. M. Bouthillette, and Y. Retter. Seattle: Bay Press, 325–338.
Rodriguez, G. 2007. Gay? Who cares? *Los Angeles Times*, November 5. http://www.latimes.com/news/printedition/opinion/la-oe-rodriguez5nov05,1,7225510.column?ctrack=3&cset=true [Accessed April 2, 2008]
Sawyer, F. A. 2007. Castro Theater. In *Love, Castro Street: Reflections of San Francisco*, edited by K. V. Forrest and J. Van Buskirk. New York: Alyson Books, 117–128.
Stein, R. 2008. It's a wrap: 'Milk' filming ends in S.F. *San Francisco Chronicle*, March 18. http://www.sfgate.com/cgi-bin/article.cgi?f=/c/a/2008/03/18/DDNDVJJHL.DTL [Accessed April 11, 2008]
Streitmatter, R. 1995. *Unspeakable: The rise of the gay and lesbian press in America*. Winchester, MA: Faber and Faber.
Sullivan, A. 2005. The end of gay culture. *The New Republic*, October 13. http://www.tnr.com/politics/story.html?id=cac6ca08-7df8-4cdd-93cc-1d20cd8b7a70 [Accessed March 28, 2008]
Sullivan, R. D. 2007. Last call—why the gay bars of Boston are disappearing, and what it says about the future of city life. *Boston Globe*, December 12. http://www.

boston.com/bostonglobe/ideas/articles/2007/12/02/last_call/ [Accessed March 18, 2008]

Towleroad. 2008. http://www.towleroad.com [Accessed March 28, 2008]

Trebay, G. 2006. Kinky chic extends its dominance. *New York Times*, June 22. http://www.nytimes.com/2006/06/22/fashion/thursdaystyles/22leather.html [Accessed March 28, 2008]

Trebay, G. 2007. These hills still talk to him. *New York Times*, August 19. http://www.nytimes.com/2007/08/19/fashion/19maupin.html [Accessed March 28, 2008]

Wanatabe, T. 2007. Clinging to a culture—Little Tokyo works to welcome a new wave of multicultural investors and residents while preserving its distinctive heritage. *Los Angeles Times*, October 28. http://articles.latimes.com/2007/oct/28/local/me-littletokyo28 [Accessed March 18, 2008]

Warner, M. 1999. *The trouble with normal: Sex, politics, and the ethics of queer life*. Cambridge, MA: Harvard University Press.

Wellman, B., Quan Haase, A., Witte, J. and Hampton, K. 2001. Does the Internet increase, decrease, or supplement social capital? Social networks, participation, and community commitment. *American Behavioral Scientist* 45(3): 436–455.

Wilkin, H. A. and Ball-Rokeach, S. J. 2006. Reaching at risk groups: The importance of health storytelling in Los Angeles Latino media. *Journalism* 7(3): 299–330.

Winerip, M. 2007. Parenting: Accepting an identity, and gaining strength. *New York Times*, April 1. http://query.nytimes.com/gst/fullpage.html?res=9807E5DC1030F932A35757C0A9619C8B63&scp=3&sq=WINERIP+gay&st=nyt [Accessed April 2, 2008]

Chapter 21

From Websites to Wal-Mart
Youth, Identity Work, and the Queering of Boundary Publics in *Small Town, USA*[1]

Mary L. Gray

Shaun was the first to arrive at the donut shop attached to the Gas-n'-Go. It was a popular spot among young people in this town of 3,000 tucked between eastern Kentucky's deep ravines and rolling hills.[2] He was there to meet with other members of the Highland Pride Alliance (HPA), an informal group of area lesbian, gay, bisexual, and transgender (LGBT) youth and their allies. White, gay-identifying men between 17 and 22 dominated HPA's leadership. While fewer than 10 members regularly attended its organizational meetings, more than 30 regularly participated in HPA's monthly activities and posted messages to its website guestbook. HPA usually held their monthly meetings in the basement of the county public library but another community group had already booked the space.

As this HPA meeting progressed, talk of their upcoming Halloween fundraiser seamlessly turned to casual chatter about the evening's post-meeting plans. Possibilities were bandied about and then dismissed as "too boring" or "too far away." Joe tossed out the idea of heading over to neighboring Springhaven, Kentucky to do some drag in the aisles of the regional Wal-Mart—the only public venue open 24 hours within 80 miles. HPA had recently turned the Super Store into a favorite backdrop for its growing photo collection of drag outings posted to the HPA website. The group's collective roar of affirming whoops and laughter drew the eyes of two bleach blonde-haired women in their mid-twenties listlessly tending to the donut display case and coffee hot plates. Shaun met their tentative smiles with a large grin and a small princess-atop-a-float hand wave. Turning back to the group, he giggled, then purred softly, "now, settle it down, y'all."

That boisterous LGBT-identifying young people scattered throughout rural Kentucky and its Appalachian borders visibly occupied and, in many ways, confounded the boundaries of sites as disparate as public libraries, gas stations, house parties, Wal-Mart, and websites surprised me. I had assumed these young people met clandestinely in friends' houses, online in chatrooms, or through instant messaging to avoid trouble or hostility from locals. I had not considered how these strategies might be combined out in the everyday spaces of their daily lives.

Indeed, their unabashed public identity ran counter to those youth studies that frame LGBT sexualities and genders as developed in isolation and endemically at risk of individual mental health crises, rather than as vibrant, collectively and publicly negotiated identities.[3]

Perhaps the overriding reason for surprise at the visibility of rural LGBT youth, from their presence in libraries and Wal-Marts to websites, is the pervasive assumption that rural environments are, by definition, hostile to queer desires and genders and, therefore, rural LGBTQ-identifying youth (at least the self-respecting ones?) must live in quiet invisibility or have already left their small towns for the BIG CITY. This chapter draws from a larger project that interrogates these assumptions. In it, I attempt to assess the importance of digital media in the lives of queer youth unable or unwilling to leave their small towns for the queer enclaves of identity that have become visible components of urban landscapes. Through 19 months of ethnographic fieldwork in rural parts of Kentucky and its border states, I studied how rural young people engage and enmesh local support agencies, peer networks, and new media as sites and technologies for what I call "queer identity work"—the collective and visible labor of identity construction and public recognition that at once chips away at *and* stabilizes coherent gay and lesbian identity categories.[4] I wanted to know what difference the Internet made to youth negotiating a "queer" sense of sexuality and gender in the rural U.S. and the raced, classed, and gendered dimensions of those negotiations. This approach shifts new media studies away from attempts to delineate a clear divide between "online" and "offline" or "actual" and "virtual" lived experience (Boellstorff 2008) toward investigations of the deeply contextual, multi-sited experiences of new media use that shape our everyday lives. In fact, an explicit goal of this chapter, as part of a collection examining queer identity formations and new online media technologies, is to press for de-centering technologies as the object of analysis in new media studies. This chapter calls for foregrounding the relationships between social contexts and media engagements as the sites of identity production and articulation rather than privileging the media apparatus itself.

Social theorists and media scholars have consistently drawn attention to the importance of studying communication technologies as an aspect of, rather than separate from, social relationships (Fischer 1992; Miller and Slater 2000; Starr 2005; Wellman and Haythornthwaite, 2002; and Woolgar 2002). As new media scholar Steve Jones poignantly argues new media scholarship must contend with "the realities (socially, politically, economically, or otherwise constructed) within which those who use [the Internet] live and within which the hardware and software, markets and marketing operate" if it is to offer itself as a critical project of intervention (Jones 2006, p. xv).

Yet, new media scholarship has a tendency to ignore what communication scholar David Beer calls the "recursive nature" of mediated experiences—the ways in which a range of media inform and shape our social concepts and cultural experiences. For example, in his critique of the widely cited, landmark special issue on social networking sites published by the *Journal of Computer-Mediated Communication* in 2007, Beer takes to task the issue's editors' distinction of online experiences as mediated and offline experiences as unmediated, questioning whether we can or should productively "imagine a 'social structure' or a 'situation' that goes unmediated" (Beer 2008, p. 521).

As Sonia Livingstone points out, "the simple distinction between offline and online no longer captures the complex practices associated with online technologies as they become thoroughly embedded in the routines of everyday life" (Livingstone 2008, pp. 393–394).[5] I argue that young people's everyday uses of new media simultaneously confound and blur boundaries among experiences of online/offline, rural/urban, and private/public. In other words, to understand the relationship between experiences and meanings of queer identities in rural places and new media we must account for not only media use but also *the nexus of sociality* that constitutes queer visibility in the public sphere of the rural United States. I will review two examples of the kinds of publics crafted by rural queer youth that illustrate this nexus: namely, the building of very personal websites for public consumption and the online posting of photos of drag performances in the aisles of Wal-Mart to produce a sense of local queer visibility. I will end with some final thoughts on both the resiliency and fragility of rural queer youth's uses of publics.

Rhetoric of the Rural

Imaginings of rural spaces as endemically inhospitable to queer difference are commonplace. To date, most historical and political renderings of queer life focus on the possibilities afforded by the public and private spaces of urban centers.[6] Narratives of urban sophistication have a history of invoking tolerance of visible queerness implicitly signaling the liberalness of the city and the backwardness of the country (Williams 1973).

As scholar Eve Sedgwick among others notes, visibility operates as a binary: in order for someone to be visible, to "come out," there must always be a closet someplace where others clamor or struggle to get out.[7] The rural United States, in effect, operates as America's perennial, tacitly, taken-for-granted closet.[8]

If access to a visible community of sexual and gender difference is central to the story of urban queer cultural formation, where, when, and how do rural youth seeking support for their sense of gender or sexual difference acquire a vocabulary for specifically LGBT identities? And, with the rapid but unequal incorporation of new information technologies into the lives of rural youth and their support agencies, what difference might the Internet's increasing presence—and presumed ubiquity—make to the possibility for queer visibility among rural LGBT and questioning youth?

If, as feminist geographer Doreen Massey argues, "the social is inexorably also spatial" (Massey 1994, p. 265) we cannot examine the social relations of power that produce the meaning of LGBT identities without a careful consideration of how locations, rural locales and their engagements with new media in this case matter to those relations. This chapter draws on the experiences of rural LGBT young people and their everyday uses of new media to illustrate its importance not as an escape route from rural life but as a means to expand experiences of local belonging. New media are experienced as social engagements that enhance young people's sense of inclusion to broader, imagined queer communities beyond their hometowns. In other words, new media come to be understood as one among several interlocked, ephemeral moments of queer visibility and public belonging. They effectively—though not without cost—suture the queer social worlds they find in their hometowns and online.

A Nexus of Publics

What constitutes a rural community is by no means a settled matter in the United States.[9] As the General Accounting Office wrote in 1993, "nonmetro/rural is…defined by exclusion—any area that is not metro/urban is nonmetro/rural" (U.S. General Accounting Office 1993). Arguably, federal definitions and cultural imaginings of rural places fix them as quaint (and isolated) premodern (traditional) moments frozen in time as modernity plays itself out in the refinement and advancement of urbane, cosmopolitan settings. Against such a backdrop, rural unemployment, underfunded public schools, and the erosion of insufficient public infrastructures of support—from healthcare to road maintenance—fade into one-dimensional accounts of "just how it is and always has been." Rural conditions are cast as inadequacies in need of urban outreach instead of as a bellwether for the nationwide dismantling of public services. New media are seen as yet another development tool to bring relief to the limits of the rural public sphere.

Rich literatures theorize both the idyllic public sphere and responsive counterpublics (Fraser 1992; Habermas 1989; Warner 2002). But neither of these analytic models effectively accounts for the experiences of rural queer and questioning youth, nor contains the theoretical pliability to imagine the permeating and fusion of multiple publics through experiences of new media engagement. Youth categorically cannot enter the discursive arena of the public sphere on an equal footing: they are not autonomous (sexual/gender/state) citizens or "social peers" to their adult counterparts; rural youth in particular live in conditions thin on "privacy" and short on public spaces in which to gather. Most critically, rural queer youth do not have access to the material or social capital to establish their own freestanding counterpublics of gay-owned or occupied neighborhoods, bookstores, gyms, or bars. Indeed, the rural communities I worked in had no bars because they were located in "dry" counties where liquor could not be legally sold. Additionally, few residents had the disposable income for gym memberships or social leisure we associate with middle-class urban or suburban living.

With the material conditions of U.S. rural, predominantly white working poor in mind, I want to offer the notion of "boundary publics" to better address the infrastructural specificities of rural communities. I define boundary publics as iterative, ephemeral experiences of belonging that happen both on the outskirts and at the center(s) of the more traditionally recognized and validated Public Sphere of civic deliberation.[10] These experiences of boundary publics travel and circulate through the Super Stores, churches, and other de facto public spaces of the rural United States and ricochet across new media sites produced by and for rural youth. Boundary publics offer moments of occupation for queer identity work and praxis to challenge local and universal expectations of queer invisibility. Rather than thinking of boundary publics as tangible buildings, specific streets, or solitary websites, I suggest that we imagine boundary publics as strategies for space making and constitutive processes for the queering of identity that increasingly, though not exclusively, incorporate new media use.

Boundary Publics

My first example of a boundary public is the personal website of a young person I met named AJ. AJ is a white, female to male trans-identifying teenager living in a town of 6,000 in Kentucky. A month after we met, AJ turned eighteen and immediately started physically transforming his body to match his sense of gender identity. He learned that it was possible to change oneself from female to male from watching a Discovery Channel documentary.[11] Since that day, he and his mother have driven regularly to the university-based hospital two hours north of their town to access the healthcare services for AJ's sex reassignment surgery.

Often in our conversations, I had to prompt AJ to repeat what he had just said as he spoke at a nearly inaudible whisper. But AJ's voice booms on the website he has created to chronicle his hormone therapy and sexual reassignment surgery. His website features updates on his mental and emotional well being written as monthly journals; an "about me" section providing a brief introduction to AJ and his feelings about his own gender identity and its origins; a "Gallery of T-effects" which documents AJ's use of testosterone hormone therapies from detailed pictures of his top (double mastectomy) surgery, photos of his growing hair organized by body area, and mp3 files of his voice recorded at monthly intervals to demonstrate the deepening effects of testosterone; a complete listing of his doctors and surgery prices; a "Links" page with hyperlinks to friends' websites and various transgender resource sites; and a third-party commercial form-generated "Guestbook" feature with entries from the last two years of the website's existence.

AJ's mother wrote the first entry in his viewable guestbook: "Great work on your site especially the educational part and family part. Remember we love you, kid. Mom!" AJ's guestbook is filled with similar remarks from his local friends and aunts on his mother's side of the family living in Ohio. But there are also comments from an international network of acquaintances and friends made though trans-friendly Internet-based chat rooms, organizational web-based mailing lists such as *FTM International*, and transgender support groups based in the Kentucky/Indiana border region.

As AJ's website illustrates, use of Internet technologies can register as both a private experience and a suspended moment of public engagement. When rural youth browse websites, they in one instance may be sneaking off to locations unimaginable to their offline peers. But, when they create and post to their own websites as AJ does to document his physical transition through hormones and reconstructive surgery, they are creating a sense of public recognition through the expression of their experiences. AJ created a detailed website giving the browser access to photos of his leg hair, recordings of his voice changing, and at various stages of the website, photos of his clitoris as it grew with testosterone, expressing a desire to help other people like himself who needed to know "how it's done." The website became a way for him to locally embody the transperson he was becoming in the absence of locations in his town for expressing or sharing the intimacy of that process with others. And it also became his way for circulating the knowledge he was accumulating from others about what it meant—for him—to be a transsexual. AJ's journaling and graphic, online documentation of physical transition extend his changing gender identity both into and beyond his rural town. In other words, AJ's website brokers the boundaries of online and offline public spaces to connect with others like him outside of his community and assert his trans presence in his community, particularly among his family.

I want to turn now to my second example of a boundary public: the aisles of the Springhaven, Kentucky Wal-Mart. Other than gas stations along an interstate for more than 30 miles away, it is the only business open 24 hours within an hour's drive of the Highland Pride Alliance's core members. I found out about the popularity of this Wal-Mart when I asked a local teen what they did for fun: "Most gay people around the county, we all go to McDonald's," Clay said with exuberance. He added casually, "and, then most people all haul up together in big carloads, put on some drag, runway walk the Super Wal-Mart in Springhaven and walk around for about 5 hours with people almost having heart attacks and conniption fits cause we're running around...we take pictures of us all and have fun with our little getaway from living in rural Kentucky."

When I asked other area youth about their experiences at Wal-Mart, it became clear that this had practically—and fairly recently—become a rite of passage for those entering the local gay scene. Joe recalled his initiation this way, "The first time I was with them, we all put on these furry jackets and we walked through the aisles. That was fun. Me and all my friends, we all gather up several cars and now we go once or twice a month." While one shy young woman said she hadn't been, she suggested that it was only a matter of time, "I have to figure out how to get off work one of these nights. The group always seems to be going when I've got a swing shift and I can't drop my hours right now."

When probed to describe how they happened to choose Wal-Mart as a social gathering spot, most of the young people present couldn't really remember the details of the first outing nor did they understand my noticeable surprise. To them, the Wal-Mart Super Center seemed an obvious place to hang out. As Shaun put it,

> Why wouldn't we go there?! It's the best place to find stuff to do drag. They've got all the wigs and make up and tight clothes and stuff. Besides, no matter how much we bug people doing what we're doing, we're still customers too. And we have friends who work there who won't let nothing happen to us if they see any trouble start.

Such comments situate Wal-Mart as a model boundary public for HPA members. Yes, it is a fabulous place to do drag complete with runways and basic drag gear. Beyond that though is the positioning of Wal-Mart as a welcoming place to all customers. No matter which Wal-Mart one enters, so the assumption goes, national guidelines that mandate the professional and friendly treatment of "guests" can also accommodate youth doing something as queer as drag in Wal-Mart's aisles. Because these young people are readable as consumer citizens—white, predominantly male locals with enough pocket money to buy the accessories they use to glamorize themselves and young enough to suggest they will grow out of their foolishness—the logic of capital will not bar them from participation in this twist on the Habermasian Public Sphere. Additionally, Wal-Mart's then recent instatement of employee domestic partnership benefits registered among gay-identifying youth that Wal-Mart was, as Clay put it, "a tolerant place where they could expect to be accepted." The boundary public of Wal-Mart was made all the more imaginable by the presence of friends working at the Super Center seen as having the authority to step in if their consumer citizenship was challenged. Without question the race and class status of these young people matters. In a county where more than 96 percent of the residents are white and the majority live just above the U.S. poverty line, these youths are reasonably recognizable consumers. The youths' whiteness and normative class presentation (wearing styles available at Wal-Mart, but nothing that signals urban chíc) secure their status as "locals" and, thus, play a pivotal role in the viability of Wal-Mart as a boundary public for their queer identity work.

Youth in HPA turned the mega-one-stop shopping locale of Wal-Mart into a favorite gathering place for their post-meeting social activities. Also, the group's website regularly featured photos snapped against Wal-Mart's aisles. HPA members struck poses in their most memorable outfits amidst a backdrop of other shoppers browsing the roll-back-the-prices bins of clothes and hair care products. Importantly, HPA's sojourns to the Super Center were not complete without the posting of the group's photos to the HPA website. According to the HPA's page "hit" counter, these photos of the drag outings were the most visited pages of the site—most likely frequented by the members reveling in their fabulous outfits. HPA had transformed Wal-Mart into its own meeting space, drag revue, and shopping excursion seamlessly rolled into one.

The experiences of AJ and HPA at Wal-Mart challenge the prevailing sense that rural terrains are void of visible non-heteronormative genders and sexualities. Additionally, the incorporation of new media into young people's local space-making projects defies the argument that these technologies simply provide escape from tormenting or bleak offline worlds, "liberating" our bodies from physical locations.

These young people also illustrate the public nature of "queer identity work" in rural places, and the importance of considering where this work takes place. In framing sexualities and genders as produced through collective labor that ensnares people, places, and media, we can more effectively grasp the modern experiences and conditions that construct discourses and articulations of identity. Identity from this perspective then reads as a dialogue rather than a reflection of a fixed essence or reality. It refuses the inclination to be lodged in a singular person, place, or thing but is contingent on the blurring of boundaries across them.

Analytically, rural youth show us that queer identity work done in rural places is differently but not necessarily less declarative than the pronunciations associated with urban LGBT communities. In short, late modern identity work needs a public no matter where you live. As public spaces atrophy in the wake of increasing privatization, youth respond by suturing the possibilities for public identity work to be found in new media like web-based journals and group websites and the commercial zones of Wal-Mart. I argue here that what this work looks like deeply depends on one's surroundings, challenging new media scholars on their uncritical presumptions about the effects of technologies and pushing queer theorists to examine our uncritical use of urban paradigms.

In closing I want to make clear that even though boundary publics mediate the availability of publics to rural queer and questioning youth, they do not circumvent or neutralize the very real possibility of violence faced for queerly standing out. In other words, rural communities are not unproblematic, idyllic spaces for queer and questioning youth engaged in identity projects. These publics can be compromised. For example, AJ has since taken down his more graphic photo essays after a heated conversation with a relative who berated him for potentially embarrassing his family; moreover, HPA members experienced their share of angry epithets in the Wal-Mart parking lot. But, arguably these rural boundary publics are no more compromised by familial pressures to conform and the violence of heteronormativity more broadly than any other cultural space in the United States. Rather, the threats are different in rural communities depending on your class, race, age, religious affiliation, and a host of other conditions. Most noted by the youth I spoke with, the threats were not anonymous. They knew very well the relatives or neighbors most likely to harass them. They faced the same threats everyday at family dinners and the county school. Unavoidable embroilments with these publics while at times harrying are, ironically, also critical to queer identity work—these engagements bring rural LGBT youth social worlds into being, shape their boundaries, and sharpen their definition. Their navigation of these boundary publics mediates both a sense of privacy so critical to self-definition and publicity needed to test out and validate constructions of selves.

The social interactions of queer youth challenge the presumption that rural queer publics are unsustainable or poor imitations when compared to an urban queer scene. There are particular queer publics rural youth bring into being, but they are brought about in ways and locations one might not likely expect. These publics occupy the centers and margins of rural communities rather than countering or rebuffing the mainstream or general public sphere. They absorb, recycle, and recuperate these spaces to make them, albeit temporarily, address their needs. And, in increasingly complicated ways, these young people take up new media to augment their queer identity work.

Against a backdrop of increasingly privatized and impoverished structural conditions that define the rural United States and the racial and class politics that shape and are shaped by these conditions, queer youth and their allies visibly—and vibrantly—work the boundaries of public spaces available to them. My hope is that this research contributes to a growing body of materially grounded studies of both new media use and sexual and gender experience and highlights what rural queer youth new media use can teach us about the politics of identity and how to better serve their needs.

Notes

1 This chapter is a revised and developed version of an earlier work of the same title (Gray 2007). We are reprinting this with permission of the copyright holder, the Mid-America American Studies Association (MAASA).
2 The names of all persons, places, websites, and organizations are pseudonyms and some community details have been changed to secure the anonymity of young people involved in this research. This is a common practice in ethnographic and qualitative research meant to respect the privacy and confidentiality of research participants. Assuring anonymity, particularly in the case of youth participants, is a requirement of many university institutional review boards (IRBs).
3 The fields of clinical and developmental psychology, public health, and social work dominate research on the lived experiences of queer and questioning youth. For work that challenges this medicalizing model of identity development see Ritch Savin-Williams (2005).

4 I am indebted to the work of Barbara Ponse (1978) and Ken Plummer (1995).
5 See Sonia Livingstone (2008). For more on this point and a critique of the literature in media studies that attempts to maintain this divide see Maria Bakardjieva (2005) and Roger Silverstone (2006).
6 John D'Emilio (1983) and George Chauncey (1994) are paradigmatic texts in gay and lesbian history. While both authors attempt to qualify their arguments so as not to negate the role of the rural in modern U.S. identity formations they simply do not take up queer rurality. As few authors have attempted to address this gap in the literature, "urbanness" has become synonymous with "gay." For a complication of this treatment in cultural, historical, and literary studies see John Howard (1997), Carlos L. Dews and Carolyn Leste Law (2001), Angelia R. Wilson (2000) and E. Patrick Johnson and Mae G. Henderson (2005).
7 Sedgwick, in *The Epistemology of the Closet* points us to such dyads as "heterosexuality/homosexuality" "urbane/provincial" or "in/out" as rich locations for cultural critique (1990, pp. 9–11).
8 Even within queer narratives of the recent rural past, private house parties serve as the central location of queer possibility and gathering—if any gathering is imagined possible at all. See, for example, John Howard (1999).
9 The Department of Commerce's Bureau of the Census, the White House's Office of Management and Budget (OMB), and the Department of Agriculture's Economic Research Service (USDA ERS) each play a hand in defining the rural.
10 I draw on Geoffrey C. Bowker and Susan Leigh Star's (1999) notion of "boundary objects."
11 See an account of AJ's engagement with this documentary in my book *Out in the Country: Youth, Media, and Queer Visibility in Rural America* (2009).

References

Bakardjieva, M. 2005. *Internet society: The internet in everyday life*. London: Sage.

Beer, D. 2008. Social network(ing) sites: Revisiting the story so far: A response to Danah Boyd & Nicole Ellison. *Journal of Computer Mediated Communication* 13(2): 516–529.

Boellstorff, T. 2008. *Coming of age in second life: An anthropologist explores the virtually human*. Princeton: Princeton University Press.

Bowker, G. C. and Leigh, S. L. 1999. *Sorting things out: Classification and its consequences*. Cambridge, MA: MIT Press.

Chauncey, G. 1994. *Gay New York: Gender, urban culture, and the makings of the gay male world, 1890–1940*. New York: Basic Books.

D'Emilio, J. 1983. *Sexual politics, sexual communities: The making of a homosexual minority in the United States 1940–1979*. Chicago: University of Chicago.

Dews, C. L. and Law, L. L. 2001. *Out in the South*. Philadelphia: Temple University Press.

Fischer, C. S. 1992. *America calling: A social history of the telephone to 1940*. Berkeley: University of California Press.

Fraser, N. 1992. Rethinking the public sphere: A contribution to the critique of actually existing democracy. In *Habermas and the public sphere: Studies in contemporary German social thought*, edited by C. J. Calhoun. Cambridge, MA: MIT Press, 109–142.

Gray, M. L. 2007. From websites to Wal-Mart: Youth, identity work, and the queering of boundary publics in *Small Town, USA*. *American Studies* 48(2) (Summer): 5–15.

Gray, M. L. 2009. *Out in the country: Youth, media, and queer visibility in rural America*. New York: NYU Press.

Habermas, J. 1989. *The structural transformation of the public sphere: An inquiry into a category of bourgeois society*. Cambridge, MA: MIT Press.

Howard, J. 1997. *Carryin' on in the lesbian and gay South*. New York: New York University Press.

Howard, J. 1999. *Men like that: A southern queer history*. Chicago: University of Chicago Press.

Johnson, E. P., and Henderson, M., eds. 2005. *Black queer studies: A critical anthology*. Durham, NC: Duke University Press.

Jones, S. 2006. Foreword: Dreams of fields: Possible trajectories of internet studies. In *Critical cyberculture studies*, edited by D. Silver and A. Massanari. New York: New York University Press, ix–xvii.

Livingstone, S. M. 2008. Taking risky opportunities in youthful content creation: Teenagers' use of social networking sites for intimacy, privacy and self-expression. *New Media and Society* 10(3): 392–411.

Massey, D. B. 1994. *Space, place and gender*. Cambridge: Polity.

Miller, D., and Slater, D. 2000. *The internet: An ethnographic approach*. Oxford and New York: Berg.

Plummer, K. 1995. *Telling sexual stories: Power, change, and social worlds*. London: New York: Routledge.

Ponse, B. 1978. *Identities in the lesbian world: The social construction of self*. Westport, CT: Greenwood Press.

Savin-Williams, R. C. 2005. *The new gay teenager*. Cambridge, MA: Harvard University Press.

Sedgwick, E. K. 1990. *Epistemology of the closet*. Berkeley: University of California Press.

Silverstone, R. 2006. Domesticating domestication: Reflections on the life of a concept. In *Domestication of media and technology*, edited by T. Berker, M. Hartmann, Y. Punie, and K. Ward. New York: Open University Press, 229–248.

Starr, P. 2005. *The creation of the media: Political origins of modern communications*. New York: Basic Books.

U.S. General Accounting Office. 1993. *Rural development: Profile of rural areas*, Fact Sheet for Congressional Requestors, GAO/RCED-93-40FS. Washington, DC: General Accounting Office, 26–30.

Warner, M. 2002. *Publics and counterpublics*. New York and Cambridge, MA: Zone Books, distributed by MIT Press.

Wellman, B., and Haythornthwaite, C. A. 2002. *The internet in everyday life*. Malden, MA: Blackwell.

Williams, R. 1973. *The country and the city*. New York: Oxford University Press.

Wilson, A. R. 2000. *Below the belt: Sexuality, religion and the American South*. New York: Cassell.

Woolgar, S. 2002. *Virtual society?: Technology, cyberbole, reality*. Oxford and New York: Oxford University Press.

Notes on Contributors

Jonathan Alexander, PhD, is Professor of English and Campus Writing Coordinator at the University of California, Irvine. His books include *Literacy, Sexuality, Pedagogy: Theory and Practice for Composition Studies*; *Digital Youth: Emerging Literacies on the World Wide Web*; *Argument Now, a Brief Rhetoric* (with Margaret Barber); *Role Play: Distance Learning and the Teaching of Writing* (edited with Marcia Dickson); *Bisexuality and Transgenderism: InterSEXions of the Others* (edited with Karen Yescavage); and *Finding Out: An Introduction to LGBT Studies* (with Deborah T. Meem and Michelle Gibson).

Ben Aslinger is an Assistant Professor of Media and Culture in the Department of English at Bentley University (Waltham, MA). His research and teaching interests include media convergence and sound studies.

Trudy Barber, PhD, created an immersive VR Sex environment in 1992 as part of her BA Fine Art studies at Central Saint Martins College of Art. She went on to gain her PhD at the University of Kent with her thesis on Computer Fetishism and Sexual Futurology. She is currently Senior Lecturer in Media at the School of Creative Arts, Film and Media, University of Portsmouth. Her current research interests include: human-computer-interaction; new media development and content; consumer generated content; online social networking; sexuality and sexual subcultures; science fiction, cyberpunk and the future; immersive and non-immersive virtuality (such as Second Life and gaming), the convergence and customization of communication technologies and issues surrounding theory and creative digital practice.

Richard Berger is currently Reader in Media & Education at the Centre for Excellence in Media Practice, Bournemouth University, UK, where he coordinates pedagogic research. His other research interests include the adaptation of literature, comic books and videogames to film and television as well as blogging, fanfic, and other forms of personal expression online. In addition he is an experienced broadcaster and journalist for BBC Online and BBC Radio, a regular contributor to the independent film magazine, *The Big Picture*, and co-editor of *The Media Research Journal*.

Joseph Clift, Ed.D., is a health educator and social scientist. He currently works for a small social justice and community research and development company. Dr. Clift's earlier education was in the environmental field, which is still a field of interest. His dissertation was an evaluation of an STD intervention aimed at gay men in Washington, DC. His results highlighted the importance that the internet played in sexual behavior. Dr. Clift currently resides in Takoma Park, Maryland with his husband and their golden retrievers. Dr. Joseph Clift can be reached via email at joseph_clift@yahoo.com.

Margaret Cooper is a sociologist at Southern Illinois University. Her current interests regard gay and lesbian rural issues, social constructionism, and gender identity. She has been involved with the LGBT movement, the women's rights movement, and inner city activism. Her work has been published internationally in academic journals, textbooks, and collections. She lives in Kentucky with her partner, their daughter, and their dogs.

Ian Davies is an independent scholar and editor living in the UK, with qualifications in education and counseling, and research interests in the media.

Bruce E. Drushel is an Assistant Professor in the Department of Communication at Miami University. He received his PhD from Ohio University in 1991. His teaching and research interests are in the areas of media economics, media audiences, and queer representation in electronic media and film. His work has appeared in *Journal of Media Economics*, *Journal of Homosexuality*, *FemSpec*, and in numerous edited collections. His is co-editor of the recently-published book *Queer Identities/Political Realities*. He currently chairs the Gay, Lesbian & Queer Studies interest group for Popular Culture Association/American Culture Association.

Kristina Dzara holds a PhD in Sociology from Southern Illinois University Carbondale and a Master's degree in Applied Sociology from the University of Central Florida. Her broad research areas are family and sexuality, with focuses on subjective well-being and relationship transitions.

Monica Edwards holds a PhD in Sociology from Loyola University, Chicago. She is currently a full-time, non-tenure track instructor at Northeastern Illinois University. Her current research focuses on media, sexuality, and everyday life; exploring the complex ways individuals come to rely upon the media as a resource in sexual identity construction, community building and boundary negotiations, and relationship building across sexual difference.

Daniel Farr is a visiting assistant professor of Sociology at Randolph College. His is pursuing his PhD at the University of Albany, SUNY with a dissertation exploring parental aspirations among young gay men. His primary areas of research explore the intersections of gender, sexualities, and families. His recent and forthcoming publications address various aspects of queer culture and media including online personal ads, gay and lesbian commercial content, and queer families in the media.

Mary L. Gray is Assistant Professor of Communication and Culture at Indiana University, Bloomington. After "aging out" as a queer youth activist, she decided to merge her love of all things geeky, queer, and political and study queerness in mass and digital media and its uses in youth culture and everyday life. Mary is the author of *In Your Face: Stories from the Lives of Queer Youth* (1999) and, more recently, *Out in the Country: Youth, Media, and Queer Visibility in Rural America* (2009). She blogs and maintains a resource list for rural LGBTQ youth at: www.queercountry.org.

Ronald Gregg is Senior Lecturer in Film Studies and Director of Film Programming at the Whitney Humanities Center at Yale University. He teaches courses on classical and contemporary Hollywood, and experimental and queer cinema (both Hollywood and avant-garde), and he has published articles on topics ranging from MGM's management of the image of its 1920s gay star William Haines to queer representation in the competing videos produced during Oregon's 1992 anti-gay rights ballot measure campaign. His most recent publications include "Alfred Hitchcock, Male 'Vertigo' and the Hollywood Apparatus in Postwar America" in the Italian publication *La Valle dell'Eden* and "Queer Performance, Youth and YouTube" in *Jump Cut*.

Rosalind Hanmer was educated in London, moving from Liverpool in 1988. She has taught at London Metropolitan University. Her academic disciplines are in Media and Cultural Communications. She has publications and articles on sexuality and identity within popular culture in the *International Journal of Sociology and Social Policy* (2003), *Feminist Media Studies Journal* (2003), and the *Graduate Journal of Social Science* (2005). She has recently completed her PhD entitled "Lesbian Internet Fandom: A Study of the Xena: Warrior Princess Phenomena" at the University of Birmingham.

Damon Lindler Lazzara is a graduate of Goucher College, Baltimore (BA, Media Studies, 2001) and of the University of South Florida (MLA, Humanities, 2004), and is a doctoral candidate at York University, Toronto, with a dissertation in progress concerning the convergence of modern poetry and myth with coming-of-age in the western tradition. His radio work has been broadcast on the National Public Radio network and affiliate stations, and he has published and performed in academic, professional, and creative capacities as a writer, editor, poet, translator, and singer.

Elizabeth Losh of University of California, Irvine, is the author of *Virtualpolitik: An Electronic History of Government Media-Making in a Time of War, Scandal, Disaster, Miscommunication, and Mistakes*. She writes about institutions as digital content-creators, the discourses of the "virtual state," the media literacy of policy makers and authority figures, and the rhetoric surrounding regulatory attempts to limit everyday digital practices. She has published articles about videogames for the military and emergency first-responders, government websites and YouTube channels, state-funded distance learning efforts, national digital libraries, political blogging, and congressional hearings on the Internet. Her current book project, *Early Adopters: The Instructional Technology Movement and the Myth of the Digital Generation*, looks at a range of digital projects in higher education and the conflicts between regulation and content-creation that universities must negotiate.

Mark McHarry is an independent scholar. In addition to contemporary and Edo-period Japanese culture, his interests include the works of Colombian author Fernando Vallejo and modern Latin American literature. With Antonia Levi and Dru Pagliassotti he is editor of the collection *Girls Doing Boys Doing Boys: Japanese Boys' Love Anime and Manga in a Globalized World*. He has contributed to *Mechademia*, *Queer Popular Culture: Literature, Media, Film, and Television*, the *Encyclopedia of Erotic Literature*, *Journal of Homosexuality*, *Z Magazine*, *Alternative Press Review*, and *Gay Community News*. He is currently researching the life of author-inventor Hiraga Gennai and his place in the *ukiyo* (floating world).

Eleanor Morrison is a Communication PhD candidate at the University of Southern California. She worked in the film industry and at a nonpartisan policy research organization before completing her MSc in Social and Public Communication at the London School of Economics and Political Science, and recently finished a year-long fellowship at the Gay & Lesbian Alliance Against Defamation. Her academic interests revolve around the intersection of media and social change, including the potential of entertainment programs to encourage tolerance and equality.

Sharif Mowlabocus is based at the University of Sussex, where he lectures in Digital Media. His research primarily focuses on digital sub-cultures and sub-cultural (mis)appropriations of contemporary media technologies. A member of the Centre for Material Digital Culture, his work touches on the themes of identity, sexual practice, and sexual politics, and chiefly discusses how such notions are manifested and negotiated across different digital platforms and within different social contexts. Dr Mowlabocus also sits on the committee of the Brighton and Sussex Sexualities Network and is a member of the Count Me In Too research team.

Christopher Pullen, PhD, is Senior Lecturer in Media Studies at Bournemouth University, UK. He is widely published in the area of sexuality and contemporary media, and is the author of *Documenting Gay Men: Identity and Performance in Reality Television and Documentary Film* (2007), and *Gay Identity, New Storytelling and the Media* (2009).

Noah Tsika is a PhD candidate in Cinema Studies at New York University, Tisch School of the Arts. He is the author of *Gods and Monsters: A Queer Film Classic*, and numerous articles and book chapters on film, television, and new media.

Nikki Usher is a PhD candidate at USC Annenberg. She is a Knight Digital Media research assistant, and received her AB from Harvard University. She was a professional journalist and has written for the *Philadelphia Inquirer*, *Boston Globe*, *Los Angeles Times*, and *Chicago Tribune*, among other outlets. Her research interests include journalism studies, LGBT studies, and the transition of traditional media to new media.

Jason Whitesel received his PhD from the Department of Sociology at the Ohio State University in 2009. Currently, he is working on a book about how members of an international social movement organization, Girth & Mirth, use allusion and campy-queer behavior to reconfigure their stigmatized identities. This ethnography documents how big gay men respond to the injuries they experience—shame, desexualization, exclusion, and marginalization—within mainstream and especially in gay society. His broader research agenda investigates social constructions of deviance and how stigma management and norm violation serve as identity-shaping practices. Along these lines, his recent article in *Sociological Focus*, "Social Smoking: An Untenable Position," (with Amy Shuman), examines how social smokers occupy untenable, but nonetheless manageable, subject positions.

Index

Abrams, Jonathan 64
Acosta, Adrian L x, xiii, 20, 24–27, 29, 32, 34
Active Youth vii, 2, 7, 15–72
Adaptation 176–177
Adorno, Theodor 134
Advertisements (see also commercials) 88, 90–91, 94–95, 126, 133, 215, 220, 224, 226
Advertisements, public service 25
Advertisers 89, 92–96, 115, 118–119, 130, 133–134, 221, 225
Advocate, The xiii, 11, 17, 18, 63, 65, 115, 119, 160
Affirmation xi, 2, 7, 9, 191, 203
AfterEllen 160, 164, 166
AfterElton 308
Agency xi, 1, 5, 7–10, 19, 23–24, 28, 30, 32–33, 43, 85, 148, 150, 153, 156, 168, 175, 182, 221, 254
AIDS/HIV 47, 93, 130, 135, 216, 223, 225–226, 237, 258, 260–262, 276–278
Alexander, Jonathan 2, 7, 37, 48, 66, 299
Almada, Nadia 132
Alwood, Edward 3
Ambivalence of online new media 10
America Online 51, 115, 279
American Psychiatric Association 127, 195–196
Amnesia Sparkles 34
And then I became Gay: Young Men's Stories 20
Angel 182

Animage 187–188
Anime (animation) 8, 25, 185–189, 195, 302
Arbuckle, Fatty 140
Armed forces 8, 130, 133, 236
Aslinger, Ben 7, 113
Aspin, Les 236
Ault, Amber 254
Autobiographical thinking 31

Bakhtin, Mikhail 173, 176, 179, 182–183
Banet-Weiser, Sarah 41
Barber, Trudy 9, 245, 299
Barry's Boot Camp 230
Barthes, Roland 174
Bass, Lance 25
Baudrillard, Jean 52
Bay Area Reporter 275, 277
BDSM 210, 246
Beemyn, Brett 4
Ben-Ze'ev, Aaron 173
Berger, Richard xiii, 8, 173, 327
Berry, Chris 2
Bersani, Leo 202
Berube, Alan 241
Best, Joel 107, 109
Big Brother 132
Bill, The 179
Bisexual/bisexuality xi, 1, 4, 10, 39, 46, 48, 62–63, 66–70, 84, 87–88, 120, 131, 142, 149, 156, 159, 161, 163–164, 170, 177, 180, 182–183, 16 41, 247, 249, 254, 265, 288
Blakes 21 177

Blog (blogging) 1, 3, 7, 27–28, 34, 38, 43, 51, 53, 56, 117, 122, 160, 230–231, 240, 280, 299, 301, 302
Blog, video (vlog/vlogging) 3, 7, 27, 56, 39, 41, 48, 51
Bloom, Luka 34
Bloustein, David 251
Body Discourses 2, 7–8, 227–268
Body image 8, 205, 208, 211, 215–216, 223, 224
Boellstorff, Tom 42
Bordo, Susan 227
Boundary public 288, 292–296
Bourdieu, Pierre 6, 22–24, 64
Bow, Clara 141, 145
Boy George 29
Boys Will be Girls 141
Broadway 145
Broadway Brevities 141
Brokeback Mountain 174
Bronski, Michael 236, 238
Broomfield, Nick 247
Bruckman, Amy 46
Buffy the Vampire Slayer 175, 178–179, 182
Butler, Judith 3, 52, 170, 185, 189

Cagney, Jimmy 142
Caitlin, Ryan 21
Caldwell, John Thornton 3, 116
Calvin Klein 128, 220–222
Campbell, John 208, 40–281
Capsuto, Steven 31
Carnival ambivalence 176
Carnivalesque 52, 127, 173–174, 176, 178
Castro 9, 186, 274–277, 279–280, 282–283
Cayne, Candis 132
Chaplin, Charlie 140
Charmed 182
Chasnoff, Deborah 33
Chauncey, George 145
Christian Science Monitor 108
Christopher Park, New York 25–26
Christopher Street, New York 25, 274, 278, 280, 283
Circuit of Culture 11

Citizenship xi, 4, 24–25, 26–28, 252–253, 294
Civic engagement 271–273, 279, 282, 283
Civil rights 120, 130–131, 165, 202
Civil rights, gay and lesbian 4
Civil rights, LGBT 25
Clerc, Susan 175, 177
Clift, Joseph 9, 158, 300
Coalescence 1, 4, 25
Cohesion xi, 4, 27, 53, 255
Collective identity 101, 106, 108–109, 165, 167, 216, 226
Coming out 1, 7, 37–48, 53, 62–63, 66, 75–78, 83–85, 104, 106, 121, 149–151, 154, 156, 202, 206, 241, 264, 279
Commercial Closet Association (CCA) 8, 125–129, 131–134
Commercials (see also advertisements) 8, 239
Commodification 126, 177, 281
Commodity Networks 2, 7, 73–136
Communication action context 272–273, 275–281
Communication infrastructure theory 271–272, 282
Communities 1, 38–39, 41–42, 44, 48, 65, 70, 75–78, 83–85, 90, 96, 100, 106, 114, 120, 122, 131, 139, 160–161, 166–167, 169, 173, 175–176, 178, 181–182, 201, 204, 216, 218, 221, 224, 231–232, 236, 245–246, 256, 262, 265, 272–274, 282–283, 291–292, 295–296
Communities, online 38, 42, 44, 65, 75–76, 83, 85, 106, 173, 178, 231–232, 283
Community organizations 272, 276, 278, 281, 283–284
Community Spaces 2, 7, 9–10, 269–298
Community, gay 2, 26, 33, 116, 133, 168, 188, 223–224, 261–262, 271, 273–274, 276, 278–283
Community, gay and lesbian 4, 25, 89, 120
Community, lesbian 85, 120, 159–161, 163–168, 170

Community, virtual 3, 42, 57, 76, 102, 150, 152
Computing 254
Confessional 3, 28
Confidential 142
Conglomeration 113, 114, 120–121
ConnectU 64
Consumption 1, 57, 118, 118, 175, 183, 203, 210, 254, 290
Convergence 3, 254, 299, 301
Convergence Culture: Where Old and New Media Collide 3
Cooper, Evan 159
Cooper, Gary 140–141
Cooper, Margaret xiii–xiv, 6–7, 9, 75, 100, 227, 300
Copresence 17, 19, 23–24, 27, 31–32
Coronation Street 132
Costello, Brigid 249
Coté, Mark 206
Counterpublics 5, 291
Courtship 7, 51–55, 58–60, 87
Coward, Noel 141, 145
Craigslist 7, 87–97
Creativity 56, 177, 246
Crossover fic. 182
Cruise, Tom 139, 142, 144
Culture Club 29
Cyber SM 250
Cyberqueer 2
Cybersex 247–248, 250
Cyberspace 11, 40, 44, 46, 49, 51–52, 78, 147, 177, 182, 211, 215, 225–226, 246, 250, 279
Cyborg 68, 225, 254–255

D'Emilio, John 4, 209, 274, 297
Database 39, 46, 47, 126, 181
Dating 1, 7–8, 76, 87, 96, 116, 166, 193, 201, 204, 208, 212, 232–235, 237, 239, 241, 279–280
Davies, Ian xiv, 8, 125, 300
Davies, Russell, T 180
De Rossi, Portia 25, 30, 34
Defense of Marriage Act of 1996 34
DeGeneres, Ellen 17, 19–20, 24–25, 30, 32–34
Democracy xii, 5, 51, 53, 60, 143

Denial 20, 32, 63, 144
Dentith, Simon 176
Design for Living 141, 145
DiCaprio, Leonardo 142, 144
Dick, Philip K. 255
Dietrich, Marlene 140
Digital images 201–202, 225
Dirty Sexy Money 132
Discovery Channel 292
Dissembedding mechanism 2
Diversity 2, 4, 17, 22–23, 25–26, 29, 32, 47, 91, 96, 125–126, 132, 148–149, 162, 225
Do You Really Want to Hurt Me? 29
Doctor Who 180, 182
Documentary 3, 9, 33, 42, 247, 275, 292, 297
Don't Ask, Don't Tell 105, 230–232, 236–238, 240, 241
Dot.com, bubble and crash 114–116, 118
Doty, Alexander 148, 156, 175
Douglas, Billy 142
DowneLink.com 65
Dozier, Raine 166
Drushel, Bruce 7, 62, 300
du Gay, Paul 11
Dubois, W.E.B. 128
Dyer, Richard 3, 8, 129–130, 139, 162, 176–177, 208, 210, 232–233
Dzara, Kristina 7, 100, 300

E. O. Green Junior High School, Oxnard (California) 30
EastEnders 179
Edwards, Monica 8, 159, 300
Ellen DeGeneres Show, The 17
Ellis, John 3
Emancipatory politics 10
Empowerment 47, 63, 153, 155, 157
Epstein, Joy 21
Exploring the Blue 25, 34

Facebook 7, 62, 64–66, 100–110, 134
Fan Cultures 2, 7–8, 137–198
Fan fiction 154–155, 160, 173, 177, 186
Fandom 147–151, 153–156, 177, 189, 301
Fanfiction.net 179, 181, 186

Farr, Daniel 7, 87, 301
Farrell, Kathleen 162
Fat bodies 226
Fat bodies, admirers of 217–218, 223, 225
Fat Studies 226
Fatvertisements 225–226
Female to Male (FTM) 90–95, 97, 165, 168, 293
Feminine 94, 127–128, 191–192, 216, 221, 237
Feminists against censorship 247
Femslash/femmeslash 182
Fetish Scene 245–248, 250, 253
Fetishes 247
54 142
Fight Club 142
Fight OUT Loud 34
Fiske, John 59, 126, 150, 175
Flynn, Errol 140
Foucault, Michel 3, 5, 11, 22, 52, 225
Fraser, Nancy 5
Friends 159
Friendster 64
Fuss, Diana 6
Futterman, Diane 21

Gamson, Joshua 3, 44, 113–114, 127, 131, 161, 164, 167, 281
Garbo, Greta 140
Gatiss, Mark 180
Gay and Lesbian Alliance Against Defamation (GLAAD) 128, 135
Gay bars 205, 274, 276, 278, 280, 283
Gay capitalism 51
Gay community 2, 26, 33, 116, 133, 168, 188, 223–224, 261–262, 271–274, 276, 278–283
Gay enclave 271, 273, 282–284
Gay identity 19, 31, 33, 53, 189, 194, 215, 261, 273, 275, 279, 282, 303
Gay Lesbian Straight Education Network (GLSEN) 20, 24–25, 27, 29–30, 32
Gay liberation 52, 59, 258, 261, 274–275
Gay marriage xii, 34, 108, 181, 235
Gay neighborhood 9, 271, 273–274, 276, 278–279, 281–284

Gay press 130–131, 135, 273
Gay son, beloved 19
Gay wealth, myth of 118
Gay youth/teen identity 17, 19–20, 32, 42, 262, 264
Gay.com 114–116, 201, 235, 237, 260, 181–282
Gaydar 8, 201–212, 235, 260
GayTube 41
Geisler, Jerry 140
Gender ambiguous identity 19, 33
Gender roles 45, 216
Genre 8, 37–38, 41, 43, 48, 53, 148, 174–180, 182, 185, 193, 195, 209, 251
Gentrification 271, 276, 278
Geo-ethnic media 271–272, 282
Giddens, Anthony 1–4, 6, 10–11, 24, 31–32, 54, 148
Glyn, Elinor 145
Goffman, Erving 21, 102–104, 106, 215, 226
Goodnight Sweetheart 179
Grant, Cary 140, 142
Gray, Mary L 9, 188, 301
Greenspan, Aaron 64
Greenstreet, Sydney 140
Gregg, Ron 8, 139, 301
Gross, Larry 3, 159, 278
Grosz, Elizabeth 186, 190
Groupings 118, 129
Guerin, Frances 23
Gundam Wing Addiction 186

Haines, William 140, 301
Hall, Stuart 163–164
Hallas, Roger 23
Halley, Janet 232, 234, 236–237
Hanmer, Rosalind 3, 147, 301
Haptic technologies 250
Haraway, Donna 255
Harry Potter 180
Hearn, Jeff 252–253, 255
Heteronormativity 5, 52, 161, 296
Highland Pride Alliance (HPA) 288–289, 293–295
Hines, Sally 161
HIV (see AIDS/HIV)

Hodkinson, Paul 250–251
Hold of the local 2, 11, 148
Hollywood 144–145, 160, 204, 275, 281, 301
Hollywood Production Code 141
Home Box Office (HBO) 179, 218
Homo Politico, The 28, 34
Homoerotic 8, 142, 173–174, 185, 191, 194, 217–218, 220–221, 230
Homophobia 8, 27, 31, 33–34, 63, 108, 135, 203, 258, 261–262, 265
Homosexual characters 140, 177
Homosexuality Identity Model 63
Hudson, Waymon 20, 25, 27, 29, 31–32, 34
Human Rights Campaign 43, 47
Humanity, common 33
Hutcheon, Linda 174, 176, 177

Identification 3–7, 17, 22–24, 31, 38, 57, 62, 91, 95, 102, 107, 129–130, 139, 147, 152, 153, 156, 191, 203, 205–206, 208, 210–211, 237, 272
Identity confusion 63
Identity ideals 1
Identity management 7, 101, 103
Identity politics xi, 2, 4, 6, 114, 117, 133
Identity tolerance 63
Identity, online 41, 46, 51, 59
Identity, sexual 2, 6, 18–19, 28, 32, 38, 45–46, 52, 62, 66–67, 69–70, 104–105, 114, 133, 147, 150, 152–153, 155–156, 167, 173, 186, 191, 193, 203, 210, 245, 249, 258, 261–262, 300
Imagined gay community 2
Interactivity 1–2, 52, 63, 133–134, 234–235, 252, 256
International Journal of Gay and Lesbian Studies 2
Internet Relay Channels (IRC) 64–65, 149, 207
Interview with the Vampire 142
Intimate citizenship 4, 24, 28
Iraq War 231, 235
Iser, Wolfgang 178
It 145

Jackson, Janet 25
Jagger, Jill 170
Jane Eyre 173
Jarhead 240
Jenkins, Henry xvii, 139, 167, 175
Jenkins, Richard 22
Jervis, John 250
Juhasz, Alexandra 38

Kappeler, Susanne 209, 211
Katyal, Sonia K. 177
Kentucky 77–78, 288–289, 292–293
Kerr, Aphra 248
Kibby, Marjorie 249
King, Greg 33
King, Lawrence v, x, 7, 17–34, 135
Kinsey, Alfred 232
Knight, T. R. 25
Knowledge of self 10, 33
Kohn, Sally 108–109
Koskela, Hille 252

L Word, The 8, 132, 159–169, 182
Late modernity 1, 10, 247
Law Enforcement Hate Crimes Act, The (also know as The Matthew Sheppard Act) xii, 33
Lawnmower Man, The 250
Lazzara, Damon Lindler 7, 51, 301
LeBesco, Kathleen 226–227
Lesbian identity 2, 42, 78, 83–84, 149, 151, 169–170, 289
Lesbian Town 76, 85
LGBT citizens 21, 125
Liberace 142
Life on the Screen 52
Life story 19
Liminal/limimality 194, 225, 227
Lincoln, Sian 250
LinkedIn 64
littleBIGGERchris 51–60
LiveJournal 186
Local media 271, 275–276, 283
Logo/Logo Online 20, 24–25, 27, 29–30, 32, 42
Lord of the Rings, The 174
Losh, Elizabeth 7, 37, 302
Lovink, Geert 47

Index

Lubitsch, Ernst 141, 145
Lunsing, Wim 186, 188, 194

Mad About the Boy 142
Male to Female (MTF) 90–97
Malibu Beach 141
Man from Uncle, The 177
Manga (graphic novels) 8, 185–186, 188–189
Manovich, Lev 47
Martin, Fran 2
Matthew Sheppard Act, The (see The Law Enforcement Hate Crimes Act)
Matthews, Mary C 43
McHarry, Mark 8, 11, 185, 302
McInerney, Brandon 17, 20, 33
McIntosh, Mary 3
McIntyre, Joey 29
McKee, Dan 175
McLelland, Mark 177, 180
Men Who Have Sex with Men (MSM) 9, 258–265
Mercer, Kobena 208, 211
Metrosexuality 52
MGM 140, 301
Milk, Harvey 275, 280, 283
Misrecognition of educational culture 22
Mobile Cultures: New Media in Queer Asia 2
Modern power 5
Moore, Candace 159
Morphing 221, 224, 226
Morrison, Eleanor 9–10, 271, 302
Morrissey 183
Mowlabocus, Sharif 8, 201, 302
Multi User Domains (MUDs) 2
Munro, Surya 4
MySpace 41, 62, 64–71, 102, 134, 206, 235

Nakamura, Lisa 44, 113, 120
Narratives 1, 3–4, 6, 8, 17, 19–20, 23–25, 27–28, 31–32, 37–40, 42–48, 55, 75, 48, 83–85, 147, 149, 150–151, 155–157, 160, 177, 179, 191, 208, 232, 236, 238, 241, 248, 250, 290, 297
Narrowcasting 120
National Day of Silence 24–25, 27

National School Climate Survey 24
Nazi Germany/regime 26, 203
New Kids on the Block 29, 182
New storytelling 4, 24
New York Native 178
Nickasarbata 51–60
Niedweiki, Anthony 34
Non-heterosexual identity 126–127
Normalcy 20, 131, 170
NSYNC 25

O'Riordan, Kate 2, 40, 44, 46, 246
O'Toole, Lawrence 208
Oak Lawn, Dallas 278
Obama, Barack 241
One Life to Live 142
Othering 147
Ourchart 160, 164
Out magazine 115
Outproud! 53
Oxnard (California) 17, 135
Oz 180

Paparazzi 144
Paramount 141
Parody/parodying 7, 37, 127, 174, 220, 238
Passeron, Jean Claude 22–24, 28–29, 32
Pedagogic action 22, 24, 28–29, 32
Pedagogic work 22
Penley, Constance 139
Performativity 9, 51–52, 147, 195, 245
Phillippe, Ryan 142–144
Photography 147, 211, 230
Pickering, Michael 128–129
Pitt, Brad 139, 142, 144–145
PlanetOut 89, 113–122, 281–282
Plant, Sadie 203
Plummer, Ken 3–4, 24, 28, 40, 43, 48, 147, 149, 156, 297
Pornography 1, 144, 177, 201, 209–211, 217
Pornography, gay 201, 209–210
Postmodern 43, 52–54, 254
Privacy 58, 60, 65, 89, 97, 144, 291, 296
Professionals, The 177
Profic 173

Prohibition 140–141
Proposition 20 (US) 178
Proposition 22 (US) 34, 108, 181
Prosthetic communication 249
Proulx, E. Annie 174
Public Health 259, 265
Public space 4, 9, 151, 170, 185, 271–273, 276, 291–292, 293, 295–296
Public sphere 1, 5, 51, 141–142, 181, 247, 290–292, 294, 296
Public sphere, oppositional/proletarian 5
Pugh, Sheenagh 177
Pullen, Christopher xi, xiii–xiv, 17, 227, 303
Pybus, Jennifer 206

Queer as Folk 159, 179
Queer identity work 289, 292, 294–296
Queer Online: Media, Technology and Sexuality 2, 40
Queer reading 8
Queer theory xi, 2–3, 11, 46, 148
Queer Webs 2

Realjock.com 230–242
Real person slash (RPS) 182–183
Reality television 32, 145, 182
Reeves, Keanu 142–143
Reflexive project of the self 6, 24
Reflexive sociology 6
Remediation 44, 48
Rhys, Jean 173
Rites of Passage 149
RKO Studios 140
Rolling Stone 142
Romance 7, 20, 52, 54, 90, 140–141, 155
Romantic metanarratives 54, 57, 59–60
Roseneil, Sasha 161–162, 170
Rural 260, 262, 265, 288–293, 295–296, 301
Rural lesbians xiii, 100
Russo, Vito 3

Said, Edward 6

San Francisco 9, 90, 92, 97, 117, 122, 186, 260, 273–278
San Francisco Bay Times 277
San Francisco Sentinel 278
Satō Masaki 188
Savin-Williams, Ritch 20, 62–63, 296
Scanner Darkly, A 255
Schindler's List 26
Science fiction 174, 181, 277, 299
Second Life 42, 147, 157, 256, 299
Section 42 (UK) 178, 181
Sedgwick, Eve Kosovsky 3, 185–186, 191, 193, 195–196, 290, 297
Seidman, Steven 3, 176, 179–180
Self amplifying 5
Self identity 4, 6
Self narratives 1
Self reflexivity xi, 10, 32
Self storytelling 7, 31
Selvin, Lowell 115–116
Semiotics 55, 59, 215, 218, 225, 236
Sender, Katherine 118, 130–131, 133
Setoodeh, Ramin 21, 33
Sewell, Edward 191, 195
Sex and the City 218
Sexual encounter 1, 10, 89, 92, 96
Sexual Freedom Coalition 247
Sexual orientation 37–38, 48–49, 53, 63, 102, 125–126, 134, 166, 193, 195, 212, 232, 236, 247, 249
Shame free 19, 32
Shepard, Matthew 17, 19, 32–33
Sheppard, Simon 188
Shernoff, Michael 108
Shojamanesh, Christian 31
Silverstone, Roger 3, 297
Simulation 51, 53, 60, 195, 209, 218
Slash fiction (slash/fic) 8, 174, 177, 181–183
Slater, Chad 144
Slater, Donald 207
Smith, Megan 115
Social awareness 130–131
Social capital 63–65, 67–71, 102, 281, 291
Social capital, bonding 64, 67–71
Social capital, bridging 64, 67–68, 70–71

Index 311

Social capital, maintained 64, 67–71
Social construction xi, 2, 3, 10–11, 22, 107, 167, 249, 300, 303
Social movements 5, 106, 167
Social networking xi, 8, 9, 27, 62, 64–66, 69, 71, 100, 102, 109–110, 117, 134, 204, 290, 299
Social types 26, 130
Spigel, Lynn 13
Springhaven 288, 293
Star Trek 173–174, 177
Stargate 182
Starsky and Hutch 177
Stay the Same 29
Steinman, Erich 4
Stereotypes 96, 126–128, 130, 159, 161–162, 165, 225, 230, 232–233
Stigma / stigmatized identity 21, 29, 83, 87, 103, 206, 217, 223, 226, 264, 303
Stonewall 25, 33, 52, 62
Storey, John 170
Storr, Merl 254
Storytelling network 271–273, 275–276, 278–279, 281, 283
Straightening 271
Streitmatter, Roger 3, 275
Subaltern public 5
Subculture 4, 26, 155, 208, 216, 224–226, 246–250, 274, 275, 299
Subvertisements 215
Superman 178–179
Swartz, David 34, 22–23
Symbolic violence 20, 22–23, 28

Tabloid journalism 142
Tambiah, Stanley J 252
Technology 2, 7, 10, 19, 65, 113, 145, 207, 221, 224, 245–246, 249, 252–255
Television 3, 8–9, 17, 54, 119–121, 126–127, 131–132, 135, 147–151, 153, 155, 157, 159–165, 167, 169, 173–183, 220, 254, 299
Thorn, Matt 188
Tijuana Bibles 141, 143, 174
Torchwood 180, 182
Toronto xii, 195, 278
Towleroad 33, 280

Transamerica 132
Transconversations 159–170
Transformation of Intimacy 1, 3–4, 32, 54
Transgender xi, 1, 4, 8–10, 19, 39, 62, 87–91, 102, 109, 120, 131–132, 159, 163–166, 168, 170, 241, 245, 247, 249, 279, 288, 192, 293
Transgressive 5–8, 131, 150–151, 173–175, 177, 180, 247, 252
Trans-persons 7, 87, 89–90, 93–96
Tsika, Noah 8, 230, 303
Turkle, Sherry 3, 44, 52

Unks, Gerald 20
Usher, Nikki 9–10, 271, 303

Velez, Lupe 141
Venture capital/capitalists 113, 115, 117–118
Victim 177
Vincent, Keith 188
Virtual reality 248
Virtual Valerie 248
Visibility 11, 90, 118–119, 129–131, 133, 142, 160, 166, 178, 202–203, 205, 211, 215–216, 218, 224, 226, 232, 251, 273–275, 250, 284, 289–292
Visual culture 120, 160, 217

Wagner, Geoffrey 176
Waites, Matthew 247
Wajcman, Judith 245
Wakeford, Nina 2
Wal-Mart 288–297
Warner, Jackie 42
Warner, Michael 5, 176
Warren, Lorna 4
Watson, Mark 120
Wayback Machine 122
Web design 113–114, 120–122
Weeks, Jeffrey 3
West Hollywood 204, 281
West Wing, The 179
Western media producers 2
Western voices, dominant 2
Whitesel, Jason 8, 215, 303

Who's a Fairy? 142
Wide Sargasso Sea 173
Wilke, Michael 119, 125
Will & Grace 159
Williams, Raymond 3
Wire, The 180
Worldmaking power 22

Xena: Warrior Princess (XWP) 8, 147–157, 179

Xenasubtexttalk (XSTT) 147–157

Yaoi 8, 185–196
Yaoi-Con 188, 193–194
YouTube 3, 7, 17, 19–20, 24–29, 33–34, 37–49, 51–60, 134, 145, 218, 239, 302
Yue, Audrey 2

Zuckerberg, Mark 64